CLASSROOM MANAGEMENT STRATEGIES

G

CORBAN
C O L L E G E

CLASSROOM MANAGEMENT STRATEGIES

GAINING AND MAINTAINING STUDENTS' COOPERATION

SECOND EDITION

J A M E S S. C A N G E L O S I

Utah State University

Longman

New York & London

Classroom Management Strategies: Gaining and Maintaining Students' Cooperation, Second Edition

Longman, 10 Bank Street, White Plains, N.Y. 10606

Associated companies:
Longman Group Ltd., London
Longman Cheshire Pty., Melbourne
Longman Paul Pty., Auckland
Copp Clark Pitman, Toronto

Senior acquisitions editor: Laura McKenna
Development editor: Virginia L. Blanford
Production editors: The Book Studio Inc., Ann P. Kearns
Cover design: Joseph DePinho
Text art: Leslie Dunlap, Marie DeJohn, Elaine Campanella
Production supervisor: Anne P. Armeny

Library of Congress Cataloging-in-Publication Data

Cangelosi, James S.
    Classroom management strategies : gaining and maintaining
students' cooperation / James S. Cangelosi.—2nd ed.
       p.   cm.
    Includes bibliographical references and index.
    ISBN 0-8013-0614-0
    1. Classroom management—United States. 2. Teacher–student
relationships—United States. 3. Rewards and punishments in
education. I. Title
LB3013.C3259   1992
371.1'024—dc20   92-34726
                                       CIP

1 2 3 4 5 6 7 8 9 10-AL-9695949392

To Casey

Contents

CHAPTER 6 **DESIGNING AND CONDUCTING
ENGAGING LEARNING ACTIVITIES   141**

Preface

The most commonly expressed concern of students, teachers, parents, and school administrators alike regarding schools involves a lack of pupil discipline, poor classroom management and control, and disruptive student behavior. A tenth grader remonstrates: "School is a joke! I don't learn anything because the teachers are so busy trying to keep order that they don't take time to teach." One sixth grade teacher's comment is indicative of the feelings of thousands of her colleagues who teach at every level: "I became a teacher because I love knowledge and I wanted to help children. But these pupils don't want my help! They won't sit still long enough to learn anything—except how to drive me out of the profession!" Another teacher's lamentations are all too common: "I used to look forward to each school day. Now, I start days hoping I can survive until school is out without being driven crazy, overly embarrassed, or physically harmed." One parent expressed his dilemma: "My taxes go to support public education, but I had to find a private school for my child where teachers controlled students with good old-fashioned discipline." A recent high school graduate suggested: "Teachers should exert more control. I just played around in school—rarely paid attention or did homework. Now I'm paying for my fooling around. I wish my teachers had made me work and learn." A school principal stated emphatically: "The number one thing I look for when hiring a new teacher is the ability to maintain discipline and order. What good does it do a teacher to know all the subject matter and pedagogy in the world if he can't keep the kids in line?"

Not surprisingly, classroom observation instruments used in virtually every public school district for assessing teachers' performances exphasize how teachers manage their students more than any other instructional variable (see, e.g., Cangelosi, 1991b, pp. 45–172). Teachers can blame student inattentiveness, lack of effort, disruptive behaviors, and general lack of cooperation on their students' own flaws or on the lack of support provided by society, families, and school administrators. But thousands of teachers do overcome seemingly impossible circumstances and elicit their students' cooperation in the face of unfavorable student attitudes and school conditions. These teachers run efficient classrooms where student cooperation is the rule rather than the exception. Students of these teachers are achieving and learning to be successful. How can teachers obtain their students' attention, effort, and cooperation? That is the question addressed by *Classroom Management Strategies: Gaining and Maintaining Students' Cooperation,* Second Edition. This text's suggestions for helping teachers to effectively obtain and maintain students on-task and engaged in lessons are an outgrowth of extensive school teaching experiences and of the findings of numerous studies in the areas of learning theory, student motivation, behavior modification, counseling psychology, student engagement, and classroom organization.

Strategies for obtaining and maintaining students' cooperation will not be understood and applied by teachers unless those teachers are exposed to a wide variety of examples demonstrating the strategies in everyday, realistic classroom situations. Thus, this book does not only explain strategies and make suggestions, it explains them and brings them to life via 254 vignettes drawn from a wide variety of teaching situations from prekindergarten to college. These vignettes (used to demonstrate principles, successful strategies, and unsuccessful strategies) are drawn from actual experiences. Many of them "get inside teachers' minds," following thought processes as solutions to discipline problems are formulated.

This second edition reflects principles for stimulating and maintaining student engagement based on research results reported since the first edition was published. Furthermore, *Classroom Management Strategies: Gaining and Maintaining Students' Cooperation* has been reorganized so that this edition is far more "user friendly" than the first. The vignettes are now numbered and stand out from the rest of the text to facilitate cross-referencing. Transitional activities at the end of each chapter serve as a self-assessment of what was learned from the chapter and as an advanced organizer for the next chapter. A glossary of technical classroom management terms has been added. The following topics have either been added or dealt with in greater detail as compared to the first edition: individual differences among students, mainstreamed students, group dynamics, instructional supervision, self-assessment, action research, and cooperative learning.

In spite of the additional content, this second edition is not appreciably longer than the first because it has been completely redone so that the writing is crisper, delivering greater information per word. As an aid to professors who incorporate this edition into their courses, an *Instructor's Manual* is available from Longman. The manual contains (1) suggestions for taking advantage of the book's features in a variety of course structures; (2) a detailed sample syllabus, including a sequence of class activities and assignments; and (3) unit tests with scoring criteria and feedback forms for each test.

Classroom Management Strategies: Gaining and Maintaining Students' Cooperation, Second Edition is presented in four parts.

- **Part I**   (Chapters 1 and 2) deals with some basic ideas that need to be understood before one is in a position to apply the practical strategies presented in the remainder of the text.
- **Part II**   (Chapters 3 through 6) presents and demonstrates ways for teachers to communicate with students, organize their classrooms, and design and conduct lessons so that students choose to be cooperative and involved. These chapters suggest measures for preventing discipline problems and inattentiveness from ever occurring.
- **Part III** (Chapters 7 through 10) presents and demonstrates teacher-initiated solutions to problems of disruptive student behaviors, lack of student engagement in lessons, and poor student cooperation.
- **Part IV**   (Chapter 11) suggests ways of cultivating one's personal teaching style to tailor classroom management strategies to unique classroom situations.

This textbook is designed for college level courses concerned with helping pre-service and in-service teachers to effectively manage student behaviors and solve classroom discipline problems.

ACKNOWLEDGMENTS

The author wishes to express his appreciation to the following reviewers, whose helpful suggestions and insight contributed to the development of this book:

Mary Anne Christenberry, College of Charleston
Carla Crippen, California State University–Stanislaus
Jane Diekman, California State University–Stanislaus
John Donaldson, Liberty University
John Moore, University of Western Kentucky
S. D. Parker, Academy of the New Church College
Gerald Pratt, St. Mary's University
Robert Richmond, Florida Institute of Technology
Toni Sills, Tulane University

PART I

What Causes Students to Cooperate? What Causes Students to Be Uncooperative?

Thinking about Your Role as a Teacher

Purpose of Chapter 1

This chapter introduces you to a model for organizing your thoughts about teaching. An understanding of this model and the terminology associated with it will help you grasp the ideas presented in Chapter 2 and will help you apply the techniques and suggestions for gaining and maintaining your students' cooperation presented in Chapters 3–11. More specifically, Chapter 1 is designed to help you

1. Organize your teaching responsibilities within the "Teaching Process Model."
2. Comprehend the following terms: *allocated time, transition time, on-task behavior, student engagement, off-task behavior, disruptive behavior,* and *individualized education program (IEP)*.
3. Reflect upon the myriad of individual differences among students within any single classroom.
4. Examine your personal commitment to gaining and maintaining students' cooperation so that you enjoy satisfying teaching experiences and your students experience optimal learning opportunities.

THE DIFFERENCE BETWEEN SATISFYING AND FRUSTRATING TEACHING EXPERIENCES

Some teachers orchestrate smoothly operating classrooms where students cooperatively and efficiently go about the business of learning with minimal disruptions, while others exhaust themselves struggling with student misbehaviors as they attempt to gain some semblance of classroom order. Those from this latter group who remain in the teaching profession eventually give up the struggle, deciding that today's students are so unmotivated and out of control that it is futile to attempt anything more than surviving the school day (Bridges, 1986, pp. 4–18; Cangelosi, Struyk, Grimes, & Duke, 1988). Whether your teaching experiences are satisfying or marked by constant, frustrating struggles trying to get students to cooperate with you depends largely on how well you apply proven classroom management strategies. Through the application of such strategies you are able to meet one of your primary instructional responsibilities: to provide students with a learning environment that is conducive to achievement and free from disruptions, distractions, and threats to their safety and well-being.

THE TEACHING PROCESS MODEL

Before examining proven classroom management strategies for gaining and maintaining students' cooperation and for effectively confronting discipline problems, your attention is briefly directed to an examination of your role as a teacher. You practice the complex art of teaching in cycles, such as teaching units. Vignette 1.1 outlines an example of a teaching unit.

The idea for Ms. Martinez's unit grew out of her belief that her students needed to improve their writing and editing abilities. Deciding to do something about that need, she determined a learning goal. To help her students achieve that goal, she designed learning activities and then prepared for them (e.g., rearranging her classroom to accommodate five cooperative groups working independently). When Ms. Martinez's students were writing paragraphs, reading them in their cooperative groups, listening to others read, discussing what was read, taking notes, and rewriting paragraphs, they were engaged in learning activities and Ms. Martinez was conducting learning activities. Finally, Ms. Martinez evaluated how successfully her students achieved the unit's goal.

You, like Ms. Martinez, design and conduct teaching units by effecting the six steps of what is referred to throughout this textbook as the *Teaching Process Model*.

1. Determine needs of students.
2. Determine learning goal.
3. Design learning activities.
4. Prepare for the learning activities.
5. Conduct the learning activities.
6. Determine how well students have achieved the learning goal.

The Teaching Process Model (see Figure 1.1) is referred to herein for two reasons: (1) to present suggestions and techniques within the context of the complex art of teaching, and (2) to provide an advanced organizer for systematically teaching students to supplant uncooperative behaviors with cooperative behaviors.

VIGNETTE 1.1

Ms. Martinez, an English teacher at Carver Street Middle School, believes her students need to improve their abilities to communicate in writing. In her opinion, they should become aware of the different ways readers interpret what they write and be able to edit their own writing to convey their messages as unambiguously as possible. Thus, for one of her classes of 32 students, Ms. Martinez designs a creative writing unit with the following learning goal: Students will be aware of the different ways their writing can be interpreted and will edit what they write in light of that awareness.

For the unit, she plans, prepares, and implements a number of learning activities over a 10-day period. For example, one day she divides the 32 students into five cooperative groups of six or seven each. Within each group, students read paragraphs written for homework while the other students discuss the meaning of the paragraph as if the writer were not present. The writer, who is not allowed to enter into the discussion, listens and takes notes on how the classmates interpreted the paragraph. The writer is to later modify the paragraph in light of the discussion. This activity continues until all students have had a chance to read their paragraphs and hear them discussed.

Near the end of the 10-day unit, Ms. Martinez uses a posttest to help her evaluate just how aware of readers' interpretations her students have become and how effectively the students learned to edit what they wrote.

FIGURE 1.1 The Teaching Process Model

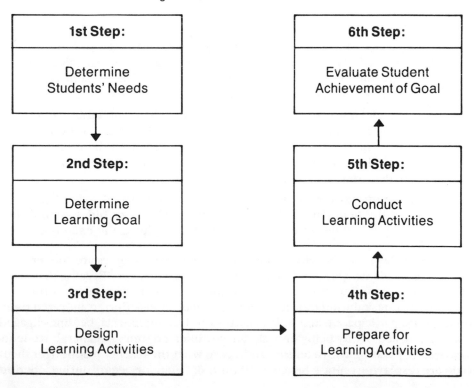

ALLOCATED TIME AND TRANSITION TIME

The third step of the Teaching Process Model requires you to design and plan your students' learning activities. Suppose that the learning activities that you plan for one school day call for one group of students to (1) read a passage from a book, (2) discuss what they read, (3) listen to you give a brief lecture, (4) respond individually in writing to questions appearing on a worksheet, and (5) read another passage and write a brief essay for homework. The time periods of the day when you intend for your students to be engaged in these learning activities are referred to as "allocated times." Obviously, allocated times cannot take up an entire school day. On the day you conduct the five learning activities, time must also be devoted to, among other things, (1) getting your students assembled and attentive, (2) assigning the reading and directing them to begin, (3) calling students' attention away from the reading and onto the lecture, (4) distributing the worksheets and directing students to answer the questions, (5) calling a halt to the worksheet activity and assigning the homework. Time periods to take care of such tasks before and after scheduled learning activities (i.e., between allocated times) are referred to as "transition times."

STUDENT COOPERATION, ENGAGEMENT, AND ON-/OFF-TASK BEHAVIORS

Consider the behaviors of the students in the following examples.

- Mr. Issac directs his 28 first graders to put on their aprons and remove their paints from their supply boxes in preparation for a learning activity. Buster puts on his apron, takes out his paints, and waits for directions. Elysia picks up a bottle of yellow paint and throws it across the room, splattering several students.

- Ms. Saunders, a high school history teacher, is in the midst of conducting a class discussion on the reasons that the U.S. Congress rescinded prohibition in 1933. Lia listens intently to the discussion, occasionally expressing her thoughts on the causes. Amy quietly sits at her desk day-dreaming about riding horses.

- Coach Murphy directs 18 of his football players to take two laps around the field. Hewitt begins running while Ricky hides behind the blocking dummies until the others have completed the exercise.

Buster's, Lia's, and Hewitt's behaviors in the three examples are cooperative. These three students were acting as their teachers had planned. Because they were attempting to follow their teachers' directions, their behaviors were "on-task." Buster was on-task during transition time. Lia was on-task during allocated time, listening and participating in the class discussion. Hewitt, like Lia, became engaged in a learning activity by being on-task during allocated time. In general, students who are cooperating with a teacher and doing what the teacher planned for them to do are displaying on-task behavior. If on-task behavior occurs during a period of allocated time, the behavior is also referred to as student "engagement" in a learning activity. On-task behavior can occur either during allocated time or transition time. Engagement can occur only during allocated time.

On the other hand, Elysia's, Amy's, and Ricky's behavior was uncooperative. Elysia was "off-task" because she was not attempting to follow Mr. Issac's directions. Amy's behavior was not as disruptive as was Elysia's, but Amy was still off-task as she was neither listening to nor contributing to the discussion. Unlike Elysia's behavior, Amy's off-task behavior occurred during allocated time, thus Amy was "disengaged" from a learning activity. Similarly, Ricky was off-task and not engaged in Coach Murphy's planned learning activity.

DISRUPTIVE BEHAVIORS

When Elysia flung her paint across Mr. Issac's room, she was not only displaying off-task behavior, she probably prevented or discouraged other students from being on-task. Amy's quiet daydreaming, however, probably did not disturb any of the other students nor interfere with their chances of being on-task. The off-task behavior exhibited by Elysia is referred to as "disruptive", while Amy's off-task behavior was not disruptive. Off-task behaviors such as students talking to one another when they should be listening to a presentation, interrupting a speaker, being generally discourteous, clowning, and acting out violently are usually thought of as disruptive. Off-task behaviors such as students allowing their minds to wander from the topic at hand, daydreaming, being quietly inattentive because of the effects of drugs, failing to complete homework assignments, skipping class, and cheating on tests are usually thought of as nondisruptive. In general, a student's behavior is disruptive when it encourages or causes other students to be off-task. (The Glossary [pp. 305–310] provides a ready reference to specialized terms introduced in this as well as other chapters.)

Disruptive behaviors are the sources of most teachers' greatest fears (Abernathy, Manera, & Wright, 1985). Teachers who are considered by their supervisors and others to have "poor classsroom control" and "discipline problems" are teachers whose students display high levels of disruptive behaviors. You have little choice but to deal with student disruptions. But unless you also deal effectively with nondisruptive off-task behaviors, (1) transition times will be inefficient, thus robbing you of allocated time, (2) disengaged students will fail to achieve your learning goals, and (3) nondisruptive off-task behaviors are likely to escalate into disruptions.

FACING THE PROBLEM OF KEEPING
STUDENTS ON-TASK AND ENGAGED

Differences among Students

Your responsibility of keeping students on-task and engaged in learning activities is compounded by the fact that each student is a unique individual. What motivates one student to be on-task does not necessarily motivate another. What discourages one from being off-task may encourage the off-task behavior of another. To say the least, teaching is a complex art. As a teacher you are confronted with more variables to concurrently manipulate than is expected in any other profession (Cangelosi, 1992a, pp. 2–35; Kobrin, 1992, pp. xii–xiv, 1–9; Mudd, 1990). In this section, you are reminded of only a minute proportion of the variables on which you can expect your students to differ.

Interest in Learning.   You are interested in teaching your students, but you will be disappointed if you anticipate they will all be equally interested in learning. Students' interests in what schools offer range from obsessive avoidance to obsessive pursuit. Major challenges of teaching include (1) motivating otherwise uninterested students to learn, and (2) preserving and fostering the enthusiasm of those who are already motivated to learn.

Self-Confidence.   Some students view learning tasks as opportunities to acquire new abilities and skills. Others approach learning tasks as competitive situations in which their existing abilities ad skills are challenged. Unlike the latter group, the former are not burdened with fears that their mistakes will be ridiculed, so they are willing to pursue perplexing tasks and to learn from their mistakes. The amount of effort students are willing to invest in a learning task is not only dependent on the value they recognize in the task, but also on their level of confidence in successfully completing the task (Ames & Ames, 1985). Problem solving, discovering relationships, analyzing academic content, and interpreting communications are cognitive tasks requiring students to work through perplexing moments. Those who are not confident in their own abilities tend to stop working on the task as soon as they become perplexed; more confident students tolerate perplexity longer and are more likely to continue with the task.

Perception of What Is Important.   Adults tend to value schools as vehicles for preparing their children for the future. "Study hard and you'll be able to get a good job and make something of yourself when you're grown!" a parent tells a child. However, most of your students are far more concerned with succeeding as children or adolescents than with succeeding as adults (Goodlad, 1984, pp. 75–81). Today seems more important than tomorrow. Thus, many of your students will need to recognize immediate benefits in what you're trying to teach them before they are motivated to engage in your learning activities. There is tremendous variation among what students consider immediately beneficial. For example, some students want to please their parents with their accomplishments; others find peer approval over their appearance far more important. There are those who seek satisfaction within themselves and do not depend on outside approval. Still others seek material rewards for their efforts. In any case, students are driven by unique combinations of motives based on a variety of things they find important.

Attitude toward School.   Some of your students will greet you as their friend, expecting to benefit from the experience you provide. Others arrive with little regard for how you might help them, and view you as an authority figure who interferes with what they would prefer to be doing.

Aptitude for Reasoning.   Many of the learning activities you design for your students confront them with high-level cognitive tasks (e.g., inductive reasoning or deductive application of syllogisms). Such requirements are quite arduous for some preadolescents and adolescents, but present no difficulty for others. Whether you teach elementary, middle, or secondary school students, you will have to contend with a wide range of students' abilities to use various reasoning processes. Students who enjoy a history of successes with reasoning tasks are more likely to engage in higher cognitive learning activities than those who come to you with a history of discouraging experiences.

Prior Achievements.   Look at the initial chapters of any textbook. Note how the book begins with remedial material that overlaps the content of books for prior grades. Apparently, the author(s) recognized that having been exposed to content in prior courses does not guarantee that content was learned by all students. Most of your students will have failed to learn some content at a learning level you consider prerequisite for what you want to teach them. However, learning gaps will vary from student to student. Furthermore, many students, although lacking some remedial skills and abilities, will have already acquired understanding of some advanced topics you are expecting to introduce to them. Your assessments of students' needs will detect differences among their motor skills as well as cognitive learning. Of particular concern to most teachers are differences in students' communication skills. Student engagement in most learning activities depends on an individual's ability to both receive messages (e.g., by listening and reading) and send messages (e.g., by speaking and writing).

Experiences upon Which You Can Build.   Different students bring vastly different backgrounds to your classroom. Participating in sports, caring for younger children, repairing motors, raising gardens, working in a salaried job, traveling, experiencing major family upheavals, playing music, suffering from illnesses, and raising animals are only a small sampling of the types of students' experiences to which you can relate the things you teach, thus motivating engagement.

Home and Social Life.   Children and adolescents are under continual domestic and social pressures. The parenting of your students will range from supportive to neglectful, from healthy to abusive, and from constant to absent. For most students peer acceptance is of paramount concern (Charles, 1989, pp. 70–87; Dreikurs, 1968). Some have friends who encourage their pursuits of learning and cooperation with your efforts. Others may perceive that they risk acceptance of those whose friendship they value most by being studious and cooperative with you. While it is important that you understand the pressures and influences with which your students live, please keep two things in mind.

- Each student is a unique individual. Do not apply the aggregate results from demographic studies in judging individuals. For example, as a group, Japanese children tend to value academic activities more than Western children (Allen, 1988), but that doesn't mean that any particular student from a Japanese family will be more motivated toward learning than a student of American heritage. Nor will any one student living in an inner-city housing project be any more inclined to abuse drugs than a student from a suburb.

- Because students live with disadvantages (e.g., abusive parents) does not mean that they cannot control their own behaviors, nor should it imply that you should expect less from them (Glasser, 1985; Pysch, 1991). However, variations in home and social life do create differences among students regarding such matters as how much time they have to devote to school work, whether or not they have a place conducive to doing homework, and whether or not you can depend on their parents' cooperation.

Cultural Background and Ethnicity.   Schools in the United States serve a pluralistic society endowed with multiethnic, multicultural communities. Your understanding of cultural diversity will serve you well as you develop strategies for motivating students to be on-task and engaged in learning activities. Furthermore, you are hardly in a position to elicit students' cooperation unless you are aware of differences that cause an action or communication to be perceived as a compliment by one subculture and as an insult by another.

Use of Drugs.   Inadequate study skills, boredom, lack of confidence, fatigue, hyperactivity, and nonacademic interests are just some of the many factors that can hinder students' willingness to engage in learning activities. Being either high or depressed from drugs at school or when trying to study is just one more factor that hinders students' academic work (Cangelosi, 1990a, pp. 64–66). Special mention of drug use is included here not because that factor is any more pervasive than others, but because (a) its influence seems to be increasing at an alarming rate among students of all ages (Brough, 1990; Elam, 1989), and (b) information on how to deal with students who abuse drugs has recently become available (see, e.g., pp. 256–263 of this book).

Special Needs.   Although you may not be a special education teacher, you can expect to have a few students mainstreamed into your classes whose special needs have been formally identified. Included among the labels are "learning disabled," "hearing impaired," "hard of hearing," "blind," "visually handicapped," "orthopedically impaired," "behaviorally disordered," "emotionally handicapped," "gifted," and "multihandicapped" (Lewis & Doorlag, 1991, pp. 49–69). The number of such exceptional students mainstreamed into "regular" classrooms increased dramatically since the U.S. Congress passed the Education for All Handicapped Children Act of 1975 (P.L. 94–142). P.L. 94–142 mandates that free, appropriate public education be available to all handicapped students between the ages of three and 18, that they be educated to the maximum extent possible, and that their education take place in the "least restrictive" learning environment. For each handicapped student, an Individualized Education Program (IEP) is to be designed in collaboration with the special education and regular classroom teachers, the parents, and the student. The IEP is a description of the student's individualized curriculum including statements of learning goals, prescriptions for educational services related to those goals, time lines for delivery of those services, and a delineation of the assessment procedures to be used for placement decisions and evaluation fo the program's success. Coolican (1988, p. 216) states

> It is important to realize that handicapped children are often socially ignored or even ridiculed by their nonhandicapped peers (see Sabornie, 1985). Teachers of mainstreamed students should therefore attempt to establish positive attitudes toward the handicapped and to encourage appropriate interactions between their disabled and nondisabled students. For example, students in a class that includes a hearing-impaired child could be taught the manual alphabet (for "finger spelling") and rudimentary sign language. To further reduce social isolation of mainstreamed students, teachers might develop a social skills training program or, if necessary, a self-care program. Such a program could be developed with the assistance of the handicapped student's special education teacher.
>
> Many of the educational needs of handicapped children are similar to the needs of other students in your classrooms. As a result of improved identification and placement procedures, emphasis is being directed toward each child's educational characteristics. This could eventually prove to be a useful way of assessing all learners. In addition, the classroom teacher is in a key position to recognize those students who have special needs. A comprehensive diagnosis, however, is not the classroom teacher's responsibility, but that of specialized personnel in the school system. You should be prepared to communicate learners' problems and work cooperatively with the professionals assigned to diagnose disabilities and prescribe treatments.

Besides addressing these students' special needs, you can be assured that your so-called "normal" students also vary considerably in their abilities to hear, see, perform mental tasks, control their emotions, concentrate, and perform physical tasks. For example, it is estimated that at any one point in time, 25 percent of students with "normal" hearing suffer a temporary hearing loss (e.g., because of an infection) serious enough to interfere with their ability to follow an oral presentation (Berg, 1987, pp. 22–38).

Taking Charge of Your Own Classroom

The problem of maintaining discipline in schools continues to be, as it has been for at least the past 20 years, the number one concern of students, teachers, parents, and school administrators (Elam, Rose, & Gallup, 1991). For typical classrooms, some research studies suggest that students are engaged in learning activities for no more than half of the time that is allocated for those learning activities (Jones, 1979). Other studies place this figure nearer 75 percent (Goodlad, 1984). The time allocated to learning activities averages only about 40 percent of the total time students spend in school. Thus, the average amount of time students spend actively engaged in learning activities ranges (depending on which study you believe) between 20 and 30 percent of the time they are in school (Latham, 1984). Why is it that, in the average classroom, students spend what appears to be an inordinate share of their time either off-task or in transition between learning activities? Should not students be engaged in learning activities for a larger portion of the school day?

When the proportion of allocated time that students spend engaged in learning activities is increased, students' achievement of learning goals increases (Fisher et al., 1980). While some reports suggest that both the school year and the school day be lengthened to accommodate more allocated time (Elam, Rose, & Gallup, 1991; National Commission on Excellence in Education, 1983), others clearly display that through effective planning and organization teachers can increase allocated time without lengthening either the school day or year by minimizing transition time (Latham, 1984; Struyk, 1990). Furthermore, by applying fundamental classroom management and discipline techniques, teachers can lead students to be engaged in learning activities for more than 90 percent of allocated time (Cangelosi, 1990a, pp. 13-20; Evertson, 1989; Fisher et al., 1980; Jones, 1979).

The goals you establish for your students to achieve; how you plan, prepare for, and conduct learning activities; how you evaluate your students' achievements; how you organize and manage the classroom setting; and the manner in which you communicate with students and their parents will be major influences on how much of your students' time is spent cooperatively engaged in learning activities. Of course other factors, many of which are out of your control, will also influence how well your students cooperate. Unsympathetic school administrators, uncaring parents, lack of needed supplies and facilities, unmotivated students, students with emotional disabilities, students with learning gaps, students with learning disabilities, overcrowded classrooms, and more work than is possible in 24-hour days are major culprits. But dwelling on causes outside of your control will not be a productive means for you to begin increasing students' time on-task and engaged in learning activities. Instead, ask yourself: "What can I, as the teacher in charge of students, do?" If you are willing to do what you can to get and keep your students' cooperation, then you are ready to work your way through the remainder of this text.

TRANSITIONAL ACTIVITIES
FROM CHAPTER 1 TO CHAPTER 2

The transitional activities from one chapter to the next are intended to (1) help you assess what you gained from the chapter so that you can identify your areas of proficiency and the topics you need to review, (2) reinforce and extend what you've learned from the chapter, and (3) set the stage for your work in the next chapter. Another purpose is to encourage you to articulate your thoughts about classroom management strategies in both writing and oral discourse. Understanding is enhanced through such activities (Santa & Havens, 1991).

   I. Analytically read Vignette 1.2. Respond to the items that follow in light of what you read.

VIGNETTE 1.2

Because Ms. Kobayashi believes that most of her 33 home economic students do not adequately practice comparison shopping, she decides to conduct a learning unit designed to better enable students to assess the cost-benefit value of products sold in stores. During one of the unit's learning activities, which involves students cutting ads out of newspapers, Corine and Gordon toss balled-up newspaper scraps at one another. Ms. Kobayashi decides to put a stop to their activity by speaking to them privately and directing them to clean up the area during the time when the rest of the class is taste-testing the fruit salad that was made during another learning activity. Both Corine and Gordon cooperatively clean up and do not disturb the class during subsequent lessons of the unit. Thus, Ms. Kobayashi concludes that they will be less likely to clown around in future class sessions. At the end of the unit, a test is given and Ms. Kobayashi decides that 11 of the 13 students who scored markedly higher than the test average are quite proficient at assessing the cost-benefit value of products.

A. In Vignette 1.2, Ms. Kobayashi completed two teaching cycles, one dealing with assessing cost-benefit values; the other, with a discipline problem.
   1. *For the cost-benefit unit:* How did Ms. Kobayashi implement the first step of the Teaching Process Model? The second step? The third step? What are some things she might have done while implementing the fourth step? The fifth step? What did she decide when implementing the sixth step?
   2. *For the discipline problem:* What decision might Ms. Kobayashi have made in carrying out the first step of the model? The second step? The third step? What are some things she might have done while implementing the fourth step? The fifth step? What did she decide when implementing the sixth step?
B. A number of instances of allocated time occurred in the vignette. What was one?
C. A number of instances of transition time were implied. What was one?

Compare your responses to Activity I with those of a colleague; discuss similarities and differences. Because the questions raised by the items are somewhat open-ended, an exact answer key cannot be provided, but evaluate your responses in light of the following comments and same responses.

In Vignette 1.2, Ms. Kobayashi followed the Teaching Process Model to plan and conduct her unit on comparison shopping and also to teach Corine and Gordon to be on-task. The application of the Teaching Process Model to discipline goals may be a strange idea to many. However, as is suggested in Chapter 7 of this text, if you treat student displays of off-task behavior as indications that students need to learn something, you are more likely to effectively deal with discipline problems when they arise.

With respect to the cost-benefit unit, Ms. Kobayashi implemented the first step of the model when she decided that most of her students needed to be able to practice comparison shopping. The second step was implemented when she set the goal for them to be able to assess cost-benefit values. The principal difference between the first and second steps is that a teacher who only determines that students have a particular need has not yet decided to do something about that need. As a teacher, you identify many needs that your students have that never lead to learning goals. You cannot, nor do you have the right or responsibility to, take care of all of your students' needs. The student needs that fall within your responsibilities as a teacher, and with which you are reasonably capable of dealing, lead to learning goals. Ms. Kobayashi could have decided that other needs should take priority over learning comparison shopping and she could have chosen not to move to the second step of the Teaching Process Model. In this example, however, she decided to act upon recognition of that particular need.

She implemented the third step by planning to have students cut out newspaper ads and carry on other activities that are not given in the example. What she did to carry out the fourth step is not described in the vignette. Try to imagine what she might have done. For example, she may have collected particular editions of newspapers with some especially helpful advertisements, distributed the papers and scissors, and grouped the students in a way that would benefit the smooth operation of the lesson. For the fifth step, she explained what the students were to do with the ads and supervised the cutting-out activities. In the sixth step, she decided, probably among other things, that 11 of the 13 students scoring markedly higher than the test average were quite proficient at assessing the cost-benefit value of products.

With respect to the way she dealt with the discipline problem, it appears that Ms. Kobayashi decided, in the first step of the model, that Corine's and Gordon's disruptive behavior should cease. There are times when a teacher may identify a need, such as that some off-task behavior should cease, and wisely choose not to deal with that need. Dealing with the unwanted behavior may, for example, itself create more disruption. But Ms. Kobayashi chose to deal with the disruption and, thus, went on to the second step of the model by deciding to get them to stop tossing paper balls. The third step was implemented by deciding to speak to them privately and directing them to the clean-up task. You really have to use your imagination to fill in a fourth step. Possibly, she saw to it that the rest of the class was able to remain busy while she directed Corine and Gordon to a private spot for the conversation. The fifth step was, of course, speaking to them and directing them to clean up. Her evaluation that they had been adequately discouraged from repeating such behavior provided the sixth step.

Regarding items I-B and I-C, there are many examples you could have given. The time Ms. Kobayashi planned to spend with students cutting out ads was an example of allocated time. Time spent directing the students from their newspaper-cutting activities and into their fruit-salad tasting activities was an example of transition time.

II. Following are some brief descriptions of student behaviors. Label each *on-task, off-task, engaged,* and/or *disruptive.*

   A. Ms. Romano directs her first graders to complete seven mathematics exercises on a tasksheet. After working only one or two of the exercises, several students begin doodling and drawing pictures.

   B. Mr. Finegan tells his third graders that it is time for them to put away the materials with which they have been working at learning centers and to get to their reading groups for the next lesson. Dale puts away his materials and immediately goes to his reading group area and waits. Adonis places some of the colored rods from the learning center on Mary's head. Mary yells at Adonis, and the two begin arguing.

   C. Charlene, Marion, and Rufus are eleventh graders engaging in a lively conversation as they wait for Mr. Bench to enter the classroom and begin chemistry class. Mr. Bench arrives, asks for silence, and asks Marion to demonstrate an experiment that had been tried for homework. Marion begins the demonstration. Except for Charlene and Rufus who continue to socialize, class members watch and listen to the demonstration.

Compare your responses to Activity II with those of a colleague; resolve differences. Evaluate your responses in light of the following comments.

Those of Ms. Romano's students who doodled during time allocated for the mathematics exercises displayed nondisruptive, off-task behavior. The second example involved transitional time rather than allocated time, so there was no opportunity for students to be engaged in learning activities as was the case in the first example. Dale's behavior was on-task, while Adonis' and Mary's behavior was both off-task and disruptive. During the transitional time before Mr. Bench called the class to order, the students' talking did not seem inappropriate. However, when Marion began the demonstration, Charlene's and Rufus' conversation became off-task and may have been disruptive, depending on whether or not others were distracted. Marion and those students who paid attention were displaying on-task, engaged behaviors during the demonstration.

III. Make a list of some of the factors that lead students in many classrooms to have an undesirably low proportion of school time engaged in learning activities. Compare your list with those of colleagues. Discuss whether or not you, as a teacher, can control or influence any of those factors. Brainstorm strategies for helping students to overcome those factors.

IV. In preparation for your work with Chapter 2, discuss the following questions with two or more of your colleagues.
   A. Why is it that some students eagerly cooperate with their teachers while others are inclined to be uncooperative, off-task, and disruptive?
   B. How does a teacher's awareness of what's going on in the classroom influence students' tendencies to be on-task?
   C. How does the manner in which a teacher responds to the behavior of one student affect the behaviors of other students?
   D. Is student engagement during a learning activity influenced by what occurred during the transition period preceding that activity?
   E. What role does a teacher's body language play in communicating expectations to students?
   F. How should praise and criticism be used to teach students to be on-task?
   G. Is is smart to call students "smart"?
   H. What accommodations should teachers make for students who display "understandable" misbehaviors?
   I. Why would some students rather be punished than ignored?
   J. To what degree should teachers expect support from parents, supervisors, and school administrators in helping them deal with discipline problems?
   K. Do teachers' needs and students' needs ever conflict?
   L. How, if at all, should behavior modification strategies be employed to maintain students engaged in learning activities?
   M. How does mainstreaming influence classroom environments?
   N. How does group dynamics influence classroom environments?

SUPPLEMENTAL READINGS

Abernathy, S., Manera, E., & Wright, R. (1985). What stresses student teachers most? *The Clearing House, 58,* 361–362.

Cangelosi, J. S. (1990). *Cooperation in the classroom: Students and teachers together* (2nd ed., pp. 9–12). Washington, DC: National Education Association.

————. (1992). *Systematic teaching strategies.* (pp. 2–37). New York: Longman.

Elam, S. M., Rose, L. C., & Gallup, A. M. (1991). The 23rd Annual Gallup Poll of the public's attitudes toward the public schools. *Phi Delta Kappan, 73,* 41–56.

Kobrin, D. (1992). *In there with the kids: Teaching in today's classrooms.* (pp. 1–46). Boston: Houghton Mifflin.

McGarity, J. R., & Butts, D. P. (1984). The relationship among teacher classroom management behavior, student engagement, and student achievement of middle and high school science students of varying aptitude. *Journal of Research in Science Teaching, 21,* 55–61.

Parker, W. C., & Gehrke, N. J. (1986). Learning activities and teacher decisionmaking: Some grounded hypotheses. *American Educational Research Journal, 23,* 227–242.

Thinking about Teaching Students to Cooperate

Purpose of Chapter 2

Chapter 2 is designed to help you

1. Realize that on-task behaviors and engagement in learning activites are learned responses that you should plan to teach your students.

2. Explain fundamental classroom management principles associated with each of the following sources: Jacob Kounin, Frederic Jones, Haim Ginott, William Glasser, Rudolph Dreikurs, Lee Canter, behaviorist theory, and the literature related to mainstreaming special students.

3. Know the meaning of the following terms and be able to comprehend communications that use them: *withitness, smoothness of transitions, assertive response, passive response, hostile response, positive reinforcer, destructive positive reinforcer, naturally occurring punishment, contrived punishment, destructive punishment, negative reinforcement, isolated behavior, behavior pattern,* and *group dynamics.*

STUDENTS LEARN TO COOPERATE

Here are some examples of student behaviors that are commonly observed in school settings.

- After being told by their second grade teacher to work out the computations on a tasksheet, Jaylene begins computing, while Fred begins doodling and drawing pictures of robots on the tasksheet.

- Instead of doing the push-ups his physical education teacher assigned for homework, Woodrow watches television and eats snacks.
- During history class, Janet listens to her teacher's lecture on the European Industrial Revolution while two of her classmates, Sophie and John, chat about their plans for going out that night.

Jaylene and Janet were on-task and engaged in learning activities; Fred, Woodrow, Sophie, and John were off-task. Which group of students displayed behaviors that were more natural for people? Think about the contrasting behaviors of the two second graders, Jaylene and Fred. Would a seven- or eight-year old, when handed a pencil and a sheet of paper containing numerals, be more inclined to begin manipulating the numerals or to begin doodling and drawing? Is it surprising that Woodrow would prefer watching television and eating snacks to doing push-ups? Isn't it normal for two adolescents, such as Sophie and John, to be more interested in talking to each other than in listening to a lecture on the European Industrial Revolution?

Sitting at a desk, thinking about academic topics, completing writing exercises, trying to memorize steps in a process, doing calisthenics, and discussing mitosis are simply not the kinds of things people are inclined to do in the absence of either the imposition of a special structure (e.g., a school) or extraordinary motivation. You should keep in mind that students must learn to be on-task and engaged in the learning activities you plan for them. On-task behaviors are typically less natural than off-task behaviors and, consequently, you can expect your students to be on-task only if you have taught them to choose on-task behaviors over off-task behaviors.

The question, of course, is: "How do you teach students to choose to be on-task?" Over many years this has been addressed by enough reports, journal articles, books, and papers to fill a library. From these works, a number of schools of thought on the general topic of student discipline and classroom management have emerged. Sometimes mistakenly thought of as being in opposition (e.g., the Ginott approach versus the behaviorist approach), these theories actually complement one another when the best ideas and insights from each are taken into consideration. Fundamentals of some of the major schools of thought on teaching students to be on-task are presented in the remainder of this chapter.

THE KOUNIN APPROACH:
WITHITNESS AND ORGANIZATION

Beginning in the 1950s and continuing into the 1970s, Jacob Kounin conducted studies examining the influence of certain teacher behaviors on the tendencies of students to be on-task (Kounin, 1970; Kounin & Doyle, 1975; Kounin & Gump, 1974; Kounin & Sherman, 1979). These studies involved classrooms from kindergarten through college level.

Withitness

One of the major implications from these studies involves the impact of teachers' "withitness" on students' behaviors. Kounin coined the term to refer to a teacher's awareness of what is going on in the classroom. The proverbial teachers with "eyes in the back of their heads" have withitness. Kounin emphasized that teachers increase the likelihood of students being on-task by demonstrating to students that they are with-it and, thus, accurately detect classroom events. He found that students tend to judge their teacher as having withitness if

- When discipline problems occur, the teacher consistently takes action to suppress misbehaviors of exactly those students who instigated the problems. (This displays that the teacher knows what is happening. If on the other hand, it appears to the students that the teacher is likely to blame the wrong person, they conclude that the teacher is not with-it.)
- When two discipline problems arise concurrently, the teacher typically deals with the more serious one first.
- The teacher decisively handles instances of off-task behaviors before the behaviors either get out of hand or are modeled by others. (For example, if third grader Bernie begins creating a tower with the colored rods he is supposed to be using to validate answers to multiplication exercises, a with-it teacher will likely take action to get Bernie back on-task before the tower tumbles over or other students begin building their own.)

The Impact of Teachers' Responses to Misbehaviors

Kounin also studied how a teacher's handling of one student's misbehavior affects the behaviors of other students. He found that when a teacher responds to the misbehavior of one student so that other students clearly understand exactly what makes the behavior unacceptable, the other students are less likely to exhibit that misbehavior in the future. This effect was stronger for elementary level students than for older ones. It was also discovered that when a teacher's response to a student's misbehavior includes anger, threats, physical handling, or indications that the teacher is stressed, other students become anxious and nervous, but the chances that they will exhibit the misbehavior themselves in the future are not reduced.

Concurrently Dealing with a Number of Events

According to Kounin, it is very important for teachers to be able to manage a classroom so that they can deal with a number of events concurrently. Compare how the two teachers in Vignettes 2.1 and 2.2 handled instances of off-task behaviors.

VIGNETTE 2.1

Ms. Farnsworth is explaining certain aspects of human digestive systems to her class of 31 tenth graders when she notices Ekpe and Ross whispering to one another. She stops her explanation and announces: "Please pay attention you two! It's very important for you to understand this . . . Now where were we? . . . Oh, yes! As I was saying . . ."

VIGNETTE 2.2

Ms. Gordin is explaining certain aspects of human digestive systems to her class of 31 tenth graders when she notices Rich and Jonathan whispering to one another. She continues with her explanations to the class as she moves nearer to Rich and Jonathan. They continue their whispering. Without the least interruption to her lecture, she moves between Rich and Jonathan and gently touches Rich on the shoulder. The two stop whispering and appear to begin attending to the lesson. She continues to observe all of the students, including Rich and Jonathan, as the explanation progresses.

How would you prefer to have handled the students' whispering—as Ms. Farnsworth did, or as Ms. Gordin did? Ms. Gordin simultaneously handled two events, her lesson and the off-task behaviors of two students. Ms. Farnsworth, on the other hand, interrupted her lecture to take time to handle the whispering. Her failure to deal with both events at the same time caused other students to become disengaged from the learning activity.

Smoothness of Transitions and Momentum

According to Kounin's studies, student engagement and on-task behaviors are dependent on how smoothly teachers move from one learning activity to another, the efficiency of transitions, and how well momentum is maintained. Examine Vignettes 2.3, 2.4, and 2.5.

In Vignette 2.3, Mr. Condie failed to get all of his students' attention before attempting to provide them with directions for an upcoming learning activity. The transition between the time allocated for the writing activity and the time allocated for answering history questions was not smooth. With some students continuing to work on the first activity, others changing activities, and still others beginning the new task, the transition time was marked by confusion.

While Mr. Condie did not attend to details and attempted to make the transition between two learning activities too rapidly, Ms. Jesundas may have never gotten her second activity underway. She wasted so much of her students' time with minute details, taking care of isolated problems of individuals, and trying to convince her students how enjoyable the activity would be, that her students got bored by what she had planned for them to do before they ever got to do it.

VIGNETTE 2.3

Mr. Condie is grading papers at a desk while his fifth grade students individually work on a writing assignment at their places. Suddenly, he announces: "Okay class, you can finish that later; let's take out our history workbooks and start answering the questions beginning at the bottom of page 74. Jean, how would you answer number one?" Some students are so involved with the writing assignment they do not comprehend and continue to write, although history questions are being read. Others stop writing, but inquire from classmates about the page number. There is quite a delay before the majority of the class is engaged in the history lesson.

VIGNETTE 2.4

Ms. Jesundas announces to her fourth grade class: "I see that everyone is finished with the calculator drill. Please see that your calculator is off and put away in its box. . . . Very good! Now, we're going to begin working on something you'll really enjoy. I want everyone to get out one sheet of paper and a pencil. . . . Joseph, get those other things off of your desk. . . . Thank you, Joseph. Okay, as I was saying, you should have just one sheet of paper. . . . That's the way to do it, Mark! . . . You should have one sheet of paper, and nothing else, except for a pencil on your desk. . . . Oh! Rachel, your pencil needs sharpening. We'll take care of that in a moment. Now, you're really going to like what we're going to do. Take your paper and . . ."

VIGNETTE 2.5

With the aid of an overhead projector, Mr. Saville is demonstrating to his accounting class one system for recording certain types of business transactions. While referring to an example involving consolidation of loans, Mr. Saville pauses.

MR. SAVILLE: Have we ever explained what consolidation of loans means?
DOROTHY: No, we never did get to that.
DAVID: Yeah! What does that mean?
MR. SAVILLE: I thought we had covered that, but I guess not. . . . Open your text to page . . . Let's see . . . Here it is! Page 139. . . . Everybody's got it? . . . Good! Now read the part under heading six dash four on consolidating loans.
GWYNN: Mr. Saville, we already read this! This was a homework assignment.

Other students express their agreement, while only a few suggest that they hadn't read the section.

MR. SAVILLE: In that case, put your books away and let's get back to our new recording system. . . . Now, as I was explaining before . . .

In Vignette 2.5, the transitions were inefficient and Mr. Saville failed to maintain momentum during learning activities. He interrupted one activity to begin another and then returned to the first while the second one was abandoned. Although such interruptions cannot always be avoided, they do make it difficult for students to remain engaged in learning activities. At least some of Mr. Saville's students could still be thinking about who was right regarding the homework assignment when he was expecting their attention to be refocused on his demonstration.

Group Focus

Kounin emphasized the importance of using strategies to keep all students in a class focused on a topic. The teacher in Vignette 2.6 seems unconcerned about maintaining the group's focus, while the one in Vignette 2.7 consciously directs all students' thinking.

Ms. Grimes did not let the group session become a private conversation between herself and only one or two students. She used strategies designed to keep the entire group focused on the topic at hand.

Kounin also found that teachers reduce boredom and increase engagement in learning activities by (1) keeping students apprised as to what they are accomplishing as lessons progress, (2) injecting challenges for the students to confront at different stages of the lesson, and (3) using a variety of approaches from one learning activity to another.

VIGNETTE 2.6

Mr. Drake is leading a discussion session with his 28 sixth graders on a short story they have just read.

MR. DRAKE: Mary, why do you think Joey didn't go back to school?
MARY: Because he thought his friends would make fun of him.
MR. DRAKE: What did the story's author say to make you think that?
MARY: Well, remember when . . .

VIGNETTE 2.7

Ms. Grimes is leading a discussion session with her 28 sixth graders on a short story they have just read.

MS. GRIMES: Think about why Joey didn't go back to school. . . . Okay, we're ready to hear what you think. Why didn't Joey go back to school, Mary?
MARY: Because he thought his friends would make fun of him.
MS. GRIMES: What in the story do you suppose made Mary believe that, Devon?
DEVON: She probably thinks . . .

Subsequent chapters of this text, especially Chapters 3, 6, 9 and 10, include material that is designed to help you put ideas emanating from Kounin's studies into practice.

THE JONES APPROACH: BODY LANGUAGE, INCENTIVES, AND EFFICIENT HELP

Studies of School Time

Utilizing the results of studies that involved hundreds of observations in elementary and secondary school classrooms in a wide variety of settings (e.g., inner city and suburban), Frederic Jones developed and promoted techniques for managing classrooms and motivating students through the Classroom Management Training Program, centered in Santa Cruz, California. Observations indicated that for typical classrooms, 50 percent of allocated time is lost because of off-task behaviors (Jones, 1979). While some teachers fear that students will be openly defiant and hostile and that violence will erupt in their schools, Jones found that 99 percent of off-task behaviors take one of several forms: students typically either talk out of turn, clown, daydream, or move about without permission. Antisocial, dangerous behaviors only represent a minute proportion of the time students spend off-task. Massive time-wasting is epidemic in schools.

Many teachers and school administrators who have participated in workshops through the Classroom Management Training Program have found that student engagement time is markedly increased when teachers adhere to Jones' suggestions regarding teachers' use of body language, incentive systems, and efficient individual help.

Body Language and Proximity

Through the use of eye contact, facial expressions, gestures, your physical proximity to students, and the way you carry yourself, you can communicate that you are in calm control of the class and expect to be taken seriously. Direct eye contact between two people often makes those people uncomfortable. Consequently, teachers and students are inclined to look away when their eyes meet. However, Jones found that control over a classroom situation is exerted when a teacher continually monitors the students, often pausing to look directly into the eyes of individual students. By focusing your eyes on individual students and managing to do this regularly for all students, you communicate that each student is personally an important part of what's going on in the classroom. Occasionally winking at, smiling with, or making a positive hand gesture (e.g., thumb up) to students when you have made eye contact helps communicate that you are very aware and interested that they are there. By taking Jones's suggestion about eye contact, you demonstrate Kounin's withitness.

As you might expect, students who see the teacher nearby are more likely to be on-task than students who are farther away. You should consider planning learning activities so that you are free to roam among your students rather than being stationary (e.g., at a lecture stand, chalkboard, or behind a lab table). Chapter 6 will provide you with practical suggestions for conducting learning activities, even lectures and demonstrations, so that you are able to move among your students and encourage engagement.

Which teacher, the one in Vignette 2.8 or 2.9, displays the more effective use of body language?

The body language displayed by Mr. Brown was more in line with Jones's suggestions than that displayed by Mr. Tramonte.

Incentives

Jones's training program encourages teachers to use systems of real incentives for students. In Vignette 2.10, Ms. Robertson uses a typical approach to motivating on-task behaviors; in Vignette 2.11, Ms. Samples uses an approach that exemplifies Jones's method.

Two factors prevented Ms. Robertson's approach from succeeding. (1) Some students may have wanted to be members of Ms. Robertson's "best class ever" and have a star on their papers; however, such incentives were probably not strong enough to maintain 17 minutes of continuous work. (2) The vast majority of

---

VIGNETTE 2.8

Mr. Tramonte's students are working on individual assignments at their desks as he moves about the room answering questions and providing help. While explaining something to Charlie, Mr. Tramonte realizes that Bonnie and John, two students seated at the back of the room, are off-task and becoming disruptive as they talk with one another. Without turning his body around, Mr. Tramonte looks over his shoulder and yells: "Knock it off! I don't want to hear any more yakking."

VIGNETTE 2.9

Mr. Brown's students are working on individual assignments at their desks as he moves about the room answering questions and providing help. While explaining something to Iris, Mr. Brown realizes that Dustin and Annie, two students seated at the back of the room, are off-task and becoming disruptive as they talk with one another. Mr. Brown softly tells Iris: "Excuse me, I'll be back within 40 seconds." Mr. Brown pivots and faces Dustin and Annie. He calmly walks directly toward them and squats down so his eye level meets theirs. With his shoulders parallel to Dustin's he looks Dustin in the eyes and softly says: "I would like you to get to work without talking." He immediately turns directly to Annie, achieves eye contact and repeats the message. Standing up, he pivots and returns to Iris.

VIGNETTE 2.10

While directing her fourth graders to answer questions to start a reading activity, Ms. Robertson announces: "I know you can be my best class ever! Let's see how quickly you can get these questions answered correctly! The first three students who show me all 12 correct answers will get stars on their papers to bring home to show their parents!"

VIGNETTE 2.11

While directing her fourth graders to answer questions to start a reading activity, Ms. Samples announces: "You have exactly 17 minutes to work on these questions. I want you to answer as many of the 12 questions as you can in that time. I will be walking around watching you work. If everyone works on the questions without stopping for the entire 17 minutes and no one disturbs anyone else, the class can pick out one video from the library and we will watch the first 30 minutes of it right after lunch." Emily asks: "Ms. Samples, what will we do after lunch if we don't watch the video?" Ms. Samples: "If we don't watch a video, I'll let you help me clean the room for 30 minutes right after lunch."

Because Ms. Samples has used this tactic before, the fourth graders know not to complain that it wouldn't be fair for the whole class to miss the video if only one or two children are uncooperative. Such complaints have been nonproductive in the past, but peer pressure has served as an effective control.

Ms. Robertson's students realized they had virtually no chance of being one of the first three successful finishers; the competition was no motivation for those who were in greatest need of motivation.

Pre-scheduled opportunities to watch a video, have free time to talk or play, or listen to music (with earphones) are usually more appealing than less tangible rewards. Ms. Samples' approach provided incentives to all students, not only the few who had a chance to be early finishers.

Providing Individual Help

Vignette 2.12 illustrates one other concern raised by Jones's research findings.

Teachers were observed providing individual help, as did Mr. Dupont-Lee, and then were asked how much time they thought they averaged with each student. The vast majority thought they spent between one and two minutes; actually, they averaged about four minutes with each student (Jones, 1979). Four uninterrupted minutes is too long to spend with one individual student while others are waiting for help. Chapter 6 will explain how you can be far more efficient than Mr. Dupont-Lee in the way you provide individual help to your students.

VIGNETTE 2.12

Mr. Dupont-Lee's eleventh graders are individually working at their places on factoring algebraic polynomials. About 12 of the 27 students have their hands raised beckoning Mr. Dupont-Lee's help as he moves among them tutoring one and then another. When he gets around to Brenda, she says: "I don't know how to do these."

MR. DUPONT-LEE: What is it you don't know how to do?
BRENDA: I don't understand enough to know what I don't know!
MR. DUPONT-LEE: Let's look at number three here. Did you look for a factor common to all the terms?
BRENDA: Well, all the terms have three as a factor.
MR. DUPONT-LEE: Then what can you . . .

In the meantime, other students are waiting and feel they cannot continue with the exercise until Mr. Dupont-Lee helps them. But he doesn't get around to all those requesting help and more and more students, bored waiting for help, become disengaged from the learning activity.

THE GINOTT APPROACH: COOPERATION THROUGH COMMUNICATION

Describing instead of Characterizing

Haim Ginott (1965, 1972) offered solutions to common communication problems that parents experience with their children and teachers experience with their students. He emphasized that the messages adults send have a profound effect on children's and adolescent's self-concepts. What may seem to be only subtle differences in the ways teachers consistently use language can be a major determinant in how students view themselves and how willing they are to cooperate. Vignettes 2.13 and 2.14 provide contrasting examples to illustrate a major Ginott theme.

Ms. Robinson addressed Theresa's character; she labeled her as "rude." Ms. Hebert, on the other hand, did not bring Lamona's personality into question, nor did she label Lamona. Instead, Ms. Hebert addressed the situation and targeted Lamona's rude behavior rather than Lamona herself. Lamona's rudeness needs to be eliminated, not Lamona herself.

Paramount in Ginott's work is this principle: Teachers should verbalize to students descriptions of situations and behaviors and never value judgments about individuals themselves. Ms. Hebert described a situation when she said: "George has the floor right now." She also described her own feelings by saying: "I am angry because your interruption stopped us from hearing what George was saying." According to Ginott, teachers should recognize both their own feelings and those expressed by students. If, as a teacher, you are not angry very often, you are more likely to have students' full attention during those times when you

---

VIGNETTE 2.13

Ms. Robinson is conducting a learning activity in which her sixth graders are describing how reading a particular poem made them feel. "I began to remember back when I was only seven years old when—," Justin is saying when he is interrupted by Theresa who blurts: "Yeah, because you still are seven! Who wants to hear what a baby like you thinks?" Ms. Robinson: "Theresa! What a rude little girl you are! Why can't you be more thoughtful? Continue, Justin. It is too bad that one discourteous person hurt your feelings! You are definitely not a baby. Please go on."

VIGNETTE 2.14

Ms. Hebert is conducting a learning activity in which her sixth graders are describing how reading a particular poem made them feel. "I began to remember back when I was only seven years old when—," George is saying when he is interrupted by Lamona who blurts: "Yeah, because you still are seven! Who wants to hear what a baby like you thinks?" Ms. Hebert turns to Lamona and firmly, but calmly says: "George has the floor right now. I am angry because you stopped us from hearing what George was saying." Turning to George, Ms. Hebert says: "George, you were saying that the poem had you remembering when you were seven. I would like you to continue."

---

are angry. Ginott suggested that you take advantage of such times to model just how you want your students to handle times when they are angry. Ms. Hebert acknowledged her anger, but displayed complete control and never resorted to name calling, insults, or sarcasm. She focused on getting back to the business at hand and getting students reengaged in the learning activity.

Avoiding Labels

Teachers are often reminded (e.g., in psychology courses and professional journals) that they should not be sarcastic with students nor associate undesirable labels with students (e.g., "dumb," "rotten," or "poor reader"). Ginott, of course, agreed that such a deplorable, but not uncommon, practice is detrimental to obtaining students' cooperation and maintaining on-task behaviors. However, Ginott also pointed out the dangers of placing any kind of characterizations or labels, even seemingly complimentary ones (e.g., "smart," "good," or "fast reader"), on students. Consider Vignette 2.15.

The Detrimental Effects of Praise

You should praise sutdents' work and their desirable behaviors, not the students themselves. Being praised motivates desirable student behavior only if students' self-esteem depends on the opinions of others. Ginott warned of the dangers of

---

VIGNETTE 2.15

Upon returning one of her students' science test papers with a high score, Ms. Johnson remarks: "Whitney, you proved you are quite a scientist. Thank you for being such a good student!" Whitney feels proud being praised in front of his peers. Jana, hearing Ms. Johnson's remark thinks: "Since I had a low test score, I must be a bad student who can't do science."

Later, Whitney gets nervous, fearing that he won't score high enough on subsequent science tests to live up to Ms. Johnson's label. When science gets difficult for him, he is tempted either not to try, lest he fail to live up to the label, or to cheat on tests and at least maintain his status in the class.

---

getting students hooked on praise. Students' self-esteem should not be dependent on how they think others perceive them. In Vignette 2.13, Ms. Robinson suggested that Theresa had hurt Justin's feelings. She assured Justin that he is not a baby. In contrast, Ms. Hebert, in Vignette 2.14, avoided suggesting for a moment that Lamona could influence how George felt about himself. She assumed that George was capable of determining for himself whether or not he was a baby.

Focusing

Call to mind two other differences between Vignettes 2.13 and 2.14. Ms. Hebert responded to Lamona's disruptive behavior by describing the situation and then directing the students back on-task. Ms. Robinson, on the other hand, raised at least one irrelevant issue when she asked Theresa: "Why can't you be more thoughtful?" Unless Ms. Robinson wanted to waste class time listening to Theresa's answer, she should not have asked that question. Why, then, did she allow the exchange to get sidetracked, thus, delaying the class' reengagement in the learning activity?

The influence of Ginott's work is ubiquitous in this text. Chapter 4, in particular, suggests practical ways for you to incorporate Ginott's principles into your own teaching practices.

THE GLASSER APPROACH: RATIONAL CHOICES

Inexcusable Behavior

In the privacy of their school's conference room, two teachers have the conversation reported in Vignette 2.16.

It was probably advantageous for Mr. Green to become aware of some aspects of Bartell's background and, thus, better understand his behavior. However, according to William Glasser (1965, 1969, 1977, 1978, 1985, 1988), understanding why

---

VIGNETTE 2.16

MR. GREEN: Thanks for meeting with me. I want to talk with you about Bartell Hopkins. Wasn't he in your class last year?

MS. MENA: Yes, and I'm glad you've got him this year instead of me! How's he getting along?

MR. GREEN: Terrible! When I asked him for his homework today, he told me, it was—pardon me, I don't mean to be gross, but I'm just quoting—

MS. MENA (interrupting): Don't worry, I've heard everything after 14 years in the classroom and most of it I heard from Bartell last year. What did he say?

MR. GREEN: He told me it was up his ass, and I was welcome to come and get it.

MS. MENA: Is that all! You should of heard some of the foul things he came out with last year. You know, Bartell is an abused child. Ever since he was a baby, he's had an uncle, his father — some father! — and heaven knows who else takes advantage of him in every grotesque way. It's a wonder the poor lad behaves as well as he does.

MR. GREEN: I didn't know! No wonder he acts like that. I'm sorry I sent him out of the room today when he mouthed off at me. I'll begin to be more tolerant with him.

---

a student exhibits undesirable behaviors is no reason to tolerate such behaviors. Glasser emphasized that students are rational beings and are quite capable of choosing to cooperate and be on-task. Mr. Green should never waiver in his insistence on high standards of conduct from Bartell in spite of Bartell's unfortunate background. Glasser would remind Mr. Green that he and other teachers may provide Bartell with his only opportunity to learn acceptable behaviors. The idea is for teachers to lead students to focus on their choices of behaviors while in school and to never accept excuses for improper behaviors.

Meetings and Conferences

Rules for governing classroom conduct and maintaining students on-task should, according to Glasser, be established cooperatively by teachers and students. It is vital for rules to be strictly enforced. Students must be able to predict the consequences, both desirable and undesirable, of their behavior choices.

Group meetings in the classroom as well as one-to-one conferences between student and teacher are important tools for leading students to rationally choose how they will behave relative to school activities. Glasser recommended that teachers routinely hold three types of classroom meetings (1) meetings concerned with students' social conduct in school, (2) open-ended meetings for discussing intellectually important subjects raised by the students, and (3) meetings concerned with how well students are progressing relative to the curricula. Class meetings, as well as one-to-one conferences, are conducted so that solutions to problems are addressed, while faultfinding and name-calling are out of order.

One-to-one conferences are used to help students identify a particular problem behavior, make a value judgment regarding that behavior, and make a commitment to supplant the problem behavior with on-task behavior. Vignette 2.17 provides an example.

VIGNETTE 2.17

For two consecutive days during the time Mr. Dean allocated for his high school industrial arts students to work on a project, Elmo either sat and stared into space or slept. Responding to this display of off-task behavior, Mr. Dean meets privately with Elmo. Mr. Dean takes a seat directly in front of Elmo so that he can readily achieve eye contact during the following conversation:

MR. DEAN: Thank you for coming. Tell me, Elmo, were you in shop class today?

ELMO: Yeah, you saw me there.

MR. DEAN: How long were you in shop class today?

ELMO: I was there the whole time; I didn't skip out or nothin'! Somebody else might of slipped out, but I didn't.

MR. DEAN: I don't want to talk about anybody else, just about what you did in shop class today.

ELMO: Maybe, Sandra was the one who — ''

MR. DEAN (interrupting): We're not going to talk about Sandra or anyone other than you and me. What did you do during the 55 minutes you spent in shop today?

ELMO: I don't know.

MR. DEAN: Tell me just one thing you remember doing in shop today.

ELMO: I watched you show us how to use that new machine.

MR. DEAN: And what did you do after I finished showing you how to use the drill press?

ELMO: I dunno, I guess I went to sleep.

MR. DEAN: Do you remember what I asked you to do right before you went to sleep?

ELMO: Work on my project, but I was tired.

MR. DEAN: I'm sorry you were tired, but would it be better for you to sleep in shop or get your project done?

ELMO: But the project is so boring!

MR. DEAN: I'm sorry you find the project boring. What happens if you don't finish your project by next Monday?

ELMO: I know, you told us. We don't pass shop.

MR. DEAN: Not passing shop, is that good or bad for you?

ELMO: That's bad, that's real bad!

MR. DEAN: Do you want to pass shop?

ELMO: Of course!

MR. DEAN: What will it take for you to pass shop?

ELMO: Do my project.

MR. DEAN: By when?

> ELMO: Monday.
> MR. DEAN: What must you do to have it done by Monday?
> ELMO: I'll have to work on it this week.
> MR. DEAN: When will you have time to work on it?
> ELMO: In class, that's the only time you let us work on it.
> MR. DEAN: And there are only two more class days for you to get it done. You don't have any time to waste. What are you going to do in class tomorrow when I direct the class to work on projects?
> ELMO: I'm going to work on my project.
> MR. DEAN: What if you're tired?
> ELMO: I'll work on my project anyway.
> MR. DEAN: You've made a smart choice. Would you be willing to write a note telling me that you will work on your project for the last 45 minutes of shop class tomorrow? I'll use the note to remind myself to leave you at least 45 minutes of class time for your project and I'll make a copy to keep to remind you of your commitment.

THE DREIKURS APPROACH: MISTAKEN BELIEFS

Democratic Classrooms

Rudolf Dreikurs (1968) stressed that teachers should be neither autocratic nor permissive if they expect students to be cooperative in the classroom. Resentment and power struggles are among the unpleasant consequences of autocratic teachers' use of coercion to control students' behaviors. Permissive teachers, who fail to establish and enforce rules for conduct, leave their students confused and lacking in guidance for being on-task. Dreikurs extolled the advantages of "democratic" classrooms where students (1) have a voice in the determination of rules, (2) suffer the logical consequences of their own misbehaviors rather than submit to arbitrary punishment administered by teachers, and (3) are motivated to be on-task because of the intrinsic benefits derived from being on-task (e.g., achieving a skill by being engaged in a learning activity) rather than because of extrinsic benefits (e.g., avoiding ridicule or reaping praise).

Mistaken Beliefs about Social Acceptance

Because students desire to be accepted members of a social group and because they are able to control their own behaviors, Dreikurs suggested that student misbehaviors are attributable to mistaken beliefs about what will obtain the recognition they seek. He identified four types of mistaken beliefs that lead to misbehaviors (1) attention getting, (2) power seeking, (3) revenge seeking, and (4) displaying inadequacy.

After failing to gain recognition as a result of on-task behavior, a student may resort to off-task behavior in an attempt to achieve the recognition of a teacher or other students. Dreikurs referred to this as the "attention-getting mechanism."

When you recognize one of your students displaying the attention-getting mechanism, you should, according to Dreikurs, see to it that the student is ignored. Attention-seeking students prefer being punished, admonished, or criticized to being ignored. Attention should be afforded students when they are on-task and cooperating.

"Power seeking" refers to the mistaken belief of students that if a teacher doesn't let them do what they want, then the teacher does not approve of them. Power-seeking students attempt to provoke teachers into struggles of wills. Teachers, who follow Dreikurs advice, refuse to play such games. Compare how the teachers in Vignettes 2.18 and 2.19 respond to students' attempts at defying authority.

Ms. Burnside allowed Steve to draw her into his power-seeking game. Consequently, valuable class time was lost. Many other students probably never got well engaged in the lesson, once it finally started, because they continued to think about the nasty exchange that had just occurred. Steve's belief that the classroom is a place to have power struggles was confirmed. Ms. Burnside may think she won the battle of wills. However, because she heightened rather than defused the game, as did Mr. Ruiz, she unwittingly challenged Steve to try her again some other time.

"Seeking revenge" is closely related to power seeking. Power-seeking students are likely to develop resentment toward those to whom they have lost battles of wills. They feel hurt by others who have displayed power over them. Consequently, they want to hurt others to display their own power and thus achieve status.

VIGNETTE 2.18

During the transition between the time Ms. Burnside's fifth graders worked on a spelling exercise and the time she planned for them to report on findings of a science experiment that was assigned for homework, Steve stands up on top of a work table in the back of the room and begins to clown. Some of the students laugh at his antics. Steve remains on the table even after Ms. Burnside directs the class to begin the science activity.

MS. BURNSIDE: Please get down and take your seat, Steve. It's time for us to share what we learned from the experiments.
STEVE: I'm not getting down.
MS. BURNSIDE: Yes you are!
STEVE: You can't make me!
MS. BURNSIDE: Oh yes I can! Who do you think you're talking to, young man?
STEVE: Who do you think I'm talking to?
MS. BURNSIDE: Boy! You have just five seconds to get off that table or you'll be mighty sorry! . . . One, . . . two, . . . three, . . . four, . . .

Steve grins as he hops off the table and slowly walks to his seat.

VIGNETTE 2.19

During the transition between the time Mr. Ruiz's fifth graders worked on a spelling exercise and the time he planned for them to report on findings of a science experiment that was assigned for homework, Rubin stands up on top of a work table in the back of the room and begins to clown. Some of the students laugh at his antics. Rubin remains on the table even after Ms. Ruiz directs the class to begin the science activity.

MR. RUIZ: Rubin, I would appreciate you taking your seat right now.
RUBIN: No, I'm staying right here. You can't make me get down!
MR. RUIZ: I'm too busy to try right now; I have a class to teach.

Mr. Ruiz directs his attention to those students sitting at their places and says, "Who would like to tell one thing that surprised them about the experiment? . . ." Some students raise their hands and nearly all become engaged in the lesson. Ignored, Rubin is left standing on the table.

After failing to achieve satisfaction through seeking attention, power, and revenge, students are likely to become so discouraged that they give up and use displays of inadequacy as an excuse for not trying. Dreikurs found it extremely difficult for teachers to effectively deal with students burdened by the last two of the four mistaken beliefs. He suggested that teachers help students recognize the mistaken beliefs under which they are operating. Examples of teachers confronting students with their mistaken beliefs in response to displays of off-task behaviors are contained in Chapters 7, 9, and 10 of this text.

THE CANTER APPROACH: ASSERTIVE DISCIPLINE

Six Suggestions

Lee and Marlene Canter studied the traits of teachers whose students displayed high levels of on-task behaviors. Their research led to a formulation of principles and techniques by which teachers take charge of their own classrooms in a forceful, but calm, manner. Thousands of teachers have participated in workshops, read literature (e.g., *Assertive Discipline: A Take-Charge Approach for Today's Educator* (Canter & Canter, 1976), attended lectures, and viewed films forwarding the Canter approach known as "assertive discipline."

With the Canter approach, teachers (1) utilize the assertive-response style that is associated with assertion training (Salter, 1949; Wolpe & Lazarus, 1966), (2) recognize fallacies in reasons for excusing off-task behaviors, (3) specify exactly what types of behaviors will be required and what types will not be tolerated, (4) develop a plan for encouraging on-task behaviors and discouraging off-task behaviors, (5) persist in following through with the plan, and (6) seek and expect support from parents, instructional supervisors, and school administrators.

The Assertive-Response Style

An assertive-response style is characterized by openness, directness, spontaneity, and appropriateness. Ms. Wilford displays an assertive-response style in Vignette 2.20.

Less assertive teachers in Ms. Wilford's situation may have feared jeopardizing their relationships with the students by not agreeing with their request. In reality, Ms. Wilford's assertive reply is likely to enhance her relationship with the students for two reasons. (1) Students begin to realize that she takes their work very seriously and that her plans for them are well thought out and not changed whimsically. (2) Had she changed her plans and not allowed herself the weekend to go over the reports, the personal inconvenience she suffered might lead to feelings of resentment directed at the students.

The recommended assertive-response style is neither hostile nor passive. Your communications are hostile when they are intimidating, insulting, or include personal innuendoes. Ms. Wilford would have displayed hostile communications if she had responded to the students' request as follows:

> "You people are always trying to get out of work! Do you think your game is more important than school work? School work will take you a lot farther in life than games. Besides, if you weren't so lazy, you'd have this paper finished in plenty of time for your game!"

Hostile communications encourage antagonistic feelings that detract from an atmosphere conducive to cooperation and learning. Passive communications erode the teacher's ability to control classroom activities. Your communications are passive when you fail to convey the message you want because you are intimidated or fearful of the reactions of the recipients of your message. Ms. Wilford's communications would have been passive if she had responded to the students' request as follows:

> "Well, we really need to have these papers done by Friday. I really should be going over them this weekend. I wish you wouldn't ask me to do this because I — But, okay, just this once — since this is an important game."

Further treatises of assertive communications (as opposed to either passive or hostile communications) are included in Chapters 4 and 7.

Inexcusable Behaviors

Like Glasser, Canter warned teachers not to let excuses deter them from insisting on appropriate student behavior. Peer pressure, inadequate parenting, learning disabilities, personal stress, and poor health are just some of the factors that make it more difficult for some students to be on-task than it is for other students. However, it is a fallacy that the presence of such factors excuses students from being responsible for their own behaviors.

VIGNETTE 2.20

RUSS (one of Ms. Wilford's history students): Mrs. Wilford, you know that report you wanted us to turn in Friday?

MS. WILFORD: Yes, Russ. What about it?

RUSS: Well — could we wait 'til Monday to give it to you?

Other students in the class chime in with comments such as, "Oh yes. Please Mrs. Wilford."

RUSS (smiling): There's a game Thursday night and I know you want us to support the team!

MARIE: You wouldn't want us to miss the game?

BARKLEY: Be nice, just this once.

Ms. Wilford is tempted to "be nice" and enjoy the applause she knows she'll receive if she gives in. However, she also realizes three things. (1) Delaying the assignment will cause the class to fall behind the planned lesson schedule. (2) If she doesn't get the reports until Monday she won't be able to read and annotate them over the weekend and consequently, she would be inconvenienced. (3) If they will adjust their own schedules, the students are quite capable of completing the report on time without missing the game.

Ms. Wilford announces to the class: "I understand that you are worried about making it to this important game and still being able to finish the report on time. You have cause for concern. Because changing the due-date will mess up our schedule and because I need the weekend to go over your papers, the reports are still due on Friday." "That's not fair!" cries Dennis. Ms. Wilford responds, "Yes, so it seems to you. Now, let's turn our books to page 122 . . ."

Teacher Needs

The needs of students are emphasized throughout educational literature. Canter emphasized the needs of teachers. He discovered that many teachers have difficulty specifying just what behaviors they need for students to exhibit and what behaviors they need for students to avoid. Ask yourself the question: "As a teacher, how do I want my students to behave so that my need to have a smoothly functioning classroom is met?" Do your answers specify observable behaviors or are they couched in vague generalities? When asked what they want from students, Canter and Canter (1976) reported the following among replies given by teachers: "I want the kids to act good." "I want them to be good citizens and have positive attitudes." "I want the children to respect me and each other." "I don't want hassles from the boys who are troublemakers."

Before you, as a teacher, are in a position to formulate plans for encouraging students to behave as you need them to behave (i.e., on-task) and discouraging them from behaving otherwise (i.e., off-task), you need to specify the desirable and undesirable behaviors. Rather than the vague, general words used by teachers in Canter's aforementioned examples, Canter recommended that the list specify conduct regarding such things as following directions, completing assignments, and not leaving the classroom without permission. Even the most clever of your plans for keeping students on-task will not work unless you persist in following through with it.

Support from Parents, Instructional Supervisors, and School Administrators

Students' parents, instructional sueprvisors, and school administrators have a vested interest in the success of classroom operations. Thus, Canter's assertion that teachers should seek and expect support from them seems quite reasonable. In many locations, school-wide systems based on Canter's assertive discipline have been instituted. One such system operating in a junior high is described in Vignette 2.21.

THE BEHAVIORIST APPROACH: CONDITIONING RESPONSES

Learned Responses

With the initial impetus from the works of Watson (1914), Dunlap (1919), and others who focused attention on learned, rather than instinctive, human behavior, behavioristic psychology has flourished and provided a research-based foundation for today's theories and principles for teaching students to be on-task. Particularly notable are the investigations of B. F. Skinner (1953, 1954), who examined the effects of stimuli on learning when the stimuli occurred after a response or act. Such investigations led to the following general conclusion that is fundamental to the behaviorist approach for managing behavior.

> Behaviors (i.e., responses) that are followed by rewards (i.e., satisfying or pleasant stimuli) are more likely to be repeated than behaviors that are not. Aversive stimuli or punishment following a behavioral response tend to discourage that response from recurring.

Behavior Modification

Student behaviors are thought of as complex sets of responses that have been conditioned by their environments. "Behavior modification" refers to the behaviorist approach by which students' environments are manipulated to increase the chances of desired behaviors being rewarded while undesirable behaviors go unrewarded. Students are thus conditioned toward being on-task.

Detractors of behavior modification complain that the goal of behavior modification programs is to condition observable behaviors, thus neglecting character development while students learn to "go through the motions" of being well-behaved. Secondly, they are bothered that highly-structured behavior modification programs often depend on extrinsic reward systems that have no natural

---

VIGNETTE 2.21

Just prior to the opening of school each year, parents of students enrolled in Alpine Junior High receive a description of the "assertive discipline" program in which students' parents', teachers', and administrators' responsibilities to the program are explained. Parents are asked to sign and return to the school office a form indicating that they have read the material and are willing to comply with the stipulations of the program. An orientation to the program is provided for the students during the first week of school.

Alpine Junior High's assertive discipline program includes the following features:

1. Each classroom teacher specifies for students the rules for classroom conduct. During the course of the year, new rules may be decided upon and occasionally an old rule may be deleted. An up-to-date list of rules is always displayed in the classroom.
2. The first time a student violates a rule during a particular class session, the teacher writes the student's name on a designated area of a chalkboard. The number of the rule that was violated is put next to the name. The teacher does not say anything about the transgression, but only writes the name and numeral on the board and continues with the planned activity.
3. The second time in the class period that same student violates a rule (not necessarily the same rule), the number of that rule is added to the name appearing on the board. Again, the teacher makes no other response to the off-task behavior.
4. Upon the third violation in the same class period, the student must leave the class and report to a detention room. Again, the teacher does not take class time to talk to the student about the matter. The teacher only indicates that a third violation has occurred and the student is already aware of the consequences.
5. There are no penalties or requirements for students who have no more than one violation during any one class period.
6. Students with two violations are required to meet with the teacher after school to discuss the violations and map out a plan for preventing recurrences.
7. The parents of students with three violations must appear at school to discuss the violations and make plans for preventing recurrences with the student, the teacher, and another school official. The student may not return to the class where the violations occurred until a plan has been worked out with the parents.

---

association with the behaviors they are designed to encourage. Students, for example, may be given trading stamps for doing homework. Consequently, the students may learn to expect such prizes for simply meeting routine responsibilities. A third complaint proposes that conditioning students' behaviors is suggestive of treating human beings as if they are robots that lack free wills.

Proponents of behavior modification answer the first of these three criticisms by noting that controlling students' behaviors cannot wait for character development. Besides, by practicing desirable behaviors, one learns self-discipline. The second criticism is contested with the argument that students often need extrinsic rewards to initially choose to be on-task. After on-task behaviors become habitual, then the students begin to recognize the intrinsic values and no longer need to be "bribed." In the aforementioned example, the students eventually will find satisfaction from what they learn by doing homework (depending on the quality of the homework assignment). Thus, the intrinsic motivation (e.g., satisfaction gained from learning) replaces the extrinsic motivation (e.g., promise of trading stamps). The third criticism, dealing with free will, involves questions that are more appropriately addressed in a treatise on philosophy.

The suggestions in this text are provided to you with confidence that they will work because of the wealth of research findings from behavioristic psychology. Before you begin considering the specific methods for gaining students' cooperation that are dealt with in subsequent chapters of this text, there are some concepts and principles with which you should be familiar.

Isolated Behaviors and Behavior Patterns

Consider these four examples of student behavior.

- While Ms. Bernstein is explaining to her sixth grade class what they will be doing in an upcoming learning activity, Harry interrupts: "Aw no! That'll be boring!" This is one of the few instances in which Harry ever interrupts a speaker in class. It is atypical for Harry to interrupt.

- While Mr. Diel is explaining to his sixth grade class what they will be doing in an upcoming learning activity, Valerie interrupts Mr. Diel with a comment as she has done on numerous other occasions over the past month.

- Dianne virtually always completes the homework that her teacher assigns.

- One night Jessica completes her homework assignment. Usually she doesn't bother with doing assignments.

By interrupting Ms. Bernstein, Harry displayed an off-task, disruptive behavior. Because such interruptions are not typical for Harry, that instance of being disruptive and off-task is said to be an isolated behavior. Valerie, on the other hand, habitually interrupts Mr. Diel and so Valerie's off-task, disruptive behavior is just one display in a continuing behavior pattern. Similarly, Dianne is simply displaying what is a regular behavior pattern for her by choosing to be on-task and do homework assignments. In the instance where Jessica did homework, she was deviating from her regular pattern and was, thus, displaying an isolated behavior.

It is important for you to differentiate between behaviors that are part of a pattern that your students have incorporated into their general conduct and behaviors that are isolated displays and are not habitual. Would you not expect Ms. Bernstein to deal with Harry's isolated instance of interruption different from the way Mr. Diel should attempt to teach Valerie to break her habit of interrupting others?

Positive Reinforcers

Here are examples of behaviors, some of which are rewarded and some which are not.

- Ever since Barry began regularly training with weights in physical education class, he really likes the way he feels. He frequently receives comments from classmates about how good he looks and how strong he is.
- During class discussions, Sandra often interrupts speakers with "put downs." Others in the class usually laugh at her remarks.
- Dale has a desire to lose weight. He attends a weight-reducing class several times with no resulting loss in weight. Dale ceases attending the class.
- A week ago, two-year-old Morris attempted to get his father, who was involved in a telephone conversation at the time, to pick him up. "Dad, Dad, hold me," Morris said in a calm voice. His father continued talking on the phone without paying attention to Morris. Morris persisted with his requests becoming louder and sounding more and more distressed. Finally, Morris was lying on the floor, screaming, and kicking so that his father could no longer hear the other party on the phone. At that point, Morris' father picked him up. Similar incidents have occurred since then. Now, when Morris wants to be picked up, he just throws himself on the floor and begins screaming and kicking.
- Nancy always does the written work assigned in Mr. Washington's class. Each paper is returned to her with comments and suggestions. Nancy hardly ever does the written work assigned in Ms. Taylor's class; Ms. Taylor never returns written work.

Barry, Sandra, Morris, and Nancy displayed voluntary behavior patterns. Barry continues to participate in weight lifting, Sandra frequently interrupts speakers, Morris routinely throws temper tantrums, and Nancy consistently completes Mr. Washington's written assignments. On the other hand, Dale no longer attends weight-reduction classes and Nancy chooses not to do Ms. Taylor's written assignments. Why are some behavior patterns formed and continued, while others are discontinued or never established? Obviously, Barry perceived that his participation in weight-training classes was paying off. Because the way he felt and the compliments he heard encouraged him to continue being engaged in weight-training, they are referred to as "positive reinforcers" of that particular behavior pattern. Similarly, Sandra's classmates' laughter served as a positive reinforcer of her habit of interrupting speakers with put-down remarks. Being picked up served to positively reinforce Morris' temper tantrums. Mr. Washington's helpful feedback on written assignments positively reinforced Nancy's behavior pattern of completing assignments.

People will not retain a behavior pattern or establish a new one in the absence of positive reinforcers. Dale no longer chose to attend weight-reducing class when he perceived his attendance went unrewarded. Nancy felt that doing Ms. Taylor's assignments was fruitless; thus, without positive reinforcement, she did not elect to do the work.

By definition, a positive reinforcer is a stimulus presented after a response that increases the probability of that response being repeated in the future. In the example about Barry, the response is Barry's engagement in weight-training sessions; the stimuli are the way Barry felt and the compliments he received from classmates.

Off-task, as well as on-task, voluntary behavior patterns, may also be established because of the presence of positive reinforcers.

Destructive Positive Reinforcers

The positive reinforcers in the following examples may have undesirable side effects:

- Ms. Coco announces to her ninth grade class: "Because you have been so cooperative with me today, I will not assign any homework for you to do tonight!"
- Students in Ms. Lambert's kindergarten class receive candy for completing assignments on time.
- Mr. Breaux asks his third graders: "Who can tell me why the man in the story did not want to leave his house in the morning?" A dozen of the students eagerly raise their hands. Mr. Breaux: "Jackie?" Jackie: "Because he didn't want to go to work." Some of the other students say: "No! Mr. Breaux, Mr. Breaux!" Mr. Breaux: "Okay, Ory can you help out Jackie?" Ory: "Because he thought his friend would come back to see him." Mr. Breaux: "Very good, Ory! That is correct! You are one of my very best readers!" Ory beams happily.

A teacher used positive reinforcement to encourage on-task behaviors in each of the examples. Ms. Coco's ninth graders were rewarded for their cooperation by being exempted from homework assignments. Ms. Coco's tactics probably served to encourage students' cooperation in the future. Unwittingly, however, she may also have taught her students that homework assignments are unimportant and not doing homework is better than doing homework.

In the second example, the motivation of anticipating a piece of candy may encourage Ms. Lambert's students to complete their assignments, but it may also teach them undesirable eating habits.

Mr. Breaux positively reinforced Ory's commendable answer with praise. However, Ginott (1972) warned against getting students hooked on praise. Also, Mr. Breaux may have unwittingly taught Ory to hope others (e.g., Jackie) will be unsuccessful in order to enhance his own opportunity to be the "star" of the class.

In each of these examples, the positive reinforcer for a targeted behavior (e.g., cooperation, finishing assignments, or comprehending a reading) had an undesirable side effect (e.g., teaching the unimportance of homework, unhealthy eating habits, or undue competitiveness among students). When a positive reinforcer for one behavior has undesirable side effects on other behaviors, it is referred to as a "destructive positive reinforcer." Selecting positive reinforcers for on-task behaviors that are not destructive is a main concern of Chapters 4, 7, 8, 9, and 10.

Punishment

By definition, punishment is a stimulus presented after a response that decreases the probability of that response being repeated in the future.

Contrived and Naturally Occurring Punishment.   Because they tend to affect students differently, you should distinguish between contrived and naturally occurring punishment. Here are two contrasting examples illustrating the differences.

- Leonard falls asleep while Mr. Tessier, his tenth grade health teacher, lectures. After the lecture, Mr. Tessier directs Leonard to bring to class the following day a 1,000-word essay entitled "Why I Should Not Sleep in Class."
- Bill falls asleep while Mr. Vasse, his tenth grade health teacher, lectures. When Bill awakens, he realizes that he does not know what was explained during the lecture. The next day, Bill's fears are confirmed as he fails a test on the content of the lecture.

Oddly enough, if Leonard happened to find that writing the essay provided him with an opportunity to be comical or to vent some frustration, the assignment might positively reinforce the off-task behavior. Please assume, however, that this was not the case and writing the essay served as punishment for getting caught sleeping in class. Mr. Tessier designed the punishment specifically to get Leonard to regret having slept in class. But having to write an essay is not a natural consequence of sleeping when one should be paying attention in class. Thus, Mr. Tessier used contrived punishment in dealing with Leonard's disengagement from the learning activity.

Bill also received punishment, but Bill's punishment was a natural consequence of his sleeping when he should have been paying attention. Hopefully, Bill will make the connection: "If I miss out on Mr. Vasse's lecture, I won't learn what will be on the test." Bill suffered naturally occurring punishment.

The Effects of Naturally Occurring Punishment Compared to Those of Contrived Punishment.   In Vignette 2.22, a teacher utilizes naturally occurring, rather than contrived, punishment.

If Ms. Brock consistently continues to use this strategy, her students will soon realize the automatic consequences of being off-task. Ms. Brock's words and manner communicated that she did not withhold the promised story because the students failed to pick up after themselves. She conveyed that the story was not read because the time set aside for the story would simply have to be used for cleaning.

The differences between contrived and naturally occurring punishment may seem so subtle as to be unimportant. But over time, the differences are monumental in terms of effects on students (Dreikurs, Grunwald, & Pepper, 1982, pp. 125–129; Weber, 1990, p. 271). In Vignette 2.23, Ms. Webb confronts a situation identical to that in Vignette 2.22; however, Ms. Webb uses contrived punishment.

Do you see the subtle differences between Ms. Brock's and Ms. Webb's handling of the situation? Ms. Webb blamed her failure to read the story on the students' failure to follow directions. She turned the incident into something personal. Consistent handling of such situations will lead to an antagonistic rather than cooperative relationship between Ms. Webb and her students. In time, students will learn to avoid getting caught while still enjoying some of the benefits of being off-task. When Ms. Webb raises irrelevant questions such as: "Why is this mess still here?" they will have ready answers such as: "I was picking up, but Otis didn't!" and "I tried to pick up, but Nadine kept bothering me!"

In contrast, Ms. Brock blamed her failure to read the story on the lack of time. Of course, the lack of time was a consequence of the area not being clean. Ms. Brock focused on what must be done. The question of why the area had not been cleaned up was not raised. Rather than communicate an "I'll get you for this" tone, Ms. Brock shared the students' unhappiness at not having time to read the story.

Frankly, some teachers use contrived instead of naturally occurring punishment because some off-task behaviors do not have undesirable naturally occurring consequences. If, for example, a teacher assigns students to do work that has

---

VIGNETTE 2.22

Ms. Brock's kindergarten class is working in two groups, the "Busy Bees" and the "Chipmunks." The busy Bees have just finished working on a project in which they used scissors, paste, and cardboard. Ms. Brock tells them: "While I show a short filmstrip to the Chipmunks, I want each of you to put away your scissors and paste and then clean up these scraps from the floor and table. When I return, I will read this story to you." Ms. Brock displays a book. The Busy Bees eagerly anticipate hearing the story.

As Ms. Brock begins showing the filmstrip to the Chipmunks, the Busy Bees start giggling and playing instead of following her directive to clean up. Six minutes later, Ms. Brock returns to the Busy Bees with the storybook in hand. "Oh, my goodness! This floor is still a mess and your scissors and paste are still out," she exclaims. "I am sorry, Busy Bees, but now I will have to help you clean up this mess and I won't have time to read the story to you." As she begins picking up along with the students, Ms. Brock continues: "I know you are disappointed. It is too bad that we still have to clean up and there won't be time left for the story."

VIGNETTE 2.23

. . . As Ms. Webb begins showing the filmstrip to the Chipmunks, the Busy Bees start giggling and playing instead of cleaning up. Six minutes later, Ms. Webb returns to the Busy Bees with the storybook in hand. "Why is this mess still here?" she asks. "Okay, because you didn't cooperate with me and pick up as I told you, I am not going to read this story. Maybe next time you'll know to listen!"

---

no meaningful benefit for them, then the students will not recognize any logical drawbacks for neglecting the work. Faced with such situations, teachers resort to the threat of contrived punishment to coerce students to cooperate.

Unwittingly Administered Punishment.   You should keep in mind that on-task, as well as off-task, behaviors can be discouraged through punishment. Teachers are ordinarily unmindful of such misfortunes when they do occur. Consider Vignette 2.24.

Might Barlow's teacher's response discourage him from making such diligent efforts in the future? How could Barlow's teacher have avoided punishing his diligent efforts and still communicated to him that 19 of the answers were incorrect? Is there something the teacher could have done to see that Barlow's efforts were actually positively reinforced although he had incorrect *final* answers? One solution is to score students' papers so that error patterns are identified, but points are awarded (i.e., "partial credit") for correct steps (see, e.g., Cangelosi, 1990b, pp. 139–145).

Destructive Punishment

A positive reinforcer is destructive if it has undesirable side effects. Punishment can also be destructive if it produces undesirable side effects in addition to discouraging some targeted behavior. Here are two examples; for each, identify the behavior being punished and a possible undesirable side effect:

- Mr. Norton is in the habit of assigning extra mathematics exercises to students who are disruptive in class.
- Ms. Chamberlain catches Quinn, one of her tenth graders, shooting paper clips across the classroom. She sends him to an assistant principal who administers three "swats" with a wooden paddle to Quinn's buttocks.

Mr. Norton's punishment of extra mathematics exercises for disruptive behavior may effectively reduce incidences of disruptive behavior. However, if it teaches students that mathematics is a form of punishment to be avoided, then Mr. Norton's punishment is destructive.

VIGNETTE 2.24

Barlow spends two hours completing a computation exercise where he is to find the products of 28 pairs of three-digit whole numbers. Barlow correctly executes almost all of the steps in the process for the 28 items. However, because he repeats a one-step error pattern in 19 of the items, only nine of his final answers are correct. Without explanation as to what he did wrong nor any indication of what he did right, Barlow's teacher returns his ''corrected'' work with 19 X-marks and ''32%/F'' at the top of the paper.

Besides discouraging him from getting caught again shooting paper clips, Quinn may learn from his experience with the assistant principal that it is okay for one human being to strike another. The undesirable effects of corporal punishment are well documented (Hyman & Wise, 1979) and are addressed in Chapter 7 of this text.

Negative Reinforcement

For many, but not nearly all, instances in which a student is off-task, negative reinforcement can be a powerful mechanism for getting a student to choose to be on-task. By definition, negative reinforcement is making the removal of punishment contingent upon a specified change in the behavior of the individual being punished. Vignette 2.25 provides an example.

How does negative reinforcement relate to punishment and to positive reinforcers? Like positive reinforcement and unlike punishment, negative reinforcement focuses on the behavior to be exhibited rather than the one to be inhibited.

VIGNETTE 2.25

Ms. Dirks directs her preschool class to put away the musical instruments they've been playing and to wash up for their mid-morning snack of bananas and carrots. Jay continues to blow his horn. Ms. Dirks goes over to Jay and says: ''It's time to put your horn away and wash your hands.'' Jay slams the horn to the floor and screams: ''No, no! I don't want to eat! I wanna play!'' Ms. Dirks: ''Jay, you don't want to eat. That's fine, but I want you to put away your horn, wash your hands, and sit with the rest of the children while they eat.'' Jay throws himself on the floor, kicks his feet and yells incoherently. Ms. Dirks remains calm as with gentle firmness she gets Jay to his feet and walks him to the back of the room over to a chair that faces away from the other students. Ms. Dirks: ''Jay, you are to sit in this chair until you have decided to get control of yourself, put away your horn, wash your hands, and sit with the rest of us. She leaves him in the chair. It takes about four minutes for Jay to calm himself down when he hops off the chair, puts away his horn, washes his hands, and joins the group.

Ms. Dirks used punishment by having Jay sit in the chair. However, she allowed Jay to choose when the punishment would be terminated. Ending the punishment served to positively reinforce the on-task behavior. Ms. Dirks would have used only punishment if she had told Jay to sit in the chair for five minutes or until she told him he could get up. Instead, she used negative reinforcement because the removal of the punishment was contingent on Jay's decision to cooperate.

Chapters 8, 9, and 10 of this text will expose you to examples of teachers using negative reinforcement to teach students to supplant off-task with on-task behaviors.

IDEAS TO CONSIDER WITH MAINSTREAMED STUDENTS

Lewis and Doorlag (1991, p. 480) define special students as "those students with special learning needs who require instructional adaptations in order to learn successfully." Handicapped students, gifted and talented students, culturally diverse students, and students at risk for school failure are included. "Mainstreaming" is sometimes used to refer to the inclusion of any special student in the general education process. However, mainstreaming is usually defined in relationship to handicapped students for which IEPs are required under P.L. 94–142. Schulz and Turnbull (1983, p. 49), for example define mainstreaming as "the social and instructional integration of handicapped students in regular education class for at least a portion of the school day."

Unless you have been afforded experiences interacting and working with handicapped persons, you may be apprehensive about having students, especially those identified with behavior disorders, mainstreamed into your classroom. Typically, teachers fear being unable to control disruptive behavior patterns of students with behavior disorders. Some worry about implementing individualized programs for students with learning disabilities. Others are unsure about adapting instruction and classrooms for students with physical impairments. Fortunately, a wealth of pre-service and in-service teacher education resources are now available in the form of college coursework (required for teacher certification in most states), workshops, literature, videotape programs, and other media sources.

The research literature on how to deal with off-task behavior patterns in the classroom emphasizes the application of behavior modification strategies. Chapter 8 of this text focuses on such strategies and how to use them to teach students (whether mainstreamed or not) to give up off-task behavior patterns in favor of on-task ones.

As you work your way through the remainder of this text, developing your own classroom management strategies, keep the following in mind regarding mainstreamed students in your classroom.

- You have access to help in working with mainstreamed students that is not ordinarily available for your regular education students. The

Authors such as Axelrod and Bailey (1979), Kauffman (1989), Smith (1981), and Walker (1979) have asked questions about the effectiveness of drugs in managing hyperactivity and other inappropriate student behaviors. These experts have concluded that additional research is needed in this area and that teachers should approach the medical management of behavioral problems with due caution. Axelrod and Bailey (1979) suggest the following guidelines for the use of drug treatment in school settings:

1. Physical examinations should be prerequisites to commencing and continuing drug treatment. This is necessary not only to monitor possible physiological problems, but also to determine whether physical anomalies might be causing problem behaviors.
2. Drugs should be considered only when there is a demonstration of inordinately inappropriate behavior. . . . The mere claim from a parent or teacher that a child's behavior warrants drug treatment is insufficient.
3. Before drug treatment is implemented, behavior modification procedures or other remedial techniques should be attempted.
4. Children who receive drugs should be exposed to two different dosage levels, a baseline phase, and a placebo condition. Whenever possible, drug and placebo conditions should be conducted in a double blind manner.
5. A continual, preferably daily, record of a child's behavior should be maintained. This should be done not only when attempting to determine a child's appropriate drug treatment, but throughout treatment.
6. The effects on at least one behavior that should increase and one behavior that should decrease should be monitored.
7. Minimal goals for each behavior of interest should be specified in advance. Only when drug treatment meets the prespecified goals should the treatment be continued.
8. During the course of drug treatment, the child should periodically be drug free. If the child's behavior again becomes disorderly, it may be concluded that the drugs were responsible for the previously noted improvement. If the child's behavior remains appropriate, it may be possible to permanently discontinue drug use.
9. Drug treatment should not be considered a permanent solution to a youngster's problems. When drug therapy is considered necessary, it might be combined with more standard educational procedures. As the package of techniques improves a student's behavior, it may be possible to wean the student from drug treatment.

FIGURE 2.1 Suggestions for Teachers Regarding the Use of Drugs in Management of Hyperactivity

SOURCE: From "Drug Treatment for Hyperactivity: Controversies, Alternatives, and Guidelines" by S. Axelrod and S. A. Bailey, 1979, *Exceptional Children, 45*, 547–548.

special education teacher assigned to work with one of your handicapped students is responsible for collaborating and consulting with you.

- The IEP for each student with a behavior disorder should include a structured plan for initiating and maintaining on-task behavior patterns. Such a plan might include a contingency contract (see, e.g., Figure 9.1) or token economy system (Kerr & Nelson, 1983, pp. 80–105). For cases in which medication has been prescribed for managing hyperactivity be particularly cautious and assertively question the rationale for the treatment. Axelrod and Bailey's guidelines are enumerated in Figure 2.1.

- To accommodate students with physical handicaps, you may need to have your classroom physically altered (e.g., to facilitate wheelchairs) and extraordinary technology installed (e.g., computers that interface with communication devices designed for visually-impaired students). Take advantage of this need to develop proposals for funds to enhance your classroom. For example, sound-enhancement equipment should be installed in classrooms in which hearing-impaired students are mainstreamed (Berg, 1987, pp. 63–87). However, research clearly demonstrates that all students, not only the hearing-impared, benefit. Attentiveness to oral communications and, thus, student engagement, is enhanced by the use of audio technology (e.g., sound-field FM devices) and acoustical enhancement of classrooms (Allen & Patton, 1990; Cangelosi, 1991a). Most educational audiologists are prepared to work with you to improve listening in your classroom.

- Mainstreamed students' need for social acceptance by classmates and integration into the classroom culture is emphasized throughout the professional literature. Strategies for promoting social acceptance between mainstreamed and regular students involve instructing students about handicaps, providing regular-class students with experiences with special people, structuring interactions between regular and special students, increasing the social skills of special students, mainstreaming students gradually, and communicating with and involving parents. As with any other instructional strategies, your strategies for promoting social acceptance should be routinely evaluated and refined. Sound, concrete suggestions for promoting social acceptance are provided by Lewis and Doorlag; their list of ideas to keep in mind is shown in Figure 2.2.

GROUP DYNAMICS

Classroom teachers interact with students in group settings far more often than they do privately on a one-to-one basis. You are responsible for orchestrating group behavior, not only teaching one student at a time to be on-task. Thus, for classroom management strategies to be effective, they must be based on an understanding of group dynamics. Group dynamics are the psychological forces and processes operating within a relatively small human group (e.g., classroom size group) that (1) determine sociological characteristics of the group as a whole, and (2) influence the individual behaviors of the group's members. As a singular term, group dynamics refers to the scientific study of group influences on individuals as well as group characteristics (e.g., organization, composition, aims, and stability).

Students conduct themselves and respond to teachers differently when in the company of their peers than when interacting privately with a teacher. For many situations, the group dynamics of a complex classroom environment can be used to enhance cooperation. How to establish healthy group dynamics in your classroom and take advantage of them are major concerns of Chapters 3–6. However, group dynamics, whether working in your favor or not, always complicate

■ Mainstreaming programs should emphasize the social acceptance of special students because rejection can damage both self-concept and academic performance.

■ Special students may be rejected if they do not look or act like their peers; another contributing factor is that some special students have poor social skills.

■ Attitudes are very important; the attitudes of teachers influence the attitudes of their students.

■ Attitudes are affected by information; the more teachers and peers know about special students, the more likely they are to accept them.

■ Regular class students, special students, and parents should be prepared for mainstreaming.

■ Sociometric measures are often used to find out how special students are perceived by their peers.

■ Behavioral rating scales and checklists are used to help assess a student's social skill performance, to identify problem areas that may require instruction, or to assess the student's progress.

■ Instruction about handicaps, experiences with special people, and structured interactions with special students can be provided to help regular class students (and teachers) gain information.

■ Special students can learn appropriate social skills; however, it is usually necessary to provide instruction in this area.

■ Parental support for the mainstreaming program can be increased by explaining the purpose of the program, letting parents know how it will affect their children, encouraging parents to participate, and keeping parents informed through frequent communication.

FIGURE 2.2   Ideas for Promoting Social Acceptance of Mainstreamed Students

SOURCE: From *Teaching Special Students in the Mainstream* (3d ed.) (p. 159) by R. B. Lewis and D. H. Doorlag, 1991, New York: Macmillan.

matters, forcing you to orchestrate more variables than you would in a private one-to-one meeting with a student. Thus, oftentimes you may want to meet privately with a student (e.g., to deal with an off-task behavior) while having to concurrently monitor the rest of the class. Scattered throughout subsequent chapters are examples (e.g., Vignette 7.3) of teachers doing just that.

TRANSITIONAL ACTIVITIES
FROM CHAPTER 2 TO CHAPTER 3

I. Select the best response for each item that either answers the question or completes the statement.
  A. A teacher's withitness, according to Kounin, refers to _____.
   1. How well students respect that teacher.
   2. How enthusiastic that teacher is about the learning activities planned.
   3. How aware the teacher is of what is going on in the classroom.
   4. How well the students remain on-task and engaged in learning activities.
  B. According to Jones' studies, which one of the following forms of off-task behavior occurs the least number of times in schools?
   1. Fighting among students.
   2. Talking out of turn.
   3. Mind-wandering and daydreaming.
   4. Clowning and showing off.

C. Jones suggested that teachers should _____.
   1. avoid direct eye contact with one student at a time to avoid displaying favoritism.
   2. not use hand gestures as a form of communication because hand gestures send ambiguous messages.
   3. avoid stationing themselves at a distance from students during learning activities.
   4. address all of a student's questions when providing individual help.
D. Ginott urged teachers to _____.
   1. avoid expressing personal feelings.
   2. praise students for being on-task.
   3. describe situations for students.
   4. tolerate misbehaviors that are a function of students' family backgrounds.
E. Which remark, made on a student's test paper, is most consistent with Ginott's suggestions?
   1. "It appears that you should review the formula for the area of a triangle."
   2. "It appears that you are quite a mathematician."
   3. "You didn't study hard enough."
   4. "Apparently you are the kind of student who diligently prepares for tests."
F. Glasser recommended that teachers _____.
   1. avoid discussing discipline problems with students.
   2. lead students to make value judgments about their own behaviors.
   3. utilize group processes to embarrass students into choosing on-task over off-task behaviors.
   4. tolerate disruptive behaviors whenever the causes are understandable.
G. According to Dreikurs, all students have a desire to _____.
   1. display power.
   2. call attention to themselves.
   3. exact revenge against authority figures.
   4. gain recognition.
H. According to Dreikurs, which one of the following is most distasteful to the "attention-seeking" student?
   1. Being punished.
   2. Being criticized.
   3. Being ignored.
   4. Being praised.
I. The assertive-response style that Canter recommends for teachers is characterized by _____.
   1. concern for students' needs.
   2. honesty.
   3. hostility.
   4. passiveness.
J. Canter suggested that with assertive discipline teachers need to _____.
   1. be independent of a need for help from students' parents.
   2. depend on help from parents.
   3. hold parents responsible for their children's behaviors.
   4. find out if parental influences are causing students to misbehave.
K. Behavior modification programs are based on the belief that _____.
   1. human conduct is influenced by positive reinforcers that follow certain acts.
   2. extrinsic motivation is more important in shaping human behavior than is intrinsic motivation.

      3. human beings are like pigeons in that their conduct is primarily a function of instincts.

      4. environmental influences can explain all forms of human behavior.

L. It is important for a teacher to identify whether a student's display of off-task behavior is isolated or is part of a behavior pattern because _____.

      1. behavior patterns are instinctive whereas isolated behaviors are learned.

      2. isolated off-task behaviors should be tolerated whereas habitual off-task behaviors should never be tolerated.

      3. students can control isolated behaviors, but others must control behavior patterns for them.

      4. a teacher should plan to confront an off-task behavior pattern differently from the way an isolated off-task behavior is confronted.

M. If a student is rewarded for an off-task behavior, the reward is a _____.

      1. positive reinforcer.

      2. negative reinforcer.

      3. contrived punishment.

      4. destructive positive reinforcer.

N. Which one of the following is NOT an example of punishment?

      1. After daydreaming during the time her teacher was giving directions, Jan feels "lost" because she doesn't know what to do.

      2. Tony is unhappy that his teacher excluded him from a discussion because he repeatedly interrupted other students.

      3. Charlie's teacher tells him he can rejoin the group whenever he decides to speak only when he has the floor.

      4. Because she started a fight, Betty was required to meet with her teacher after school when she preferred to be socializing with her friends.

O. Which one of the following is NOT an example of positive reinforcement?

      1. Lloyd talks to Carol in history class instead of being engaged in the learning activity. As a result of their conversation, Carol accepts an invitation to go out with Lloyd.

      2. After studying diligently for an exam, Cynthia receives an "A."

      3. Tom enjoys the candy his teacher gave him for paying attention during class.

      4. Issac is relieved to find out that his teacher forgot to collect the homework Issac failed to complete.

P. Ted's teacher detects him talking and clowning during time allocated for quietly doing exercises in a workbook. The teacher tells Ted: "Go to the time-out area for 10 minutes. Maybe by then you will have decided to settle down and quietly do your work." Which one of the following ideas did Ted's teacher apply?

      1. Positive reinforcement.

      2. Negative reinforcement.

      3. Contrived punishment.

      4. Naturally occurring punishment.

Q. A positive reinforcer is destructive when it.

      1. Encourages an off-task behavior.

      2. Discourages on-task behavior.

      3. Fails to increase the frequency of the target behavior.

      4. Has undesirable side effects.

Compare your responses to the following key: A-3, B-1, C-3, D-3, E-1, F-2, G-4, H-3, I-2, J-2, K-1, L-4, M-1, N-3, O-4, P-3, and Q-4.

II. Chapter 2 contains the statement, "On-task behaviors are typically less natural than off-task behaviors. . . ." What did the author mean? Explain why you agree or disagree with the statement. If the statement is true, what are some of the major implications for how teachers plan their learning activities? Compare your response to those of colleagues. Discuss the similarities and differences among what you and the others wrote. Here is one sample response.

The author referred to on-task behaviors as typically less natural than off-task behaviors because what students are directed to do in schools (e.g., quietly pay attention, solve computational exercises, do calisthenics, discuss economics) are not what children and adolescents are usually inclined to do. Thus, teachers must devise plans to teach students to be on-task and engaged in learning activities.

III. Give an example of a teacher dealing with a student's daydreaming in class via contrived punishment. Compare your example to those of colleagues. Here is another example.

Upon discovering Amy daydreaming in class, Mr. Benson tells her: "Write a 500 word composition on what you were daydreaming about and turn it in to me tomorrow."

IV. Give an example of a teacher dealing with a student's daydreaming in class via naturally occurring punishment. Compare your example to those of colleagues. Here is another example.

Allison catches herself daydreaming and realizes that she's missed a critical portion of Ms. Thompson's lecture. Consequently, she does extra work to make up for what she missed.

V. Give an example of a teacher dealing with a student's daydreaming in class via negative reinforcement. Compare your example to those of colleagues. Here is another example.

Mr. Damato calls Amanda up to his desk and begins describing what she did correctly and what she did incorrectly regarding a paper she had previously turned in. As he explains, he notices Amanda daydreaming instead of listening. He abruptly stops his explanation and says: "Here Amanda! Take your paper to your desk and figure this out for yourself until you can come back up here and attend to what I'm saying. I'll explain this only when you're ready to listen."

VI. Give an example in which a student's on-task behavior is effectively encouraged by a destructive positive reinforcer. Explain why the positive reinforcer is destructive. Compare your example to those of colleagues. Here is another example.

Ms. Byrnes holds a spelling contest between the boys and girls in her third grade class. Keith's diligent studying pays off because he leads the boys to victory. The victory positively reinforces his diligent study habits, but is also destructive because it plants the idea that boys are smarter than girls.

VII. Explain how one suggestion associated with Jones' approach might help a teacher more effectively apply Kounin's approach to keeping students on-task. Compare your response to that of a colleague. Here is a sample response.

Teachers who heed Jones' suggestions and continually use their eyes to monitor students will be more aware of what is going on. Thus, those teachers will be displaying Kounin's withitness.

VIII. Explain how one suggestion associated with Ginott's approach might help a teacher more effectively apply Glasser's approach for dealing with off-task student behaviors. Compare your response to that of a colleague. Here is a sample response.

Glasser advised teachers to confer with students who have misbehaved and lead those students to make rational choices about subsequent behaviors. Ginott suggested that teachers should describe situations rather than labeling students. Because a teacher focuses on the situation rather than on characterizations of a student, the student is less likely to feel under attack, and, thus, be more reasonable in assessing behaviors.

IX. Reread Vignette 2.15. with a colleague, discuss how the effects of Ms. Johnson's praise of Whitney might differ if she had praised him privately rather than in front of the class.

Here are some thoughts to consider:

According to Ginott, praising students themselves rather than only their work is a mistake whether done publicly or privately. But group dynamics may even compound the undesirable effects. Because she called him a "good student" in front of peers, Whitney may not only feel compelled to maintain the label in Ms. Johnson's eyes, but also in those of his classmates. Another unfortunate possibility is for the group to begin resenting Whitney as a "teacher's pet" (Charles, 1989, p. 14). Whitney may then respond to the group's resentment by demonstrating that he's really not a "good student."

X. Reread Vignettes 2.18 and 2.19. With a colleague, discuss how group dynamics might have worked against Ms. Burnside's tactics, whereas, Mr. Ruiz worked group dynamics in his favor.

Here are some thoughts to consider:

Ms. Burnside may have worried that if Steve won the power game played out in front of the class, other students would be encouraged to defy her authority also. However, by perpetuating the confrontation, she provided Steve with an audience (thus, positively reinforcing the disruptive conduct) and risked escalating the nasty episode. Look ahead to Vignette 7.10; it illustrates the danger of playing out power games. In Vignette 2.19, Mr. Ruiz simply refused to play Rubin's power game, turning his attention to group business. Group dynamics worked in Mr. Ruiz's favor as once the class became engaged in the group activity, Rubin was left with no audience to impress. Mr. Ruiz communicated that the business of the group takes priority over individual power games.

XI. Reread Vignettes 2.22 and 2.23. With a colleague, discuss how Ms. Brock's use of naturally occurring punishment took advantage of group dynamics, whereas, group dynamics might work against Ms. Webb's use of contrived punishment.

Here are some thoughts to consider:

While manipulating events so that students perceived their punishment for failing to clean up as naturally occurring, Ms. Brock remained a benevolent, helpful leader working within the group. Rather than take a position against the group goal of listening to the story, she expressed disappointment at not being able to enjoy the story and helped the group rid itself of the cause of the punishment (i.e., the mess in the room). Peer pressure within the group should encourage individuals to follow Ms. Brock's directions in the future.

XII. The integration of mainstreamed students into a classroom culture may be hindered by some regular education students' resistance to accepting peers whom they consider different from themselves. Discuss with a colleague how a failure to integrate mainstreamed students into the classroom culture compounds the teacher's problem of maintaining students on-task and engaged in learning activities. Here are some thoughts to consider:

Once again, group dynamics are major factors. When exclusionary attitudes prevail in a classroom, resentment builds and self-concepts are influenced negatively. Any semblance of a healthy classroom environment conducive to learning and cooperation is poisoned. As explained in Chapter 3, a comfortable, non-threatening environment where students feel accepted and secure is a necessary condition to on-task, engaged behaviors.

XII. With your colleague, brainstorm strategies for taking advantage of group dynamics to build social acceptance of mainstreamed students in your classrooms. Keep in mind that whenever dealing with people, the success of what you attempt is likely to depend more on the manner in which you do it than on what you actually choose to do. Thus, a general list of broad suggestions is not very valuable until you have refined your abilities to apply those suggestions to unique situations. Having acknowledged that complication, here's a few broad suggestions to consider. (1) Individually work on the attitudes of key members of the class and utilize their influence over the group. (2) Assign activities with group goals that depend on collaboration among both mainstreamed and regular students. (3) While openly recognizing that no two students enjoy the same capabilities, balance your attention among all students' needs. Convey that different students have different needs, but no one person's needs are any more important than anyone else's. (4) Keep in mind Lewis and Doorlag's (1991, p. 159) list shown in Figure 2.2.

XIII. In preparation for your work with Chapter 3, discuss the following questions with two or more of your colleagues.
   A. How does the climate of a classroom (i.e., the prevalent attitudes of the students and the teacher about one another and the business of learning) influence students' inclinations to cooperate with one another and be on-task?
   B. What are some of the strategies employed by teachers to build and maintain a classroom climate that is conducive to cooperation and engagement in learning activities?
   C. What are some of the strategies employed by teachers to minimize transition time and maximize allocated time?
   D. How is the classroom climate affected by students becoming embarrassed due to their failure to succeed with learning goals or being criticized in front of their peers?

SUPPLEMENTAL READINGS

Adkins, G. (1990). Educating the handicapped in the regular classroom. *The Educational Digest, 56,* 24–27.

Azrin, N. H., Hake, D. G., Holz, W. C., & Hutchinson, R. R. (1965). Motivational aspects of escape from punishment. *Journal of Experimental Analysis of Behavior, 8,* 31–44.

Biehler, R. F., & Snowman, J. (1990). *Psychology applied to teaching* (6th ed., pp. 648–689). Boston: Houghton Mifflin.

Canter, L. (1978). Be an assertive teacher. *Instructor, 88,* 60.

Canter, L., & Canter, M. (1976). *Assertive discipline: A take-charge approach for today's educator.* Seal Beach, CA: Canter and Associates.

Chandler, T. A., & Kindsvatter, R. (1991). Complementary approaches for effective discipline. *Middle School Journal, 22,* 34–37.

Doyle, W. (1986). Classroom organization and management. In M. C. Wittrock (Ed.), *Handbook of research on teaching* (3rd ed., pp. 392–431). New York: Macmillan.

Ginott, H. G. (1965). *Parent and child.* New York: Avon.

———. (1972). *Teacher and child.* New York: Avon.

Glasser, W. (1985). *Control theory in the classroom.* New York: Perennial Library.

———. (1988). On students' needs and team learning: A conversation with William Glasser. *Educational Leadership, 45,* 38–41.

Jones, F. (1979). The gentle art of classroom discipline. *National Elementary Principal, 58,* 26–32.

Kounin, J., & Sherman, L. (1979). School environments as behavior settings. *Theory into Practice, 18,* 145–151.

Krumboltz, J. D., & Krumboltz, H. B. (1972). *Changing children's behavior* (pp. 180–201). Englewood Cliffs, NJ: Prentice-Hall.

Lewis, R. B., & Doorlag, D. H. (1991). *Teaching special students in the mainstream* (3rd ed., pp. 22–187). New York: Macmillan.

Margolis, H., & Schwartz, E. (1989). Facilitating mainstreaming through cooperative learning. *The High School Journal, 72,* 83–88.

Pysch, R. (1991). Discipline improves as students take responsibility. *NASSP Bulletin, 75,* 117–118.

Weber, W. A. (1990). Classroom management. In J. M. Cooper (Ed.), *Classroom teaching skills* (4th ed., pp. 229–306). Lexington, MA: D. C. Heath.

How Do You Get Students to Cooperate? How Do You Keep Discipline Problems from Occurring?

Creating a Favorable Climate

Purpose of Chapter 3

Chapter 3 is designed to help you

1. Understand that students are more likely to be on-task and engaged in learning activities in a classroom where (a) a businesslike climate exists so that the task of achieving learning goals is of paramount concern, (b) transition time is minimized and students are busy, (c) students are free from the threats of embarrassment and harassment, and (d) expectations for conduct are clearly established.

2. Develop organizational techniques that will aid you in establishing a businesslike atmosphere in your own classrooms.

3. Discover how transition time can be minimized by (a) using methods for dispensing with administrative tasks, (b) using methods for distributing materials and giving directions, (c) selecting audio-visual aids, (d) utilizing intraclass grouping, and (e) planning for students working at different rates.

4. Understand how to take advantage of the beginning of a new school year or new school term in order to establish a classroom environment that encourages student cooperation, on-task behaviors, and engagement.

5. Begin thinking about how you can establish a classroom atmosphere in which students (a) fear neither being embarrassed nor harassed, and (b) clearly understand how they are expected to conduct themselves as well as understand the consequences of their behaviors.

CREATING A BUSINESSLIKE ATMOSPHERE

The Advantages of a Businesslike Atmosphere

Why would you want your classroom to have a businesslike atmosphere? I want a businesslike atmosphere in my classroom because I want to make life easier for myself. Of the classroom situations described in Vignettes 3.1, 3.2, 3.3, and 3.4, in which two would you find it easier to teach?

VIGNETTE 3.1

Ms. Richard's 28 third graders are working in four reading groups when she calls a halt to the activity to begin a whole group Spanish lesson. Ms. Richard: "Okay, class! Class, listen up. Put your reading things away and get ready — Ilone, please listen to me! Margo, leave Frankie alone; he doesn't like that! Okay class, put your reading things away and set your desks up in one big group so we can start Spanish." Joey: "Misses Richard, I didn't get a turn to read; you said we'd all have a turn!" Francine: "Get you desk out'a my way! We're supposed to be startin' Spanish." Ms. Richard: "I'm waiting, class. — Let's get these desks lined up. — You're going to love what we're — Fred, put your reading things away and . . . ."

VIGNETTE 3.2

Ms. Morrison's 28 third graders are working in four reading groups when she strikes a small gong situated on her desk. The students look up as she points to the word "Spanish" on a colorful poster displayed on a wall. Ms. Morrison then points to a sketch that symbolizes a large group arrangement for the students. The students immediately put their reading materials away and go about rearranging their desks for a large group session. They communicate with one another in whispers. Within four minutes Ms. Morrison is conducting the Spanish lesson.

VIGNETTE 3.3

As the bell for third period rings at Fort George High, Mr. McMahon enters his room ready to teach Latin. "All right, enough already! Let's get in our seats, we've got a lot of work to do today," he shouts above the din in the room. Some students begin to move to their places, but others continue to be involved in conversation. "Shh, hush-up!" is heard from some of the students. Mr. McMahon: "Hey, in here! Knock it off ladies! Take your homework out and let's begin. . . ."

VIGNETTE 3.4

As the bell for the third period rings at Green Mountain High, Ms. Losavio enters her room ready to teach Latin. The students, who have been milling around and socializing, stop what they've been doing as soon as one student spots her and says: "She's here." Quietly they go to their places. Without a word from Ms. Losavio, they place their homework on their desks.

I assume that you like yourself well enough to prefer to teach in either Ms. Morrison's or Ms. Losavio's situations rather than in those of the other two. Neither Ms. Morrison nor Ms. Losavio had to struggle to get students to begin a learning activity, as did both Ms. Richard and Mr. McMahon. Are some teachers simply fortunate to operate classrooms where students seem to automatically go about the business of learning, while other teachers' struggles fail to achieve even a semblance of order and efficiency? Good fortune, although occcasionally playing a role, is undependable. You, like Ms. Morrison and Ms. Losavio, must rely on your own initiatives to establish an efficiently operating, businesslike classroom.

The Meaning of "Businesslike"

For some people, the term "businesslike" connotes formality in manner and dress. Please do not use such an interpretation in this context. A businesslike classroom refers to a learning environment in which the students and the teacher conduct themselves as if achieving specified learning goals takes priority over other concerns. Surely, even with a businesslike atmosphere, activities other than learning activities take place. Lunch money may be collected, attendance may be taken, school announcements may be heard, visits may be made to the toilet, pleasant socializing may take place, a printer may be repaired, the room may be rearranged, and a joke may evoke laughter. However, in a businesslike classroom, such deviations from the business of learning are dispatched efficiently. Engagement in learning activities may be fun for some, but pure drudgery for others. In either case, engagement is considered important, serious business. Purposefulness characterizes a businesslike atmosphere.

Five Steps toward a Businesslike Atmosphere

How do you teach your students to consider their engagement in learning activities as serious, important business? How do you establish a smoothly operating classroom with a businesslike atmosphere? First of all, you must sincerely believe that the learning activities you plan for your students are vital to the achievement of worthwhile learning goals. Do not expect your students to place any more importance on learning activities than you do. However, telling students that a learning activity is important is usually a waste of time. You communicate the importance of learning activity by the behaviors you model and the attitudes you display.

You establish a businesslike atmosphere in your classroom by (1) taking advantage of the beginning of a new school year or term to set the stage for cooperation; (2) being particularly prepared and organized; (3) minimizing transition time; (4) utilizing a communication style that encourages a comfortable, nonthreatening environment where students are free to go about the business of learning without fear of embarrassment or harassment; and (5) clearly establishing expectations for conduct.

BEGINNING A NEW YEAR

Students' Perceived Notions

Students arrive in your class on the first day of school with some preconceived notions on what to expect and what is expected of them. Even the vast majority of beginning-kindergarten students know that they will be required to follow a teacher's directions and that certain antisocial behaviors (e.g., fighting) are unacceptable. Experience has taught older students that screaming, talking out of turn, leaving a classroom without permission, and blatant rudeness are among the things that teachers don't appreciate. Experience has also taught older students that teachers vary considerably regarding (1) how seriously they take their role of helping students to learn; (2) the specific student behaviors that are expected, demanded, tolerated, not tolerated, appreciated, unappreciated, recognized, punished, or rewarded; and (3) consistency with which a teacher reacts to certain student behaviors (i.e., Given a situation, can the teacher's behavior be predicted?).

Taking Advantage of Initial Uncertainty

No matter what age-group you teach, your students come to you for the first time filled with uncertainties. Some will have developed a distaste for school and are hoping that somehow you might provide them with a different sort of experience. Others will expect a continuation of what they perceive to be meaningless, boring, and inane stupidities thrust upon them by previous teachers. Then there are those who are appreciative of previous contacts with school and meet you with high expectations.

Because students are uncertain about you at the very beginning of a new school session, they will be watching your reactions, evaluating your attitudes, predicting what the relationships among you and the students will be, assessing their individual places in the social order of the classroom community, and determining how they will conduct themselves. Take advantage of the attention that students afford you on the first days of a school session to begin establishing on-task and cooperative behavior patterns. During the beginning of a school year or term, you should strictly adhere to suggestions (e.g., display withitness, consistently enforce rules, and be highly organized) from this text and from other sources that you choose to incorporate into your teaching. Later, after students better understand what to expect from you, allowing yourself an occasional transgression from the standards you've set for yourself may not harm the smooth operation fo your classroom.

Planning for a Favorable Beginning

Do not simply hope for a favorable beginning; plan for it to happen. At least a week before you prepare for the first class meeting, spend some time alone in your classroom. While there, visualize exactly what you want to be going on in that classroom during the middle of the upcoming school session. Picture yourself conducting different learning activities and managing transition times. What traffic patterns for student movement do you want followed? What sounds (e.g., one person talking at a time during large group meetings and soft tones of several students talking at once during small group activities) should be heard? How should nonlearning activities (e.g., pencil sharpening, collecting money, and visits to the drinking fountain) be conducted? How should supplies get into and out of students' hands? How will evaluation fo achievement occur? What modes of communication will be used? When do you want to spend time planning and completing aspects of your instructional work that does not involve interacting with students?

Use the Teaching Process Model (Figure 1.1) as a mechanism for organizing your thoughts about your responsibilities. You need to plan your operation so that you can efficiently meet those responsibilities. Anticipate problems that might arise (e.g., supplies that don't arrive and students refusing to follow directions) and simulate alternative ways for you to respond to those problems. Evaluate the different alternatives. Only after you've had a week or so reflecting on exactly how you want your class to operate are you ready to plan for the new school year or term. Vignette 3.5 is an example of a teacher systematically planning for a favorable beginning.

Most of the questions in Mr. Martin's list are dealt with in subsequent sections of this text (e.g., room arrangements in Chapter 6, rules for conduct in Chapter 5, and supportive-response styles in Chapter 4). At this time, turn your attention to his three questions under the heading, "III. Reminders for the First Week's Learning Activities." Read them over once again.

Learning Activities Conducive to a Favorable Beginning

Only learning activities with easy-to-follow, uncomplicated directions should be used in the early part of a new school session so that (1) your students can immediately get to the business of learning without experiencing bewilderment over "What are we supposed to be doing?" (2) Students learn that your directions are understandable and, consequently, will be willing to attend to them in the future. If students are confused by your initial directions, they are less likely to bother trying to understand subsequent ones. Later, after students have developed a pattern of attending to the directions for learning activities, you can gradually introduce more complex procedures to be followed.

VIGNETTE 3.5

Mr. Martin made this checklist before planning to meet his middle school social studies class for the first time.

I. Classroom Organization and On-Going Routines
   A. What different types of learning activities (e.g., video presentations, whole class demonstrations, small-group cooperative-learning sessions, and independent project work) do I expect to conduct this term?
   B. How should the room be organized (e.g., placement of furniture, screens, and displays) to accommodate the different types of learning activities and the corresponding transition times?
   C. What rules of conduct and routine procedures will be needed to maximize engagement during the different types of learning activities and to maximize on-task behaviors during transition times?
   D. What rules of conduct and routine procedures will be needed to discourage disruptions to other classes or persons located in or near the school?
   E. What rules of conduct and routine procedures are needed to provide a safe, secure environment in which students and other persons need not fear embarrassment or harassment?
   F. How will rules and procedures be determined (e.g., strictly by me, by me with input from the students, democratically, or some combination of these)?
   G. When will rules and procedures be determined (e.g., from the very beginning, as needs arise, or both)?
   H. How will rules and procedures be taught to students?
   I. How will rules be enforced?
   J. What other parts of the building (e.g., detention room or other classrooms) can be utilized for separating students from the rest of the class?
   K. Whom, among building personnel, can I depend on to help handle short-ranged and long-ranged discipline problems?
   L. How do I want to utilize the help of parents?
   M. What ongoing routine tasks (e.g., reporting daily attendance) will I be expected to carry out for the school administration?
   N. What events on the school calendar will need to be considered as I schedule learning activities?
   O. What possible emergencies (e.g., fire or student suffering physical trauma) might be anticipated and, considering school policies, how should I handle them?
II. One-Time-Only Tasks
   A. How should I communicate the general school policies to my students?
   B. What special administrative tasks will I be required to complete (e.g., identifying number of students on reduced-payment lunch program and checking health records)?
   C. What supplies (e.g., textbooks) will have to be distributed?
   D. Are supplies available and ready for distribution in adequate quantities?
   E. How will I distribute and account for supplies?

F. Are display cards with students' names ready?

G. How should I handle students who appear on the first day, but are not on the roll?

H. What procedures will be used to initially direct students into the classroom and to assigned places?

I. Which students might need special provisions or assistance for certain types of activities (e.g., students with hearing losses and students confined to wheelchairs)?

J. For which students will I need to schedule IEP conferences and, for each, who is the relevant special education resource person?

III. Reminders for the First Week's Learning Activities

A. Do lesson plans for the first week call primarily for learning activities that each have (1) uncomplicated directions that are simple to follow; (2) challenge, but with which all students will experience success; (3) built-in positive reinforcers for engagement; (4) all students involved at the same time?

B. Do the first week's lesson plans allow me to spend adequate time observing students, getting to know them, identifying needs, and collecting information that will help me make curricula decisions and design future learning activities?

C. Do plans allow me to be free during the first week to closely monitor student activities and be in a particularly advantageous position to discourage off-task behaviors before off-task patterns emerge, and positively reinforce on-task behaviors so that on-task patterns emerge.

IV. Personal Reminders for Myself

A. Am I prepared to pause and reflect for a moment on what I should say to students before I say it?

B. Am I prepared to observe exactly what students are doing and hear exactly what they are saying before making a hasty response?

C. Am I prepared to use descriptive, rather than judgmental, language as I interact with my students?

D. Am I prepared to consistently act and communicate assertively, being neither hostile nor passive?

E. Am I prepared to use a supportive-response style?

F. Am I prepared to model a businesslike attitude?

Students should find their first engagements with your learning activities satisfying. You want to leave them with the impression: "I learned something; I can be successful!" The idea, of course, is to make sure engagement is positively reinforced so that patterns of engaged behaviors are formed.

Later in a school session, it will be advantageous for you to have students work on individual levels, with some engaged in one learning activity while others are involved in a different learning activity. However, it is advisable to involve all students in the same learning activity in the first stages of a school session. Having all students work on the same task allows you to keep directions simple, monitor the class as a whole, and compare how different individuals approach a common task. Besides, until you get to know your students, you hardly have a basis for deciding how to individualize. In Vignettes 3.6 and 3.7 teachers conduct learning activities that are ideal for students' initial experiences in a new school session.

VIGNETTE 3.6

It is the opening day of a new term at Blackhawk Trail High School. The bell ending the second period rings and the bell to indicate the beginning of third period will ring in five minutes. Mr. Stockton, in preparation for the arrival of his third period earth science class, turns on a video player showing a tape on a prominently displayed monitor with the audio volume control turned up rather loudly. As required by school policy, Mr. Stockton stations himself just outside the classroom door between second and third period. As students enter the room, they hear Mr. Stockton's voice coming from the video monitor, "Please have a seat at the desk displaying a card with your name. If no desk has a card with your name, please sit in one of the desks with a blank card. There you will find a marking pen for you to print and display your first name. Once seated at your desk, please take out one sheet of paper and a pen or pencil. You will need them when the third period begins. I would appreciate you clearing your desk top of everything except your name card, pencil or pen, and paper. This message will be repeated until the beginning of third period. After the bell, the directions for today's first lesson will appear on the screen." The message, which is printed on the screen while it can be heard in Mr. Stockton's voice, is repeated continually until five seconds after the third period bell. Mr. Stockton has moved into the room. He moves among the students, gently tapping one inattentive student on the shoulder and pointing toward the monitor. Several times he gestures to the monitor in response to students trying to talk to him.

The message on the video changes. Mr. Stockton's image appears on the screen with this message: "I am about to perform an experiment. It will take six and a half minutes. During that time, carefully watch what happens. When the experiment is completed, you will be asked to describe in writing just what you observed. Remember those two words, 'describe' and 'observe.' They will be very important during this course in earth science." . . .

As the experiment appears on the screen, Mr. Stockton watches the students. At the end of the experiment, the students are directed to spend seven minutes writing a paragraph describing what they saw. Mr. Stockton circulates around the room reading over students' shoulders as they write. At the end of the seven minutes, he calls on several students to read their paragraphs. Other students are then brought into a discussion session in which a distinction is made between describing observations and making judgments.

Mr. Stockton judges the lesson a success because all students seemed to realize that they had made and described observations. Mr. Stockton distributes copies of the course syllabus and goes over it item by item. Frequent references to observing and recording experiments, such as the one everyone had just commonly shared, are made as the goals of the earth science course are discussed.

Textbooks are distributed and some administrative tasks are taken care of before the period ends. Mr. Stockton indicates that classroom rules and organizational procedures will be discussed at the very next meeting.

By the way, while the students were viewing the videotape, Mr. Stockton checked the role and posted the attendance report outside the classroom door for school office personnel to collect.

Mr. Stockton Getting His Class Off to a Businesslike Start

Ms. Phegley Uses Visual Cues to Keep Students On-Task

VIGNETTE 3.7

Ms. Phegley spent most of the first two days of the school year helping her first graders get accustomed to their new surroundings. She spent the majority of the time getting to know these six-year-olds and teaching them how to follow rules of conduct and some basic routines (e.g., procedures for cleaning up after themselves and getting to and from the cafeteria).

On the third day, as the students are seated at their places, Ms. Phegley announces: "Everyone put your hands on your head like this." She puts both her hands atop her head and the students follow along. Ms. Phegley: "Now keep your hands up there until you see me take mine off of my head." Smiling brightly, she surveys their faces with deliberation. Ms. Phegley: "Taped under your table is an envelope containing your very own word." Roger and Ethan begin to reach under their tables. Ms. Phegley: "My hands are still on top of my head. — Thank you for waiting. Now, look around the room. What do you see on the wall just above the boards?" "Posters!" "Cards!" "Words!" are some of the replies. Ms. Phegley: "Yes, I agree! There are posters and cards hanging all around the room with words on them. How many are there?" "Too many!" "One, two, three, four, . . . ten, there are ten!" "No, more than ten!" Ms Phegley (interrupting): "I'll tell you how many there are. There are as many words on the wall as there are of you. There's one for each of you. One of those words belongs to Louise, and one belongs to Granville, and one belongs to Marva . . ." "And one belongs to me!" shouts Mickey. "Which one is mine?" asks Gwynn. "Oh! I know," says Claudia, "the envelopes under our tables will tell us!" Ms. Phegley: "That's right; they will. When I take my hands off of my head that is the signal for you to take the envelope from under your desk and — Tamara, look where my hands are — and find out which word on the wall it matches. Once you've found your word, you are to go quietly stand under it. I'll tell you what we'll do next after you are all quietly standing under your own word. Do you want to ask me anything before I take my hands from my head? . . ."

The learning activity continues, culminating with students comparing similarities and differences in their words. Ms. Phegley chose this activity for the first week of school, not only because it helps students develop some reading readiness skills, but also because it gets them used to following her directions, and is one with which all would achieve success. Some students were quicker than others to match the letters and locate their words. But this made it easier for those who were slower with this task because it reduced the number of places left to stand and, thus, the number of comparisons to be made.

BEING PREPARED AND ORGANIZED

The Importance of the Third and Fourth Steps of the Teaching Process Model

Mr. Stockton and Ms. Phegley left their students with the impression that directions are to be taken seriously. Reread Vignettes 3.6 and 3.7 and list some of the specific steps that Mr. Stockton and Ms. Phegley took that helped convey this impression to students. Now, classify each step in your list according to its placement in the Teaching Process Model. For example (1) Mr. Stockton was operating within the third phase of the Teaching Process Model when he decided to demonstrate an experiment at the very beginning of the class period. (2) Mr. Stockton was operating within the fourth phase when he videotaped the experiment in preparation for the class meeting. (3) Ms. Phegley operated within the fourth phase when she prepared the posters and hung them on the walls. (4) She was also within the fourth phase when she taped the envelopes under students' tables prior to meeting her class.

I would guess that a large share of the steps in your list fall within the purview of the third and fourth phases (i.e., determining and preparing for learning activities) of the Teaching Process Model. The way Mr. Stockton and Ms. Phegley organized and prepared for their classes contributed to their smooth classroom operations and the desirable impressions left on students.

The Effects of Preparation on Classroom Climate and Efficiency

It took more preparation time for Mr. Stockton to demonstrate the science experiment via video presentation than it would have had he conducted the experiment "live." However, the extra effort made it much easier for Mr. Stockton to start the first class session smoothly and have students engaged in a learning activity while he was free to manage the setting. The video presentation also added a professional touch that told students: "This is serious business. This teacher is serious enough to make the extra effort to thoroughly organize and prepare. The same is expected of students."

Compare the message such well-prepared sessions send to students to that sent by sessions in which a teacher is prepared only with a piece of chalk and a resolution that "students had better pay attention or else!" Or else what? Such teachers should listen to today's adolescents when they use the popular expression: "Get serious!"

Preparing name cards for students was a simple matter for Mr. Stockton that made a major difference in how his initial meeting with students went. Name tags designating seating arrangements provide students with a hint of order in the classroom. Even though Mr. Stockton has approximately 150 students per term at Blackhawk Trail High, the name tags enabled him to call each student by name on the very first day of school. Suppose, for example, that while he was going over the course syllabus, he noticed a student's attention drifting away; he would be readily able to work that student's name into the explanations. Such a tactic can serve to cue a student back on-task. "The guy in the green shirt . . ." is not nearly as effective as "Ralph . . ."

Secondary school teachers typically present information about course expectations at the beginning of a school term. Mr. Stockton prepared a course syllabus for distribution on the first day. Such documents, if professionally prepared, can provide at least four advantages in helping students to be on-task. (1) A course syllabus suggests to students that the learning activities are purposeful and gives them an idea of how it will benefit them. (2) A well-organized syllabus gives the impression that the course is well-organized and will be conducted in a businesslike manner. (3) Throughout the term, the teacher can use the syllabus as a point of focus (e.g., Mr. Stockton can reference it saying such things as: "Tonight's homework will move you to Section XI on page 9 of your syllabus."). (4) The syllabus provides an outline for the class meetings (e.g., Mr. Stockton's first meeting) and for course expectations.

Figure 3.1 displays a syllabus developed by Nancy Fisher, a history teacher.

Course Syllabus
for
U.S.History

WHAT IS THIS COURSE ALL ABOUT?

The course is all about the **history of the United States:**
- Journeying through time taking us from the origins of our country to where we are today
- Discovering how to utilize the lessons of history to deal with today's issues and problems

WHAT IS HISTORY?

There are three aspects of history:
- All actual past events
- Methods used by historians to discover and describe past events and explain their causes and influences
- Documented references resulting from the work of historians

WHY SHOULD YOU LEARN U.S. HISTORY?

Everyday of your life you make decisions about how to behave, what to do, where to go, who to see, what to eat, what to wear, and so on and so forth. Those decisions are influenced by your understanding of events in your past life (i.e., your own history). For example, you are more likely to choose to go places you found enjoyable in the past than to places where you were bored. Your understanding of past events help you to control present and future events.

As a world citizen, especially one living in the United States, you have an influence over present and future events in this country. Those events influence your everyday life. Understand events in this country's past and you'll be better able to influence its future.

There are also some more mundane reasons:
- Your success in other courses you take in high school as well as in any vocational school, technical school, or college you might attend depends on your understanding of history.
- A full year credit in U.S. history is required for a high school diploma in this state.
- An understanding of at least some U.S. history is expected of literate citizens in today's society and is needed in many occupations.

WITH WHOM WILL YOU BE WORKING IN THIS COURSE?

You will be working with Nancy Fisher, who is responsible for helping you and your classmates learn U.S. history. You will also be working with your classmates, each of whom will be making a unique contribution to what you get out of this course. In turn, you will contribute to what they learn by sharing your ideas, discoveries, insights, problems, and solutions.

WHERE WILL YOU BE LEARNING U.S. HISTORY?

You will draw your understanding of history from your entire environment whether at home, school, or anywhere else. Your classroom, room 203, at Rainbow High is the place where ideas about history are brought together and formalized. Room 203 is a place of business for learning history.

HOW WILL YOU BE EXPECTED TO BEHAVE IN THIS CLASS?

You and your classmates have the right to go about the business of learning history free from fear of being harmed, intimidated, or embarrassed. Ms. Fisher has the right to go about the business of helping you and your classmates learn history without disruption or interference. Thus, you are expected to follow five rules of conduct:

(continued)

FIGURE 3.1 Sample Course Syllabus Developed by Nancy Fisher

SOURCE: From *Systematic Teaching Strategies* (pp. 341–343) by J. S. Cangelosi, 1992, New York: Longman. Copyright 1991 by Longman. Reprinted by permission.)

1. Give yourself a complete opportunity to learn history.
2. Do not interfere with the opportunities of your classmates to learn history.
3. Respect the rights of all members of this class (they include, you, your classmates, and Ms. Fisher).
4. Follow Ms. Fisher's directions for lessons and classroom procedures.
5. Adhere to the rules and policies of Rainbow High as listed on pages 11–15 of the **Student Handbook.**

WHAT MATERIALS WILL YOU NEED FOR CLASS?

Bring the following with you to every class meeting:
- The course textbook:
  DiBacco, T. V., Mason, L. C., & Appy, C. G. (1991). **History of the United States.** Boston: Houghton Mifflin.
- A four-part notebook:
  1. Part 1 is for class notes.
  2. Part 2 is for homework and class assignments.
  3. Part 3 is for saving artifacts from independent and cooperative-group activities.
  4. Part 4 is for maintaining a reference for definitions and facts.
- A scratch pad
- Pencils, pens, and an eraser

You will also need five 5.25" computer diskettes in a storage case. You will not have to bring these to class every day, but have them available at school (e.g., in your locker).

A textbook has been checked out to you for the school year. You are responsible for maintaining it in good condition and returning it to Ms. Fisher on the last day of class. The other materials can be purchased at the Rainbow High Bookstore or at other retail outlets.

WHAT WILL YOU BE DOING FOR THIS CLASS?

The course is organized into 22 units between one to three weeks each. During each unit you will be:
- Participating in class meetings
  Depending on the agenda for the meetings you will be:
  - Listening to Ms. Fisher speak and seeing her illustrations as you take notes on what is being explained
  - Listening to classmates speak and seeing their illustrations as you take notes on what is being explained
  - Explaining things to the class as your classmates take notes on what you say and show them
  - Asking questions, answering questions, and discussing issues with members of the class during questioning/discussion sessions
  - Working closely with your classmates as part of small task-groups
  - Working independently on assigned exercises
  - Taking brief tests
- Completing homework assignments
- Taking a unit test

WHAT WILL YOU LEARN FROM THIS CLASS?

Each unit will either introduce you to a new historical topic or extend your understanding of a previous topic. During the unit you will:
- Discover an idea or relationship

FIGURE 3.1 (continued)

- Add to your ability to use historical methods
- Acquire new information or add depth of understanding to previously acquired information
- Extend your ability to utilize the lessons in history to solve today's problems

Here are the titles of the 22 units:
1. Looking Ahead in Light of Past Lessons; Historical Methods
2. The First Americans, Exploration, and Colonization
3. A New Nation
4. The U.S. Constitution and the New Republic
5. Expansion
6. The Civil War and Reconstruction Eras
7. Emergence of Industrial America, New Frontiers
8. Urban Society and Gilded-Age Politics
9. Protests and the Progressive Movement
10. Expansionism
11. World War I
12. The Roaring Twenties
13. The Great Depression and the New Deal
14. A Search for Peace and World War II
15. A Cold Peace
16. The Politics of Conflict and Hope
17. The Civil Rights Movement
18. The Vietnam War
19. Dirty Politics
20. Toward a Global (and cleaner) Society
21. The New Nationalism
22. Extending What You've Learned into a New Century

Units 1–12 are planned for the first semester, Units 13–22 for the second semester.

HOW WILL YOU KNOW WHEN YOU'VE LEARNED U.S. HISTORY?

Everyone knows at least some history, but no one ever learns it completely. History is being discovered. You will use what you learn in this course to further develop your ability to apply the lessons of history to everyday decision making.

The question is not whether or not you've learned history, but how well you are learning it. During this course, you will be given feedback on your progress through comments Ms. Fisher makes about work you complete, scores you achieve on brief tests, and the grades you achieve based on unit, midsemester, and semester tests.

HOW WILL YOUR GRADES FOR THE COURSE BE DETERMINED?

Your grade for the first semester will be based on 12 unit tests, a midsemester test scheduled between the sixth and seventh units, and a semester test. Your scores on these tests will influence your first semester grade according to the following scale:

- The 12 unit tests .... 60% (5% each)
- The midsemester test 15%
- The semester test 25%

Your grade for the second semester will be based on 10 unit tests, a midsemester test scheduled between the 17th and 18th units, and a semester test. Your scores on these tests will influence your second semester grade according to the following scale:

- The 10 unit tests .... 60% (6% each)
- The midsemester test 15%
- The semester test 25%

FIGURE 3.1 (continued)

Now let's take a look at the effects of Ms. Phegley's preparations. Instead of simply distributing the word cards to her students, she placed them in envelopes before class started and taped them under table tops where they would be out of sight. What advantages did she gain by going to this extra trouble? (1) The first graders were able to discover "their very own" words at the same time without waiting for them to be handed out one at a time. (2) By being taped under the table tops, the word cards were kept out of sight and thus did not become distracting toys before Ms. Phegley was ready for the students to work with them. (3) Having an unknown word located in an unusual place added an air of mystery that helped hold students' attention while Ms. Phegley related the directions for the learning activity. (4) Having the words already distributed before class left Ms. Phegley more freedom during class to supervise and orchestrate the activities.

Generally speaking, the more work you put into your preparation, the less work you will need to do to maintain a smooth operation during class. The benefits also increase over time for at least two reasons. (1) Materials prepared for one class (e.g., Mr. Stockton's videotape and Ms. Phegley's posters for displaying words) can be reused with or refined for subsequent classes. (2) The businesslike attitude a well-prepared, highly organized teacher models for students has a lasting effect that will help establish on-task and engaged student behavior patterns.

MINIMIZING TRANSITION TIME

By minimizing transition time, you maximize allocated time. The more allocated time you have available, the more time your students have for being engaged in learning activities (Borg, 1980; Latham, 1984). Of course, making more allocated time available does not necessarily result in greater achievement unless the learning activities are worthwhile, and the additional allocated time actually results in additional engaged time.

Keeping transition time to a minimum has benefits in addition to making more allocated time available. Students' engagement levels are likely to be better when there is a smooth and rapid transition between learning activities than when transition time is extended or when learning activities are interrupted (Kounin, 1970; Struyk, 1990). By efficiently moving from one lesson to another and by streamlining your procedures for dispensing with non-teaching, managerial, and administrative tasks, you can avoid wasting your students time waiting for the business of learning to start. Students waiting to get busy develop their own devices for relieving their boredom, such as, attention-getting disruptions and daydreaming (Cangelosi, 1990a, pp. 13–19). Disruptive behaviors tend to extend the transition periods between learning activities and, consequently, amplify the initial cause of the problem. Daydreaming, while not disruptive, makes it difficult for a student to become engaged in the learning activity when transition time stops and allocated time begins. Switching the focus of one's thoughts cannot always occur on cue.

Ideas on how to minimize transition time are provided in the next five sections.

DISPENSING WITH ADMINISTRATIVE DUTIES

Inefficient Use of Classroom Time

Vignette 3.8 would be incredible if if were not indicative of commonplace, everyday occurrences in thousands of classrooms.

VIGNETTE 3.8

Ms. Rolando teaches fourth grade. Each day, she reports to the main office the names of absentees and the number of students planning to eat lunch in the cafeteria that day (categorized by free lunch, reduced-payment lunch, and full-payment lunch). Students who were absent the previous day are required to display an "admit slip" signed by a school secretary before Ms. Rolando may permit their participation in class. Students not in the classroom by the "second bell" must possess a signed "late slip" before being accepted into class. Every Monday, Ms. Rolando is required to check students for head lice and report the names of students displaying symptoms.

A typical Monday morning may go something like this.

Twenty-five of Ms. Rolando's 31 students are seated in their desks by the second bell. Four others come in during public address announcements which are followed by the "Pledge of Allegiance." Ms. Rolando then begins calling the roll: "Raymond?" "Here." "Melinda?" "Here." "Turner? — Turner! — Are you here, Turner?" "Oh! Yes Ma'am, I'm here." "Barbara? — I see Barbara's absent. — Frank?" "Yea, I guess so!" "Frank, that's no way to answer the roll! Okay, Melanie? — Where's . . ." It takes nine minutes to complete the roll call, during which time students sit idly or find ways to entertain themselves.

Ms. Rolando then asks: "Which of you on free lunch are eating in the cafeteria today? Okay, keep your hands high! One, two, three — Ralph, is your hand up? — six, seven. — Okay, raise your hand if you're on reduced lunch." Turner: "I'm on reduced lunch, but I brought my lunch today. Should I raise my hand?" Ms. Rolando: "You know what I mean! No, Turner, keep your hand down unless you're eating in the cafeteria today." Turner: "What if I just want to get milk today?" Ms. Rolando: "Never mind, Turner, one, two — Willie, put your hand down, you're not on reduced lunch — three, four, six, eight. Now, the rest of you who are eating . . ." Six minutes later, Ms. Rolando has her lunch tallies and is ready to check for head lice. She says, "Everybody settle down and stay in your places while I check your heads." . . . Twelve minutes later, Ms. Rolando discovers that only Pam's name needs to be included on the head lice list.

"Those of you who came in late or who were absent yesterday, bring your passes to me now," Ms. Rolando says as she dispenses with the admit and late slips in four minutes. All this time, her students are waiting for the business of the day to begin. As they wait, they are becoming more and more restless and their moods are changing so that they are becoming less and less ready to become engaged in learning activities.

Forty-four minutes after the second bell, Ms. Rolando starts her mathematics lesson with, "Take out your homework so I can come around and check on who did it and who did not."

VIGNETTE 3.9

Ms. Drexler teaches fourth grade at the same school, and so must perform the same morning administrative duties as Ms. Rolando. However, a typical Monday morning in Ms. Drexler's class is somewhat different.

Twenty-six of Ms. Drexler's 33 students are seated as the second bell rings and public address announcements begin. As soon as the announcements and the "Pledge of Allegiance" are completed, Ms. Drexler directs her students to place their mathematics homework papers on top of their desks with "Yes" written in the upper left corner of the first page if they plan to eat in the cafeteria that day and "No" if they will not. She then distributes a written-response mathematics quiz which students begin immediately. As they respond to the quiz, Ms. Drexler circulates among the students filling out a chart which she carries on a clipboard (see Figure 3.2).

Because Ms. Drexler's chart indicates the lunch status of each student, the simple "Yes" or "No" written on the homework paper is sufficient for her to provide the office with the lunch tallies. As she stops by each student and fills out the chart, she checks for head lice and collects admit slips and late slips from those who are required to have them.

Ms. Drexler checks for homework, completes the head lice check, transfers information from her chart to the form that the main office expects, and takes care of other administrative duties before the students finish the mathematics quiz.

Efficient Use of Classroom Time

Most public school teachers are burdened with administrative tasks that tend to extend transition time and detract from student engagement. However, many teachers cope with this burden with only a minimal loss in allocated time. Vignette 3.9 provides an example.

SAVING TIME WHEN DISTRIBUTING MATERIALS AND GIVING DIRECTIONS

Inefficient and Efficient Methods

Compare the efficiency of the transitions in Vignette 3.10 to that in Vignette 3.11.

Freedom from Having to Speak to the Whole Class

In Vignette 3.10, Mr. Hansen tried to speak to his entire class at once to direct students into a planned learning activity. Students who were ready to listen for the directions right away had to wait for everyone else to be situated before finding out what to do. On the other hand, in Vignette 3.11 Mr. Jukola had the directions for students to read printed and duplicated on cards and on notes sealed inside envelopes. By not having to tell everyone at once what to do, Mr. Jukola was

DATE _____

NAME	LUNCH TYPE - YES/NO	ABSENT	TARDY	LICE	HOMEWORK
Amarillo, P.	free				
Bing, D.	full				
Bundy, V.	full				
Cafarell, P.	full				
Church, P.	free				
Costello, A.	part				
D'Armond, R.	full				
Epstein, S.	full				
Gale, R.	free				
Gambino, S.	part				
Grimes, Ma.	part				
Grimes, Mi.	full				
Gustofson, A.	full				
Heidingstelder, L.	part				
Jacobsen, D.	full				
Javier, J.	full				
Johnson, D.	full				
Johnson, C.	free				
Johnson, J.	full				
Luidzinski, M.	part				
Marchand, B.	free				
Mayberry, M.	free				
Nun-Sung, S.	full				
Osborne, B.	full				
Ramad, A.	full				
Sorenson, K.	free				
Sudiaski, J.	part				
Tyler, W.	full				
Tyung, S.	free				
Whitman, V.	part				

FIGURE 3.2 Ms. Drexler's Chart

VIGNETTE 3.10

Mr. Hansen's 28 fifth graders are filing into their classroom just after a recess break. He has planned a learning activity that involves pairs of students working with $250 in play money. Mr. Hansen believes that the students will enjoy and profit from what he has planned and eagerly waits for everyone to be seated so he can explain what to do. Speaking above the mild noise level created by the movement of bodies and a few conversations left over from recess, Mr. Hansen begins: "As soon as everyone's seated, I want your attention. — Okay! Listen up. — Hey, Bob, over here! Listen up. — Okay, now. Find yourself a partner. Pull your desk next to his. The . . ." "What if it's not a 'him'?" asks Deborah. "That's right. Make that him or her," Mr. Hansen responds. He continues, "When everyone and his or her partner are seated together, I'll pass out some materials and tell you what we'll be doing."

Students move around identifying partners. Initially, some have no partners and others have two. Some friendly pushing occurs and comments such as, "I wanna be with Allison!" and "I always get stuck with Caesar!" are heard. Thirteen minutes after the start of the period, everyone seems to be with a partner, but the confusion concerns Mr. Hansen. Speaking louder than before, he says, "I have $250 of play money for you and your partner. You will be needing this for the problem you'll have to solve together." While he counts and distributes the money, students begin making remarks: "What are we going to do?" "Oh shoot! This isn't real money!" "Yeah, Mr. Hansen, give us real money!" "Hey! Mr. Hansen, you only gave us $210!"

During the 14 minutes it takes for each pair to obtain the right amount, some students begin daydreaming, others doodle, and others pick up their conversations from recess. By the time Mr. Hansen is ready to explain the directions for the learning activity, enthusiasm for becoming engaged has waned.

SOURCE: Adapted from *Cooperation in the Classroom: Students and Teachers Together* (pp. 13–15) by James S. Cangelosi, 1990, Washington: National Education Association.

VIGNETTE 3.11

Mr. Jukola wants to conduct the same learning activity with his class of 30 fifth graders. However, Mr. Jukola is better prepared than was Mr. Hansen. Before the students return from recess, Mr. Jukola places 15 different numerals (e.g., 62) at each of 15 work stations he set up in the classroom. Thirty index cards (e.g., the one in Figure 3.3) are prepared so that each has a different numerical expression at the top, but the same directions printed below. There is only one other card in the deck that has an equivalent numerical expression. For example, a card with $(8 \times 8) - (3 \times 4)$ would match the card in Figure 3.3 since $(8 \times 8) - (3 \times 4) = 52$ as does 50% of $((303 + 9)/3)$.

As the students begin filing into the room, Mr. Jukola gives a card to each and softly announces to about five or six students at a time, "Please follow the directions on the card." Upon entering the room, the students are busy reading and computing. Because Mr. Jukola is not busy trying to provide directions to the entire class, he is able to move among the students and respond to any indications of off-task behaviors.

50% of ((303+9)/3)

Go to the work station that is labeled with a number equal to the expression at the top of this card. There you will meet your partner. Next, find the envelope taped under the table top. Remove the envelope and open it. Inside you will find $250 in play money and instructions on what you and your partner should do with it. Good luck!

FIGURE 3.3   One of Mr. Jukola's 30 Index Cards

Six minutes after the first student entered the room, all are busy working with their partners. Some started with the learning activity before others arrived as they did not have to wait for directions from Mr. Jukola. The very process for locating their materials and finding out the directions involved them in reading, computing, and acquiring a curiosity about the learning activity.

---

free to move about the room to help, prod, and encourage individuals. Often, you can achieve smoother, quicker transitions, free of hassles and off-task behaviors, by using modes other than oral directions to the whole group. Sometimes alternatives to oral, whole group directions are not feasible. However, when directions are complicated or inidividualized, and students are able to read, approaches similar to Mr. Jukola's are usually more time efficient than Mr. Hansen's. In any case, giving directions in a manner that doesn't depend on you having to speak to the class all at once has its advantages. (1) You are freer to supervise and manage the transition time before the learning activity begins. (2) Students do not have to wait for everyone else to be attentive before they begin the activity. (3) You can save your voice and energy for times when it is more important to speak to the group as a whole. (4) The less you speak, the more attentive students will be when you do speak. (5) You can more efficiently clear up some students' misunderstanding of the directions. The next two contrasting vignettes (Vignette 3.12 and Vignette 3.13) illustrate this fifth advantage.

Instead of repeating the directions over and over, as did Ms. McDaniel, Mr. Johnson referred unsure students back to the printed directions.

VIGNETTE 3.12

Ms. McDaniel announces to her 25 science students: "Each of you is to take your scale and individually weigh the five substances beginning with the lightest colored one, then the next lighter one, and so on until you've weighed the darkest colored one last. Any questions?" Xavier: "Then what do we do?" Ms. McDaniel: "I was coming to that." Carmen: "Why do we start with the lightest one?" Ms. McDaniel: "You'll see. Now, plot each weight on the sheet of graph paper. It is marked with the shades of colors on the vertical axis and the weights on the horizontal. Okay, get busy!"

  Some students misunderstand the directions and begin weighing the substances according to which one feels lightest in weight, not by shade of color. April beckons Ms. McDaniel to help her: "I don't know what to do." Ms. McDaniel: "What don't you understand?" April: "What to do!" Ms. McDaniel: "I told you to weigh these substances, beginning with the one with the lightest color and . . ."

  Ms. McDaniel repeats the directions several more times before the end of the activity.

VIGNETTE 3.13

Mr. Johnson wants his eighth grade science class to carry out the same activity as did Ms. McDaniel. However, he has a copy of the directions printed on a slip of paper at each work station along with the substances and the graph paper. Students read the directions for themselves, and Mr. Johnson observes how well they are followed. When a student appears to misunderstand, Mr. Johnson simply points to the directive on that student's slip that is not being followed.

  Mickey says to Mr. Johnson: "I don't understand what we're supposed to be doing." Mr. Johnson: "Read the second sentence just loud enough for me to hear." Mickey: "Line the substances up so that the darkest colored one is fifth, the next darker one is fourth, and so on until the lightest colored one is first." Having already observed that Mickey had not yet done that, Mr. Johnson says: "Do what it says, and then do what the third sentence says."

Distributing Materials ahead of Time

Distributing materials (e.g., play money or documents) before they are needed for student use can reduce transition time. Mr. Jukola, in Vignette 3.11, took advantage of a recess break to distribute materials. In Vignette 3.14, Ms. Salley uses time near the end of one learning activity to distribute materials for the next.

Cues for Efficient Routines

Once you have established a consistent, predictable routine for giving directions and distributing materials, student cooperation can be achieved with only a minimal effort on your part. Because certain directions (e.g., "Everyone is to look

at the overhead projector screen''; ''Cluster into small groups of five or six'';
''Take out your notebooks.'') occur over and over, you may want to teach your
students to respond to cues or signals for beginning certain routine procedures.
Vignettes 3.15 and 3.16 are two examples.

VIGNETTE 3.14

As Ms. Salley's health science students write their answers to questions during a
reading activity on diseases of the ear, she circulates among them silently reading
their answers and placing a closed box containing an otoscope under every other
student's desk. She plans for partners to use the otoscope to examine each other's
ears in the learning activity following this one. Because she has used this procedure
for distributing materials before, the students know not to open the boxes without
further directions and they know not to ask: ''What's this for?''

VIGNETTE 3.15

The variety of learning activities that Ms. Morrison uses in teaching her 28 third
graders frequently necessitates the students changing from one type of grouping
arrangement to another. To facilitate these transitions, Ms. Morrison has several
posters clustered together on one wall of the classroom. When she is ready for
her students to stop one activity and begin another, she strikes a small gong
located near the cluster of posters. Her students have learned that this is the
cue for them to stop whatever they are doing and silently pay attention. Once
Ms. Morrison has their attention, she uses the posters to give directions for the
next learning activity.

   For example, she may point to the poster pictured in Figure 3.4 to indicate
whether or not talking is allowed. Pointing to one of the numerals in Figure 3.5
indicates the size of the group students are to form. If Ms. Morrison points to ''1,''
the students know to work individually at their places. Pointing to ''3'' means they
work in groups of three; ''Whole Class'' means there will be a large group session
of the whole class.

VIGNETTE 3.16

Mr. Bowie reserves one section of the chalkboard for in-class assignments and another
for homework assignments. His industrial arts students know where to find the
assignments without waiting to be told.

FIGURE 3.4 Ms. Morrison's Poster for Signaling Whether or Not Talking Is Allowed

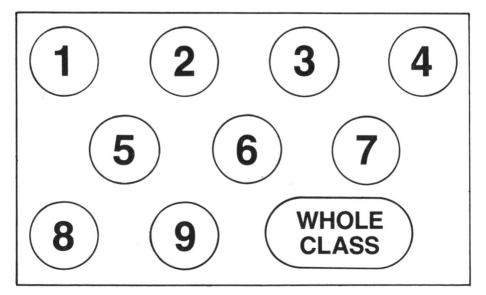

FIGURE 3.5 Ms. Morrison's Poster for Signaling How to Group for a Learning Activity

SAVING TIME BY USING AUDIO-VISUAL AIDS

Compare Vignette 3.17 to Vignette 3.18.

VIGNETTE 3.17

Ms. Steel announces to her social studies class: "There are seven major features of the Bill of Rights with which I want you to be familiar. Please jot each down in your notebooks as I put it on the chalkboard. Then we'll discuss the feature in some detail." With her back to the class, Ms. Steele lists the first feature on the board. The students try to copy from the board as she writes, but they must wait for her to finish writing and move out of their lines of vision. Ms. Steel turns around ready to discuss the first feature, but the students are still copying. Some finish sooner than others. Ms. Steele begins her explanation of the feature after most students look up from their notebooks, leaving only a few still writing.

   With the discussion of the first feature completed, Ms. Steele turns her back again to the class, and starts repeating the process for the second through the seventh features. By the time she gets to the fourth feature, the chalkboard area that could be readily viewed by the students is exhausted, so she erases the first several features to make room. Erasing, besides taking time, prevents her from using that information later in the discussion. During the periods when Ms. Steele was writing on the board, some students amused themselves by daydreaming or whispering among themselves. Some of those students had difficulty getting reengaged in the discussion each time Ms. Steele faced the class to explain and discuss another one of the seven features.

VIGNETTE 3.18

Mr. Piowaty announces to his social studies class: "There are seven major features of the Bill of Rights with which I want you to be familiar. Please jot each down in your notebooks as I display it on the overhead screen. Then we'll discuss the feature in some detail." Mr. Piowaty observes the students readying their notebooks and then flips on the overhead projector. The first feature is displayed; he watches as the students make their copies. During the ensuing explanation and discussion, Mr. Piowaty makes notes on the overhead transparency and highlights phrases in the description. He does this without ever turning his attention from the class.

   The class is cued that it is time to attend to the second feature when Mr. Piowaty replaces the first transparency with a second one. The process is repeated again and again without Mr. Piowaty ever having to turn away from the class, or the students having to wait for either the description to be written out or for their lines of sight to be cleared. Throughout the learning activity, Mr. Piowaty is able to control what the students view on the screen. Features not being discussed are not displayed. However, Mr. Piowaty is able to bring back into view, previously discussed features if he wants to draw comparisons or raise other points about them.

Ms. Steele Writes on the Chalkboard, Her Back to the Class

Whenever feasible and practical, consider using visual displays and even audio presentations to minimize transition time and keep students engaged. Overhead projectors, video cassette recorders, microcomputers, computer display projectors, laserdisc players, and ELMO visual presenters are only some of the widely available and cost-effective devices that make it easier for you to conduct high quality, professional demonstrations and presentations that (1) enhance the businesslike atmosphere of your classroom, (2) require little transition time, and (3) make it easier for you to supervise and attend to your students while they are engaged in learning activities.

SAVING TIME BY USING INTRACLASS GROUPING

Intraclass grouping is the subdividing of the students within a class into individual task groups for a learning activity. In Vignette 3.19, students waste time waiting their turns to be engaged in a learning activity. In Vignette 3.20, the teacher uses intraclass grouping to keep students busily engaged.

Mr. Piowaty Illustrates Points on the Overhead Projector While Maintaining Eye Contact with the Class

---

VIGNETTE 3.19

Coach McCreary is conducting drills on throwing two-hand chest passes with 13 junior high basketball players. The players are in a single line as Coach McCreary tosses the ball to Jan who is first. Jan passes the ball to Coach McCreary who exclaims: "Good job, Jan! Next!" Jan returns to the back of the line and the next player has a try. As players take turns, Coach McCreary encourages them, acknowledges properly executed passes, and points out flaws in techniques.

VIGNETTE 3.20

Coach Adomitis is conducting drills on throwing two-hand chest passes with 13 junior high basketball players. The players are divided into five groups of two and one group of three. Each of the six groups has a ball. As each group practices, Coach Adomitis circulates among the groups, encouraging players, acknowledging properly executed passes, and pointing out flaws in techniques.

While Coach McCreary's students spent more time waiting than practicing, Coach Adomitis kept all of her students busy by using intraclass grouping. Intraclass grouping is an especially effective means for accommodating individual differences among students within the same class (see, e.g., Vignettes 6.6 and 6.7).

ACCOMMODATING STUDENTS' COMPLETING WORK AT DIFFERING TIMES

Consider the dilemma Mr. Uter faces in Vignette 3.21.

VIGNETTE 3.21

Mr. Uter distributes copies of a tasksheet containing 18 questions to his sixth graders to individually answer using their geography textbooks as a reference. The students have 35 minutes to complete and turn in the assignment before discussing the questions in a large group session.

After 15 minutes, several students have completed the work, while others are only through the first four questions. Those who finished sit idly waiting for the others. As more students complete the assignment, the noise level in the room increases and becomes disturbing to those still working. The noise bothers Mr. Uter and he finally puts an end to the exercise by saying: "Okay, it looks like most of you are finished. Everybody turn in your papers and we'll discuss the answers."

How could Mr. Uter have planned the assignment so his students' time would be more efficiently utilized? As one of many options, Mr. Uter might have made this a two-part assignment. The first part would consist of the 18 questions to be turned in at the end of the 35 minutes. Time permitting, the second part would be begun in class, but would not be due until the next day (i.e., homework). As a precaution against students rushing through the first part in order to take advantage of the class time for homework, Mr. Uter could make the assignment such that successful completion of the second part is dependent on the first part having been done well. At the end of the 35 minutes, work on either part of the assignment ceases, the first part is turned in, students put the second part away and out of sight, and then the first part questions are discussed in a large group session.

In general, your classroom will operate more efficiently if you sequence your learning activities so that independent tasks that need to be finished in class are followed by independent work that has flexible beginning and ending times. Mr. Uter made the mistake of scheduling the large group discussion immediately after the independent work without accommodating for some students finishing before others.

CREATING A COMFORTABLE, NONTHREATENING ATMOSPHERE

A Frightening Place

A classroom climate that encourages on-task, engaged student behaviors can be cultivated by (1) creating a businesslike atmosphere; (2) being exceptionally prepared and organized, especially in the beginning of a new school term; and (3) minimizing transition time by efficiently dispensing with administrative tasks, efficiently distributing materials and giving directions, prudently choosing and preparing audio-visual aids, taking advantage of intraclass grouping, and sequencing learning activities to accommodate students finishing work at differing times. However, unless students feel that it is safe for them to wholeheartedly participate in learning activities without being ridiculed, embarrassed, or harmed, the classroom climate will not be as conducive to on-task, engaged behaviors as you would like.

Why would a student ever be fearful of putting forth a concerted effort (i.e., becoming highly engaged) in a learning activity? The reasons are complex and varied. Some preadolescent and adolescent students may fear that their efforts to achieve learning goals will be ridiculed by peers who do not value academic achievement. Being accepted by a peer group is typically more important in the minds of students in this age-group than is achieving a learning goal determined by a teacher. Oftentimes, academic learning goals appear long-ranged, whereas a peer-acceptance goal seems immediate and urgent. Consequently, in a case where a student feels that peers do not value school achievement, the student may fear separation from peers as a consequence of engagement in learning activities.

If students feel that a teacher has challenged or embarrassed them in front of their peers, they may consider engagement in learning activities to be tantamount to collaborating with a resented authority figure. Fears related to labeling compound the problems. Some students believe that if they put an effort into learning activities and still fail to achieve learning goals, they will either be labeled "stupid" or fail to live up to a previously acquired label of "smart." Consequently, they are afraid to risk failure, so they do not try.

Due to threats by schoolyard bullies or outbursts of antisocial conduct (e.g., gang-related violence), school may be such a frightening place for some students that they worry more about protecting themselves than they do about learning. Students can hardly be concerned with academics when in fear for their lives.

The lack of familiarity with a new school environment is a source of fear for many primary grade children. School confronts some with their first extended period of time away from the familiar surroundings of their homes and families.

The presence of these sources of fear does not excuse misbehavior or disengagement from learning activities. However, being aware of them is the first step in developing and implementing strategies for mitigating their influences. Such strategies are suggested in subsequent chapters.

Risking Self-Respect

From their earliest moments, most children are inundated with storybook tales, television programs, poems, songs, and talks from adults and other sources that leave them feeling: "The degree to which a person is loved, appreciated, and respected by others and the worth of that person are dependent on how well that person performs, accomplishes commendable deeds, and achieves desirable goals." "Rudolph, the Red-Nosed Reindeer," for example, was an object of scorn for his peers until he achieved an act of heroism one Christmas Eve. Then he was loved and respected.

Many well-meaning but misguided parents attempt to motivate their children to achieve by displaying greater signs of love after the children have been successful in an endeavor than after the children have failed in an endeavor. Consequently, the vast majority of students enter school believing that their own personal worth and self-esteem depend on how well they perform in school. On the surface, such a phenomenon would seem to motivate students to be engaged in learning activities so that they will achieve. In reality, the phenomenon poses one of the greater hindrances to students willingly engaging in learning activities. As a positive reinforcer for on-task behavior, the promise of love and self-respect can be effective over a short term, but it virtually always produces undesirable side effects over time (Ginott, 1972). Thus, rewards for achievement or on-task behaviors that communicate the message: "You are a better, more loved person because you have succeeded or behaved as someone else wants you to behave," are destructive positive reinforcers. Similarly, the withholding of love and displays of disrespect following off-task behaviors are destructive punishments.

In order to understand why using love and respect as a reward is a destructive positive reinforcer that should be avoided, as should the destructive punishment of withdrawing love and respect, consider these two generalizations. (1) The acquisition and maintenance of love and esteem is one of social person's more basic and compelling drives (Maslow, 1962). (2) Different students achieve learning goals at differing rates and to different degrees (Anderson, 1976, Corno & Snow, 1986). When students are led to believe that the more successful among them will be loved and respected more than the less successful, their ego defense mechanisms discourage their participation in what seems to be a game with excessively high stakes and few winners (Lessinger, 1970). Why should anyone other than the highly apt students be willing to jeopardize their self-esteem in a competition in which they cannot be best? Students who believe that they are worth less in the eyes of others when they are less than successful in school-related activities are very defensive about engaging in those activities. Such defensiveness precludes the attitude of open cooperation that you would like to prevail in your classroom. Vignettes 3.22, 3.23, and 3.24 illustrate the problem.

VIGNETTE 3.22

Ms. Davilio would like to find out just how well each of her Spanish-language students has achieved the learning objectives of an instructional unit. Such as evaluation will help Ms. Davilio make wiser decisions regarding what should be retaught, what new objectives should be established, and who needs help with what. Like most teachers, Ms. Davilio uses tests to help her assess student achievement. However, she has difficulty obtaining valid test results because many of her students feel that their personal prestige and Ms. Davilio's fondness for them are dependent on their test scores. Consequently, some of these students display such anxiety when taking tests that their scores do not accurately indicate their achievement levels. Other students do not put forth the effort they should to prepare for tests because, consciously or unconsciously, they do not want to risk "losing face" by trying and failing. Other students even attempt to deceive Ms. Davilio into believing that they have achieved more than they actually have by either faking their way through test questions or directly cheating.

VIGNETTE 3.23

Maunsell believes that his self-worth depends on his achievements. In time, he begins to resent Mr. Iverson and other teachers who seem to be continually judging him (whereas in reality some of those teachers were only judging Maunsell's achievement, not Maunsell himself). While using Socratic methods for one learning activity, Mr. Iverson asks Maunsell a question. Maunsell suddenly snaps: "Pick on somebody else, you're always trying to make me look bad!"

VIGNETTE 3.24

Ms. Whalen assigns homework to her chemistry class in which students are to balance some equations. Theresa attempts the exercises at home and finds that she has difficulty completing them. Rather than return to school without the equations properly balanced, she feigns illness and does not attend school when the assignment is due. She prefers to miss class and not achieve the objective than to face what she perceives to be a potentially embarrassing situation.

Disassociating Self-Respect from Achievement

Students would be much less defensive and, thus, more likely to cooperate if adults did not give them the idea that they risk their self-respect whenever they undertake tasks or are expected to behave in a prescribed manner. The destructive message from an authority figure that leads to student defensiveness is: "I love and respect you when you are successful (or behave properly)." Or in other words, "I do not love and respect you when you are unsuccessful (or misbehave)."

You can mollify a student's defensiveness by communicating: "I am happy when you are successful (or behave properly) because I love and respect you." Or in other words, "I am unhappy when you are unsuccessful (or misbehave) because I love and respect you."

It is not easy for teachers to effectively communicate that their jobs involve judging behaviors and achievement exhibited by students rather than judging students themselves. Chapter 4 of this book is designed to help you develop a particular style for communicating with students that, when consistently practiced, breaks through defensive student attitudes and leads to the type of classroom climate where students feel free to enthusiastically cooperate and engage in learning activities. Through appropriate communication techniques, you can (1) avoid the characterizations and labels (e.g., "smart," "dumb," "bright," "slow," and "good") that lead students to be defensive about engaging in learning activities; (2) gain students' trust so that they understand that they are not gambling with their self-esteem by cooperating with you and engaging in the learning activities you plan; and (3) avoid the resentment and power struggles that occur as a consequence of students' feeling embarrassed in the classroom.

TRANSITIONAL ACTIVITIES
FROM CHAPTER 3 TO CHAPTER 4

I. Write one paragraph suggesting how the incident in Vignette 3.25 might influence, both positively and negatively, the businesslike atmosphere of Ms. Schott's class.
   Exchange your paragraph with that of a colleague. Discuss the implications, including the impressions students might infer regarding the priority Ms. Schott affords the business of learning. "Avoiding Unintended Messages" in Chapter 4 elaborates further on these issues.

VIGNETTE 3.25

While conducting a questioning strategy session with her class, Ms. Schott notices Ms. Byung-Lee, the school principal, beckoning her to the doorway of the classroom. Ms. Schott calls a halt to the learning activity by telling her class: "Excuse me class, but I have some business with Ms. Byung-Lee. We'll finish up shortly. While I'm busy, please confine your talk to whispers." After six minutes in which Ms. Schott and Ms. Byung-Lee confer at the doorway, Ms. Schott directs the class: "Okay, now let's get back . . ."

   II. Write two paragraphs explaining why the beginning of a new school year is an opportune time for establishing a classroom climate that is conducive to on-task behaviors. Compare your response to that of a colleague.
  III. Imagine yourself as a teacher about to begin a school year. Answer the first nine questions from Mr. Martin's list in Vignette 3.5.
  IV. Develop a lesson plan for one day during the first week of school that fits Mr. Martin's three "Reminders for the First Week's Learning Activities" in Vignette 3.5.
   V. Write a paragraph explaining why you agree or disagree with this statement. "The harder a teacher works within the fourth stage of the Teaching Process Model, the less that teacher will have to work within the fifth stage to make learning activities effective." Discuss your response with a colleague.
  VI. Tell about a teacher you once had who used an inefficient method of taking roll. Tell about a second teacher you had who took roll more efficiently.
 VII. List some of the difficulties teachers make for themselves by spending too much class time distributing materials. Compare your list to that of a colleague.
VIII. List some of the advantages, relative to keeping students on-task, of directing students into learning activities using techniques other than personally speaking to the entire class at once. Compare your list to that of a colleague.
  IX. Describe two contrasting examples in which a teacher uses an audio-visual device (e.g., a chalkboard or video cassette recorder) in communicating information to students during a learning activity. Write the second example so that the teacher's choice of device results in a more efficient use of students' time than in the first example. Discuss your examples with a colleague.
   X. Plan a learning activity in which intraclass grouping is used to maximize allocated time and minimize transition time.
  XI. Describe an example in which students in a classroom complete an assignment at differing times. Devise and describe a plan for that teacher to use so that students who finish the assignment before others are kept busy with productive activities. Exchange and discuss examples with a colleague.
 XII. Carlotta is a student who feels more loved after scoring high on tests than she does after scoring low. Discuss with colleagues why such a feeling may eventually discourage Carlotta from enthusiastically engaging in learning activities.
XIII. In preparation for your work with Chapter 4, discuss the following questions with two or more of your colleagues.
   A. How does a teacher's style of communication (i.e., whether the teacher tends to describe situations or judge people) affect the classroom climate?

    B. What strategies can teachers employ to condition students to attentively listen to what is said?

    C. How can teachers help students deal with their frustrations and get on with the business of learning?

    D. How can teachers avoid being misinterpreted by students?

    E. Can teachers be disruptive?

    F. How can teachers consistently send the message that students are responsible for their own conduct?

    G. What are some of the strategies employed by teachers to elicit the cooperation of students' parents?

    H. What role do grades play in motivating student engagement?

    I. What are teachers' professional responsibilities regarding privileged information about students?

SUPPLEMENTAL READINGS

Boynton, P., Di Geronimo, J., & Gustafson, G. (1985). A basic survival guide for new teachers. *The Clearing House, 59,* 101–103.

Cangelosi, J. S. (1990). *Cooperation in the classroom: Students and teachers together* (2nd ed., pp. 13–19). Washington, DC: National Education Association.

Emmer, E. T., Evertson, C. M., & Anderson, L. M. (1980). Effective classroom management at the beginning of the school year. *Elementary School Journal, 80,* 219–231.

Ginott, H. (1972). *Teacher and Child.* (pp. 123–144). New York: Avon.

Jones, V. F., & Jones, L. S. (1990). *Comprehensive classroom management: Motivating and managing students* (3rd ed., pp. 61–99). Boston: Allyn and Bacon.

Petreshene, S. (1986, October). What can you do in 10 minutes? Transition activities that make kids think! *Instructor, 96* (3), 68–70.

Smith, H. A. (1985). The marking of transitions by more and less effective teachers. *Theory into Practice, 24,* 57–62.

CHAPTER **4**

Communicating with Students

Purpose of Chapter 4

Chapter 4 is designed to help you

1. Develop a descriptive, rather than judgmental, language style in communications with your students so that you (a) avoid the characterizations and labeling that lead students to be defensive about engaging in learning activities, (b) gain students' trust so that they understand that they are not gambling with their self-esteem by cooperating with you and engaging in the learning activities you plan, and (c) avoid the resentment and power struggles that occur as a consequence of students feeling embarrassed in the classroom.

2. Understand how to carefully select what to say and when to say it, utilize body language, utilize listening techniques, and utilize supportive replies so that your students will choose to pay attention to you when you speak.

3. Avoid communicating unintended messages that lead your students to misunderstand how you expect them to behave.

4. Leave no doubt in your students' minds that each person is responsible to his or her own conduct.

5. Emphasize formative, rather than summative, evaluations when communicating with students and parents about students' achievement of learning goals.

6. Recognize that the level of professionalism you display in your communications with and about your students influences the trust and confidence students have in you.

7. Develop an assertive communication style, avoiding both hostile and passive responses to students.

USING DESCRIPTIVE RATHER THAN JUDGMENTAL LANGUAGE

Differences between Descriptive and Judgmental Language

Research studies indicate that students feel less threatened, less defensive, and more willing to engage in learning activities when working with teachers who consistently use descriptive language than with teachers who use a more judgmental language style (Van Horn, 1982). Descriptive language verbally portrays a situation, a behavior, an achievement, or a feeling. Judgmental language verbally labels behavior, achievement, or person. Judgmental language that focuses on personalities is particularly detrimental to a climate of cooperation (Ginott, 1972).

Notice how descriptive language is used in these examples.

- Four-year-old Justin shows one of his paintings to Ms. Maeger who exclaims: "The greens and browns in your painting make me think of being outside in a forest!"
- Mr. Zelezak turns to Joe, who has just interrupted Katrina while she is speaking, and says: "I cannot concentrate on what Katrina is saying while you are talking."

Here are examples of teachers using judgmental language.

- Four-year-old Caroline shows one of her paintings to Ms. Murphy who exclaims: "Why Caroline, that's a beautiful picture! You are a great artist!"
- Ms. Gordon turns to Mindy, who has just interrupted Greg while he was speaking, and says: "You are very rude for interrupting Greg!"

The Consequences of Judgmental Language

To consistently use a descriptive language style, you must resist even silent thoughts that label students "smart," "slow," "good reader," "well behaved," "problem child," "honest," "intelligent," "underachiever," and the paradoxical "overachiever" (Cangelosi, 1982, pp. 73–74). Instead of thinking of students according to labels, focus on learning tasks, circumstances, and situations.

Recall the failure of the teacher in Vignette 2.15 to separate judgments about what students do and accomplish from her judgments of students themselves; she again uses judgmental language in Vignette 4.1.

VIGNETTE 4.1

Ms. Johnson is a fifth grade teacher who tends to characterize her students and communicate her evaluations of them. For example, while orally giving directions to her class, Ms. Johnson notices Ursala talking to a neighbor instead of paying attention. Ms. Johnson tells her: "Ursala, you're always talking when you shouldn't! Why are you such a pain?" Ursala begins to feel uncomfortable in Ms. Johnson's presence as she now believes that Ms. Johnson has little respect for her. Ms. Johnson continues to respond to Ursala's displays of disruptive behaviors with judgmental language. In time, Ursala develops a disruptive behavior pattern as she lives up to what she perceives to be Ms. Johnson's expectations (Rosenthal & Jacobsen, 1968).

In a parent-teacher conference, Ms. Johnson tells Leo's father, "Leo is quite bright, but he tends to be lazy."

Avoiding Labels

By consistently following their successes with ego builders and following their failures with attacks on their personalities, Ms. Johnson reinforces the misconception that personal self-worth depends on successes. Even those students who do not care about Ms. Johnson's opinions are impacted by the constant association between achievement levels and character judgments.

Compare Ms. Johnson's labeling of students in Vignettes 2.15 and 4.1 to Mr. Ramirez's use of descriptive language in Vignette 4.2.

VIGNETTE 4.2

Mr. Ramirez is a fifth grade teacher who distinguishes between a student's accomplishments and the value of that student. He does not view a student's display of off-task behavior as a reflection of character flaws. Mr. Ramirez believes that he is responsible for teaching each student to be on-task and to achieve learning goals. He does not include judgment of students' characters among his responsibilities. His use of descriptive language focuses on learning tasks, not on personalities.

Upon returning one of his student's science test papers with a high score, Mr. Ramirez remarks: "Mickey, this paper indicates that you understand the dependence of animal respiration on plant respiration."

While orally giving directions to his class, Mr. Ramirez notices Mary Frances talking to a neighbor instead of paying attention. Mr. Ramirez tells her: "Mary Frances, I would like you to stop talking and listen to these directions."

In a parent-teacher conference, Mr. Ramirez tells Nettie's father: "Nettie grasped the idea of multiplication right away. However, she does not have all of the multiplication facts memorized because she sometimes does not take the time to complete the drills that I assign in class."

Mr. Ramirez makes a concerted effort to use language that addresses specifically what has or has not been achieved, specific behaviors he expects students to exhibit, and specific behaviors that are unacceptable. He avoids implications that label or characterize personalities. Mr. Ramirez does not hesitate to communicate his feelings about specific behaviors or achievements of students; however, he never allows those feelings to influence the degree to which he respects, cares for, and values students.

The Fallacy of Labels

If a student does not comprehend a reading passage, it does not necessarily imply that the student is a "slow learner" or a "poor reader." It only means that the student did not comprehend that passage. The lack of comprehension might stem from a lack of interest in the content, from thought patterns that diverge from those of the author, from misconceptions regarding the content, or from a myriad of other reasons that do not fall under a general label such as "poor reader." If, however, students acquire the idea that they are poor readers, they usually avoid engaging in reading even when they are interested in the content, do not think divergently from the author, have no misconceptions to overcome, and suffer no other interferences specific to that particular reading selection. Rather than blame the lack of reading comprehension on "poor reading," the teacher should focus on designing and helping students engage in learning activities that improve reading comprehension skills.

If a student readily grasps what is generally a difficult-to-grasp scientific principle, it does not necessarily imply that the student is especially "bright" or has a "scientific mind." It only means that the student has a grasp of that particular scientific principle. To label students "scientifically-minded" is to ask them to live up to someone else's image and to encourage elitism. To label such students "bright" is to unwittingly label those who do not grasp the concept "dull."

A student who is misbehaving is not a behavior problem; the misbehavior, not the student, is the problem. The distinction may seen trivial. However, for you to be able to apply the suggestions for dealing with misbehaviors that are presented in Chapters 7–10, you need to perceive the behavior, not the student, as the problem to be eliminated. Students who perceive themselves as "behavior problems" cannot do away with the problem without doing away with themselves. Unless such students resort to suicide, they tend to protect themselves by wearing their "behavior problem" label with pride. On the other hand, students who learn that they are "okay" (Harris, 1969), but that they display certain behaviors that are problems, may be willing to alter those behaviors.

TEACHING STUDENTS TO LISTEN TO YOU

The Richness of Descriptive Language

Descriptive language is richer in information than judgmental language. In Vignette 4.3, Mr. Allred's comment is descriptive, while in Vignette 4.4, Ms. Mustaphos's comment is judgmental. Which is more informative to students?

VIGNETTE 4.3

Mr. Allred and his second graders have just returned to their classroom from the schoolyard where they conducted an experiment on erosion. He announces to the class: "After we finished the experiment, it took us only four minutes to collect our equipment and return to our places here in the room. We didn't disturb any other classes during that time. We will go outside again tomorrow and conduct an experiment with water."

VIGNETTE 4.4

Ms. Mustaphos and her second graders have just returned to their classroom from the schoolyard where they conducted an experiment on erosion. She announces to the class: "You are such good boys and girls! I'm so proud of you! Next time we do something like this, I know you'll be just as cooperative."

By listening to Mr. Allred, students gained specific knowledge about what they did and what they would be doing. They were able to associate how their specific behaviors (e.g., taking only four minutes to get situated) influence future plans and opportunities (e.g., they will get to perform another experiment outside the next day). By listening to Ms. Mustaphos, students only found out that their teacher was pleased with them. While important, her message did not tell them anything they didn't already know. Hopefully, students already know they are "good." Ms. Mustaphos can't really know that they will be just as cooperative next time, so why did she say that? Was that her attempt to improve the chances that they would be cooperative next time? If so, there was a hint of dishonesty in her statement. Students don't care to listen to teachers who are not being forthright.

The Judicious Use of Words

In general, students are likely to pay attention to what you say if they have learned that, whenever you speak you really have something to say. By judiciously using words that inform and avoiding inane talk, you leave your students with the idea that they miss something by not hearing you when you speak to them.

Unfortunately, students readily learn to be deaf to may teachers because the majority of them are frequently exposed to meaningless talk from adults. Look at this example.

Five-year-old Holly is drinking a glass of milk. Her father sees her and says: "Don't spill your milk."

Holly's father's words neither taught nor reminded Holly that milk is not to be spilled. She was drinking her milk with no intention of spilling it. She already knew that milk-spilling is not allowed. Her father's words taught Holly that he sometimes says uninformative things, thus she does not always need to pay attention to him. If, on the other hand, Holly's father notices her being careless with the milk by swinging the glass around with one hand, he might have said: "Holly, it would be safer to hold that glass with two hands." Those words acknowledge that Holly already knows that milk should not be spilled and help her to think of ways to prevent spilling.

Here's another all too typical example of inane talk.

> Joshua is working on an individual assignment in Mr. Green's psychology class when he gets up and begins walking across the room. Mr. Green sees him and says: "Joshua, don't get up."

When Mr. Green spoke to Joshua, he was already up and walking. At that time, it was possible for Joshua to sit down, but impossible for him to have never stood up. By giving a command that he could not possibly obey, Mr. Green was unwittingly teaching Joshua to ignore him. Mr. Green could have told Joshua to return to his place. Rather than reacting with the first words that come to mind, it is usually wiser for teachers to pause and carefully frame words before speaking to students.

Thinking before Talking

Often, adults send inane messages to children because they react before becoming aware of some relevant circumstances. Vignette 4.5 gives an example.

Had Amanda's mother first observed where Amanda was going before ordering her back to bed, she might have avoided that unnecessary exchange. Over time, Amanda might learn to attend to her mother's talk if the circumstances under which she is allowed to get out of bed (e.g., having to go to the bathroom) are initially clarified. The same type of situation occurs in Vignette 4.6.

Exchanges such as the one between Maureen and Mr. Prenn cannot always be avoided. However, if they become common occurrences, they condition students to ignore what a teacher is saying. if Maureen was only telling Walt the page number, the talking would have terminated without Mr. Prenn's intervention. Had he first waited to see if the talk would quickly stop, he could have avoided the exchange of useless words.

Vignette 4.7 illustrates how teachers and other adults teach students to be "deaf" to them by acting as if they are terminating self-terminating behaviors.

VIGNETTE 4.5

As three-year-old Amanda goes to bed her mother tells her: "Now, don't get up! You stay in bed." Several minutes later, Amanda's mother sees her out of bed and in the hall. She exclaims: "I thought I told you to stay in bed! Get back to bed this instant!" Amanda: "But Momma, I have to make pee-pee!" Mother: "Okay, go to the bathroom and then get back to bed."

VIGNETTE 4.6

Mr. Prenn directs his fourth grade class to silently read pages 17 through 21. He notices Maureen talking to Walt and says: "Maureen, this is supposed to be silent reading. You know you're not to be talking." Maureen replies: "I'm sorry, but I was just telling Walt the page number." Mr. Prenn: "Then that's okay."

VIGNETTE 4.7

Peabody Junior High teachers are expected to stand in their doorways to enforce hall regulations which include "no running." Mr. Adams notices Carol and Mark running toward a room. Just as the two students get to their room, they hear Mr. Adams yell: "Stop that running!" They were already about to stop running, not because of what Mr. Adams yelled, but because they had reached their destination.

The incident in Vignette 4.7 was relatively harmless, but a more positive impact could have been realized had he either said nothing about the running or acted decisively to prevent such running from recurring. Mr. Adams's words only served to remind the students that adults say a lot of meaningless things.

Why are adults sometimes so unthinking in their use of language? If they understood their reasons, they might be more careful with words. Here is one hypothesis as to why Mr. Adams chose such an ineffectual approach:

> From his location in the classroom doorway with a hall crowded with students, Mr. Adams is not in an advantageous position to enforce hall regulations. If he leaves his post to effectively deal with Carol's and Mark's running, he no longer will be serving as a reminder to the scores of other students in the hallway to follow regulations. He realizes that his mere presence is a cue to many students. Mr. Adams may not consider Carol's and Mark's running offensive enough to exert time and energy to deal with it effectively. They were only running, not fighting. On the other hand, he doesn't simply ignore the self-terminating behavior because he feels obliged to announce to anyone in earshot that he is doing his duty. If Carol and Mark collide with something and injuries result, he can at least say: "I told them to stop running."

More and More Useless Words

Students also learn to ignore "teacher-talk" when teachers act as if they are initiating self-initiating behaviors, as in Vignette 4.8.

The unnecessary words that interrupted their engagement lead Mr. Chapman's students to place less importance on what he says. As a teacher, you should limit what you say to only what you intend to be heard.

VIGNETTE 4.8

Mr. Chapman's fourth graders eagerly begin working on a learning activity he has just explained to them. He then says: "Okay, get to work."

VIGNETTE 4.9

Ms. White is introducing a learning activity to her fifth graders. She says: "You're going to love this! This'll be more fun than what we've been doing! You won't want to stop after we begin to . . ."

Students may begin tuning a teacher out when that teacher makes judgments that only the students can make. Ms. White makes judgments for her students in Vignette 4.9.

How long will Ms. White go on? Whether or not the students will enjoy the activity, find it fun, or will want to stop is something for them to individually judge for themselves. Probably some will enjoy the activity, while others won't. Shouldn't Ms. White get on with the directions and quit trying to sell the activity to them? If the activity is truly enjoyable for the students, they will find this out for themselves when she stops talking and they become engaged. If Ms. White thinks she will enjoy the activity, she should quickly pass that information to the students by telling them: "I'm going to enjoy this; I hope you will also." The students would probably like to know how she feels. But she only wasted time and words by trying to inform them of their own feelings.

Speaking Only to Intended Listeners

The teacher in Vignette 4.10 is conditioning students to ignore him.

VIGNETTE 4.10

Mr. Brunoski is sitting at his desk as his business law students silently read assigned passages from a textbook. Mr. Brunoski notices that Ali is doing chemistry homework instead. From his place at the front of the room, Mr. Brunoski says: "What do you think you're doing, Ali?" Ali: "I wasn't doing anything!" Mr. Brunoski: "Well, you sure weren't reading your business law! Put that stuff away, before I confiscate it. Do the reading like everybody else." Ali: "Yes, sir."

Ali needed to be engaged in the reading and that was the message he, not the others in the class, needed to hear. Shirley, for example, stopped reading when Mr. Brunoski spoke. She then waited for the exchange between Mr. Brunoski and Ali to cease before becoming reengaged. The other students had to either ignore what Mr. Brunoski said or become disengaged in the learning activity. Had Mr. Brunoski dealt with the situation similar to Ms. Lowe in Vignette 4.11, students would be more inclined to listen to him in the future.

Ms. Lowe made it clear that what she had to say was meant only for Woody. Other students didn't need to interrupt their work to find out that Ms. Lowe's message didn't apply to them. Ms. Lowe doesn't speak to the entire class unless she expects all of them to listen. Her students are conditioned to stop and listen when she addresses them because they haven't had to block out her voice when the message was for someone else.

Body Language

In Vignette 4.11, Ms. Lowe effectively used body language to let her class know to whom she was speaking and to gain Woody's attention before speaking. As Jones (1979) and other researchers have discovered, how you position your body when speaking to students has a major impact on what messages students receive. Because Ms. Lowe got out of her seat, squatted directly in front of Woody, and made eye contact, Woody was likely to listen to Ms. Lowe and realize that she meant business.

Sometimes teachers also make the mistake of saying one thing, but communicating another as a consequence of their body language (Cangelosi, 1992b, pp. 135–136). Vignette 4.12 is an example.

Ms. Nagle's students didn't really take what she said very seriously. Her voice provided a hint of stress and indicated to them that she was not really in control. Her body language indicated that she was willing to continue with the learning activity although she hadn't obtained their cooperation. Because she didn't bother to face them and command their attention, they didn't attend to her demand of "no more talking." Do you think Ms. Terrell, in Vignette 4.13, will be more successful in getting her students to follow her directions than did Ms. Nagle?

VIGNETTE 4.11

Ms. Lowe is sitting at her desk as her business law students silently read assigned passages from a textbook. Ms. Lowe notices that Woody is doing chemistry homework instead. Ms. Lowe walks over to Woody, squats down directly in front of him, and makes eye contact. She whispers: "Woody, it is time for you to be reading your business law text." She stands, pivots, and returns to her desk as Woody puts away the chemistry homework and appears to read the business law text.

VIGNETTE 4.12

At the chalkboard, Ms. Nagle is writing some sentences that she has directed her students to classify as either simple or compound. As she writes with her back to the class, she is disturbed by loud talking from the class. "No more talking!" she says without pausing from her writing task. The students quit talking momentarily, but soon the noise level increases again. Continuing to write, but now looking over her shoulder toward the class she shouts: "I've had it with all this noise! I said, 'No more talking!'"

VIGNETTE 4.13

At the chalkboard, Ms. Terrell is writing some sentences that she has directed her students to classify as either simple or compound. As she writes with her back to the class, she is disturbed by loud talking from the class. Ms. Terrell puts the chalk down, pivots, and directly faces the class. She pans her eyes across the class, making eye contact with one student and then another. Momentarily, she feels they are ready to listen and says: "The talking is disturbing me and those of you who are trying to analyze these sentences." She pauses and observes them briefly before turning around to continue with the task at hand.

Speaking Only to the Attentive

Ms. Terrell obtained her students' attention before trying to speak to them. Sometimes, students may not be ready to listen to you because they do not think you understand them well enough to tell them anything that they would consider important. In other cases, they may be preoccupied by thoughts with which they must dispense before attending to your message. Speak to people when they are ready to listen.

LISTENING TO STUDENTS

Effective communication with students involves, not only sending them messages, but also receiving their messages. Students become bored with monologues sooner than with verbal interchanges. They are more likely to be attentive to a conversation than a speech to which they are expected to listen passively.

Listening to students, observing their actions, and reading what they write are opportunities for you to learn what they think, believe, feel, know, understand, misunderstand, value, are willing to try, and are unwilling to try. A reasonably accurate understanding of your students' thoughts and attitudes is vital to your ability to identify students' needs, decide learning goals, design learning activities, and evaluate how well learning goals are achieved. You also need to understand students' thoughts and attitudes to decide what messages to communicate and when and how each message is to be communicated. By listening to them, you will discover how to get students to listen to you. Contrast Vignettes 4.14 and 4.15.

Lois was too upset to follow Ms. Medlyn's initial directions to the class. However, because Ms. Medlyn actively listened, she was able to detect a key to obtaining Lois' attention. By saying something that Lois wanted to hear, Ms. Medlyn was

---

VIGNETTE 4.14

Except for Billy, Ms. Lye's kindergarten students are following her directions to put away the materials with which they've been working and to gather around her in the reading corner. Billy throws himself on the floor and screams: "I'm hungry! I wanna eat my candy!" Ms. Lye goes over to Billy who is now yelling and crying incoherently. He flails his arms and legs and seems out of control. Ms. Lye grabs him and says: "Stop that Billy! Get hold of yourself. What's the matter with you anyway?" Billy continues crying, unintelligibly screaming something about candy. Ms. Lye is on her knees with Billy. Speaking loudly to be heard above the screams, she says: "That's enough! You know you can't have any candy right now! You haven't even had lunch yet! Please calm down. I know you will like this story; you can sit on my lap while I read it." Billy doesn't even hear her as he continues the tantrum.

VIGNETTE 4.15

Except for Lois, Ms. Medlyn's kindergarten students are following her directions to put away the materials with which they've been working and to gather around her in the reading corner. Lois throws herself on the floor and screams: "I'm hungry! I wanna eat my candy!" Ms. Medlyn goes over to Lois who is now yelling and crying incoherently. Louis flails her arms and legs and seems out of control. Ms. Medlyn gets down on her knees and gently, but firmly, takes Lois by the shoulders and turns her so that the two are face to face. Without speaking, Ms. Medlyn observes and listens for some indications of what's on Lois' mind. Soon, she catches the word candy among all the sounds emanating from Lois. Speaking loudly, calmly, slowly, and distinctly and maintaining direct eye contact, Ms. Medlyn says: "You want some candy." Hearing the word candy seems to strike a chord with Lois and she momentarily gains a semblance of composure. Ms. Medlyn seizes the opportunity to say: "As soon as you get control of yourself, we will talk about getting some candy." "But, I want my candy!" Lois says as she again starts to get upset. Ms. Medlyn: "Oh! You have some candy. Where is your candy?" Lois: "I left it." Ms. Medlyn: "You left it where?" Lois: "I don't know." Ms. Medlyn: "May I help you find it?" Lois is now relatively calm as she answers: "Yes." "Okay, I will. You put away your things and after I finish reading the story, we'll talk about finding your candy."

able to help Lois calm down enough to hear what Ms. Medlyn had to say. Ms. Medlyn did not try to get her own message across (i.e., put the materials away and prepare for the story) until Lois was able to receive that message. Please note that Ms. Medlyn never promised Lois anything she was not prepared to deliver. When she said: "You want some candy," in order to get Lois' attention, she was not telling Lois that she would give her candy or that Lois could eat candy before the materials were put away, the story was read, and lunch was eaten.

USING SUPPORTIVE REPLIES

Accepting Feelings

Consider Vignette 4.16.

Ms. Leonard tried to encourage Paul and help him build his confidence. What impact do you think her response had on Paul's thinking? Ms. Leonard's response denied Paul's feelings. He said the problems were hard; she said they were simple. She indicated that such problems were easy for smart people like him. Will he conclude that he is dumb? Will he conclude that when Ms. Leonard discovers that he can't do them, she'll think he's not smart and she will no longer like and respect him? As Ms. Leonard tries to explain the algebraic process to Paul, he may not attentively listen because he feels she didn't hear him. In his mind, Ms. Leonard doesn't understand the difficulty and frustration he is experiencing.

Ms. Leonard's response to Paul's expression of frustration was an example of a nonsupportive response because the response did not indicate that she understood and accepted his feelings. Expressions of feelings receive a supportive response when the listener indicates that the expression has been understood and accepted (Gordon, 1974, pp. 66–77).

Relieving Frustration

Ms. Palcic uses a supportive response in Vignette 4.17.

Before trying to help Bruce with the factoring problems, Ms. Palcic let him know that she understood what he was going through and that he was perfectly fine although he was experiencing difficulties with the problems. Frustration can be quite incapacitating and sometimes must be relieved before the source of

---

VIGNETTE 4.16

Ms. Leonard is walking among her algebra students as they individually work on factoring polynomials. Paul tells her as she passes near his desk: "I can't figure these out! They're just too hard for me." Ms. Leonard replies: "Paul, these should be a piece of cake for a smart guy like you! Just do them like the example we did on the board. They're really simple. Let me show you. First, begin by . . ."

VIGNETTE 4.17

Ms. Palcic is walking among her algebra students as they individually work on factoring polynomials. Bruce tells her as she passes near his desk: "I can't figure these out! They're just too hard for me." Ms. Palcic replies: "Factoring polynomials can really be difficult. I see that you're having trouble with these. Read number five to me. . . ."

---

the frustration can be addressed. Having another person's empathy can relieve frustration. Vignettes 4.18 and 4.19 contrast the nonempathetic nonsupportive response style to the empathetic supportive response style.

Eva's husband's reply was supportive. He let Eva know that he heard her, and it was okay to feel as she did. Theresa's husband, with his nonsupportive reply, found flaws in Theresa's statement and attempted to propose a solution to the problem before indicating that he understood the problem. Theresa, like Eva, needed understanding and the knowledge that her husband did not think less of her for feeling the way she did.

Defusing Conflict

In Vignette 4.20, the parent uses a nonsupportive response, while the response in Vignette 4.21 is supportive.

Both Krisilen and Allison simply expressed a desire for ice cream. In his supportive reply, Allison's father acknowledged that Allison wanted ice cream before he reminded Allison of the rule. Instead of acknowledging her desire for ice cream, Mr. Drake argued with Krisilen and perpetuated an unnecessary conflict.

VIGNETTE 4.18

Theresa tells her husband: "I feel so tied down! The children have been off-the-wall all day long and I'm just sick of being with them!" "Oh, come on! You know you love those kids," replies her husband. Theresa: "I never get a chance to get away from them and be with adults." Her husband: "Now, didn't I take you out to dinner Tuesday? Saturday, I'll stay home so you can go out and do whatever you like. You'll feel better."

VIGNETTE 4.19

Eva tells her husband: "I feel so tied down! The children have been off-the-wall all day long and I'm just sick of being with them. I never get a chance to get away from them and be with adults." Her husband: "I don't know how you manage to do what you do all day. I got a taste of what you're talking about last Saturday, and you've been putting up with it practically every day!"

VIGNETTE 4.20

Mr. Drake is driving his four-year-old daughter, Krisilen, home from preschool when they approach an ice cream shop. Krisilen: "I want some ice cream! I want some ice cream!" Mr. Drake: "No you don't! You haven't had your supper, and you never have sweets before supper." Krisilen: "Momma let me have some gum before supper one time!" Mr. Drake: "Don't argue with me; you're not getting any!" They drive past the ice cream shop, but Krisilen continues to mutter: "I do want some."

VIGNETTE 4.21

Mr. Fisher is driving his four-year-old daughter, Allison, home from preschool when they approach an ice cream shop. Allison: "I want some ice cream! I want some ice cream!" Mr. Fisher: "Yes, I bet you do. Ice cream would really taste good right now! It's too bad we haven't had supper yet." They drive past the ice cream shop. Allison: "Can I watch 'Sesame Street' when we get home?"

By acknowledging students' feelings with supportive replies, you can often avoid arguments and dispense with excuses for not being on-task. In Vignette 4.22, Mr. Layton's nonsupportive reply leads to a useless argument. In Vignette 4.23, Ms. Malone's supportive reply avoids an argument while clearly communicating an expectation.

VIGNETTE 4.22

Adrian to Mr. Layton, his physical education teacher: "Do I have to dress out today? I feel so stupid in these baggy gym shorts. My legs are too skinny!" Mr. Layton: "Why Adrian, you look good in shorts. You have nice legs. Of course you want to dress out! Do you want to mess up your regular clothes?" Adrian: "I don't have nice legs!" Mr. Layton: "They're not skinny by any means." Adrian: "I don't mind messing up my clothes."

VIGNETTE 4.23

Frank to Ms. Malone, his physical education teacher: "Do I have to dress out today? I feel so stupid in these baggy gym shorts. My legs are too skinny!" Ms. Malone: "You don't like the way you look in those gym shorts. I wish I didn't have to wear these shorts either. Better hurry and get dressed; we're starting volleyball in six minutes."

AVOIDING UNINTENDED MESSAGES

The Risk of Misinterpretation

As a teacher, you deal with many students at once. Some students' interpretations of what you say and do are likely to differ from those of other students. Obviously, you are continually risking being misinterpreted. Unintended messages, unwittingly communicated to students by teachers, can cause many of the misunderstandings that lead students to be off-task. Miscommunicating with your students cannot be completely avoided. However, you can reduce the frequency by (1) modeling a businesslike attitude, (2) avoiding disruptions of your own learning activities, (3) avoiding destructive positive reinforcers, and (4) avoiding destructive punishments.

In Vignette 4.24, a teacher fails to display an adequate businesslike attitude with her students and consequently communicates that engagement in learning activities is not the highest priority.

VIGNETTE 4.24

Ms. Coonley is conducting a lecture-discussion for her eleventh grade health science class when her principal, Ms. Rodriguez, appears in the classroom doorway and beckons Ms. Coonley to her. Ms. Coonley tells her class: "Excuse me, I have some business with Ms. Rodriguez. Please be quiet until I'm through." Ms. Rodriguez engages Ms. Coonley in a nine-minute conversation about a meeting to be held that night. In the meantime, the students' thoughts turn to other things. When Ms. Rodriguez leaves, Ms. Coonley turns to her class and says: "Okay, let's get back to our discussion. Where were we?"

Modeling a Businesslike Attitude

In Vignette 2.25, Mr. Chenier's businesslike attitude tends to convince students that what goes on in class is of primary importance.

VIGNETTE 4.25

Mr. Chenier is conducting a lecture-discussion for his eleventh grade health science class when his principal, Ms. Meador, appears in the classroom doorway and beckons Mr. Chenier to her. Mr. Chenier turns to Ms. Meador and says: "Just a moment, Ms. Meador; Phil is just responding to a comment about the sensibility of taking decongestants." Phil takes 30 seconds for his response while Mr. Chenier listens intently. Mr. Chenier: "Class, keep Phil's thought in mind while I quickly check with Ms. Meador." Ms. Meador then tries to involve Mr. Chenier in a conversation about

---

VIGNETTE 4.25 (continued)

a meeting that night, but Mr. Chenier instead uses 40 seconds to arrange to speak with her another time. Mr. Chenier turns to the class: "Now that you've had a little time to think about Phil's concerns regarding the dangers of decongestants, do you think the warning label we looked at earlier is adequate? Okay, Audrey." Audrey: "Like Phil said, ..."

Avoiding Disruptive Teacher Behavior

Teachers fail to model businesslike attitudes when they disrupt their own learning activities. Such disruptions carry the unintended message that disruptive behavior is acceptable. Compare Vignettes 4.26 to 4.27.

Mr. Miller disturbed his entire class, leading them to become disengaged, in order to help Robert and Chad get back on-task. Ms. Toney, on the other hand, dealt with the disruptive talking without disrupting students who remained on-task.

Avoiding Destructive Positive Reinforcers

Please reread "Destructive Positive Reinforcers" in Chapter 2.

The side effects of destructive positive reinforcers are often unintended messages such as "Homework is unimportant" or "A student is worthy of more respect for knowing an answer." The use of positive reinforcers to encourage on-task behaviors is dealt with throughout the remainder of the text. Whenever considering a positive reinforcer, reflect on the possibility of side effects that may lead to unintended messages.

Avoiding Destructive Punishment

Please reread "Destructive Punishment" in Chapter 2.

Punishment that leads to unintended messages is destructive. Consider Vignettes 4.28 and 4.29.

The embarrassment he felt may have served to discourage Virgil from again being caught without his homework. The pain suffered by Vern may teach him

---

VIGNETTE 4.26

Mr. Miller's sixth grade students are busy with an interdisciplinary writing assignment in which each proposes a solution to a problem. The room is quiet when Robert and Chad begin talking to one another from their places in the back of the room. Mr. Miller, seated at his desk in the front, notices them and in a loud voice announces: "This work is supposed to be done on your own. I don't want any talking until everyone is finished. Chad and Robert, cut the talking out right now." During Mr. Miller's announcement, all the students look up and listen. Some turn to see what Chad and Robert are doing when he mentions their names. Some continue to watch them for awhile to see if they'll talk again.

VIGNETTE 4.27

Ms. Toney's sixth grade students are busy with an interdisciplinary writing assignment in which each proposes a solution to a problem. The room is quiet when Andrew and Julius begin talking to one another from their places in the back of the room. Ms. Toney quietly and discreetly walks over to them, catches their eyes and whispers in a very businesslike tone, "Get back to work." Only the students very near Andrew and Julius notice Ms. Toney's actions.

VIGNETTE 4.28

In class, Mr. Fabian directs Virgil: "Please read your answer for number six." Virgil: "I didn't get to my homework." Mr. Fabian: "You didn't get to your homework! And why not?" Virgil: "Well, we had a basketball game last night and . . ." Mr. Fabian: "Oh! That's right. You're a hotshot basketball player. You're too important to do your homework. You think you'll ever make a living playing basketball? . . ." Virgil feels humiliated in front of his peers as Mr. Fabian continues.

VIGNETTE 4.29

Ms. Jennings notices Vern, one of her third graders, playing with some string instead of reading the passage she just assigned. She comes up behind Vern and raps him on the head with her knuckles. Vern winces in pain. His head still hurts as he appears to begin reading.

---

not to play with string where Ms. Jennings will see him. Thus, both examples of punishment may have effectively discouraged those off-task behaviors. However, might they also be destructive because they communicated unintended messages? The embarrassment may have taught Virgil not to trust Mr. Fabian and it distracted from the businesslike atmosphere of the classroom. After all, the business at hand did not involve whether or not Virgil was a "hotshot." Unfortunately, Ms. Jennings' actions communicated to Vern that violent behavior is acceptable within the confines of the classroom. Vern learned an effective, but uncivil, means for getting someone's attention and convincing another to do what you want.

The use of punishment is dealt with in Part III of this book. Possible side effects should always be considered before punishment is selected as a means for discouraging off-task behaviors.

BEING RESPONSIBLE FOR ONE'S OWN CONDUCT

Canter (1978), Ginott (1972), Glasser (1985), Gordon (1974), and most other purveyors of thought on classroom discipline emphasize that individuals are responsible and held accountable for their own behaviors. Except for the relatively unusual cases where one person physically accosts another, one person cannot make another do something. Once students realize this, they are disarmed of virtually all of their excuses for misconduct. To lead students to understand that only they are in control of their own conduct, you should consistently use language that is free of suggestions that one person can control another. In other words, purge your language of statements such as these. "Be careful of what you say or you'll make Mia feel bad." "He made me lose control." "You made Allen cry." "Fred, don't get Tommy into trouble." "She got me so mad." "Vernon just can't get along without Martha." "She makes me happy."

Such language should be replaced with, "Be careful of what you say or Mia may think you don't enjoy her company"; "I didn't maintain control when I saw what he did"; "Allen was so unhappy with what you said, that he cried"; "Fred, don't encourage Tommy to do something he shouldn't"; "I got so mad when I thought of what she did"; "Vernon depends on Martha for help"; "I'm happy to be with her."

Remind students that they control their own behaviors when they say such things as, "I did it because they wanted me to"; "She hurt my feelings"; "Make me happy."

FORMATIVE VERSUS SUMMATIVE EVALUATIONS

Two Reasons for Evaluating Student Achievement

The sixth step in the Teaching Process Model deals with evaluation of achievement. There are two types of evaluations teachers use to appraise student achievement of learning goals. (1) *Formative evaluations* assess students' progress relative to specific objectives during an instructional unit and help teachers decide how to design learning activities, when students are ready for certain learning activities, and which learning activities should be repeated. (2) *Summative evaluations* provide periodic judgments on how well students have done as a result of instructional units that have been completed. (Cangelosi, 1990b, pp. 2–3). Report card grades result from summative evaluations.

In which vignette, 4.30 or 4.31, is the teacher communicating a formative evaluation?

Mr. Jones indicated that he used his evaluations to influence the design of a learning activity. Thus, Mr. Jones' evaluation was formative. Effective teachers

---

VIGNETTE 4.30

Jay asks Ms. Motta, his basic chemistry teacher, do you think if I sign up for advanced placement chemistry, I'll do okay?'' Ms. Motta: "I don't know. That's really up to you. But I am confident that you understand almost everything we've covered in basic chemistry."

VIGNETTE 4.31

Larry asks Mr. Jones, his basic chemistry teacher: "Why did you give us so many problems for homework? You usually don't give half that many." Mr. Jones: "You seem to conceptualize the formulas very well, but you've been making a lot of computational errors. The only way I know for you to overcome that difficulty is to practice."

---

design learning activities in light of ongoing, frequent formative evaluations that are regularly communicated to students (Rosenshine & Stevens, 1986). Summative evaluations occur periodically (e.g., at the end of a learning unit) and not as frequently as formative evaluations. However, when students and their parents think of teacher evaluations, they are nearly always thinking of the summative variety (because they're thinking of grading).

Emphasizing Formative Evaluations

The grade consciousness that many students and their parents display can interfere with how well teachers are able to communicate formative evaluations to students. Consider Vignette 4.32.

All Mr. Wedington wanted to do was to diagnose Stephanie's skill with long division so he would be in a better position to help. But Stephanie was so used to having teachers grade the outcomes of her efforts, that she just didn't understand that Mr. Wedington was trying to help her, not grade her.

VIGNETTE 4.32

Mr. Wedington wants to find out exactly which steps in a long-division process his fifth graders can do and on which steps he needs to provide help. Thus, he meets with each student individually and has the student think aloud while working out a long-division computation. It is Stephanie's turn to demonstrate her skill with the process. Mr. Wedington: "Stephanie, I want to watch you divide 753 by 12. As you work it out on your paper, tell me what you are thinking." Stephanie writes down $12\overline{)753}$ but stops and says: "I don't know the answer." Mr. Wedington: "Neither do I. But I do know how to find the answer. I'd like you to begin to find the answer." Stephanie: "I can't while you're watching me!" Mr. Wedington: "Why not?" Stephanie: "Because I'll make a mistake and you'll count off." Mr. Wedington: "This has nothing to do with your grade. I just want to see how you divide, so I can help you divide better." Stephanie writes 6 as a partial quotient above the 5 in 753. Quickly, she puts down her pencil and asks: "Is that right?" Mr. Wedington: "Tell me why you decided to put 6 there." Stephanie begins to erase the 6 as she exclaims: "Oh! It's not right!" Mr. Wedington gently grabs her hand and stops her from erasing her correct response. Stephanie: "Oh! We're not allowed to erase...."

How can you help students overcome their defensiveness toward "being evaluated" and gain the cooperation you need to conduct ongoing formative evaluations? Here are three suggestions. (1) Use descriptive rather than judgmental language. (2) Clearly distinguish those relatively infrequent tests you use to make summative evaluations from the nearly continual observations and tests used for formative evaluations. (3) Do not collect data for summative evaluations during learning activities.

Descriptive language helps convince students that you evaluate only their levels of achievement of specific learning goals and you do not evaluate them.

Frequent assessments that are used to keep students apprised of their progress throughout learning units, but that do not influence their grades, help students to conceptualize, and thus cooperate in , formative evaluations. Those less frequent assessments that do influence students' grades should be distinguished as extraordinary events for which their engagements in your learning activities and formative evaluations have prepared them.

You, like many teachers, may value student-centered learning activities in which students respond to your questions (e.g., with Socratic methods), solve problems, or have discussions. Sometimes, students are reluctant to engage in such activities because they feel they're being graded. A comment of one seventh grader is typical: "Sure, Mr. Burke says, 'We learn by our mistakes.' But when we make mistakes, he's right there to take off points!" The conversations in Vignettes 4.33 and 4.34 discourage students from feeling free to ask questions, try out answers, and make mistakes during learning activities.

GRADES AS A FORM OF COMMUNICATION

Although formative evaluations should be emphasized more than summative evaluations, summative evaluations must still be periodically communicated to students and their parents. Grades and report cards are common vehicles for such communications. Unfortunately, many teachers use grades for other purposes. For example:

VIGNETTE 4.33

Byron: "Mrs. Thomas, I was surprised to get only a 'C' in sociology. My test scores weren't that bad." Ms. Thomas: "Well, I had to take into account your participation in class. You really struggled, missing a lot of questions."

VIGNETTE 4.34

Sam: "Thanks for the 'A'." Mr. McHale: "You got it because you've been so sharp in class lately. You really do a good job of contributing to discussions."

- Ms. Carter bases 40 percent of her students' history grades on attendance. She believes this will motivate students to come to class.
- Ms. Albright lowers a student's reading grade by one letter for every 10 demerits received during a term. A student gets demerits for getting caught exhibiting disruptive behaviors.

When teachers make grades directly contingent on attendance, effort, level of cooperation, or other factors different from student achievement of academic learning goals, the meaning of grades is lost. Is a "B" in history an indication of how well a student has achieved the goals specified by the history course syllabus, or is the "B" a reflection of effort, willingness to cooperate with the teacher, faithfulness to assignments, or what? There are far more effective ways to motivate students to be on-task than artificially rewarding on-task behaviors with high grades and artificially punishing off-task behaviors with low grades. Specific suggestions for positively reinforcing on-task behaviors and punishing off-task behaviors, without distorting the meaning of grades, are included throughout the remainder of this text. In general, there is no need for you to artificially manipulate grades as long as you (1) make sure your learning activities provide students with effective means for achieving the stated learning goals, and (2) use summative evaluations that are valid indicators of how well students achieved those same learning goals.

COMMUNICATING WITH PARENTS

Focusing on Formative Evaluations

You should, but may not always be able to, depend on help from parents to help secure students' cooperation. Often, you may want to discuss formative evaluations with parents to help them understand what you're trying to get their children to accomplish and how they can help. Sometimes communications are thwarted by parents who think all teacher evaluations are summative. In Vignette 4.35, Mr. Perkins attempts to gain Rolando's mother's cooperation. To do so, he must assertively steer the conversation away from summative and toward formative evaluations.

Conferences

Conferences between parents and teachers are more common in elementary schools than in secondary schools. Although elementary school teachers are involved with fewer students than secondary school teachers, they have greater responsibilities for each student. It is quite common for elementary schools to periodically devote entire school days for parent conferences. This practice is less common for secondary schools, but there are times when even secondary teachers must find time for conferences with parents. Consider these suggestions whenever you meet with a parent for a scheduled conference.

VIGNETTE 4.35

Mr. Perkins does not have the time to confer with his fifth graders' parents as frequently as he would like. He does, however, maintain contact by routinely phoning one or two parents each school day. In this way, he is able to speak with a parent of each student at least once every three weeks. It normally takes two conversations before parents understand that Mr. Perkins' intentions are to inform them about what their children are doing and not to either praise or criticize the student. Here is an account of Mr. Perkins' first telephone conversation with Rolando Mitchell's mother.

MS. MITCHELL: Hello.

MR. PERKINS: Hello, Ms. Mitchell. This is Sal Perkins, Rolando's teacher. I hope you are doing well.

MS. MITCHELL: Oh, yes. And what about you?

MR. PERKINS: Just great! I'd like to take five to six minutes to let you know what Rolando's working on in fifth grade. If this is an inconvenient time, I can call back later.

MS. MITCHELL: I can talk now, but what kinda trouble is that boy giving you? You just let me know, and I'll lay it on him.

MR. PERKINS: Rolando's not giving me any trouble. I just wanted to let you know about some things Rolando is working on in school.

MS. MITCHELL: I'm glad he's not troubling you. Is he going to pass? How are his grades?

MR. PERKINS: We're just beginning a lesson on how to use mathematics to find the best prices when shopping.

MS. MITCHELL: That's interesting. Do you think he'll learn it?

MR. PERKINS: Yes, and he should improve both his reading and mathematical skills as we start examining newspaper ads.

MS. MITCHELL: It'd be good for him to do more reading. He'd rather watch TV. I'm always telling him to turn off that boob-tube and go do some reading. But he just keeps watching.

MR. PERKINS: You've just given me an idea! Let's use his liking for TV to build his interest in relating mathematics and reading to shopping. I'll ask Rolando to record price-related information that he finds in TV commercials. We'll use his notes during our mathematics lessons.

MS. MITCHELL: I'll make sure he has a pad and pencil with him when he's in front of the television.

MR. PERKINS: That'll be a help. Thank you.

MS. MITCHELL: Anything else?

MR. PERKINS: He'll be working on expanding his writing vocabulary and using a dictionary for another week.

MS. MITCHELL: How's his writing?

MR. PERKINS: Each day this week, I'll give him a list of between five and 10 new words and, for homework, ask him to write sentences using them. It should take him about 20 minutes a night to look up the words in his dictionary and write the sentences.

MS. MITCHELL: I'll see that he does it.

> MR. PERKINS: Thank you. I'll call again in about three weeks and we can further discuss what Rolando is doing in school.
>
> MS. MITCHELL: That would be very nice. Thank you for calling.

1. Prepare an agenda for the conference that specifies: (a) the purpose of the meeting (e.g., to communicate summative evaluations relative to achievement of learning goals for the previous nine weeks or to develop a plan to increase the rate at which the student completes homework assignments); (b) a sequence of topics to be discussed; and (c) beginning and ending times for the conference.
2. Except for special situations, invite the student to attend and participant in the conference. Healthier, more open attitudes are more likely to emerge when the student is included.
3. Schedule the meeting in a small conference room or other setting where distractions (e.g., a telephone) are minimal and there is little chance for outsiders to overhear the conversation.
4. Provide a copy of the agenda to each person in attendance. During the meeting, direct attention to the topic at hand by referring to the appropriate agenda item and by using other visuals (e.g., report card or tests).
5. During the conference, concentrate remarks on descriptions of events, behaviors, and circumstances. Focus on needs, goals, and plans for accomplishing goals. Completely avoid characterizations and personality judgments.
6. During the conference, be an active listener so that you facilitate communication and, thus increase the likelihood that you (a) get your planned message across, and (b) learn from the others at the meeting and pick up ideas for more effectively working with the student.

Written Communications

Besides conferences with parents, which out of necessity are infrequent, some teachers send home weekly or monthly newsletters that are designed to apprise parents of what their children's classes are doing. Figure 4.1 is an example.

By taking the time to write such form letters, you foster the goodwill and understanding of parents. Their understanding of what you, as a teacher, are trying to accomplish with their children will serve you well when you need to call on them to help you deal with behavior problems.

PROFESSIONAL CONFIDENCE AND STUDENTS' RIGHTS

Unprofessional Behavior

What, if anything, bothers you about the behaviors of the teachers in Vignettes 4.36, 4.37, and 4.38?

PARENTS' NEWSLETTER FOR AMERICAN HISTORY II,

3RD PERIOD

From Jake Bertolli, Teacher

Vol. 1, No. 24, Week of March 16–20

Looking Back

Our last letter mentioned that we had begun a unit on late 19th century industrialism in the United States. I think a majority of the class were a bit bored with the material dealing with some of the major personalities (e.g., Carnegie and Rockefeller) that influenced industrialization in that era. However, I was quite pleased with the enthusiasm nearly everyone showed for the lessons on worker–management issues, especially when we studied the problems that led to the enactment of child labor laws. Based on my statistical analysis of the results, the test the class took last Friday seemed to provide a pretty accurate indicator of what most students achieved during the week. The class average on the test was 37.3, slightly higher than I had anticipated.

This Week

This week we will be discussing the rise of trusts in this country and move into the presidency of Woodrow Wilson. The relationship between the economic climate in the United States and the fighting of World War I will be a major focus of the class. One of the goals of the lesson is to help your daughter or son to understand how one event (e.g., a corporation in the U.S. decides to expand) influences another (e.g., strategic plans for a battle in Europe).

Homework assignments will include: (1) Read pp. 588–661 from the textbook for Thursday's class; (2) Watch the show from 8:30 to 9:30 on Channel 7, Tues. night, and be prepared to discuss its content on Wednesday; (3) Complete a worksheet, to be distributed Thursday, and attach it to the test to be given on Friday; (4) Prepare for Friday's test.

Looking Forward

Next week, we will compare what we learned about the rise of industries and corporations near the turn of the century to today's world economic situation. In subsequent weeks, we'll return our attention to the 1920s and examine some causes of war and ways to achieve peace.

FIGURE 4.1 Sample Monthly Newsletter for Parents

VIGNETTE 4.36

Two teachers, Mr. Bates and Ms. Saddler, are talking in the faculty room. Mr. Bates: "How's it going?" Ms. Saddler: "There must be a full moon! The kids are a bit nutsy today. Just hope you never have Arla Neville. She can't follow what's going on, so she entertains herself by bugging me. Why do I have to have all the retards?"

VIGNETTE 4.37

Bill Kresie, a high school coach and social science teacher, meets one of his friends, Vickie Dobson, in the grocery store. Mr. Kresie: "Hi, Vickie." Ms. Dobson: "Well, hello, Bill. It's nice to see you. What've you been up to?" Mr. Kresie: "Same old stuff. How about you?" Ms. Dobson: "Well, you know my daughter, Christine . . ." Mr. Kresie: "Yes, lovely girl. How's she doing?" Ms. Dobson: "She just broke up with Ronald Boher and has taken up with Don Palmer." Mr. Kresie: "Really! Good move on her part. Ronald's a real loser. He went out for football, you know, and showed no guts at all. I had Don in American history. Bright, bright kid!"

VIGNETTE 4.38

In a parent-teacher conference with Gary Matorini's father, Ms. Mauger tells him: "You know Gary is doing quite well. I wish all my students were like him. If I could get Elmo Thompson to cooperate like Gary, I'd jump for joy!"

Trust between a teacher and a student is an important ingredient in establishing a classroom climate that is conducive to cooperation, on-task behaviors, and engagement in learning activities. Teachers violate that trust when they gossip about students or share information with people who need not be privy to that information. Ms. Saddler in Vignette 4.36 was frustrated and obviously needed to talk about her difficult day. Her behavior was understandable, but was it professional? Was it excusable? Her baneful use of the label "retards" displayed Ms. Saddler's disregard for at least some accepted professional standards. If all the teachers at her school understand that the faculty room is a place for teachers to vent some of their frustrations and what is said does not leave the room, then Ms. Saddler's comments may never get back to students. Once students acquire the idea that teachers gossip about them, they are unlikely to trust those teachers. In Vignettes 4.37 and 4.38, Mr. Kresie and Ms. Mauger can hardly hope that their comments about students will not be spread by the outsiders to whom they spoke.

Privileged Information

Surely, there are times when teachers should communicate information and express their judgments about students' achievement levels and behaviors. Who should be privileged to those communications? Typically, the following are considered to have a right and a need to know.

1. For most cases, the student needs to be kept apprised of his or her achievement of learning goals and evaluations of school conduct.
2. The parents need to be aware of their child's level of achievement and behaviors for two reasons.
   a. Parents who are informed about their child's accomplishments in school are in an advantageous position to help their child cooperate and achieve.
   b. Parents are legally responsible for their child's welfare. They delegate and entrust some of their responsibilities to teachers. They have a right to know how the school is impacting their child.
3. *Professional personnel (e.g., a guidance counselor or another of the student's teachers) who are responsible for a particular student* sometimes need to know about the student's achievement and behaviors so that they are in a better position to help that student.
4. *Professional personnel who supervise and evaluate the teacher's performance or provide the teacher with formative feedback and help in improving instruction* sometimes need to understand specifics about individual students to meet their responsibilities to the teacher (see, e.g., Cangelosi, 1991b, pp. 3–14).
5. *Professional personnel (e.g., the principal, subject-area supervisor, or curriculum director) whose judgments impact the curricula and conduct of the school* sometimes need to be aware of an individual student's achievements or behaviors so that they will be in an advantageous position to make school-level decisions.
6. Because a school often acts as an agency that qualifies students for occupations, as students at other institutions, or for other privileges (e.g., scholarships), it may sometimes be necessary for a representative of an institution to which a student has applied (e.g., employment college, scholarship) to have knowledge of that student's achievements and behaviors. However, school personnel should seriously consider following a policy that they release such information on an individual student's achievements or behaviors to such representatives only with that student's and her or his parents' authorization.

COMMUNICATING ASSERTIVELY

Studies examining traits of teachers whose students display high levels of on-task behaviors suggest that students are more likely to cooperate with teachers if they consistently communicate in an assertive manner rather than in a hostile or passive manner (Canter & Canter, 1976). The teacher in Vignette 4.39 displays an assertive response; hostile and passive responses are displayed in Vignettes 4.40 and 4.41 respectively.

To gain control over your professional life, you must be assertive, not only with students, but also with colleagues and administrators (as illustrated by Vignette 4.25) and with parents (as illustrated by Vignette 4.35 and further elaborated upon in "Utilizing the Help of Parents and Instructional Supervisors" in Chapter 7). Vignette 4.42 relates a conversation between a beginning mathematics teacher, Casey, and an experienced colleague, Vanessa, who confers with him as he strives to be more assertive in his classroom.

VIGNETTE 4.39

Lori loudly yells out during an independent work session: "Help! Mr. Clark, I can't do these!" Mr. Clark: "We don't shout out in here. Quietly raise your hand if you want me to help you."

VIGNETTE 4.40

David loudly yells out during an independent work session: "Help! Ms. Lancy, I can't do these!" Ms. Lancy: "You screech like a little girl! If you yell like that again, you're gone, Buster!"

VIGNETTE 4.41

Tamara loudly yells out during an independent work session: "Help! Ms. Slovaki, I can't do these!" Ms. Slovaki: "Why must you yell at me? I hope you try and raise your hand next time."

VIGNETTE 4.42

CASEY: Some days, I'd just love to walk into class and discuss mathematics without having to worry about Frankie falling asleep unless I'm either right on top of her or we're discussing a problem that strikes within the limited range of what she fancies! Or just once, getting through a lesson without having to deal with Brad's showing off or Christi's yakking with anyone who'll listen to her. Wouldn't that be nice?

VANESSA: Obviously, you've had one of those days!

VIGNETTE 4.42 (continued)

CASEY: It's just that we were getting into our first formal proof today, and they seemed so enthusiastic. But then they started to get a little noisy—some off-task talking. I let it go at first because I didn't want to put a damper on their enthusiasm. Then, it became obvious that Christi and Livonia's conversation had nothing to do with geometry—right in the middle of my explanation!

VANESSA: What did you do?

CASEY: I kept on explaining the theorem, and just moved over to them and caught their eyes—that usually works for me.

VANESSA: And it didn't this time?

CASEY: Oh, the two of them stopped as long as I stood there, but then other conversations broke out, and Christi and Livonia started up again as soon as I moved away. Five minutes later, I'd had enough and made the mistake of threatening the class.

VANESSA: What'd you say?

CASEY: I told them if they didn't pipe down, they'd be sorry when the test came around. I knew that wasn't the best thing to say, but the noise just got to me, and I reacted.

VANESSA: Did they quiet down?

CASEY: Yes, but then Brad whispered something to Lin-Tau who started giggling. That's when I jumped on them, calling Brad a show-off. In other words, I handled it all wrong and made matters worse.

VANESSA: So, you weren't Mr. Perfect. You let things go too far and reacted with hostility instead of assertiveness—the way most of us react when things go too far.

CASEY: But I know better. I applied none of the stuff that's worked for me in the past—assertiveness, descriptive language, reinforcement principles—all out the window!

VANESSA: I don't think you threw your principles out of the window; I think you waited too long to respond decisively. Most teachers wait until they are too near their annoyance threshold before dealing with off-task students.

CASEY: You're saying I should have stepped in and dealt with the earlier minor incidence before things escalated. I was passive in the beginning instead of being assertive. Then things got out of hand.

VANESSA: And when things get out of hand it's natural to be hostile.

CASEY: And that's really why I'm upset—at my own hostile behavior. I'm afraid I've lost some of the control and good will I established up to this point. I don't have much enthusiasm for tomorrow's class.

VANESSA: What do you have planned?

CASEY: Before this, I was going to continue the session on proofs.

VANESSA: I think you have two choices. You either go on with your original plan and conduct the class as if none of this had happened, but be ready with an alternate plan to go to as soon as they become uncooperative—you know, one where they have to work on their own while you monitor their every move.

CASEY: What's my second choice?

VANESSA: The second choice is to start the period off expressing your feelings about what happened, even indicating that you're disappointed in your own behavior for letting things go too far and then acting with hostility. But if you use this tactic, make sure to assertively demand their cooperation. If it turns out you don't get it even after clearing the air, then go immediately to the alternative lesson plan.

SOURCE: Adapted from *Teaching Mathematics in Secondary and Middle School: Research-based Approaches* (pp. 258–259) by James S. Cangelosi, 1992, New York: Macmillan.

No teacher is capable of applying principles of classroom management all of the time. With experience, they learn to apply them well enough to gain and maintain sufficient student cooperation to enjoy their profession and provide students with productive learning experiences.

TRANSITIONAL ACTIVITIES
FROM CHAPTER 4 TO CHAPTER 5

I. Below is a list of statements by teachers. Label them *D* for *descriptive, JP* for *judgmental of a person,* or *J* for *judgmental of a behavior, achievement, or situation.*
   A. "Xavier, you are very polite."
   B. "Xavier, that was a very polite thing for you to do for Richard."
   C. "Xavier, you allowed Richard to go first."
   D. "I am having trouble concentrating because of the noise in here."
   E. "All this noise shows that some people in here are inconsiderate."
   F. "Your score on this test makes you one of my best students."
   G. "Your score on this test was the highest in the class."
   H. "You did better on this test than anyone else in the class."
   I. "Pushing Ryan like that is not acceptable behavior."
   J. "Pushing Ryan like that is a violation of class rules."
   K. "I am angry because you pushed Ryan like that."
   L. "You're a bully for pushing Ryan!"

   Compare your responses to these answers. A—*JP*, B—*J*, C—*D*, D—*D*, E—*JP*, F—*JP*, G—*D*, H—*J*, I—*J*, J—*D*, K—*D*, L—*JP*.

II. Write a paragraph suggesting how Ms. Price's tactics in Vignette 4.43 can backfire on her and eventually encourage students to be off-task in her class.

   Compare your response to that of a colleague.

VIGNETTE 4.43

Ms. Taylor asks Ms. Price in the faculty lounge: "How do you get your students to do their homework?" Ms. Price: "I embarrass the hell out of them in front of their buddies if they come to class unprepared. I can make them feel like less than nothing for not doing what I assign."

III. Students sometimes don't bother to listen to teachers because they've learned that adults often speak to them without really having anything of consequence to say. Categorize each statement below as either inane or informative.
A. "Karl, your milk is dripping down the side of your glass."
B. "I am really enjoying myself!"
C. "You should behave while we're visiting the library."
D. "You really had a good time!"
E. Mr. Ballam notices one student in his class of 28 looking around during a written-response test. Mr. Ballam announces to the class: "Keep your eyes on your own paper."
F. "Until we get back to the room, remain close enough to touch your partner."
   Compare your responses to these. *A*, *B*, and *F* are informative; *C*, *D*, and *E* are inane.

IV. Marcia, a sixth-grader, comments to her teacher: "I don't want to take this test. I'll just flunk it." Provide a supportive and a nonsupportive response Marcia's teacher could make. In both responses, let Marcia know that she is expected to take the test as scheduled.
   Compare your responses to those of colleagues and to these samples. Supportive response: "You seem nervous about taking the test and it starts in only 40 seconds." Nonsupportive response: "Oh, come on, Marcia! You'll do just fine! Just relax; you'll see."

V. Vignettes 4.24, 4.26, 4.28, and 4.29 are examples of teachers unwittingly miscommunicating with students. Develop and describe five more realistic examples of such unfortunate events. Compare your examples to those of colleagues.

VI. Write the letter of each comment below that suggests that individuals are not completely responsible for their own conduct.
A. "Marla's had trouble regaining her composure after Davalon spat on her."
B. "Evelyn's clowning in class is due to her lack of attention at home."
C. "He made me so ashamed!"
D. "Fred, your behavior will embarrass your mother!"
E. "I'm embarrassed!"
F. "Study hard and make me proud."
G. "I'll be very pleased to see you do well."
H. "He made me hit him."
I. "I was running so I wouldn't be late."
   Did you list *B*, *C*, *D*, *F*, and *H*?

VII. Label each of these teacher-made evaluations as either formative or summative.
A. Mr. Jones decides to give Brenda a "C" in physical education.
B. Ms. Tempelton judges that her learning unit on China went very well.
C. Ms. Blackstone decides that she should spend another day on an inductive activity for discovering a formula for the area of a triangle.
D. Ms. Collier decides not to allow Marcus to use paints for the rest of the week.
E. Mr. Larusso decides to cut the homework assignment in half.
F. Ms. Banker decides that Juanita has made satisfactory progress.
   A, *B*, and *F* are summative; *C*, *D*, and *E* are formative.

VIII. Write a one-page essay that presents both positions for and against this policy.

A grade a student receives in a course should *only* reflect how well that student achieved the specified course goals.

Exchange your essay with that of a colleague and discuss similarities and differences in your responses.

IX. Write a paragraph explaining the advantages you, as a teacher, gain by maintaining a routine flow of information about your class to parents.

   Compare your paragraph to that of a colleague.

X. Describe two examples in which teachers' gossip about their students result in a loss of students' trust of those teachers. Compare your examples with those of colleagues.

XI. Ms. Jung's chemistry students are working in the laboratory when one student, Troy, turns up a Bunsen burner so that the flame is dangerously high. Troy laughs saying: "Let's see how high this thing can go!"

   A. Write a passive verbal response Ms. Jung might make.

   B. Write a hostile verbal response Ms. Jung might make.

   C. Write an assertive verbal response Ms. Jung might make.

   Compare your examples with those of colleagues and these samples. Passive response: "Troy, I really wish you wouldn't do that. That could be dangerous." Hostile response: "Troy, you're a menace to the safety of this class. What's the matter with you? Don't you have any sense at all?" Assertive response: "Troy, turn down that flame immediately. . . . Thank you. Now, shut off the Bunsen burner and come see me at my desk."

XII. In preparation for your work with Chapter 5, discuss the following questions with two or more of your colleagues.

   A. Why are classroom rules and procedures necessary?

   B. Why is it important to distinguish between rules for conduct and classroom procedures?

   C. Why should teachers avoid having unnecessary rules for conduct?

   D. Who should determine classroom rules for conduct?

   E. What strategies do teachers employ to teach classroom rules of conduct and procedures to students?

   F. How should school-wide solutions to discipline problems be formulated and enforced?

SUPPLEMENTAL READINGS

Cangelosi, J. S. (1990). *Designing tests for evaluating student achievement* (pp. 196–202). New York: Longman.

———. (1992). *Systematic teaching strategies* (pp. 295–301, 344–351). New York: Longman.

Ginott, H. (1972). *Teacher and child* (pp. 35–120). New York: Avon.

Gordon, T. (1974). *T.E.T.: Teacher effectiveness training.* New York: Peter H. Wyden.

Harris, T. A. (1969). *I'm OK — You're OK: A practical guide to transactional analysis.* New York: Harper & Row.

Morganett, L. (1991). Good teacher-student relationship: A key element in classroom motivation and management. *Education, 112,* 260–264.

Paley, V. G. (1986). On listening to what children say. *Harvard Educational Review, 56,* 122–131.

CHAPTER 5

Establishing Procedures and Rules for Conduct

Purpose of Chapter 5

Chapter 5 is designed to help you

1. Distinguish functional rules from specific procedures and understand how to use a combination of the two for managing your classroom.
2. Distinguish between necessary and unnecessary classroom rules of conduct.
3. Understand how the existence of unnecessary rules of conduct encourages off-task student behaviors.
4. Understand why a failure to enforce existing rules, both necessary and unnecessary, encourages off-task student behaviors.
5. Be thoughtful about your methods for establishing rules (i.e., when, by whom, and how).
6. Apply the Teaching Process Model to help students comprehend rules, know how to follow them, and predict the consequences of not following them.
7. Develop a plan for establishing rules of conduct and specific procedures for (a) maximizing on-task behaviors; (b) increasing safety and security; (c) preventing activities within your classroom from disturbing others outside; and (d) maintaining acceptable standards of decorum among students, school personnel, and visitors to the school campus.

STATING FUNCTIONAL RULES

Semantics

Classroom rules of conduct are formalized statements that provide students with general guidelines for the types of behaviors that are required and the types of behaviors that are prohibited. Some teachers attempt to soften the restrictive nature of rules by stating them as behaviors that are allowed (e.g., "You may talk when recognized."). These teachers avoid both negative statements (e.g., "Do not talk without first being recognized.") and imperative statements (e.g., "Remain silent until you are recognized."). Stating formal rules in this manner suggests that nothing is allowed unless it is included in the list. However, "You may talk when recognized" does not imply not to talk when unrecognized. Telling students what they may do might be advantageous in ordinary, everyday conversations. However, negative and imperative statements are quite appropriate for formal rules.

If you are going to have formalized classroom rules of conduct, you and your students should be prepared to take them very seriously. Word rules so that they denote exactly what is intended. A list of "do's and don'ts" will more accurately communicate than a list of what is permitted. After all, permissible behaviors are far too numerous to include in any list.

Mr. Redden's imprecisely worded rule, indicating what may be done, contributes to the unnecessary confrontation in Vignette 5.1.

Don probably did know what the rule meant, but he is right; the rule did not say what was intended. You need not use legal language when stating rules, but by wording them accurately and to the point, you encourage students to take rules seriously.

Focusing on the Rule's Purpose

Classroom rules of conduct may also be stated so narrowly that they become nonfunctional. Consider Vignette 5.2.

VIGNETTE 5.1

Mr. Redden's sixth graders are working on individual assignments at their places when Don quickly gets up and exits the room. In four minutes he reenters and Mr. Redden asks: "Where have you been, Don?" Don: "To the bathroom." Mr. Redden: "It wasn't time for you to go to the restroom." Don: "Why not?" Mr. Redden: "Read rule number 12 on the bulletin board." Don: "It says, 'You may go to the restroom during the last five minutes of the class period.'" Mr. Redden: "There's still 20 minutes left." Don: "But, the rule doesn't say we can't go before the last five minutes." Mr. Redden: "Don, you know what the rule means . . ."

VIGNETTE 5.2

"All students are to remain seated during group-administered tests until the teacher has given the signal that all of the papers have been collected," is included among the rules of conduct for Mr. Blanton's eighth grade classroom. Thau is taking one such test, sitting between Nikita and Kay both of whom have finished the test and are waiting for the others. Kay rises up and leans over Thau and hands Nikita a pencil (see Figure 5.1). Mr. Blanton notices the disturbance and motions Kay up to his desk where he asks: "Kay, what is the rule about getting out of your seat during a test?" Kay: "I was only returning the pencil I borrowed from Nikita. And besides, I never left my desk." Mr. Blanton: "How is it possible for you to give Nikita the pencil without leaving your seat?" Kay: "I leaned way over so my knee stayed on my seat." Mr. Blanton: "That's the same as leaving your desk." Kay: "Not if my knee was still touching. . . ."

FIGURE 5.1   Kay Manages to Stay in Her Seat but Still Disturb Thau

The time Mr. Blanton wasted with that inane conversation with Kay should have been more purposefully spent. It is ridiculous to argue over whether or not Kay left her seat. The concern should be with preventing disturbances to students who are still taking the test. Mr. Blanton's rule to "stay in your seat" is too narrow to serve the purpose of "not disturbing others who are still taking the test." Instead of being thoughtful about not creating a disturbance, Kay focused on remaining in her seat. Mr. Blanton's rule is not stated in functional terms. A rule stated in functional terms focuses on the purposes or function for having the rule in the first place. Examples of rules stated in functional terms include: "Be careful not to distract others while they are being tested." "Allow others an opportunity to speak without being interrupted." "Do nothing that would risk a person being injured, harmed, or uncomfortable." "Respect the property of others."

The Number of Functionally Stated Rules

A few (less than 10) functionally stated rules are generally preferable to a large number of narrow rules, each applicable to a specific situation (e.g., "Do not sharpen your pencil while the video player is on"), for the following reasons. (1) A few rules are easier to remember than many rules. (2) Each rule in a small set of rules is more likely to appear important than is each rule in a large set of rules. (3) Functional rules appeal to the common sense of students and lead students to be thoughtful about their behaviors (e.g., "Would handling this pencil to Nikita disturb Thau?"). (4) Functional rules focus attention on purposeful behaviors (e.g., how to be considerate) rather than on dysfunctional technicalities (e.g., whether or not a student was seated). Teachers sometimes establish too many, narrowly focused rules because they confuse rules of conduct with routine procedures applicable to only specific situations (e.g., during group testing or while videotapes are being viewed).

PROCEDURES FOR SMOOTHLY OPERATING CLASSROOMS

Routine procedures, like rules, should communicate expectations for behavior. Unlike a rule, however, a routine procedure applies only to a particular type of activity and does not define a general standard for conduct. Rules for classroom conduct should be written down and prominently displayed in the classroom. Except for particularly complex activities, procedures are usually learned through participation and need not be displayed in written form. Procedures are simply the mechanisms by which students move through transition periods and learning activities.

Well-designed, efficient procedures are necessary for a smoothly operating classroom. Here are some of the types of routine classroom activities for which procedures need to be established: (1) students arriving in the classroom at the beginning of a school day or class period; (2) taking roll; (3) completing administrative duties (e.g., collecting lunch money); (4) collecting assignments; (5) students desiring to speak aloud in class; (6) going to lunch; (7) sharpening pencils; (8) getting a drink; (9) going to the bathroom; (10) removing items from the storage area; (11) making transitions from large group to small group sessions; (12) cleaning up after oneself; (13) leaving the room during class; (14) returning to class following an absence; (15) taking tests; (16) retaking tests; (17) borrowing materials; (18) requesting individual help; (19) scheduling conferences outside of class hours; (20) having guests in the classroom (e.g., guest lecturer, visiting parent, supervisor, or observer from a college); (21) using computers; (22) visiting the library; (23) turning in reports; (24) fire and disaster drills; (25) listening to announcements; (26) leaving the room at the end of the school day.

The list, of course, could be extended indefinitely. It may be helpful for you to begin with some general categories and list specific activities under each. Categories might include (1) Room use. (2) Use of supplies. (3) Large group learning activities. (4) Small group learning activities. (5) Independent learning activities. (6) Transitions between learning activities. (7) Administrative duties.

To help you think further about establishing routine procedures for your own classroom, classify each of the 25 activities from the given sample according to the aforementioned seven categories. Modify, delete, and add categories to fit your needs.

NECESSARY RULES OF CONDUCT

Four Purposes for Rules

Does Vignette 5.3 seem familiar?

Teachers, as well as school administrators, sometimes establish unnecessary rules of conduct. A necessary classroom rule of conduct serves at least one of the following purposes (Cangelosi, 1990a, pp. 28–29):

1. To maximize on-task behaviors and minimize off-task, especially disruptive, behaviors.
2. To secure the safety and comfort of the learning environment.
3. To prevent the activities of the class from disturbing other classes and persons outside of the class.
4. To maintain acceptable standards of decorum among students, school personnel, and visitors to the school campus.

Justification of a Rule

Which one, if any, of the four purposes does Mr. Tuft's no-hat-wearing rule serve?

Purpose 1.   Ordinarily, wearing hats does not interfere with students being on-task. Of course, you can think of exceptions, but such exceptions can be covered under general functional rules, such as, "Dress for class so that your apparel does not cause distractions that make it difficult for others to concentrate."

VIGNETTE 5.3

As a youth, Mr. Tuft learned that hats are not to be worn indoors. He remembers his father yelling at him: "Take that hat off of your head! What kind of place do you think you're in? There're ladies present!" He remembers his parents laughing at "Old Mr. Busby" for forgetting to take his hat off when he visited their home.

When Mr. Tuft became a teacher, it seemed natural for him to establish a rule prohibiting the wearing of hats in the classroom. He didn't give it much thought. Now, Mr. Tuft frequently finds himself interrupting his own learning activities to enforce his no-hat-wearing rule.

Purpose 2. Hat wearing is usually unrelated to the safety and security of most classroom situations. Again, there are exceptions. A hat dislodged from a student's head during a volleyball game could cause someone to slip. During contact drills, football coaches would be negligent if they didn't require their students to wear helmets. Such exceptions can be effectively handled under procedures for specific learning activities.

Purpose 3. Rules designed around this purpose are concerned with having consideration for persons who are not in the class, but who are on or near the school campus. Even a lively on-task discussion can be disturbing to a neighboring class. Establish rules such as "Be considerate of other classes by holding down your voices," and procedures for specific activities, such as, "While walking past those houses on the way to visit the science center, stay on the sidewalk and away from people's lawns." Prohibiting the wearing of hats does not seem to serve this purpose.

Purpose 4. If Mr. Tuft could justify his no-hat-wearing rule at all, he'd probably relate it to this purpose. Maintaining acceptable standards of decorum is surely necessary to the development of a healthy, businesslike climate. Common courtesy is a critical ingredient in a smoothly operating classroom. However, Mr. Tuft and other teachers should be cautious that they do not use this fourth purpose as an excuse for imposing their personal biases and tastes on student.

Politeness and Courtesy

The bases for the fourth purpose are (1) Impolite interactions among students and teachers lead to ill feelings that diminish the likelihood of cooperation in the classroom. (2) Polite interactions among students and teachers help maintain a classroom that is conducive to cooperation. (3) The community within which a class exists expects that class to exhibit certain standards of courtesy.

One of the problems you, as a teacher, face with this fourth purpose is how to decide which behaviors are polite and which are impolite. In all probability, your students come to you from a variety of backgrounds and subcultures. While hat-wearing in a building may be distasteful to one, it may be in vogue to another, and required by the religion of yet another. One approach is to define politeness and courtesy as behavior that is exhibited as the result of thoughtful consideration for the rights and feelings of others. Such a liberal definition, as opposed to conventional dictionary definitions (e.g., "showing good manners, cultured, refined"), focuses on thoughtfulness toward others, rather than on one group's opinion on what constitutes "good" taste.

Even this advisable approach can also lead to some difficulties in the complex classroom environment. Consider Vignette 5.4.

Did Dick violate rule number four? Whether or not his use of a word that is socially unacceptable to many people violated the rule depends on the degree to which others found his expression offensive. Ms. Oskoei did indicate to him that she, for one, found the term offensive. If you feel that Dick was within his rights in saying what he pleases as long as no one is really hurt or prevented from being on-task, then you may not want to include any rules for the fourth purpose dealing with standards of decorum. On the other hand, if you find it important to uphold community standards of courtesy in your classroom, then establish rules for the fourth purpose. However, please proceed with care. You want to make sure that you do not allow unnecessary rules to be established under the guise of maintaining acceptable standards of decorum. This mistake of establishing unnecessary rules can cause you more problems than the mistake of failing to establish necessary rules.

VIGNETTE 5.4

During a discussion on nutrition in Ms. Oskoei's health class, Julie says: "There was something in the newspaper yesterday about some scientists saying we should be careful not to eat too much red meat." Dick: "I don't give a shit what any scientists say, I'm not gonna stop eating meat." Ms. Oskoei: "Dick, please don't use words like that while we're having class."

After class, Ms. Oskoei meets with Dick privately and says, "Which one of our classroom rules did you violate today?" Dick: "I don't know." Ms. Oskoei: "I have one in mind that I think you did violate and I want you to read through the list and guess at which one I have in mind." Dick begins to read the list of rules that are displayed on the wall. Dick: "I don't know. Are you talking about the fourth one?" Ms. Oskoei: "Please read it aloud." Dick reads, "Before you act or speak, think of how your actions and words influence others. Act and talk in ways that others appreciate and not in ways they find offensive." Ms. Oskoei: "Yes, that is the one." Dick: "Because of what I said! Aw! Everybody says 'shit.' That doesn't hurt anybody." Ms. Oskoei: "I agree that it's no big deal. But there are people, including me, who just don't like to say or hear that word during class. Since you are quite capable of substituting words that others don't find offensive, I do not expect you to violate rule number four again." Dick: "But Ms. Oskoei, we talk about bowel movements and urine in health class. Why is that okay?" Ms. Oskoei: "You've made an excellent point. I can't argue with your logic. However, while our society considers it acceptable to refer to human waste material on television, such as in laxative commercials, our society generally considers it unacceptable to say the word 'shit' on television. In fact, saying that word on television or in public places is a violation of obscenity laws in many locations. As long as our society frowns upon public use of such words, people are going to feel uncomfortable hearing them spoken or written in formal, businesslike settings such as our classroom. I happen to be one of those people. Right or wrong, we violate rule number four by using words like 'shit' when other words that don't offend anyone can be used instead." Dick: "It doesn't seem right that something is okay in one place, but not in another." Ms. Oskoei: "It's like belching. Most everyone has a good healthy belch now and then. But most people in our society find other people's belching to be disgusting." Dick: "So belching is a violation of rule four also." Ms. Oskoei: "A public display of belching, when it could be avoided, would indeed be a violation of rule number four."

THE CONSEQUENCES OF UNNECESSARY RULES

When considering the inclusion of a particular rule in your classroom, ask yourself: "Which of the four purposes for having rules does this one serve?" If the answer is "none," then that rule is unnecessary and should not be included. If you do include unnecessary rules, you will be faced with three unpleasant consequences.

1. You will be responsible for enforcing a rule that does not have a defensible rationale. Thus, you put yourself in the position of teaching students to submit to unjustified regulations.
2. Once your students realize that a rule you enforce serves no important purpose, they will tend to generalize that other rules must be unimportant also.
3. Students who are penalized for resisting unnecessary rules are likely to become disenchanted with school. Such students are often distracted from the business of learning because time that could be allocated for learning activities is used to deal with rule violations.

Of course, you could choose to enforce only the necessary rules and ignore the unnecessary ones. This is inadvisable. Unenforced rules, even unnecessary ones, teach students that rules need not be taken seriously. It is more difficult to teach students to be on-task when they feel they can be selective about which rules to follow and which rules to ignore.

WHEN TO DETERMINE RULES
AND ROUTINE PROCEDURES

Some teachers prefer to determine all rules for conduct and a large share of routine procedures at the very beginning of a school year or term. Others establish both rules for conduct and routine procedures as the need for them becomes apparent.

The advantages of establishing rules and routine procedures at the outset of a school term include (1) When expectations are formally communicated from the beginning, some off-task behavior patterns do not have time to emerge. (2) Students are more receptive to learning rules and procedures at the beginning of a school term than they are once they've become accustomed to a situation. (3) The sooner students know about rules and procedures, the more time they have to practice following them.

The advantages of establishing rules and routine procedures throughout the school term include (1) Waiting to establish some rules avoids prescribing rule-breaking behaviors for students who were positively reinforced for breaking rules in previous classes. (2) Students are more likely to understand a rule or a procedure when it is established in response to a need that has just become apparent. (3) Students are more likely to appreciate the importance of individual rules and procedures that are established gradually, rather that those being thrust on them all at once.

You will probably want to use some combination of the approaches by establishing several functional rules of conduct and some basic routine procedures at the outset, and then developing a more comprehensive list over time. The younger your students, the more time you will need to establish and teach rules and procedures at the very beginning of a school year.

WHO SHOULD DETERMINE RULES?

Do rules more effectively serve their four purposes when teachers determine them or when students themselves agree on them? Should you use an authoritarian process, a democratic process, or some combination of the two to establish rules? Research studies have addressed that question (Evertson & Emmer, 1982; Glickman & Wolfgang, 1979). Considering the conclusions from a number of such studies, it appears that there are four ways for you to establish rules. How well each method works depends more on how you go about implementing the method, than it does on the method itself. The four methods are:

1. You decide all rules, making sure that each is functional, necessary, and not confused with a routine procedure.
2. You determine all rules yourself, but your determinations are influenced by the recommendations of students.
3. Rules are proposed and voted upon by students. You are responsible for establishing the structure for democratic decision-making, for providing leadership to encourage the establishment of necessary functional rules, and for ensuring that every student has the opportunity to participate in the decisions.
4. Some combination of the other three methods is used. Typically, you impose a few fundamental guidelines for behavior, and students participate in decisions about more specific rules that fall within the purview of those guidelines.

TEACHING RULES TO STUDENTS

Establishing rules for conduct and routine procedures for activities is one thing. Teaching students to follow those rules and procedures is quite another. Students must first learn what the rules and procedures are and how to follow them; then, they must become willing to follow them. The Teaching Process Model applies to the teaching of rules and procedures just as it does to the teaching of academic subjects.

TEACHERS WHO EFFICIENTLY ESTABLISH, TEACH, AND ENFORCE RULES AND PROCEDURES

Vignettes 5.5, 5.6 (p. 135), and 5.7 (p. 136) provide examples of teachers successfully establishing, teaching, and utilizing rules and procedures.

Because of her arrangement with Mr. Demery, Ms. Williams has a very useful structure for dealing with rule violations and failure to follow procedures. Rules and procedures that are not enforced are counterproductive. How Ms. Williams conducts the student conferences is, of course, quite a critical factor influencing the effectiveness of her rules and procedures. The question of how to deal with students after they have violated a rule or failed to follow a procedures is addressed in Chapters 7–10.

Vignette 5.6 provides an example of a teacher who allows students' suggestions to influence her decisions regarding procedures.

VIGNETTE 5.5

Ms. Williams autocratically establishes some basic routine procedures and functional rules of conduct for her second grade class at the very beginning of the school year. She plans to spend a major share of the first two weeks teaching rules and procedures.

On the second day of the new school year, Ms. Williams announces to her 27 students: "There are four rules that you are required to follow anytime you are at school. Here is the first one." Ms. Williams displays a bright orange poster with "Respect the Rights of Others" boldly printed and a drawing of a cluster of happy faces. Touching each word on the poster as she read it, Ms. Williams continues: "'Respect the rights of others!' That is our first rule. I will hang this reminder for you right here on the wall. Connie, please help me with this." The bright orange poster is permanently displayed. "Now read this with me as I point to each word," Ms. Williams directs the class. Together the class recites with her: "Respect the rights of others."

MS. WILLIAMS: What does it say, Allen?

Several students, including Allen, shout out, "Respect the rights of others!"

VIGNETTE 5.5 (continued)

MS. WILLIAMS: I'm sorry; there were too many people talking for me to understand Allen. Allen?

ALLEN: It says, "Respect the rights of others."

MS. WILLIAMS: Thank you. Now I want everybody to quietly think to themselves
what the rule means before we discuss it.

Ms. Williams waits 30 seconds, and says: "Okay, let's share our ideas on what it
means to respect the right of others. We'll begin with Reginald."

REGINALD: Well, respecting others is being nice to them.

MS. WILLIAMS: And what are some of the ways that we can be nice to others?
What do you say, Jaylene?

JAYLENE: You don't pick on 'em.

MS. WILLIAMS: Who wants to tell me what they think Jaylene means? . . .

The discussion about the first rule continues until Ms. Williams is satisfied that
her students have a reasonable understanding of the types of behaviors this rule
requires and the types it forbids. Ms. Williams then tells her students how she will
deal with violations of rule number one.

To deal with rule violations, Ms. Williams has made arrangements with
Mr. Demery, who teaches another second grade class at her school, to combine their
two classes for 40 minutes every afternoon just prior to dismissal. During that
40-minute period, some type of activity that the students find especially enjoyable
is conducted. One day there may be supervised recreation in the gym, playground,
or auditorium. Another day, the children may view a videotape or play games in
the computer lab. Only Mr. Demery supervises the combined classes for the first
20 minutes of these sessions. Ms. Williams reserves that time to individually meet
with any of her students who have violated rules or failed to follow procedures.
At these conferences, Ms. Williams and the students work out a plan for preventing
such violations or failures in the future. Ms. Williams supervises the second half of
these 40-minute periods to allow Mr. Demery to work out plans with any of his
students who violated rules or failed to follow procedures.

In explaining this to her students, Ms. Williams does not, of course, attempt
to relate all the details of the arrangement with Mr. Demery. In time, they will
learn this for themselves. She does tell them: "Anytime I recognize someone not
respecting the rights of another, I will simply tell them, 'Meet with me to discuss
the first rule when it's time to join Mr. Demery's class.' We won't discuss it until
that time comes."

On the third day of the new school year, Ms. Williams introduces the second
rule, "Respect Your Own Rights," displayed on a bright green poster with one happy
face. Ms. Williams' experiences have taught her that she should include this second
rule to urge students to be more assertive in protecting their own rights and not
allowing themselves to be abused. She uses role-playing learning activities to teach
this rule. The following is an example of one such lesson.

Ms. Williams announces to her class: "Ron and Frankie will perform a skit to
help us better understand the second rule. Imagine that they're out in the schoolyard
waiting for the first bell to ring. Ron will be playing the part of Joe, who is a fourth
grader. Frankie will be Bob, a second grader. Okay fellows, you're on!"

Holding his lunch pail, Bob walks near Joe. Joe grabs Bob by the shoulder and says: "Hey! Where are you going, Buddy?"

BOB: To my room.

Joe lets go of Bob and asks: "You wanna be my friend?"

BOB: I guess so.
JOE: Good! I'd like to be your friend, too. Watcha got in the box?
BOB: My lunch.
JOE: Let me look at it. You might have something for me.
BOB: Naw! I gotta get to my room.
JOE (holding up his fist to Bob): Look! You'd better let me check out your lunch or you'll be sorry.

Ms. Williams interrupts the skit at that point saying: "Thank you. Let's stop the drama for a few minutes to discuss what we've seen. I want each of you to think of what Bob can do so that he won't break the second rule." A discussion ensues in which suggestions are made as to how Bob can protect his rights from Joe's bullying behavior. Later, Ms. Williams has Ron and Frankie act out two different endings to the skit. In one, Bob violates the second rule by allowing Joe to take his lunch. In the second, Bob protects his rights.

On subsequent days, Ms. Williams introduces and teaches two other rules: "Give Everyone a Chance to Learn" and "Follow Procedures."

Ms. Williams' third rule is primarily concerned with preventing disruptive behaviors during learning activities. This particular rule serves as a general guideline that leads to many of the procedures governing both transitional and allocated time. The following episode illustrates this relationship.

During the second week of school, Ms. Williams directs her students to individually complete a journal–writing activity at their places. As they work, students begin to yell out for Ms. Williams to help them or to interrupt her while she is helping another. Other students grow impatient waiting for Ms. Williams to get to them and they begin talking among themselves. The noise disturbs those trying to complete the tasks.

Having observed the chaos, Ms. Williams develops a procedure for independent work sessions and decides to teach it to her students the next time such a session is scheduled. Ms. Williams: "Class, may I have your attention please?" She looks directly into students' eyes until everyone appears to be ready to listen. Ms. Williams: "Thank you. Do you remember what happened the last time we wrote in our journals in class?" Because Ms. Williams had previously established a procedure for speaking in a large group arrangement, students raise their hands to signal that they would like to answer her question. No one yells out a response. Ms. Williams: "Sadi, what do you remember?" Sadi: "It got very noisy and you couldn't get to help all of us." Other students provide more detail as Ms. Williams conducts a discussion in which the problems with which she wants to deal are articulated by the students. Finally, Ms. Williams says: "It seems to me that we didn't give everyone a chance to learn last time. We need a procedure so we won't break the third rule when we are working individually at our places. I'll explain the procedure now." She takes a bag from the storage closet and holds it up for the class to see. Ms. Williams:

VIGNETTE 5.5 (continued)

"In here is something to help us give everyone a chance to learn when we are working at our places." Barbara: "Is it candy? Are you going to give us candy for cooperating?" Ms. Williams looks directly at Barbara sternly and raises her finger to her lips. Barbara receives the message and does not pursue her question. Ms. Williams pulls a device from the bag that the students have never before seen (see Figure 5.2). The device consists of a holder with a clip that can be attached to a student's desk. The holder contains three flags — a red, a blue and a yellow. Each flag can be rotated up or down. Ms. Williams distributes the devices and explains how to use them.

On-task students who do not want to be disturbed display the yellow flag. Students who want help display a red flag. Students who have completed the work and are willing to provide help to others display a blue flag. Ms. Williams quietly moves from one student displaying a red flag to another. She also directs students displaying blue flags to provide help.

Ms. Williams chose this seemingly elaborate flag raising procedure over a more conventional "raise your hand" procedure because she believed that (1) The formality of the flags would help teach students just how seriously she expects them to follow the procedure. (2) Students who want help could simply display their red flags and continue to work without having to hold their hands up. (3) It provides a quiet, efficient method for utilizing cooperative learning strategies with students who finish the assignment before others.

FIGURE 5.2   Ms. Williams' Flag-Raising Device

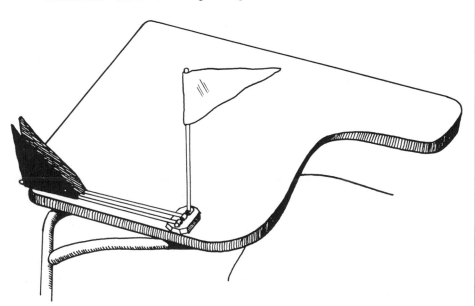

Ms. Williams' Students Using Her Flag-Raising Procedure Activity

---

VIGNETTE 5.6

Ms. Clifford tells her seventh grade class: "I received three separate complaints from other teachers that their lessons were disturbed by some of us who were making trips to the library. If those reports are accurate, we were in violation of our rule against bothering people outside our group. We still need to make trips to the library. Do I need to develop a procedure that guards against our bothering other classes?" Some students raise their hands.

MS. CLIFFORD: Dale?

DALE: The trouble is three or four of us go at once. Maybe you should allow only one to go at a time.

MS. CLIFFORD: I will seriously consider that. Jim?

JIM: Find who's causing the trouble and don't let them ever go to the library again.

VIGNETTE 5.6 (continued)

YOLANDA: But we really weren't doing anything wrong! Mrs. Crooks, she's always trying to get us in trouble.

MS. CLIFFORD: That's not relevant. I really don't care about what has already happened. I just want to make sure we don't disturb others in the future.

JEAN: Do we really need a special procedure if we just promise to keep quiet from now on?

Ms. Clifford: "That's what I'd like to decide. How many of you think we need a special procedure for going to the library? Raise your hands. One, two, three, . . . most of you believe we need one. Okay, I would like each of you to take out a sheet of paper and suggest what I should do in one to three sentences. Please do not put your name on the paper. I'll take your papers home tonight and consider your suggestions. I'll have a decision for you tomorrow."

In Vignette 5.7, a teacher uses a democratic process for determining procedures.

VIGNETTE 5.7

Mr. Cooper has 12 hand-held, battery-powered calculators available for use by his 32 eighth graders. The calculators are kept in a box on a supply table in the back of the room. Except for certain learning and assessing activities, students generally have free access to the calculators. Class treasury funds are used to maintain a supply of calculator batteries.

Mr. Cooper notices that calculators are being left on when not in use and that students are failing to return them promptly after using them. Students complain that they have trouble obtaining a working calculator when needed. To address the complaints, Mr. Cooper calls a "class community meeting." Whenever such meetings are held, the students know that they operate under *Robert's Rules of Order* (Robert, 1970) and can raise issues of common concern. At this meeting, Mr. Cooper describes the recurring difficulty with calculator use; he proposes that the problems be resolved.

After a discussion, the group agrees that procedures governing the use of calculators will be formulated. Roy moves and Gertrude seconds a motion that anyone who leaves on a calculator, or who doesn't promptly return one to the supply box, may never again be allowed to use one. After some discussion, the motion is amended to change the penalty from banning calculator use for life to a week for the first offense, two weeks for the second, and so forth. Mr. Cooper and several students speak against the motion, arguing that other proposals that do not restrict calculator use should be considered. They contend that work will be impaired if the calculators are not available to all students and that such a rule will sometimes place Mr. Cooper in the position of trying to find out who left a calculator on or who failed to return one to the box.

The motion fails 14 to 15 with two abstentions and one student absent. Amanda then proposes that students be allowed to use calculators only while standing at the supply table. She argues that students should be able to use them without removing them from the area, and that the machines could be secured to the table. The motion is defeated after students argue that the table would become congested and that they need calculators at their desks. After further discussion, the following motion finally passes.

> The batteries will be removed from calculators and held in storage. Four unused batteries will be distributed to each student from those already in storage and from additional ones purchased using the class treasury. Each calculator will be marked with an identification numeral and kept in the supply box without batteries. Students may obtain calculators by checking them out—writing their names, the time, date, and the calculator's numeral on a signout–signin sheet left on the supply table. To use the calculators, the students install their own batteries, which are removed and retained by the students upon returning the calculators. Students are required to maintain their own supply of batteries, just as they do their own pencils and paper. Batteries will be kept on hand for sale at a profit for the class treasury.

The motion seems a bit complicated, but Mr. Cooper helps students work out the necessary details. Once the procedure is in effect for a week, students acquire behavior patterns and follow the procedure with little thought given to the complex written description that appears in the minutes of the class community meeting.

SOURCE: Adapted from *Cooperation in the Classroom: Students and Teachers Together* (pp. 33–35), by James S. Cangelosi, 1990, Washington: National Education Association.

SCHOOL-WIDE DISCIPLINE POLICIES

Classroom rules of conduct and procedures should not be in conflict with school-wide policies. Unfortunately, students in many departmentalized schools (e.g., most high schools) have to deal with rules that are inconsistent from teacher to teacher (Cangelosi, 1980). Many schools have rules that are unnecessary, according to the definition presented herein. Banning hats, prohibiting boys from wearing earrings, and regulating boys' hair length are typical examples of school-wide regulations that are difficult to justify under the four purposes for classroom rules of conduct. Thus, the responsibilities of a teacher are further complicated by being required to enforce unnecessary rules.

More and more, schools are moving toward a uniform discipline policy that allows teachers to establish their own classroom rules of conduct, but provides two major advantages over having no school-wide policy at all. First of all, the school-wide discipline policy can establish general guidelines for individual teacher's classroom rules for conduct. Ideally, these guidelines are flexible enough to allow teachers autonomy while providing enough direction to prevent one teacher's rules from conflicting with those of another. Secondly, the school-wide discipline policy can establish a support service for enforcing individual teacher's classroom rules of conduct. Vignette 5.8 is an example.

VIGNETTE 5.8

A month prior to the opening of a new school year, the faculty of Unity High School meets for five days to develop policies and plans for the year. Two agenda items are to agree on (1) Guidelines for teachers to follow in establishing classroom rules of conduct. (2) How the school administration can support teachers' enforcement of their rules of conduct.

After sharing ideas and working with a consultant on student discipline, Unity High's teachers and administrators develop these policies.

1. All teachers are responsible for establishing rules of conduct for their own classes. Those rules should only focus on (a) maximizing on-task behaviors; (b) increasing safety and security; (c) preventing class activities from disturbing others outside that class; and (d) maintaining acceptable standards of decorum.
2. Assistant Principal Coombs will serve as the chief administrator of the school-wide discipline program.
3. Teachers should print out rules as they are established and share them with Ms. Coombs so that she is able to provide support services for teachers enforcing those rules.
4. The school will maintain a time-out room to which each teacher may send no more than two students to wait until the beginning of the next period of the day. A paraprofessional will supervise the time-out room.
5. There will be an in-school suspension program in which students officially suspended from a class spend that class time in a special supervised classroom. There they complete independent-work assignments for the class they are missing. The following steps lead to an in-school suspension.
   a. Because of an alleged rule violation, a teacher chooses to write up the violation on a form supplied by Ms. Coombs' office.
   b. The student takes a copy of the form to Ms. Coombs' office where an appointment is set up with the student and Ms. Coombs.
   c. If the appointment cannot be arranged before the student is scheduled to return to that class, the student spends that period in the in-school suspension classroom until the conference can be held.
   d. At the conference, the student and Ms. Coombs attempt to work out a plan for returning to class.
   e. The plan, which is designed to prevent a recurrence of the incident, is forwarded by Ms. Coombs' office to the teacher. If the teacher agrees to the plan, the student is readmitted and is no longer on in-school suspension.
   f. If the teacher does not agree to the plan, then a meeting of the three parties (i.e., the student, the teacher, and Ms. Coombs) is held to work one out.
   g. If a plan still cannot be agreed upon, the student's parents are involved. In the meantime, the student remains in in-school suspension.

It should be noted that the plan may involve the teacher altering behaviors as well as the student. If it appears that no reasonable plan will be worked out in the very near future, arrangements are made for the student to be transferred out of that class.

TRANSITIONAL ACTIVITIES
FROM CHAPTER 5 TO CHAPTER 6

   I. In a short paragraph, explain the differences between a classroom rule of conduct and a routine procedure.

  II. In a short paragraph, explain why the literal meaning of this statement fails to communicate anything about expected conduct. "You are allowed to come into the room after the first bell."

 III. Which of the following rules or procedures are stated in functional terms?

     A. When you have been recognized to speak during a large group meeting, speak so that everyone in the room can hear you.

     B. Do not chew gum in the classroom.

     C. Avoid doing anything that dirties, mars, or damages the classroom, its furniture, and its equipment.

     D. Sit straight with both feet on the floor.

     E. Use expressions like "thank you," "pardon me," and "please"; refer to adults as "sir" and "ma'am."

     F. Do not bring toys to school.

     G. Respect everyone's right to learn.

     H. Be considerate of others' feelings.

       Statement A, C, G, and H are stated in functional terms.

  IV. Using two short paragraphs, describe two alternative procedures you would consider for routinely checking your students' homework.

   V. According to this text, what is the difference between a necessary and unnecessary rule of conduct?

  VI. Obtain a list of the rules of conduct established by another classroom teacher. In your opinion, which ones are necessary?

 VII. Write a paragraph explaining why you either agree or disagree with this statement. "The mistake of establishing unnecessary rules can cause a teacher more problems than the mistake of failing to establish necessary rules." Compare your response with that of a colleague. Discuss similarities and differences.

VIII. With a colleague, discuss the advantages and disadvantages of establishing all rules and procedures at the very beginning of a school term.

  IX. With a colleague, discuss the advantages and disadvantages of having students democratically determine rules of conduct.

   X. Design a school-wide discipline policy for the type of school in which you are or will be teaching. Have a colleague critique your plan.

  XI. In preparation for your work with Chapter 6, discuss the following questions with two or more of your colleagues.

     A. What strategies do teachers employ to motivate students to be on-task and engaged in learning activities?

     B. Why is it that a subject that seems so boring in the hands of one teacher is so exciting and interesting in the hands of another teacher?

     C. What strategies do teachers employ to help students understand and follow directions?

     D. What strategies do teachers employ to keep students engaged in these types of learning activities?

       • Lecture

       • Cooperative learning

       • Discussion

- Questioning
- Independent work

E. What are the preferable methods of motivating students to do homework assignments?

F. How should classrooms be arranged for smooth, efficient, businesslike learning?

SUPPLEMENTAL READINGS

Boostrom, R. (1991). The nature and functions of classroom rules. *Curriculum Inquiry, 21,* 193–216.

Brophy, J. E., & Putnam, J. G. (1979). Classroom management in the elementary school. In D. L. Duke (Ed.). *Classroom Management: The Seventy-eighth Yearbook of the National Society for the Study of Education* (pp. 182–216). Chicago: The University of Chicago Press.

Jones, V. F., & Jones, L.S. (1990). *Comprehensive classroom management: Motivating and managing students* (3rd ed., pp. 391–415). Boston: Allyn and Bacon.

Lasley, T. J. (1985). Fostering nonaggression in the classroom: An anthropological perspective. *Theory Into Practice, 24,* 247–255.

MacNaughton, R. H., & Jones, F. A. (1991). Developing a successful schoolwide discipline program. *NASSP Bulletin, 75,* 47–57.

CHAPTER **6**

Designing and Conducting Engaging Learning Activities

Purpose of Chapter 6

Chapter 6 is designed to help you

1. Distinguish between examples of students being intrinsically and extrinsically motivated to engage in learning activities.
2. Develop ideas for designing learning activities in which students are intrinsically motivated.
3. Develop techniques that encourage students to be on-task when you are giving directions.
4. Develop techniques that encourage students to be engaged during (a) lecture sessions, (b) cooperative learning sessions, (c) discussion sessions, (d) questioning sessions, (e) independent-work sessions, (f) homework assignments.
5. Develop ideas for creating classroom arrangements that facilitate students' being on-task and engaged in learning activities.

Part 1: Ideas for Motivation and Giving Directions

INTRINSIC AND EXTRINSIC MOTIVATION

Student Disinterest

"School is boring." "I hate history! Names, facts, dates — Who cares?" "My teacher says geometry is supposed to teach us logical thinking, but all we do is memorize somebody else's proofs." "Why do we have to learn this? Nobody ever uses it!"

"Why can't we study something we care about?" "The best thing happened today! There was a fire drill, so we didn't have to go to reading!" "Tomorrow, we don't have to study science 'cause we're going on a field trip." Do these comments sound all too familiar? Often, students do not cooperatively engage in learning activities because they find the activities uninteresting and of no immediate value to them (Wittrock, 1986). Teachers need not be entertainers and learning activities should probably be more work than fun for students. However, there are designs for learning activities that stimulate enthusiastic student engagement. Such designs are based on strategies for motivating students to be on-task.

Intrinsic Motivation

Students are intrinsically motivated to engage in a learning activity if they recognize that by experiencing the learning activity they will satisfy a need. Intrinsically motivated students value engagement as directly beneficial. The learning activity itself is perceived to be valuable. The students are intrinsically motivated to engage in learning activities in these two examples.

- Casey wants to stay healthy and avoid illness. He believes that a proper diet will contribute to his health. Thus, when his seventh grade teacher directs his class to read a chapter on nutrition, Casey willingly completes the assignment.

- Samantha believes strongly that people should not hunt and kill wild animals. When her English teacher gives a lecture on how to write creatively, Samantha listens intently because she wants to become an effective writer able to use her writing to convince others not to hunt.

Students learn to recognize the value of learning activities from having been positively reinforced as a direct result of being engaged.

Extrinsic Motivation

Students are extrinsically motivated to engage in learning activities if they desire to receive rewards that have been artificially associated with engagement or if they want to avoid consequences artificially imposed for being off-task. Here are two examples of students extrinsically motivated to engage in learning activities.

- James's seventh grade teacher directs his class to read a chapter on nutrition. James completes the assignment because he wants to please his dad by making high grades in school. James believes that reading the chapter on nutrition will enhance his chances of raising his grades.

- Roy listens intently while his English teacher lectures on creative writing because he fears that if he doesn't listen, he will be embarrassed by not knowing answers when asked questions in class.

Students become extrinsically motivated to be engaged through experiences in which engaged behaviors are positively reinforced with rewards that are not directly related to the learning activity itself. Similarly, contrived punishments following off-task behaviors can teach a student to be extrinsically motivated to avoid being off-task.

Honor rolls, academic scholarships, academic competitions, letter jackets for students with high grade-point averages, and honor societies are just some of the incentives provided by teachers and school administrators for being engaged in learning activities. Typically, such incentives do not extrinsically motivate those students who are in greatest need of motivation because such rewards are only vied for by students who have a history of academic success and, thus feel they have a reasonable chance of winning. Teachers can, however, design learning activities with built-in extrinsic motivators for all students. Vignettes 6.1 and 6.2 are examples.

The Preferred Type of Motivation

Ms. Malaker's and Mr. Landry's methods for extrinsically motivating student engagement were, of course, superior to not motivating students at all, but inferior to having students intrinsically motivated (Brody, 1983, pp. 202–207). Students can be intrinsically motivated to engage in learning activities only if those activities

---

VIGNETTE 6.1

To motivate her 28 second graders to study spelling words, Ms. Malaker holds team spelling tournaments. The class is divided into four teams, the "Protectors," "Gobots," "Starriors," and "Bird People." On Monday, the Protectors stand in line in the front of the classroom. Ms. Malaker calls out the word "harp." The first Protector says "H." The second says "U." Ms. Malaker: "No, that's not it." The second Protector exclaims: "Oh, shoot!" and looks in anticipation to the third Protector, who says "A." The fourth one says "R." The fifth says "R." Ms. Malaker: "No." The sixth says "P." Ms. Malaker: "Very well, the Protectors got four right and two wrong. Four minus two is two. So the Protectors have two points. The second word is 'tap.'" The seventh Protector says "T." The first says "A" and the second, "P." Ms. Malaker: "That's three right and zero wrong. So, that's three more points, giving the Protectors a total of five points. The next word is "biggest." The third Protector says, "B." . . .

The Gobots have their turn on Tuesday, the Starriors on Wednesday, and the Bird People on Thursday. On Friday, all seven members of the highest-scoring team receive free passes to the zoo.

Ms. Malaker prefers this type of spelling contest to traditional spelling bees for three reasons. (1) Even the least skilled spellers can contribute and be rewarded for a winning effort. (2) To compete, team members must listen to one another as letters are called out. (3) Students are not eliminated from the spelling drill for missing a letter as they are in traditional spelling bees.

VIGNETTE 6.2

Mr. Landry meets individually with each of his 26 fifth graders once every two weeks. He spreads the conferences over two weeks so he is not overloaded at any one time. During a conference, Mr. Landry and the student agree on a set of goals and rewards the student will receive if the goals are accomplished.

During one such conference, Mr. Landry and Mindy review how well previous goals were accomplished, and begin establishing new ones. He shows Mindy a page from their science text and says: "I would like you to choose an experiment from this section. Figure out how to do it, set it up, and demonstrate it to the class on Wednesday. You'll get 20 science points just for doing it and another 15 points for following the steps exactly the way they are in the book. Do you agree?" Mindy: "I don't know if I can do it by Wednesday." Mr. Landry: "That's okay, but you won't get the points unless you do." Mindy: "Okay, I'll try." Mr. Landry hands Mindy a test paper and says: "You scored 14 on this pretest. Monday, we'll have the posttest. You bring that pretest score up at least 10 points to a 24 or better and you get a 'B.' Bring it up more that 20 points and you get an 'A.'" Mindy takes notes on the goals and the rewards as the conversation moves to other subjects and other goals.

---

are designed to help students achieve objectives that clearly meet their needs (i.e., The Teaching Process Model is followed). However, just because the connection between your learning activities and your students' needs is obvious to you, do not assume your students will be intrinsically motivated. To stimulate students' interest and intrinsically motivate engagement, design so-called "problem-solving" learning activities (Cangelosi, 1990a, pp. 21–24).

PROBLEM-SOLVING LEARNING ACTIVITIES

The Non-Problem-solving Approach

Vignette 6.3 is purely fictitious; it never happened and, hopefully, never will.

What do you think of Mr. Doe's fictitious course? It is organized ridiculously. Real industrial arts teachers don't teach skills in isolation from one another. Typically, students learn necessary skills as they work on some project. Projects are usually individualized, so that while one student is building a bookcase, another is building a doghouse. In some cases, the entire class may focus on one large project, such as constructing a portable classroom building. Unlike Mr. Doe, real industrial arts teachers provide students with learning activities that teach them to apply special skills to solve real-life problems (e.g., how to build something people care about having).

Like all vignettes in this text other than Vignette 6.3, Vignette 6.4 reflects an actual event.

VIGNETTE 6.3

Mr. Doe teaches a high school carpentry course by first conducting a unit on hammering nails into wood. The second unit is on sawing lumber. Subsequent lessons include measuring planks, squaring corners, joining ends, selecting materials, sanding, inserting screws, the care of a drill, workshop safety, and using a drill press. Mr. Doe's students study and practice the skills from each unit in isolation from one another.

VIGNETTE 6.4

Mr. Ullrich conducts a mathematics unit on equivalent fractions for his sixth graders by (1) lecturing on the importance of understanding fractions, (2) explaining the rules for expressing fractional equivalents, (3) demonstrating several examples on the overhead, (4) assigning practice exercises, (5) providing individual help with exercises, (6) assigning textbook exercises for homework, and (7) reviewing the homework in class.

Mr. Ullrich's learning activities were fairly standard for academic subjects (Jesunathadas, 1990). Like Mr. Doe's fictional lesson, techniques and ideas are often taught in isolation from their real-world applications. Mr. Ullrich lectured students on the importance of what they were to learn, but do you really think his students will be intrinsically motivated to be engaged in the learning activities on fractions because of what he said? Had Mr. Ullrich followed the example of most industrial arts teachers and designed his unit so that it focused on problems with which students are concerned, then students would have discovered the value of learning about fractions for themselves.

The Problem-solving Approach

In Vignette 6.5, the problem-solving approach is used to teach sixth graders about equivalent fractions.

VIGNETTE 6.5

Ms. Olson has observed her 23 sixth graders at Westside School long enough to understand what interests them. In planning a mathematics unit on equivalent fractions, she decides to take advantage of the interest some have in the basketball season, a class social for which they are planning to bake some cakes, and physical education activities in which students are running various distances for time.

VIGNETTE 6.5 (continued)

She begins by assigning six students to the basketball group, nine to the cake group, and eight to the running group. While the other 18 are working on assignments, she engages the basketball group in a conversation.

MS. OLSON: How do you think our Westside boys' basketball team is doing this year?

ANTOINE: Oh! We're doin' okay. We're gonna beat Sixth Avenue today. You watch!

MS. OLSON: I will. What's our record?

MARY: We've won three.

GENE: Yea, and lost two.

ANTOINE: Yea, but we would've won those if it wasn't for the refs.

MS. OLSON: What's your favorite NBA team, Alphonse?

ALPHONSE: The Utah Jazz! I like the Utah Jazz!

ANTOINE: Aw, I like the Lakers.

MS. OLSON: Who's doing better this year, the Jazz or Westside?

ANTOINE: The Jazz may be better, but we win more.

MARY: You're crazy! The Jazz have won a lot more games.

ANTOINE: Well sure! They play more.

MARCIA: Yea, they also lose more.

MS. OLSON: Okay, wait a minute. We have a game today. Antoine, your mathematics assignment is to report Westside's won-loss record to the class tomorrow.

ANTOINE: I can tell you that now. It'll be four and two; you watch!

MS. OLSON: Alphonse, your job is to look up the Jazz's record in the morning paper and report it to the class.

MARY: What for?

MS. OLSON: We're going to figure who's having a better year, Westside or the Jazz.

In a similar fashion, Ms. Olson meets with the cake group. She directs some of those students to bring in recipes for cakes that serve eight. One recipe will be chosen to use for the class social.

Her meeting with the running group leads them to report times for different distances they are to run during physical education that afternoon.

The following day, Ms. Olson uses the groups' data to present the class with three problems. (1) Which team is doing better, Westside in their six games or the Jazz in their 44 games? (2) According to the recipe for eight, how much flour should the class buy to have enough cake to serve 24? (3) Do we run faster in a 30-meter race or in a 60-meter race? Ms. Olson uses inductive questioning techniques to help her students discover that such problems can be efficiently solved using equivalent fractions.

Later in the unit, Ms. Olson explains the rules for expressing fractional equivalents, demonstrates examples, and assigns and reviews exercises. At no point does she bother to tell students how important it is for them to be able to skillfully use equivalent fractions. They have already discovered that for themselves.

According to *Webster's Third New International Dictionary* (1986, p. 1807), a "problem" is a perplexing or difficult question that needs to be answered or something difficult that must be worked out. Because problems suggest difficulties, people are often inclined to think of them as undesirable. However, the existence of problems serves as a strong motivator for human endeavor. A perfectly satisfied person, one who recognizes no problems, lacks motivation to change, and, thus learn. Why would anyone want to learn to read unless that person felt a need to understand written communication? Why would someone want to learn how to drive nails unless there was a need to build or repair something? Do people ever write unless they have something to communicate? Do people ever work with equivalent fractions without first being confronted with a problem they are motivated to solve?

Intrinsic Motivation via the Problem-solving Approach

Students can be intrinsically motivated to engage cooperatively in learning activities when those activities focus on problems the students have a felt need to solve. Learning activities, such as those typically conducted by industrial arts teachers and by Ms. Olson in Vignette 6.5, that are initiated by presenting students with real-world problems are known as problem-solving learning activities. The goals of some teaching units may not lend themselves to problem-solving learning activities. For such situations, you need to utilize extrinsic motivators to ensure student engagement. However, when well organized problem-solving activities are used, obtaining students' cooperation and engagement is usually a much easier task for a teacher.

Vignettes 6.6 and 6.7 are examples of problem-solving learning activities:

VIGNETTE 6.6

Ms. Piscatelli designs a two-week unit to help her high school history students better understand the activities of the U.S. Congress in the first third of the twentieth century. Ms. Piscatelli observes her students so as to identify current issues that concern them. She decides to focus on the following problems. (1) Should marijuana be legalized? (2) What should the federal government do about unemployment? (3) What should Congress do to ensure the rights of ethnic minorities? (4) Does the United States need an Equal Rights Amendment? (5) What should the federal government do about the abortion issue? (6) What stand should the federal government take on combating pollution?

The learning activities include the following:

1. Ms. Piscatelli assigns each class member to one of six cooperative groups. One group, consisting of five students, is directed to examine how Congress handled the prohibition of alcohol in the first third of the twentieth century

---

VIGNETTE 6.6 (continued)

and then relate those lessons of history to the current question about marijuana. The group is to report on Congress' rationale for repealing prohibition and to identify both similarities and differences between the question of alcohol prohibition then and marijuana prohibition now. Each of the other five task groups examines one of the other problems in a similar manner.

2. Each cooperative group is provided with an organizational structure within which to operate, a list of resources from which to acquire information, a list of deadlines for specific subtasks, and directions on how findings are to be reported to the rest of the class and to Ms. Piscatelli.

3. To obtain an overall picture of the climate within which the Congress operated in the first third of the twentieth century, and thus be better able to compare problems of that era to current problems, all students are assigned to read the text chapter dealing with the period from 1901 to 1935.

4. Each group reports to the class according to the schedule.

5. After each group reports, class members who are not members of that group discuss the report and propose a solution for solving the current problem.

SOURCE: Adapted from *Cooperation in the Classroom: Students and Teachers Together,* Second Edition (pp. 22–24) by J. S. Cangelosi, 1990, Washington: National Education Association.

VIGNETTE 6.7

Mr. Cefalo often combines intraclass grouping techniques with problem-solving learning activities to accommodate the variety of achievement levels and interests displayed by the 34 tenth graders in his English class. As part of a unit designed to improve students' creative-writing abilities, he groups students into pairs and assigns each pair a topic on which information is to be gathered and reported upon in writing.

Mr. Cefalo utilizes what he has learned about the students to design the assignment. Herb, for example, is an avid motorcycle racing fan who has not displayed much desire or ability to write. Ron, on the other hand, displays both a knack for and interest in writing, but knows hardly anything about motorcycle racing. Therefore, Mr. Cefalo pairs Herb with Ron and directs them to write a report on motorcycle racing in the local community.

Mr. Cefalo figures that Herb will tend to be engaged in the activity because his knowledge of motorcycle racing is needed by Ron. Ron, who already possesses quality writing skills, should be challenged by the problem of having to write about an unfamiliar topic. Because of the diversity of interests and achievement levels, both Herb and Ron contribute to the completion of the task.

The strategy of confronting students with real-life problems to intrinsically motivate engagement has proven successful at virtually every grade level and school subject (see, e.g., Cangelosi, 1992b, pp. 25–27). Here are some additional examples:

- Mr. Byers involves his fourth grade students in a project to build a scale model of the schoolyard in order to teach them about ratios and proportions.

- Ms. Groves discovers that 12 of the juniors in her literature class read below the third grade level. Realizing that nine of them want to pursue a driver's license, she provides them with the state driver's manual and uses it as a textbook for improving their reading skills. While they focus on learning how to pass the test for a driver's license, they steadily improve their reading levels.

- Mr. Gervin takes advantage of his fifth graders' desire to decide upon their own rules for classroom conduct to teach them principles of democratic government.

- Ms. Robique's kindergarten students are making greeting cards for their parents in a learning activity designed to teach them to form manuscript letters.

- Ms. Jones's students discover the rules of multiplying signed numbers while trying to figure out how drivers can avoid speed traps.

- While some second grade students manage a classroom store and others make purchases from it, they acquire some needed computational and reading skills.

- Mr. Orborson realizes that his seventh graders have an avid interest in television, but virtually no interest in history. To stimulate their interest in history, he designs a learning activity in which they are to analyze certain TV shows for historical accuracy. For example, one student is to compare the dress of the actors on two "Old West" shows to the dress of persons from that era who appear in history book photographs.

- While caring for and feeding the inhabitants of the classroom aquarium, preschoolers polish their counting and grouping skills.

IDEAS FOR GIVING DIRECTIONS

Explicitness, Specificity, and Directness

Indirect and inexplicit communications are appropriate for learning activities that stimulate students to reason, appreciate, discover, or create. Vignette 6.8 gives an example.

Ms. Southworth knew the answer to Judy's question, but instead of answering it directly, she probed with another question. This indefinite, evasive communication was appropriate in this type of situation because Ms. Southworth's objective was to get Judy to reason, not simply to know the answer. However, when instead of stimulating thinking, you are providing directions for an upcoming learning activity, your communications should be extremely explicit, specific, and directly to the point.

VIGNETTE 6.8

During a problem-solving learning activity, Ms. Southworth is trying to help her junior high students discover principles of physics that make it possible for airplanes to fly. At one point in the lesson, Judy asks: "What would happen if the wings of the plane were curved on the bottom like they are on top?" Ms. Southworth: "Hmmm, I wonder. Let's think about it. In that case, would the air pass over the top surface faster or slower than it would over the bottom surface?" Judy: "I guess that . . . ."

Ordinarily, you give directions during transition periods, just before the start of a learning activity. Directions must be explicit, precise, and concise so that transition time is minimized and allocated time is not wasted. Consider Vignettes 6.9, 6.10, 6.11, and 6.12. In which two are the teachers' directions clear and to the point? In which two will student engagement in the upcoming learning activity be impaired because the directions don't fully communicate exactly what is to be done?

VIGNETTE 6.9

Ms. Aldomat is holding a gymnastics class on the basketball court of the Saddle Hill School gym. Just as her 18 third graders complete their warmup exercises, Ms. Aldomat briskly walks to the middle of one foul line, pivots, faces her students, and blows her whistle for an instant. As shown in Figure 6.1, she holds her hand high above her head with the palm facing the students. The students have learned from previous class periods that the whistle signals an end to one activity, and Ms. Aldomat's hand signal means to line up in front of her to wait for directions. As the students quickly move toward her, she says: "Line up facing me on the half-court line, one arm's length apart." She watches them intently as they line up facing her. As soon as everyone is in position, she drops her hand and points to Jenny who is standing first. Ms. Aldomat: "Jenny, please do four cartwheels directly forward and then wait facing us on the baseline behind me." Jenny obliges. Ms. Aldomat: "Thank you. Stay there, Jenny." She continues speaking to the group: "When I say 'start,' I want the rest of you to take turns doing four cartwheels and wait on the line as Jenny did. We'll begin on this end with Frank. As soon as Frank starts his third cartwheel, Freda goes, then Tamara, and so on down the line. Remember to watch the person to your left. You go as soon as that person begins the third cartwheel. Ready, start!"

   As the students take their turns, Ms. Aldomat positions herself so that she is just out of the way of the student who is about to begin. That helps signal the students to wait for their turns. If a student is late starting, she says nothing, but simply gestures with her hand.

FIGURE 6.1 Ms. Aldomat Provides Her Students with Explicit, Specific Directions

---

VIGNETTE 6.10

Ms. Duncan is holding a gymnastics class on the basketball court of the Westdale School gym. Just as her 18 third graders complete their warmup exercises, Ms. Duncan announces: "Okay, okay, that's enough. All right, listen up. Let's do something else now." The last student stops stretching and the students gather around Ms. Duncan as she says: "We're going to practice our cartwheels now." "Good! Good!" Rhonda yells, jumping up and down. Tommy: "I hate cartwheels! Can't we jump on the tramp?" "Yea! Yea! Let's jump on the tramp, Miss Duncan," exclaims Dustin. Ms. Duncan: "We'll do the tramp another time; it's time to work on cartwheels. Here's what we'll do. Go over to the middle of the court and . . ." Several students run over to the center circle of the basketball court. The others, not knowing what to do, hesitate before rushing over themselves. Ms. Duncan reluctantly follows and

VIGNETTE 6.10 (continued)

says: "I didn't say to go yet. Now listen. I'm only going to say this once. Form a line." The students line up in somewhat of a semi-circle as they tend to bunch themselves around the center court circle. Ms. Duncan: "Spread out. Come on! You know what I mean." Finally, the students are positioned and ready to hear Ms. Duncan who says: "Now, one at a time, I want you to do several cartwheels. We'll start on one end and go one at a time. It's your turn when the one ahead of you is halfway through. Okay, let's go."

VIGNETTE 6.11

Mr. Boudreaux wants to lead his third period English students through the literal, interpretative, and analytical stages of reading poems. After completing a brief lecture on reading poetry, he distributes copies of Edwin A. Robinson's poem "Richard Cory" saying: "I want you to carefully read this wonderful poem and be prepared to discuss it when everyone is finished." Some of the students are beginning to read the poem as Mr. Boudreaux continues to provide direction. Mr. Boudreaux: "Now wait, don't start yet—Anthony, pay attention! Thank you. Okay, now as I was about to tell you, when you come across a word in the poem that you don't know, look it up in the dictionary and write down the definition." Denise: "Where should we write them?" Mr. Boudreaux: "Just on a sheet of paper—No! I've got a better idea. Write them on the back of the poem. Then you'll have them together for our discussion. Any other questions? Good! Let's get started."

VIGNETTE 6.12

Mr. Rice wants to lead his third period English students through the literal, interpretative, and analytical stages of reading poems. After completing a brief lecture on reading poetry, he distributes a three-page document to each student. The first page contains directions; the second page, the poem "Richard Cory"; and the third page, a list of questions for discussion. Watching their faces closely and seeing that they all have the document, Mr. Rice raises his hand signaling their attention. Mr. Rice: "Thank you. Let's go through the directions on the first page." Seeing that Blanche is thumbing through the pages, he gently taps her desktop and whispers: "First page." With everyone appearing attentive, he reads the following directions aloud, occasionally pausing to clarify or emphasize points.

"After receiving the signal to start, you have 14 minutes to

1. Take out your pocket dictionary.
2. Read the poem 'Richard Cory' on the next page. As you read it, circle each unfamiliar word. Look it up in your dictionary. Decide for yourself which of the meanings Robinson meant for that word. Get the number of the page from your dictionary where that word appears. Jot that page number just

over the word on your copy of the poem. Be ready to explain your choice of definitions to the class.

3. Read through the questions on the third page of this document.
4. Reread the poem. But, this time, read it so that you are prepared to discuss the answers to the questions with the class.
5. After the 14 minutes are up, we will have a two-part class discussion. The first part will focus on the vocabulary. The second part will focus on the questions.''

''Richard Cory'' is rather brief; the third page consists of three questions.

1. What did Robinson mean by
   ''. . . he was always human when he talked''? (line 6)
   ''. . . he glittered when he walked''? (line 8)
   ''And went without meat and cursed the bread''? (line 14)
2. Was Richard Cory a happy man? Why or why not?
3. How did others think of him? Did they think he was happy? What lines from the poem support your answer?''

Nine Points about Directions

Ms. Aldomat's and Mr. Rice's explicit directions more efficiently communicated what students were to do than did either Ms. Duncan's or Mr. Boudreaux's. Keep these nine points in mind when giving directions.

1. The students of teachers who display businesslike attitudes are more likely to efficiently follow directions than those of teachers who seem lackadaisical and less organized. Both Ms. Aldomat and Mr. Rice knew exactly what tasks they wanted students to complete, and had well-organized plans for accomplishing those tasks.
2. Body language is a powerful medium for communicating expectations to students (Jones, 1979). By briskly walking to the point where she wanted to give directions, deliberately positioning herself, directly facing students, establishing eye contact with shoulders paralleling the students', Ms. Aldomat communicated that her directions were to be heard and strictly followed.
3. Signals or cues that instantaneously communicate certain recurring expectations to students minimize transition time, streamline communication procedures, display a more businesslike attitude, and reduce the amount of ''teacher talk'' in classrooms. Non-verbal signals are particularly effective. From their prior experiences in her class, Ms. Aldomat's students knew exactly how to respond to her whistle, her hand over her head, and even her body language. Similarly, Mr. Rice had conditioned his students to appropriately react to certain signals.
4. Deliberately gain at least the appearance of everyone's attention before providing directions. This communicates the seriousness of the directions and increases the chances that the directions will be followed. Speaking to students who are not attentively listening is not only a waste of time

and energy, but it also encourages inattentive behavior patterns. Both Ms. Aldomat and Mr. Rice achieved eye contact with students to ascertain that students were ready to listen and to signal that they expected to be heard before beginning to speak. Had students' attention not been obtained quickly, they would have resorted to more decisive methods for dealing with student inattentiveness. (Methods for dealing with off-task behaviors are suggested in subsequent chapters of this text.)

5. Students who have learned that their teacher says things only once tend to listen the first time the teacher speaks. Ms. Duncan said: "I'm only going to say this once," but she probably repeated herself anyway, because her initial directions were so vague.

6. Students are more likely to carefully listen to the directions of teachers who restrict their remarks to exactly what students need to know. Neither Ms. Aldomat nor Mr. Rice mixed uninformative, inane words with directions, as did Mr. Boudreaux who included, "Okay, now as I was about to tell you . . . ."

7. Efficiently communicated directions do not normally allow time for students to debate the pros and cons of what is to be done. Unlike Ms. Duncan, Ms. Aldomat never provided students with an opening for arguing about the upcoming learning activity. She had Jenny demonstrate the cartwheels before the class even knew they would be doing cartwheels instead of jumping on the trampoline.

8. Students are far more likely to follow directions that provide very specific guidelines than they are ambiguously worded general directions. Ms. Aldomat told her students: "Line up facing me on the half-court line, one arm's-length apart," rather than: "Form a line." She directed students to do "four" cartwheels instead of "several." Mr. Rice's time limit of "14 minutes" communicates something more specific to students than "in a while," "several minutes," "when everyone is finished," "10 minutes," or "15 minutes." (Numbers like 10 and 15 appear rounded and less specific.) Unlike Mr. Boudreaux who only told his students to be prepared to discuss the poem, Mr. Rice provided very specific guidelines for how to prepare for the discussion.

9. The more senses (e.g., seeing and hearing) that are stimulated by the directions, the more likely students are to understand them. Besides telling her students what to do, Ms. Aldomat had Jenny demonstrate the activity. Mr. Rice's students heard and read his directions. If students had questions about the directions or appeared to misunderstand them, Mr. Rice could simply point to the relevant statements on the first page of the document he distributed.

A VARIETY OF LEARNING ACTIVITIES

In Vignette 6.12, Mr. Rice conducted a lesson consisting of a variety of learning activities. He began with a brief lecture followed by a 14-minute independent work session and a two-part discussion session. If you incorporate too many types of learning activities into a single lesson, you'll find yourself spending an inordinate amount of time giving directions in transitional periods. However, an optimum mix of different types of sessions (e.g., in Vignette 6.12) guards against monotony leading to student boredom.

TRANSITIONAL ACTIVITIES
FROM PART 1 TO PART 2

Part 2 of this chapter presents ideas for keeping students engaged during various types of learning activities (lectures, cooperative learning, discussions, questioning, independent work, and homework). Before studying those sections, please complete the following activities.

 I. Tell whether each student is intrinsically or extrinsically motivated.
   A. Clyde carefully listens to the questions his teacher raises in class to avoid the embarrassment he feels when he's called on and doesn't provide an acceptable response.
   B. Lynnae's mother tells her she can adopt a new kitten only if she does well on her next spelling test. Because of this, Lynnae diligently works on her spelling homework.
   C. To impress her coach, Carmen spends extra time during basketball practice running up and down the bleachers.
   D. To build up her endurance, Noel spends extra time during basketball practice running up and down the bleachers.
   E. Because he wants to converse easily with his Spanish-speaking friends, Damien diligently works on assigned exercises in his Spanish class.
   F. Madison carefully listens to and watches his teacher as she shows him how to write his name. He is anxious to write it himself on the Mother's Day card he's prepared.
   G. To avoid being criticized by her teacher, Marnae carefully follows directions when completing a writing assignment.
   H. To increase the chances that her teacher will display her essay on the bulletin board, Nadine carefully follows directions when completing a writing assignment.
   I. Convinced that by learning arithmetic he can increase his chances of purchasing a better bicycle for less money, Anthony raises questions in class about how to complete a computation.
      Students are intrinsically motivated in D, E, F, and I. Students are extrinsically motivated in A, B, C, G, and H.
 II. In two paragraphs, describe the associations between (A) positive reinforcement and whether motivation is intrinsic or extrinsic; (B) contrived and naturally occurring punishment and whether motivation is intrinsic or extrinsic.
      Compare your paragraphs with those of colleagues. They should include the following points. (1) When a behavior is positively reinforced by a naturally occurring reward, one tends to be intrinsically motivated to repeat that behavior. (2) When a behavior is positively reinforced by a contrived reward, one tends to be extrinsically motivated to repeat that behavior. (3) When a behavior is followed by naturally occurring punishment, one tends to be intrinsically motivated to avoid that behavior. (4) When a behavior is followed by contrived punishment, one tends to be extrinsically motivated to avoid that behavior.

III. Revisit Vignette 6.6. With a colleague, discuss why you agree or disagree with these statements.

    A. The variety of learning activities in Ms. Piscatelli's unit prevents lessons from being monotonous.

    B. Ms. Piscatelli's problem-solving approach to unit design leads to lessons that are more complex than traditional lessons. Thus to students engaged in the various types of learning activities, she needs to be even more explicit with her directions than do teachers whose practices are more traditional.

IV. Develop two unit plans for teaching a four-year-old how to count from 1 to 20. Design the first plan so that is does NOT use problem-solving learning activities. Design the second plan so that it does utilize problem-solving learning activities.

    Compare your plans with those of colleagues. In general, problem-solving learning activities focus on real-life questions, tasks, or concerns of the students, while the non-problem-solving activities focus on what is to be learned.

V. Write a paragraph comparing the advantages and disadvantages of problem-solving and non-problem-solving learning activities.

    Compare your responses with those of colleagues. In general, students tend to be intrinsically motivated to engage in problem-solving learning activities because they discover they can accomplish some of the things that are important to them via engagement in the learning activities. Because problem-solving learning activities tend to be more student centered and indirect than traditional styles of teaching (non-problem-solving activities), students may initially perceive them to be weird and unstructured. Consequently, they may tend to be off-task until they are taught on-task behaviors for this seemingly new type of activity. Problem-solving learning activities should not be thrust on students who are not used to them.

VI. Develop a lesson plan for teaching one objective involving your own teaching specialty. Describe in one or two paragraphs how you would provide your students with directions for that learning activity.

    Compare your lesson plan and directions with those of colleagues. Analyze the directions for consistency with the nine points enumerated on pages 153–154.

Part 2: Ideas for Instruction

IDEAS FOR LECTURE SESSIONS

Student Engagement during Lectures

For students to be engaged in a lecture-type learning activity, they must attentively listen to what a teacher is saying. Taking notes and attempting to follow a teacher-prescribed thought pattern may also be involved. Such engagement requires students to be congnitively active, while physically inactive. This is not easy for older students and virtually impossible for younger students.

    In Vignette 6.13, the teacher is not likely to maintain even older students' attention during her lectures. In contrast, the teacher in Vignette 6.14 utilizes lecture techniques designed to obtain and maintain student engagement.

VIGNETTE 6.13

Ms. Haenszel has prepared a lecture designed to help her junior high mathematics class understand, know, and apply the arithmetic mean statistic (i.e., averaging numbers). The 28 students quietly sit at their desks, 12 of them poised with paper and pencil for note taking, as Ms. Haenszel begins from her station near the chalkboard at the front of the room. Ms. Haenszel: "Today, class, we are going to learn about a statistic for averaging data. It is called the arithmetic mean; many of you are probably already familiar with it. Here's the definition." She turns to the chalkboard and writes as she says: "The arithmetic mean of N scores equals the sum of the scores divided by N." She keeps her side to the class so that she can easily look over her shoulder at the class and still see what she writes on the board. Continuing she says: "For example, to compute the mean of 30, 25, 20, 30, 40, 30, 60, 10, 0, and 15, we would first add all the numbers to find the sum. Let's see, adding those 10 numbers on my calculator I get . . . 260. Since three are 10 scores, we divide 260 by 10 and get 26.0. The mean in this case is 26. The arithmetic mean is a very important statistic. For example, if we had a second set of data, say 25, 18, 15, 20, 70, 10, 10, 8, 30, and 15, and we wanted to know which of the two sets is greater, then we could compare their means to find out. In the second case, the sum is . . . 221. And 221 divided by the number of scores, which like before is also 10, is 22.1. So the arithmetic mean of the first group of scores, although containing a zero and no number as large as 70, is, on the average greater. This is because 26.0 is greater that 22.1."

VIGNETTE 6.14

Mr. Dwyer has prepared a lecture designed to help his junior high mathematics class understand, know, and apply the arithmetic mean statistic. After directing students to have their calculators available and distributing the form appearing in Figure 6.2, he faces the class from a position near the overhead projector and says: "I'm looking at you people and I just can't get one question out of my mind." Very deliberately he walks in front of the fourth row of students and quickly, but obviously, looks at their feet. Then he moves in front of the first row and repeats the odd behavior with those students. "I just don't know!" he says shaking his head as he returns to his position by the overhead.

He switches on the overhead displaying the first line of Figure 6.2, and says: "In the first blank on your form, please write: Do the people sitting in the fourth row have bigger feet than those in the first row?" He moves closer to the students, obviously monitoring how well his directions are followed. Back by the overhead as they complete the chore, he says: "Now, I've got to figure a way to gather data that will help me answer that question." Grabbing his head with a hand and closing his eyes, he appears to be in deep thought for a few seconds and then suddenly exclaims: "I've got it! We'll use shoe sizes as a measure. That'll be a lot easier than using a ruler on smelly feet!" Some students laugh, and one begins to speak while two others raise their hands. But Mr. Dwyer quickly says: "Not now, please, we need to collect some data."

VIGNETTE 6.14 (continued)

Question to be answered: _____

_____

Data for Row 4: _____

Data for Row 1: _____

Treatment for Row 4's data:

Treatment for Row 1's data:

Treatment to compare the two sets of data:

Results: _____

_____

Conclusions: _____

_____

FIGURE 6.2 Form Mr. Dwyer Uses During an Interactive Lecture Session

He flips an overlay off of the second line of the transparency, exposing "Data for Row 4." Mr. Dwyer: "Starting with Jason in the back and moving up to Becky in the front, those of you in the fourth row call out your shoe sizes one at a time so we can write them down in this blank at our places. If you don't know it, either guess or read it off your shoe if you can do it quickly. . . . ." As the students volunteer the sizes, he fills in the blank on the transparency: 6, 10.5, 8, 5.5, 6, 9. Exposing the next line on the transparency, "Data for Row 1," he asks: "What do you suppose we're going to do now, Melanie?" Melanie: "Do the same for row one." Mr. Dwyer: "Okay, you heard her; row one, give it to us from the back so we can fill in this blank." The numbers 8.5, 8, 7, 5.5, 6.5, 6.5, 9, and 8 are recorded and displayed on the overhead.

Mr. Dwyer: "Now, I've got to figure out what to do with these numbers to help me answer the question." Several students raise their hands, but he responds: "Thank you for offering to help, but I want to figure this out for myself." Pointing to the appropriate numbers on the transparency, he seems to think aloud saying:

"It's easy enough to compare one number to another. David's 8.5 from row one is greater than Jason's 6 from row four. But I don't want to just compare one individual's number to another. I want to compare this whole bunch of numbers [he circles row four's set of numbers with an overhead pen] to this bunch [he circles row one's]. . . . I guess we could add all of row four's numbers together and all of row one's numbers together and compare the two sums—the one with the greater sum would have the larger group of feet."

A couple of students try to interrupt with: "But that won't wor . . . ," but Mr. Dwyer motions them to stop speaking and asks: "What's the sum from row four, Terri?" Terri: ". . . 45." Mr. Dwyer: "Thank you. And what's the sum for row one, Haeja?" Haeja: "59." "Thank you. So the people in row one have bigger feet since 59 is greater than 45," Mr. Dwyer says as he writes: "59 > 45" on the transparency. Mr. Dwyer: "I'll pause to hear what those of you with your hands up have to say. Vanessa?" Vanessa: "That's not right; it doesn't work." Mr. Dwyer: "You mean 59 isn't greater than 45, Vanessa?" Vanessa: "59 is greater than 45, but there's more feet in row one." Mr. Dwyer: "All the people in row one have only two feet just like the people in row four. I carefully counted. [students laugh] Now that we've taken care of that concern, how about other comments or questions—Jeremy?" Jeremy: "You know what Vanessa meant! There's more people in row one. So what you did isn't right." Mr. Dwyer: "Let me see if I now understand Vanessa's point. She said we don't want our indicator of how big the feet are to be affected by how many feet, just the size of the feet. . . . So, I've got to figure out a way to compare the sizes of these two groups of numbers, when one has more numbers. I'm open for suggestions. . . . Jung?"

Jung: "You could drop the two extra numbers from row one; then they'd both have six." Mr. Dwyer: "That seems like a reasonable approach. I like that, but first let's hear another idea—maybe one where we can use all the data. . . . Alice?" Alice: "Why not do an average?" Mr. Dwyer: "What do you mean?" Alice: "You know, divide row four's total by 6 and row one's total by 8." Mr. Dwyer: "How will dividing help? It seems like just an unnecessary step. . . . Cito." Cito: "It evens up the two groups." Mr Dwyer: "Oh, I see what you people have been trying to tell me! Dividing row four's sum of 45 by 6 counts each number one-sixth. And dividing row four's sum of 59 by 8 counts each number one-eighth. And that's fair since six one-sixths is whole, just like eight one-eighths is a whole. How am I doing, Jason?" Jason: "A lot better than you were."

Flipping over another overlay, he displays the next two lines of Figure 6.2 and says: "Let's write: The sum of row four's numbers is 45. . . . 45 divided by 6 is what, Becky?" Becky: "7.5." Mr. Dwyer: "Thanks. And on the next line we write: The sum of row one's numbers is 59. . . . 59 divided by 8 is what, Henry?" Henry: "7.375." Mr. Dwyer: "Since 7.5 is greater than 7.375, I guess we could say that row four's feet are larger than row one's feet. That is, of course, if you're willing to trust this particular statistic—which is known as the VAJJ. Any questions? . . . Yes, Haeja." Haeja: "Why VAJJ?" Mr. Dwyer: "Because I just named it after its four inventors, Vanessa, Alice, Jung, and Jeremy. They're the ones who came up with the idea of dividing the sum." The class breaks into laughter.

Mr. Dwyer shifts to direct instruction to help students remember the formula, practice using it, and remember its more conventional name, "arithmetic mean," during the remainder of the session.

Fourteen Points about Lectures

Please consider the following thoughts when designing lectures.

1. Students are more likely to be engaged during a lecture session if the teacher has provided clear directions for behavior. Students need to have learned how to attend a lecture. Questions about how to take notes, if at all, should be answered before the lecture begins.

2. Some sort of advanced organizer to direct students' thinking helps students to actively listen during a lecture. A written outline of topics to be covered or problems to be addressed, such as the form that Mr. Dwyer distributed in Vignette 6.14, can be useful in focusing students' thoughts.

3. Signals, especially nonverbal ones, can efficiently focus students' attention during a lecture. Mr. Dwyer utilized at least two such signals. He directed students to a particular item on the form and had them write down specific things from time to time. This helped students stay on track, preventing mind wandering. His use of the overhead projector also helped maintain students' focus. Turning the projector on signals students to look, turning it off signals students to focus their eyes elsewhere. The use of transparency overlays controls what students see.

4. Lectures are useful learning activities for teachers who want to have a group of students concurrently follow a common thought pattern. Lectures, such as Mr. Dwyer's, that are designed to do more than just feed information to students, run the risk of becoming discussion or questioning sessions. Thus, some means for staying on track should be considered. One method is to have signals worked out with students so that they clearly discriminate between times when the teacher is strictly lecturing and times when discussion or questions are welcome. Mr. Dwyer divided his lecture into two parts. In the first part, he presented the problem to be addressed, collected data, and focused thoughts on how to manipulate the data. During this first part, he had students speak, but they did not enter into a discussion or raise questions. They simply provided him with data that he used in the lecture. Between the first and second parts of the lecture, Mr. Dwyer conducted a brief discussion session in which the students discovered the formula for the arithmetic mean. After the discussion, when he was again lecturing, he did entertain Haeja's question, but he had set the students up to ask such a question to achieve a smooth transition into the formal statement of the formula. Mr. Dwyer let his students know when their comments and questions were welcome by saying such things as: "But let me try and figure this one out myself . . ." and "I'll pause to hear what those of you with your hands up have to say . . ."

5. Voice volume, inflection, pitch, rhythm, and pace should be strategically modulated according to the message you want to send and according to the level of the students. Even when the message itself is important and exciting, a monotone speech is a recipe for boredom. Punctuate

key sentences with voice variations. Follow key statements and questions with strategic pauses. Pauses indicate points to ponder. Pace your speech so that sessions move briskly, but so that students still have time to absorb your messages and take notes. The type of lesson you're teaching, of course, should influence pace. A lecture for an inquiry learning activity would ordinarily proceed at a slower pace than one using direct instruction. Quina (1989, p. 143) suggested that between 110 and 130 words per minute is optimal.

6. Students are more likely to follow lectures that utilize professional quality media and technology. Students can hardly be engaged when the learning activity requires them to read, see, or hear something that is unintelligible. Recent technological advances make computerized, multimedia, and sound-enhanced presentations cost effective for everyday classroom use.

7. At least three advantages can be gained by videotaping lectures ahead of time and playing them for students in class. (1) Videotaped lectures avoid some of the interruptions in thought that occur when students make comments or ask questions. (2) The teacher can more attentively monitor students' behavior and effectively respond to indications of disengagement. (3) Kinks and mistakes in the presentation can be corrected and improvements made before the lecture is played for the class. With videotape and other record-and-play devices (e.g., video laser discs), teachers can easily start, interrupt, replay, terminate, modify, and repeat presentations.

8. Entertaining is not teaching. However, lectures that interject a bit of humor or contain other attention-getting devices help keep students more alert than a straight monologue. Care must be taken that the attention-getting devices don't distract attention from the goal of the lesson.

9. Students are more likely to follow a lecture when the lecturer maintains eye contact with them. This, of course, was one of the advantages Mr. Dwyer's use of the overhead had over Ms. Haenszel's use of the chalkboard.

10. Mind wandering and daydreaming are major causes of student disengagement during lectures. Teachers can deal more effectively with these behaviors when they move about the room as they lecture. Rather than standing behind a lectern, Quina (1989, pp. 141–142) suggested purposeful movements with the room divided into quadrants.

> Beginning teachers sometimes unconsciously pace the floor, moving from one side of the room to another. The observing students' heads move as though they are watching a tennis match. To avoid this, think where you want to be standing as you develop parts of your lecture. You can divide the room into quadrants and intentionally move into each quadrant at different stages of your lecture. For example, after introducing the question: "Why do we need to communicate?" the teacher may move to the left side of the room, give some information on communicating in pantomime, provide a quick pantomime, then

move to the right side of the room, discuss ways people designate things, illustrate by pointing to objects, and then ask a related question: "How is pointing and acting things out like using words?" The teacher may then walk to the back of the room and ask even more pointed questions. "What would happen if we did not have words? What would it be like if words were not available right now?"

The shift in position in the room corresponds to the development of the lecture, providing a spatial metaphor for organization. As the teacher walks back to the front of the room to sum up, the very return to the front of the room, to the beginning point, suggests a completion, a completed square, circle, or other shape. These movements are intentional. They can be planned in advance or they can be used spontaneously. Either way, they are intentional—not random pacing.

11. Students who hear their names are usually alerted to listen to what is being said. Thus many teachers purposefully interject the names of individual students into their lectures. For example, during a lecture in a Spanish class, a teacher might say, "Suppose George wanted to tell Louise that her hair had just caught on fire. He could begin by . . ."

12. To be engaged in lectures, students need to do more than just passively sit and listen. They need to listen actively, trying to follow the teacher's thought patterns. Mr. Dwyer realized this, so he appeared to be thinking and reasoning aloud. Teachers can facilitate engagement by verbally walking students through cognitive processes that lead to information and answers. Such an approach is akin to the spirit of the problem-solving learning activities.

13. As teachers lecture, they should frequently monitor their students' comprehension of what is being said. Planned breaks, in which students are asked questions, may provide the teacher with formative evaluation information that can guide subsequent stages of the lecture.

14. Sometimes, students become disengaged during a lecture because the teacher uses an unfamiliar word, expression, formula, or symbol. The teacher continues, assuming the students understand; the students are no longer listening to what the teacher is saying because they are busy trying to figure out what they don't understand. Teachers should be aware of the prerequisite knowledge and skills needed to follow a lecture and should teach those prerequisites before giving the lecture.

IDEAS FOR COOPERATIVE LEARNING SESSIONS

Students Learning from One Another

For some learning activities, it may be more efficient for you to organize your class into several subgroups rather than into a single large group. Intraclass grouping arrangements in which students in each group work on a common task provide greater opportunities than whole class activities for students to interact with one another, for tasks to be tailored to special interests or needs, and for a wide variety of tasks to be addressed during class.

Cooperative learning activities in which students learn from one another have proven to be quite successful (Augustine, Gruber, & Hanson, 1990, Lyman & Foyle, 1990; Slavin, 1991a, 1991b; Voorhies, 1989). Students can engage in cooperative learning activities in large group settings, but small task-group sessions are particularly well suited for students teaching one another. A variety of task-group patterns are commonly used to facilitate cooperative learning. (1) In peer instruction groups, one student teaches others, either presenting a brief lesson, tutoring, or providing help with a particular exercise. (2) In practice groups, students review, drill, and provide one another with feedback as part of a knowledge-level or skill-level lesson. (3) Interest or achievement-level groups are organized around interests (as in Vignette 6.5), achievement levels, or combinations of the two (as in Vignette 6.7). In problem-solving groups, students use a team approach to undertake projects or formulate solutions (as in Vignette 6.6).

Guidance and Structure
for Maintaining Engagement

Research studies examining how students spend their time in classrooms indicate that students tend to have poor engagement levels in small group learning activities unless the teacher is actively involved in the session (Fisher, Berliner, Filby, Marliave, Cahen, & Dishaw, 1980). But a teacher cannot be in the middle of several groups at once and oftentimes subgroups fail to address their tasks due to a lack of guidance. Consider Vignette 6.15.

VIGNETTE 6.15

As part of a science lesson for her 24 fourth graders, Ms. Keene demonstrates the property of density by adding oil and then maple syrup to a container of water. She then organized her students into four groups of six to discuss why the syrup settles below the water while the oil floated on the water's surface.

After six minutes, the students in one group discontinue their discussion and begin to socialize with one another. Ms. Keene, who is working with another group, hardly notices that they're off-task. A third group becomes quite noisy, and Ms. Keene raises her voice from her position with the second group and announces: "Better keep it down in here. You won't discover a very important property of matter unless you keep your discussion on-task." In the fourth group, Terri dominates the first five minutes, explaining to the others why heavier substances sink. She stimulates Shirley's interest and the two of them engage in a conversation about the demonstration. The other four members of the group are doing things unrelated to the lesson's topic.

VIGNETTE 6.15 (continued)

After managing to get the second group on track, Ms. Keene moves to the noisy third group, saying: "You people aren't following directions; you're supposed to be discussing your observations of the experiment." She then tells the group about the property of density, a concept she intended for them to discover by themselves.

After spending four minutes with the second group, Ms. Keene calls a halt to the activity and announces: "Okay, class, let's rearrange our desks back. . . . Now that you understand the idea of density, I want to show you how to . . ."

Ms. Keene failed to initiate student engagement because her directions did not spell out the tasks each group was to address and just how to go about completing the task. Contrast her strategies to those of Ms. Hensler in Vignette 6.16.

VIGNETTE 6.16

Ms. Hensler is in the midst of a science unit with her fourth graders. Convinced that the students have adequately achieved objectives involving weight, mass, and volume, she introduces the concept of density (without using the word "density") by displaying two identical sealed cardboard boxes, each with dimensions 60 cm × 37 cm × 30 cm. Unknown to the students, Ms. Hensler has tightly packed one box with a neat stack of newspapers. The other box is filled with loosely crumpled balls of newspaper.

Students examine the two boxes without touching them, agreeing that the boxes appear to have the same capacity. Ms. Hensler announces that both boxes are filled from top-to-bottom and from side-to-side with newspapers. After instructing them on how to carefully lift heavy objects (back straight, knees bent), she directs students to lift one box and then the other. They agree that one is much heavier than the other, but they don't understand why.

The following day, as students enter the room, Ms. Hensler hands each a blue, green, orange, or pink card with directions to go directly to the work station matching the color on the card. (Her strategy for getting students organized into small task-groups is similar to that employed by Mr. Jukola in Vignette 3.11.) Each card also spells out the role of the student in the group. (1) The "chairperson" is responsible for conducting the group's activities and reminding group members to stay on task. (2) The "communicator of directions" reads the directions for completing the task to the group and answers questions regarding what to do. (3) The "custodian of materials" cares for, distributes, and collects the materials Ms. Hensler has made available at the work station. (4) The "reporter" writes up the group's activities and finalizes the report to be presented to the rest of the class. (5 & 6) Two "workers" actually carry out the physical aspects of the assigned task.

Ms. Hensler has arranged the work stations so that each group of six students is able to perform its individual task out of sight of the other three.

The Blue Group is provided with two identical boxes, 100 soft rubber balls, a roll of packaging tape, and a scale for weighing the boxes. Each member of the group is assigned a specific role. As directed, they completely fill one box with 25 balls and cram the remaining 75 balls into the second box, squeezing the balls nearly flat to fit. The students are motivated to keep their voices low because Ms. Hensler's directions indicate that their activities are to be kept secret from the other three groups in the room. They seal and weigh both boxes. The "reporter" records the procedures and results of the experiment in a written report.

The Green Group operates similarly, except one box is one-third the size of the other and students are directed to completely fill both boxes with the same number of balls, thus having to cram them into the smaller box. Both boxes are sealed and weighed and a brief report written.

The Orange Group operates much like the Blue Group, but instead of filling boxes with balls, they fill two garbage bags of equal capacity, one with empty round aluminum cans, the other with flattened aluminum cans. The bags are sealed.

The Pink Group operated much like the Green Group, but fills one large garbage bag with unaltered aluminum cans and one small garbage bag with the same number of flattened aluminum cans. The bags are sealed.

As the groups work, Ms. Hensler moves about the room occasionally prompting chairpersons to remind group members to stick to their roles, but never allowing herself to become part of the group. For example, as she passes by the Orange Group, Zach asks: "Ms. Hensler, how many of the cans are we supposed to stuff in here. Ms. Hensler, turns to Sara who's chairing the group, and says: "You'd better have your communicator of directions make a decision on Zach's questions."

Later, after moving to a large group arrangement, the products of each group's experiment are examined (without unsealing the containers) by the other three groups. Ms. Hensler then conducts an inductive questioning session in which students make conjectures about what the groups did to create the observed phenomena (two objects with equal volume, but different mass). Using probing questions, Ms. Hensler leads students to discover the concept of density. No one uses the word "density," but the students agree to name the idea "squishiness." The students formulate a definition of "squishiness" in terms of volume and mass. They apply their newly formulated concept to explain the mystery of the two boxes they worked with the previous day.

Ten Points about Cooperative Learning Sessions

Consider the following when designing cooperative learning sessions.

1. Expect the sort of off-task behaviors Ms. Keene's students exhibited in Vignette 6.15 unless you clearly define not only tasks for each group, but also the individual responsibilities of each group member.
2. As in Vignette 6.16, all group members should be jointly accountable for completing the shared task, with each member responsible for fulfilling an individual role.
3. Efficient routine procedures for making transitions into and out of small group activities, such as Mr. Jukola's in Vignette 3.11, Ms. Morrison's in Vignette 3.15, and Ms. Williams' flag-raising routine in Vignette 5.5, avoid the time-wasting chaos following a direction such as: "Let's move our desks so that we have four groups of five or six each."

4. Tasksheets and advanced organizers such as Ms. Hensler's in Vignette 6.16, direct students' focus and provide them with an overall picture of what they are expected to accomplish in their groups.
5. To avoid interrupting cooperative group work to clarify directions the whole class should hear, specify the task and directions for everyone before attentions are turned to individual group activities.
6. Monitor groups' activities, providing guidance as needed without usurping individual students' responsibilities for designated tasks. In Vignette 6.16, Ms. Hensler moved from one group to another, cuing students on-task without actually becoming a member of any one group.
7. Model active listening techniques. Students do not automatically know how to listen to one another without you showing them. From classes they take with teachers other than you, they may have acquired the misperception that anything of academic importance (i.e., will be on the test) is said by teachers, not peers. Thus you should demonstrate that you intently listen to them and make use of what they say. Vignette 6.17 is an example.
8. Use formative feedback to regulate activities. Engaged behaviors during cooperative task-group sessions are observable. Thus, formative feedback for regulating the activities is relatively easy to obtain.
9. Closure points are needed for lengthy sessions. As with other types of sessions, students need to experience climactic moments to positively reinforce engagement. Having a sequence of subtasks rather than simply one overall task facilitates this need if you provide students feedback as they complete the subtasks.
10. Individual group work should be followed up and utilized during subsequent learning activities. In Vignette 6.16, Ms. Hensler brought together the products of the four groups to induct a concept in the follow-up activity with the whole class.

VIGNETTE 6.17

As he monitors a cooperative learning activity in which his marketing education class is organized into five task-groups, Mr. Lau-Chou stops and sits in with one group as they struggle with one of the questions from a tasksheet. As Malinda is commenting, Horace attempts to engage Mr. Lau-Chou with his own private question: "Mr. Lau-Chou, this doesn't make . . ." But Mr. Lau-Chou uses a frown and a hand motion to cue Horace to be quiet, and then says to the group: "Excuse me, Malinda, would you repeat that last part about adding the two prices? I missed what you said about that." Malinda repeats and finishes her comment. Mr. Lau-Chou says: "Thank you. That should shed some light on Horace's concern. Horace raise your concern with the group." Horace: "To me, the question ought to be . . ." Later, in the large group session, Mr. Lau-Chou plays off different comments students made in their groups.

IDEAS FOR DISCUSSION SESSIONS

Student Engagement during Discussions

The success of cooperative learning strategies typically depends on students focusing on a particular topic during discussion sessions. For students to be engaged in a discussion-type learning activity, they must attentively listen to what classmates say and be willing to make comments and raise questions pertinent to the topic. Discussion can be conducted in small intraclass groups or in large group meetings of a whole class. Vignette 6.18 provides examples of both.

VIGNETTE 6.18

To help her 26 third graders develop both their skills and interest in reading, Ms. Torres directs the class to silently read a three-line story entitled "Making Things" from page 97 of one of their readers. In 35 seconds, everyone is finished and Ms. Torres begins a brief questioning session that leads into a large group discussion.

    Ms. Torres stands in front of the class holding her copy of the reader open to page 97 in one hand and her bookmark high over her head with her other hand. Ms. Torres: "Please put your bookmark on page 97, close your book, and keep it on your desk." She demonstratively follows her own directions with her copy of the reader she watches the class do the same. Ms. Torres: "I would like everyone to think about the answer to the question I'm about to ask. What was the reading about?" Most of the students raise their hands. Ms. Torres recognizes Gail who says: "Making things." Ms. Torres moves about the room as she asks: "What did Gail say? Doris."

> DORIS: She said, "making things."
> MS. TORRES: Why would anyone want to make things? Jamal.
> JAMAL: It's fun.
> MS. TORRES: Todd?
> TODD: You don't have to pay for them.
> MS. TORRES: Put your hand up if you never, ever like to make anything.

No hands are raised. Ms. Torres: "It looks like we agree that we sometimes like to make things. We are about to have a discussion on making surprises for other people. Who remembers what we do when we have a class discussion?" About half the class raise hands.

> MS. TORRES says: First we'll hear from Veda, then Morris, and Simon.
> VEDA: Only one talks at a time.
> MORRIS: You hafta raise your hand to talk.

There's a pause, so Ms. Torres motions to Simon who says: "That's what I was going to say."

> MS. TORRES: Tell me, who calls on people who raise their hands to talk? Jessie.
> JESSIE: The last one that talked.

VIGNETTE 6.18 (continued)

MS. TORRES: Thank you. Remember in a discussion, I don't call on you. Whoever has the floor calls on the next person to speak.

Ms. Torres: "Let's talk about making things, but not just anything. Let's talk about making things to surprise other people with things they like. We'll begin the discussion with Marvell. Marvell, you have the floor to start the discussion on making surprises for others to enjoy." Fourteen students eagerly raise their hands beckoning Marvell to call on them. Marvell: "I like to make drawings and surprise my Momma. She hangs them up on the wall. Okay, Lydia." Lydia, who is seated near Ms. Torres, begins speaking directly to her: "My brother lost the pick for his guitar, so I cut out a piece of this stuff and wrapped it up in a box for him." As Lydia speaks, Ms. Torres moves across the room so that most of the other students are positioned between her and Lydia. This encourages Lydia to project her voice and speak to the class rather than to just Ms. Torres. The discussion continues for 12 minutes, with Ms. Torres continually moving about the classroom, occasionally motioning students to speak up and politely reminding them of the topic.

After the discussion, students take turns reading aloud from a three-page story entitled "Surprise Pancakes." Ms. Torres then divides the class into four groups. Each group is assigned a section of the room in which they are to meet, sitting on the floor in a circle. After all four groups are in place, Ms. Torres says to all of the groups at once, using body language and gestures to help students understand her directions: "Austin, you are the discussion leader for this group. Veda, you're the leader there. Marvell, here. Zeke, there. Your group is to think of five things we could make to bring home as surprises for your parents. The surprises have to be something that we could all make here at school. You have nine minutes to decide and we've already used four seconds."

Ms. Torres moves from one group to another. Stopping to listen to the discussion in Veda's group, Jo asks her: "Is it okay if we cook something, like the kids did in the story?" Ms. Torres: "What do the rest of you think about cooking something?" Veda: "I didn't think we could, but . . ." Seeing that Veda's group is again talking to one another, Ms. Torres quickly moves to Austin's group where Mary Jo and Freda are involved in a private conversation about cats. The other five appear to be on-task. Ms. Torres: "What are you thinking about making?" Austin answers, as Mary Jo and Freda continue their conversation: "Greg thinks we should make up a song." Zane: "That's stupid!" Ms. Torres: "Freda, what do you think about us making up a song?" Freda: "What?" Ms. Torres: "Explain your idea to Freda one more time, Greg." Ms. Torres sees that everyone in the group is now listening to Greg, so she moves over to another group.

After nine minutes, the alarm of the chronograph on Ms. Torres' wrist rings and she says: "Time's up. Just stay where you are and we'll have each group give us its list. She positions herself by a chalkboard and makes a list of the 16 items as they are told to her. Only one group has exactly five suggestions; the others have one, three, and seven respectively. Several suggestions appear in the list more than once. Ms. Torres: "I will leave this list on the board until tomorrow when we decide which ones to make as surprises for your parents. Right now, I would like for you to return to your places and open your readers to page 101." Once the students are in their places with their books open and ready to listen, Ms. Torres says: "What is the name of the story beginning on page 101? Barton.'' Barton reads: ''Things to Make at School.'' Ms. Torres: ''Thank you. Class, I want you to take this reader home tonight and read 'Things to Make at School.' We will discuss it tomorrow before we decide which things from our list we will make.''

Six Points about Discussion Sessions

Keep these thoughts in mind when planning discussion sessions.

1. Efficient use of time in a discussion session partially depends on how clearly the directions communicate the exact procedures to be followed. If a teacher consistently follows the same procedures for all discussions, students learn from repeated experiences to automatically follow those procedures without elaborate directions. For the first few discussion sessions with her class, Ms. Torres needed to spend time directly teaching her procedure for speaking to the group; now only occasional reminders are necessary.

2. Student talk is likely to stray from the topic unless that topic is specified and the purpose of the discussion is understood. Ms. Torres led into the large group discussion with a questioning session in which she controlled the subject about which students talked. She had her students thinking about ''making things'' before she began the discussion that was to specifically deal with ''making things to surprise someone.'' The small discussion groups were directed to complete a specific task.

3. The focus of a discussion is more likely to be maintained when students perceive that the discussion is purposeful. The purposefulness of discussions can be appreciated by students when the teacher uses lead-in activities to set the stage for the discussion and outcomes of the discussion are used in activities subsequent to the discussion. The readings and the questioning session had Ms. Torres' students focusing on the topic prior to the discussion. She used the list produced during discussions the following day.

4. Students have a tendency to direct their comments to the teacher. Seating arrangements in which students face one another and the teacher is not a focal point encourage students to speak and listen to one another. During the large group discussion, Ms. Torres moved about so that most of the class was between her and whoever had the floor at the time.

5. With only a minimal disruption to discussion, teachers can silently use hand signals to remind individuals to attend to a speaker or to motion a speaker to direct comments to the group, speak up, or slow down.

6. By using the comment of one student to involve another, teachers model active listening behavior while encouraging participation. Ms. Torres, for example, asked Freda about Greg's idea.

IDEAS FOR QUESTIONING SESSIONS

Student Engagement during Questioning Sessions

For students to be engaged in a questioning-type learning activity, they must attentively listen to each question asked by their teacher, attempt to formulate answers to that question, and either express their answers in a manner prescribed by the teacher or listen to others express their answers. Recitation is one type of questioning session which teachers use to help students memorize. Vignette 6.19 is an example.

Generally more interesting and helpful to students than recitations are higher-level questioning sessions that are designed to stimulate students to think, discover, and reason. Vignette 6.20 is an example.

VIGNETTE 6.19

Ms. Caldaron asks her fourth graders: "What is the capital of Mississippi? Eva." Eva: "Jackson." Ms. Caldaron: "What is the capital of Louisiana? Vincent." Vincent: "New Orleans." A number of students raise their hands and Ms. Caldaron calls on Rosalie who says: "Baton Rouge." Ms. Caldaron: "That is correct, Baton Rouge is the capital of Louisiana. Now, what about the capital of . . ."

VIGNETTE 6.20

Mr. Becnel is conducting a high-level questioning session for the purpose of helping his 28 eighth graders understand how writers use facts to support their opinions. He displays an overhead transparency listing eight statements taken from a magazine article the class has just read. The list, as it appears on the transparency, is given in Figure 6.3.

Mr. Becnel to the class: "The eight statements on the screen are from the reading. Each is marked with either an O or an X. Can anyone tell me why the X statements belong together and why the O statements belong together? How are the X statements like each other, but different from the O statements?" Jamal, Tracy, and Sidney eagerly have their hands up; they raised them even before Mr. Becnel had completed his questions. Without pausing after his questions, Mr. Becnel calls on Sidney. Sidney: "The ones with the Xs have numbers in them." "No, no!" cries Jamal. Tracy is waving her hand trying to get Mr. Becnel's attention as three other students raise their hands. Mr. Becnel: "Easy, Jamal. Let's give Sidney a chance. Does the fourth one have a number in it?" Sidney: "No." Mr. Becnel: "But, is it an X statement?" Sidney: "Yes." Mr. Becnel: "Then what can you conclude?" Sidney: "My idea's not right." Mr. Becnel: "I agree that you've managed to disprove your hypothesis. Jamal?" Jamal: "The ones with the Os are things that everyone doesn't agree on." Mr. Becnel: "What do you mean? Give us an example." Jamal: "My aunt doesn't think fishing is exciting. She

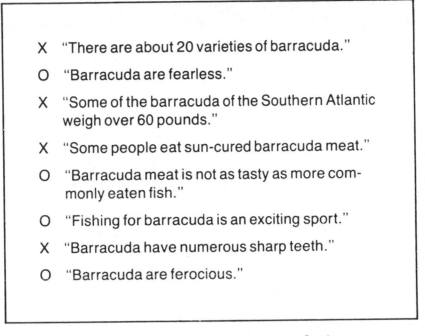

X   "There are about 20 varieties of barracuda."

O   "Barracuda are fearless."

X   "Some of the barracuda of the Southern Atlantic weigh over 60 pounds."

X   "Some people eat sun-cured barracuda meat."

O   "Barracuda meat is not as tasty as more commonly eaten fish."

O   "Fishing for barracuda is an exciting sport."

X   "Barracuda have numerous sharp teeth."

O   "Barracuda are ferocious."

FIGURE 6.3 List of Statetments Used in Questioning Sessions Conducted by Mr. Becnel, Mr. Mongar, Ms. Kranz, and Ms. Dzildahl

hates fishing. And who knows if barracuda are fearless. Did anyone ever ask a barracuda?'' Mr. Becnel: ''Can't the same thing be said for the *X* statements?'' Sidney: ''No, because each of the *X* ones we can know for sure.'' Mr. Becnel: ''For example?'' Sidney: ''You can weigh a barracuda and count his teeth.'' Murray: ''Not me! I'm not gonna count no monster's teeth!'' Laughter erupts in the class. Mr. Becnel: ''Barracuda are monsters. Is that an *X* statement or an *O* statement? Okay, Jamal.'' Jamal: ''That's an *O* statement, because that's just what Murray thinks. Some people may think they're pretty.'' Mr. Becnel: ''Statements of what some people think, but that can't be determined as true or false, are statements of what? What is the word for ideas we don't all agree to—for all the *O* statements?'' Tracy: ''Opinions! *O* for opinions.'' Mr. Becnel: ''Are all the *O*s statements of opinion?'' Jamal: ''Yes.'' Sidney: ''What do the *X*'s stand for?'' Mr. Becnel to Sidney: ''Think of a word for something we know to be true. It doesn't begin with *X*, but it fits all the *X* statements.'' Sidney: ''Theories?'' Tracy and Jamal raise their hands. Mr. Becnel: ''But do we know all theories to be true?'' Tracy: ''Facts.'' Mr. Becnel: ''Who agrees with Tracy?'' Sidney, Jamal, and two others raise their hands. Mr. Becnel: ''I agree also. All of the *X* statements are called what?'' Jamal: ''Facts.''

As the questioning session continues, the relation between the author's use of facts and opinions is discovered by a number of Mr. Becnel's 28 students.

What did you think of Mr. Becnel's use of questioning or Socratic methods for stimulating students to reason? The session was probably very valuable to Jamal, Sidney, and Tracy. However, what about the other 25 students; what did they learn? Mr. Becnel seemed to know how to effectively utilize questioning strategies, but only a relatively small portion of his class seemed involved. For high-level questioning sessions to be effective for all students, each student must attempt to answer the questions posed by the teacher. It is unnecessary for all students to express their answers to the teachers, but they should at least attempt to formulate answers in their minds. Because Mr. Becnel called on Sidney immediately after asking his first set of questions, most students did not have enough time to even try to answer the questions. They quit thinking of their own answers to hear Sidney's answer and the ensuing discussion.

Mr. Becnel, like most teachers, did not allow enough time to elapse before accepting a student response. The average time teachers, as a group, wait for students to respond to their in-class questions is less than two seconds (Arnold, Atwood, & Rogers, 1974; Doenau, 1987). After experiencing a few sessions like Mr. Becnel's, in which they are asked questions that they don't have the opportunity to answer, most students learn to not even attempt to formulate their own responses. Some will politely listen to the responses of the few; others entertain themselves with off-task thoughts; and others, if allowed, entertain themselves with disruptive behaviors.

Mr. Becnel should not discard Socratic methods. High-level questioning sessions are the only type of learning activities for helping students achieve certain types of learning objectives (Cangelosi, 1992a, pp. 68–115). What Mr. Becnel should do is reorganize his questioning sessions and apply techniques that lead all students to address all questions raised. Such techniques are demonstrated in Vignettes 6.21, 6.22, and 6.23.

VIGNETTE 6.21

Mr. Mongar is conducting a high-level questioning session for the purpose of helping his 28 eighth graders understand how writers use facts to support their opinions. He displays an overhead transparency listing eight statements taken from a magazine article the class has just read. The list, as it appears on the transparency, is given in Figure 6.3.

Mr. Mongar says: "I am going to ask you some questions, but I don't want anyone to answer aloud until I call on someone. Answer each question in your mind. Here are the first two questions. How do you think the X statements are alike, but different from the O statements? How are the Os alike but different from the Xs?"

Two students eagerly raise their hands and say: "Oh, Mr. Mongar!" Mr. Mongar is tempted to call on them and positively reinforce their enthusiasm, but he resists and they sit quietly after seeing his stern look and gesture. He waits, watching the students' faces. Finally, he says: "Tom do you have an answer?" Tom nods.

MR. MONGAR: Good! How about you, Linda?
LINDA: Yes.
MR. MONGAR: Fine. Are your ready, Thelma?
THELMA: No, I don't know.
MR. MONGAR: I'd like you to just think aloud. What are your thoughts about how the X statements and O statements are different.

THELMA: I don't see any difference; they're all about barracuda.

MR. MONGAR: That's an important similarity among all the statements. Now, I'd like some volunteers to share their answers with us. Okay, Rita.

RITA: Well, it seems to me that . . .

VIGNETTE 6.22

Ms. Kranz is helping her 26 eighth graders understand how writers use facts to support their opinions. She distributes to each student a list of eight statements taken from a magazine article the class has just read. The list, as it appears on the handout, is given in Figure 6.3.

Ms. Kranz: "At the bottom of the handout you just received, each of you is to write one paragraph describing why you think the X statements go together and why the O statements go together. How are the Xs alike, but different from the Os? How are the Os alike, but different from the Xs?" As the students think and write out answers, Ms. Kranz moves about the room, reading what students write from over their shoulders. Some students write nothing until Ms. Kranz comes by their desk and silently motions for them to write. After noticing that everyone has written something, she asks: "Would you please read to us what you wrote, Pete?" Pete reads: "The ones with the Xs are more specific. The other ones, with the Os, are general."

MS. KRANZ: Judy, please read yours.

JUDY: I don't think this is right, I wasn't . . .

Ms. Kranz interrupts and says: "I would appreciate you just reading exactly what you wrote."

JUDY: The O statements are more critical of barracuda than the other ones are. The X statements are more straight-forward.

MS. KRANZ: Crystal, I'd like you to compare what Pete read to what Judy read. Is there anything about Judy's answer that is similar to Pete's?

CRYSTAL: It seems that . . .

After discussing her first set of questions, Ms. Kranz raises follow-up questions and again has the students silently write out answers. Because she reads some responses as she circulates around the room, she can select the responses to be read that will better stimulate discussion and help make points she wants made.

VIGNETTE 6.23

After subdividing her class of eighth graders into five cooperative groups of five or six each, Ms. Dzildahl distributes to each group a list of eight statements (see Figure 6.3) taken from a magazine article the class has just read. She directs each group to decide on the differences and similarities between the X and O statements and gives them 11 minutes to prepare and present their decisions to the rest of the class. Ms. Dzildahl moves from one group to the other and monitors them as they work.

Six Points about Questioning Sessions

Here are some thoughts to keep in mind when designing questioning sessions.

1. Provide for periods of silent thinking during high-level questioning sessions. Unlike recitation sessions, student engagement during high-level questioning sessions requires students to take time to ponder and think about questions posed by teachers before expressing answers.

2. Have all students write out their responses to your questions. This technique has at least four advantages over only having students who are called on express answers. (a) Students have to organize their thoughts to write out answers, thus, providing an additional learning experience. (b) Allowing time for students to write serves as a silent period for all students to be thinking about how to respond to questions. (c) Written responses makes it possible for teachers to preview students' answers and decide which ones should be read to the class. (d) Having written responses available to read to the class avoids some of the stammering and grasping for words that are typical of students answering aloud in front of their peers.

3. Avoid directing a question to a particular student before articulating the question. The teachers in Vignettes 6.20–6.23 posed most of their questions before designating someone to answer aloud. None of them, for example, phrased questions like: "Johnny, is this an *X* or an *O* statement?" If they had, students other than Johnny may not have bothered to listen to the question.

4. Teachers need to move quickly from one student to another so that as many students as possible express answers aloud. However, with high-level questions, some students' answers are complex and need to be discussed in some detail; answers are not simply right or wrong. To involve more students, maintain a single focus, and yet have some particular answers fully discussed, teachers should use the responses of some students to formulate subsequent questions for other students. Mr. Becnel applied this technique by using Murray's characterization of barracuda as "monsters" in his next question for the class. Ms. Kranz asked Crystal to compare Pete's response to Judy's.

5. Students are more likely to engage in questioning sessions in which: (a) questions relate to one another and focus on a central theme or problem rather than appear isolated and unrelated; (b) questions are specific rather than vague. The teacher-raised questions in Vignettes 6.20–6.23 focused on the relation between facts and opinions as used in a particular selection that all students had read. Vague questions, such as, "Do you understand?" hardly focus thought as well as, "Is the statement 'Barracuda are monsters' an *X* or an *O* statement?"

6. Learning activities conducted prior to questioning sessions can serve to maintain the focus of the questioning session. Also, students learn the importance of engaging in questioning sessions when the sessions culminate in problem resolutions that are applied in subsequent learning

activities. In Vignettes 6.20–6.23, the reading of the passage on barracuda set the stage for the questions. What students discover about how the author supported opinions with facts should be used in follow-up assignments. Subsequent activities might include (a) an assignment in which students read a new passage and analyze it, pointing out where the author supported opinions with facts; (b) an assignment in which students are directed to write an opinion piece in which they use facts to support their positions.

IDEAS FOR INDEPENDENT WORK SESSIONS

Student Engagement during Independent Work Sessions

Engagement in an independent work session requires a student to complete some assigned task without disturbing others also working on the task. Typically, students work individually with the teacher available for help (e.g., Vignette 5.5 in which Ms. Williams introduced the "flag raising" procedure for independent work sessions). When you plan for such sessions, two potential problems should be taken into account: (1) How can you efficiently provide the individual help that students may need to remain engaged with the task? (2) How do you accommodate students' completing the task at differing times?

The first problem was experienced by Mr. Dupont-Lee in Vignette 2.12. The second led to the disruption of Mr. Uter's learning activity in Vignette 3.21. Ms. Evans solved these problems for the independent work session of Vignette 6.24.

VIGNETTE 6.24

Ms. Evans distributes a tasksheet with the following directions to each of the 34 students in her Spanish I class.

1. Please take out your translation notebook, pencil, textbook, and Spanish-English dictionary.
2. Translate into English each of the six sentences under the heading "A orillas del lago" on page 63 of your test. Use these five steps.
   (a) Look at the entire sentence. Lightly circle, with your pencil, each word whose meaning you don't remember.
   (b) Look up the meaning of each circled word in your dictionary and write down the "short" meaning in your notebook.
   (c) Locate the verb in the sentence. Determine the tense of the verb. If you need help, turn to page 39 and follow the directions for "Verb Tenses."
   (d) Write a literal, word-by-word translation of the sentence in your notebook.
   (e) Write an interpretative translation of the sentence right under the literal one in your notebook.

VIGNETTE 6.24 (continued)

3. In 17 minutes we will go over the translations of the six sentences.
4. If you finish the six sentences before 17 minutes are up, please begin your homework assignment which appears in the usual place on the whiteboard.

Ms. Evans reads through the directions with the students, and the students begin the task at their desks. Soon several students raise their hands. Ms. Evans walks over to Brad who tells her: "I can't do these." Ms. Evans notices that Brad has all of his materials out with the text and notebook open to the appropriate pages, but that he has neither circled any words nor written anything down. She says: "I'll be back to see what you've done in 70 seconds. In the meantime, do this." She points to Line 2a on his copy of the directions. Ms. Evans goes over to Anna Mae who says: "What's 'lugar' mean?" Ms. Evans says nothing, but points to the words 'Lightly circle, with your pencil, each word that you don't remember' in Line 2a of the directions. As Anna Mae circles 'lugar,' Ms. Evans picks up Anna Mae's dictionary, hands it to her, and moves to another student.

Four Points about Independent Work Sessions

By keeping the following thoughts in mind, you may improve the chances that your students enjoy high levels of engagement during the independent work sessions that you plan and conduct.

1. Clearly define the task. In this way you will avoid many of the nagging questions about what to do and requests for reiterating directions that can be observed in many classrooms during independent work sessions. Ms. Evans' extra effort to specify her directions beforehand, prevented her from wasting allocated time repeating or clarifying directions.

2. To efficiently provide real help (Jones, 1979) so that all students can remain engaged in an independent work session, avoid spending too much time with any one student. For students with adequate reading skills, having the steps in writing allows the teacher to quickly refer students to what they need to do to help themselves. Ms. Evans used this technique and avoided lengthy exchanges with students. For students who cannot read (e.g., some kindergartners), tasks for independent sessions should be kept extremely simple. If there are, for example, three steps in the completion of a task, the teacher might consider conducting three separate brief independent work sessions, devoting a session to each step.

3. To avoid having finished students idly waiting for others to complete the task, sequence independent work sessions so that they are followed by other independent activities with flexible beginning and ending times. The homework assignment Ms. Evans directed her students to begin after they translated the sentences could easily be interrupted when class is ready to go over the translations.

4. Establish some sort of formal routine for requesting help. This mini-
   mizes the time students spend waiting and maximizes the time they have
   for working on the task. Ms. Williams's "flag raising" procedure in
   Vignette 5.5 is an example of such a formal routine.

IDEAS FOR HOMEWORK ASSIGNMENTS

Student Engagement in Homework

Unlike most other types of learning activities, students typically must allocate
their own time for engaging in homework assignments. Some students may even
have parents nearby encouraging them to be on-task. However, parental supervision varies according to circumstances in the home, the ages of the students,
and a myriad of other factors (Cangelosi, 1992a, p.20–22). Engagement in a
homework assignment usually requires students to (1) understand the directions
for the assignment, (2) schedule time away from school for the assignment, (3)
resist out-of-school distractions while completing the assigned task, (4) deliver
the completed work by a specified deadline.

Many teachers find it so difficult to have students diligently complete homework assignments, that they have given up and no longer expect students to do
homework. But for most academic subjects, homework is a critical form of
learning activity that provides students with needed opportunities for solitary
thinking, studying, practicing, and problem solving. The crowded social setting
of a classroom is not very conducive to the type of concentrated, undisturbed
thinking in which individuals must engage to achieve certain cognitive learning
objectives (e.g., being creative or analytical). To teach your students to complete
the homework you assign, you must make sure that engagement in this relatively
unsupervised type of learning activity is positively reinforced. In Vignettes 6.25
and 6.27, Mr. Davis and Ms. Salsevon try both contrived positive reinforcement
and contrived punishment to extrinsically motivate students to do homework.
Ms. Hanzlik and Mr. Sampson, in Vignettes 6.26 and 6.28, utilize intrinsic motivation because the positive reinforcers for doing homework and the punishment
for not doing it are naturally occurring.

VIGNETTE 6.25

Mr. Davis directs his 28 third graders to complete 25 multiplication exercises in their
mathematics workbook for homework. The next day, he collects the workbooks
and returns them, having placed a smiling-face sticker on the homework of each
student who had at least 20 correct answers. Four students who did not even attempt
to exercise are verbally reprimanded in front of the class.

VIGNETTE 6.26

Ms. Hanzlik carefully examines the 25 multiplication computations from Exercise 8-6 of her third graders mathematics workbooks. For their homework, she selects the 12 computational exercises from the 25 she thinks will provide her students with practice in each of the possible problem areas typically encountered by students attempting this particular computational process. The next day she collects the work and does a quick error pattern analysis (Ashlock, 1990). The papers are returned to the students with a clear indication of the steps they did correctly and the steps they did incorrectly. Because she had carefully selected the computations, she is able to provide more helpful feedback with fewer computations that she would have on all 25 computations or on randomly assigned ones.

While the rest of the students are going over her error pattern analysis, correcting their mistakes, and beginning another assignment, Ms. Hanzlik calls the four students, Tim, Gail, Mary Jo, and Phil, who did not complete the assignment aside to speak with them. Ms. Hanzlik: "I'm sorry you didn't give me the opportunity to help you learn how to do this kind of multiplication." Phil: "I would've done it, but . . ." Ms. Hanzlik interrupts saying: "It doesn't make any difference why you didn't do it. Let's just figure out when you can get this done so I can analyze it and get it back to you before you leave school today. I need to do that for you before you can continue to learn math." Gail: "I forgot . . ." Ms. Hanzlik: "Please, just let me think about how I can help you . . . I know! Here's what we'll do. I'll let you do those 12 exercises right after lunch today. That's when the rest of the class will be baking pumpkin bread. You can finish it then, and I'll go over it right after school and get it back to you just in time for you to catch your buses."

VIGNETTE 6.27

As part of a unit on writing library papers, Ms. Salsevon directs her eighth grade English students to each choose a topic, find at least four references from the library on that topic, develop an outline for writing a report on the topic, and write an essay of five to eight pages following the outline. The assignment is due in two weeks and, in the meantime, procedures for using the library, using references, outlining, and writing essays will be explained in class. The students are told that 40 percent of their grade for the unit will be based on whether or not this homework assignment is turned in on time. The other part of the grade will be from the exam to be given at the end of the unit.

VIGNETTE 6.28

As part of a unit on writing library papers, Mr. Sampson provides his 26 eighth grade English students with a list of topics and assigns the following homework: "Examine the list of topics. Pick three topics that interest you more than the others. For each of the three, write one paragraph explaining why that topic is more interesting to you than some of the others. Bring your paragraphs to class tomorrow.''

The next day, Mr. Sampson has his students name the three topics they wrote about and read their favorite paragraphs to the class. The nine students who do not have the assignment completed exactly as directed are not asked to read. After the last of 17 students read, Mr. Sampson collects the papers and makes the following announcement: "Based on what you read to the class and what I read in these papers, I will assign each of you a topic for a project to be completed in the next two weeks."

The next day, Mr. Sampson assigns topics. Students who had followed Mr. Sampson's directions with the previous homework assignment are given the popular, favored topics for their projects. Those who did not write paragraphs expressing their preferences are assigned the leftover topics. Mr. Sampson announces to the class: "For homework, go to the library and find four references about your topic. Write the title of each reference, its author, and one sentence on what the reference is about. Bring your list to class tomorrow." Six students raise their hands. Mr. Sampson calls on Allison. Allison: "What's a reference?" Mr. Sampson: "I'm glad you asked that! What did you want to say, Jessie?" Jessie: "I don't know what we're supposed to do." Mr. Sampson: "Allison doesn't know what a reference is and Jessie doesn't know what to do for homework because I haven't explained these things to you yet. We're going to spend the rest of today's class explaining just how to do tonight's homework assignment." The rest of the day's English period is devoted to learning activities on how to find and report on references in the library.

The next day, the learning activities focus on the lists of library references that the students bring to class. Some time is spent in explaining how to develop outlines for writing library papers. The homework assignment for the next day involves refining the reference lists and developing the first drafts of the outlines. This inextricable association between homework assignments and in-class learning activities continues throughout the unit until writing the final draft of the library paper is assigned for homework.

Students' grades for the unit are determined strictly by their performances on the in-class examination given at the end of the unit. However, items on the exam require students to refer to how they used library references for their project, to refer to their outlines, to refer to their final library paper, and to attach a copy of both their outlines and the library paper to their exam.

Eight Points about Homework Assignments

Your students are more likely to complete homework assignments on time if you keep the following thoughts in mind when planning those assignments.

1. Plan learning activities, especially early in a school term, that teach students how to budget time for homework and procedures for completing homework. Students do not automatically know how to schedule their time for homework, to efficiently study, or to present homework as a teacher expects it.
2. Simple, uncomplicated homework assignments are more likely to be followed than complex ones. Unlike Ms. Salsevon, Mr. Sampson divided a rather complex, multi-step assignment into numerous simple assignments.

3. Students tend to delay the completion of assignments until just before they are due. Thus, for long-ranged assignments, teachers should set short-ranged deadline dates for completion of intermediate steps that eventually lead to final completion. Rather than simply require the library paper to be completed at the end of the two-week period, Mr. Sampson had students complete specific tasks leading to the final paper throughout the two-week period.

4. All homework assignments should clearly be an integral part of an overall plan of learning activities designed to help students achieve worthwhile goals. Some teachers assign homework only because it's expected. Consequently, the assignment does not tie in very well to in-class learning activities. These teachers' students learn to consider homework as a useless waste of their time. Using homework as punishment or withholding homework assignments as a reward are highly destructive forms of punishment or positive reinforcement that teach students to resent having to do homework.

5. Student behavior patterns of diligently doing homework assignments are encouraged when their efforts are positively reinforced by feedback provided by their teachers. Mr. Davis's students only found out whether the final answers on their homework were right or wrong. Ms. Hanzlik, on the other hand, provided her students with helpful information.

6. Ms. Salsevon attempted to motivate her students to complete a homework assignment by making students' grades contingent on whether or not the assignment was completed on time. Mr. Sampson, on the other hand, treated the assignment as a learning activity, not a test. However, Mr. Sampson made it clear that the homework assignment helped the students achieve exactly the same learning goals that the graded examination would test. Students can learn the importance of diligently doing homework when there is a clear link between homework assignments and tests. To help students make this association early in the school year, consider giving tests requiring students to complete tasks that are nearly identical to those assigned for homework. Do this early in a school term, and until students develop behavior patterns of doing homework, virtually always test after every homework assignment.

7. By utilizing homework in the class session in which it is due, students failing to complete the assignment can experience naturally occurring punishment by being unable to fully participate in class. Similarly, students who have completed the assignment on time can be positively reinforced by the success they experience in class. Mr. Sampson tied each homework assignment in his unit on writing library papers to in-class learning activities. Students who failed to complete homework as specified by his directions felt clearly disadvantaged in the class period when the assignment was due.

8. If the potential for parents to encourage or supervise their children's homework is ever to be realized, teachers, at the very least, must keep parents apprised of homework expectations. Some teachers have parents sign agreements indicating that they will supervise and encourage children to do homework.

CLASSROOM DESIGNS THAT ENHANCE STUDENT ENGAGEMENT

To implement some of the ideas presented herein for conducting engaging learning activities, you must be able to easily and quickly move about in your classroom. Your classroom's acoustical characteristics need to be such that students can hear what you intend for them to hear without disturbing reverberations and background noise. Students can hardly be engaged in a learning activity in which visual presentations are used if they cannot comfortably see what is displayed. Transition time can hardly be minimized when major rearrangements of furniture are required between learning activities. Furthermore, it is difficult for you to take one or several students aside and hold a conference if there is no convenient area for doing so while still supervising the rest of the students.

Questions regarding optimum classroom size and ideal room shape have been studied (Loo, 1977). Classroom acoustics can be vastly improved by the installation of sound-absorbing material on walls, carpet, and FM amplification equipment (Berg, 1987, 1990; Worner, 1988). On-task student behaviors tend to improve with such installations (Allen & Patton, 1990). Unfortunately, teachers typically have virtually no control over the size and shape of their own classrooms nor over any equipment that is permanently installed in them. Teachers are assigned rooms that they did not design to accommodate groups of students whom they did not select. In spite of unfavorable conditions, many teachers maximize their resources and enhance their learning environments by carefully and creatively arranging their classrooms (Cangelosi, 1992a, pp. 9–15; Evertson, 1989; Ornstein, 1990, pp. 401–408; Weinstein, 1987). Vignette 6.29 is a case in point.

VIGNETTE 6.29

In her first year as an English and Spanish teacher at Vanguard High School, Ms. Del Rio is assigned room 129 for homeroom and for teaching two remedial reading classes with 23 and 27 students respectively, one American literature class of 30, and two Spanish I classes with 29 and 30 students respectively. Room 129's initial arrangement and the way Ms. Del Rio utilizes it for the first month is depicted in Figure 6.4.

Because Ms. Del Rio stresses problem-solving and student-centered learning activities, she finds the room's initial arrangement inconvenient. It is difficult for her and the students to move about. She laments: "I have to negotiate an obstacle course to provide individual help to students located near the center of the room. I jab myself at least twice a day on the corners of these desks!" She is unable to conveniently and smoothly move towards students drifting off-task. Furthermore, the arrangement does not provide for separation between sound-producing group activity areas (e.g., where lectures and videos are presented) and quiet areas (e.g., where individual reading or computer assisted instruction is taking place).

Dissatisfied with the inflexible arrangement, Ms. Del Rio makes a list of the accommodations she wants her room to provide.

VIGNETTE 6.29 (continued)

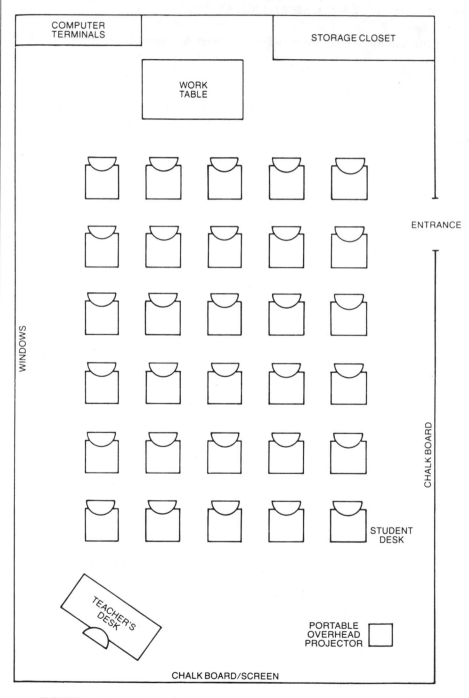

FIGURE 6.4 Room 129's Initial Arrangement

1. Quick and easy access between any two points in the room.
2. A designated quiet area for students to engage in individualized work.
3. A designated large group activity area for an entire class to congregate for discussion, lectures, tutorial sessions, and media presentations.
4. Small group activity areas for cooperative groups to conduct their business.
5. Storage space for equipment and materials to be kept out of sight.
6. A secure teacher's desk in a location with a favorable vantage point.
7. A silent reading room and minilibrary that can comfortably accommodate several students at a time.
8. A time-out room for isolating students.
9. A private room in which Ms. Del Rio can hold uninterrupted conferences with individuals (e.g., students with their parents) when a class is not in session.

Ms. Del Rio doesn't believe she can possibly build all the features on her "wish list" into her classroom, but she does begin modifying the room to more closely resemble her ideal classroom. In the third month of the school year, she manages to have the school administration exchange the 30 traditional student desks for 10 6.5-ft.-by-2.67-ft. elliptically shaped tables and 30 folding chairs. Her arrangement, with three students per table, is diagrammed in Figure 6.5. Although she would prefer students to have their own desks rather than sharing tables, this new arrangement provides more work areas in the back of the room and makes it easier for her to move about the room from one student to another. For small group discussions, she can quickly have students rearrange tables and chairs to follow the pattern given in Figure 6.6.

Ms. Del Rio needs the storage space provided by the large closet in the back of the room. However, she also needs more area in the back of the room for the quiet work section. To remedy that situation, she gets one of the school's custodians to install a closet with a chalkboard and projection screen on the doors in each of the two corners in the front of the room. She had observed that these two front corners had been dead space. With this latest modification, depicted in Figure 6.7, Room 129 has more viewable board and screen areas, storage space is maintained, and additional floor areas are available in the back of the room.

During the summer break after her first year, Ms. Del Rio calls on the generosity and skills of some of her students and their parents. They partition off an 8-ft.-by-10-ft. area in the back of the room to serve as a combination minilibrary, reading room, time-out room, conference room, and out-of-class-hours escape room for Ms. Del Rio to work undisturbed. Used book shelves, a coffee table, a sofa, and two chairs, all labeled "surplus" in the school district's warehouse, furnish the new room. While the volunteer carpenters are working, Ms. Del Rio mentions that it would be nice to have individual work stations with the computers in the "quiet" area in the back of the room. Mr. Singleton, a cabinetmaker by profession, custom-makes the stations to her specifications. Figure 6.8 depicts how Room 129 appears on the first day of Ms. Del Rio's second year at Vanguard.

Ms. Del Rio now finds it much easier to keep her students on-task. The additional year's experience plays a major role as do the modifications to the room. However, she sometimes finds the noise from the learning activities in the front of the room disturbing to the individualized activities in the rear. The problem is mitigated as a result of the tour of her room and presentation she makes for Vanguard's Home and School Association. Members are so impressed with her initiative and need for

VIGNETTE 6.29 (continued)

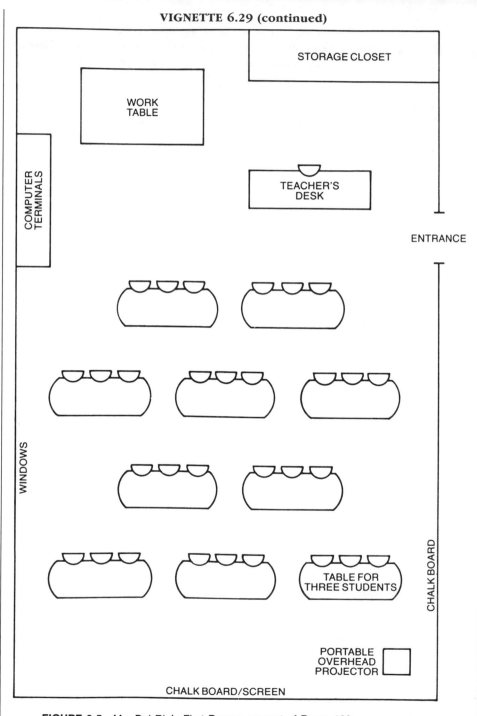

FIGURE 6.5   Ms. Del Rio's First Rearrangement of Room 129

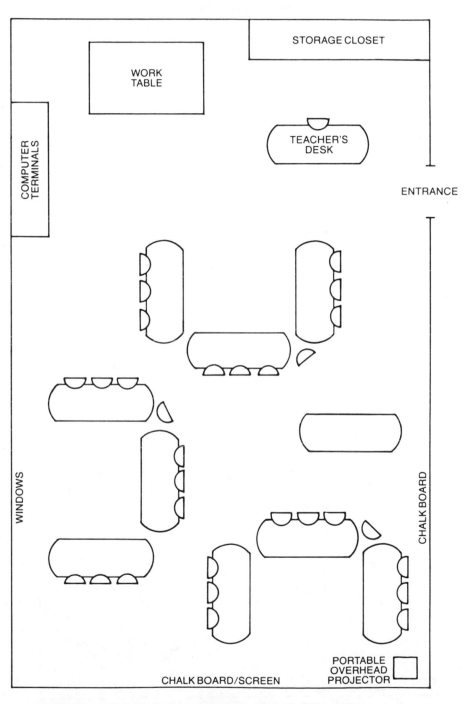

FIGURE 6.6 A Small Group Activity Arrangement in Room 129

VIGNETTE 6.29 (continued)

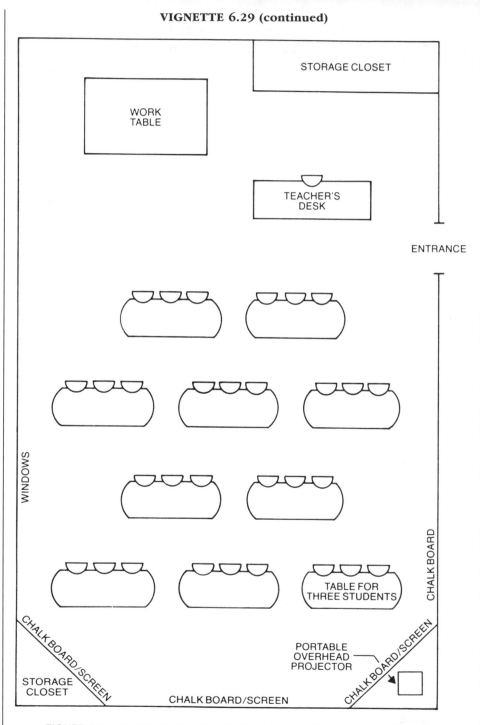

FIGURE 6.7   Ms. Del Rio Provides for More Room in Rear of Room 129

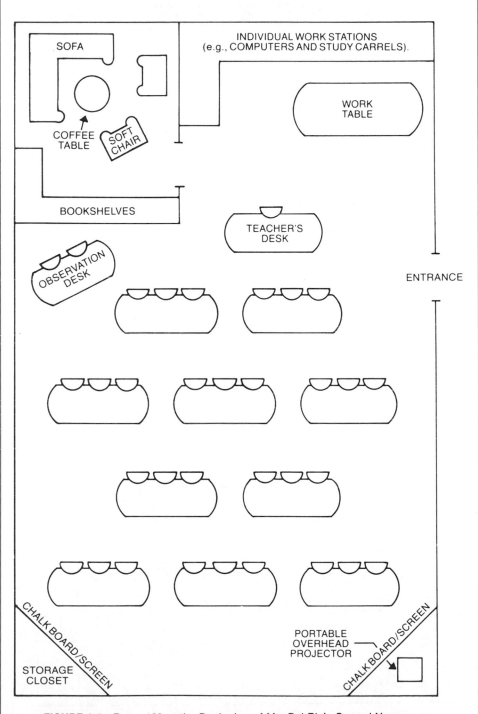

FIGURE 6.8 Room 129 at the Beginning of Ms. Del Rio's Second Year

VIGNETTE 6.29 (continued)

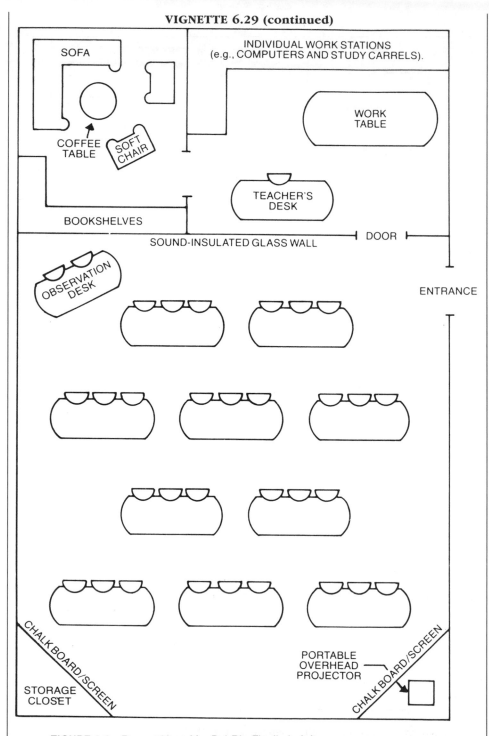

FIGURE 6.9   Room 129 as Ms. Del Rio Finally Left It

sound separation that they appropriate funds for installing two doors and a sound-insulated glass wall. The project is completed over the December holiday break and Room 129 appears as depicted in Figure 6.9.

Ms. Del Rio would have continued to improve Room 129 had she not accepted a position for the following year at Rose Park High. She will be assigned Room 244 at Rose Park, a room similar to the one depicted in Figure 6.4.

Vignette 6.30 illustrates modifications to an elementary school classroom before and after it was modified.

VIGNETTE 6.30

Figure 6.10 is a diagram of Room 9 in P.S. 157 where Mr. Hawkoos is assigned to teach 26 third graders. Through tactics similar to those used by Ms. Del Rio, Mr. Hawkoos's room is modified as diagrammed in Figure 6.11.

TRANSITIONAL ACTIVITIES
FROM CHAPTER 6 TO CHAPTER 7

I. Design a lecture-type learning activity within one of your teaching specialties. In one or two paragraphs, describe your plan for conducting the lecture.

Compare your lecture plan to those of colleagues. Also, analyze the plans for consistency with the 14 points about lectures on pages 160–162.

II. Design a cooperative group learning activity within one of your teaching specialties. In one or two paragraphs, describe your plan for conducting the activity.

Compare your plan to those of colleagues. Also, analyze the plans for consistency with the 10 points about cooperative learning sessions on pages 165–166.

III. Design a high-level questioning activity within one of your teaching specialties. In one or two paragraphs, describe your plan for conducting the session.

Compare your plan to those of others. Also, analyze the plans for consistency with the six points about questioning sessions on pages 174–175.

IV. Design an independent work learning activity within one of your teaching specialties. In one or two paragraphs, describe your plan for conducting the session.

Compare your plan to those of colleagues. Also, analyze the plans for consistency with the four points about independent work sessions on pages 176–177.

V. Design a homework learning activity within one of your teaching specialties. What is the assignment?

Compare your assignment to those of colleagues. Also, analyze them for consistency with the eight points about homework assignments on pages 179–180.

VI. Design a classroom you feel would be conducive to keeping students on-task. Make a detailed sketch of the room arrangement.

Compare your classroom arrangement to those of colleagues. Which features from Ms. Del Rio's list (Vignette 6.29) did you incorporate?

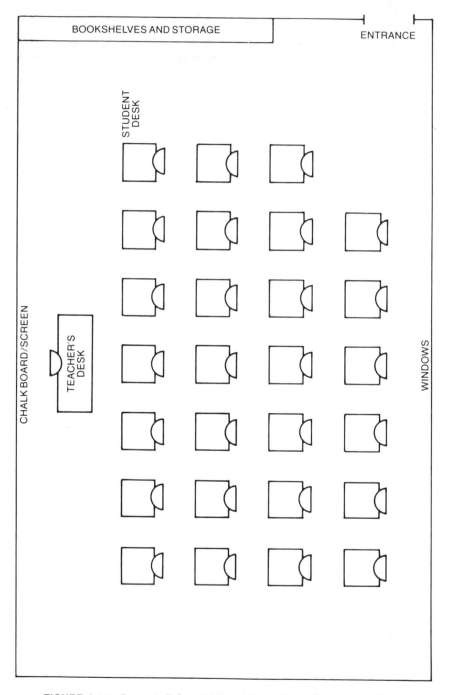

FIGURE 6.10 Room 9, P.S. 157 When Mr. Hawkoos First Took It Over

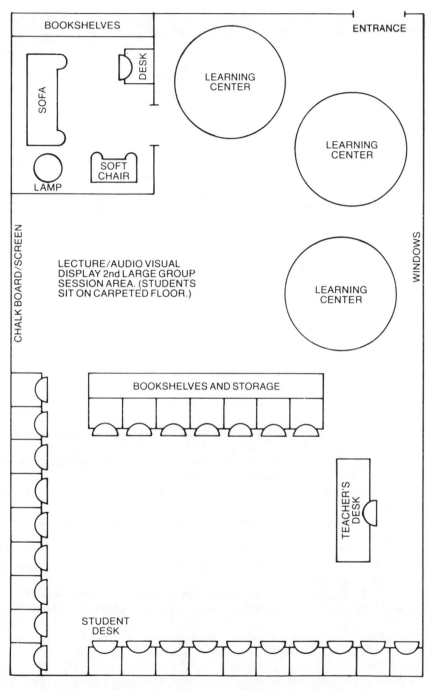

FIGURE 6.11 Room 9 in P.S. 157 After Mr. Hawkoos's Alterations

VII. In preparation for your work with Chapter 7, discuss the following questions with two or more of your colleagues.
   A. What are some strategies for decisively and effectively dealing with student misbehaviors?
   B. What responsibilities do teachers have regarding building the character of their students?
   C. How do effective strategies for dealing with isolated incidents of off-task behavior differ from effective strategies for dealing with off-task behavior patterns?
   D. How can teachers act as classroom disciplinarians without having students feel they're being robbed of their dignities?
   E. What are some strategies teachers employ to discourage student misbehavior when misbehaving students are not readily identified?
   F. Is corporal punishment ever an appropriate response to student misbehavior?
   G. How far does the authority of a teacher extend when dealing with student discipline problems?

SUPPLEMENTAL READINGS

Alderman, M. K. (1990). Motivation for at-risk students. *Educational Leadership, 48,* 27–30.

Biehler, R. F., & Snowman, J. (1990). *Psychology applied to teaching* (6th ed., pp. 514–579). Boston: Houghton Mifflin.

Brophy, J. E. (1987). Synthesis on strategies for motivating students to learn. *Educational Leadership, 45,* 40–48.

Cangelosi, J. S. (1992). *Systematic teaching strategies* (pp. 167–228). New York: Longman.

Cooper, H. (1989). *Homework.* New York: Longman.

——— (1989). Synthesis of research on homework. *Educational Leadership, 47,* 85–91.

Doenau, S. J. (1987). Soliciting. In M. J. Dunkin (Ed.). *The international encyclopedia of teaching and teacher education* (pp. 407–413). Oxford: Pergamon Press.

Foyle, H. C., Lyman, L., & Thies, S. A. (1991). *Cooperative learning in the early childhood classroom.* Washington: National Education Association.

Hilke, E. V. (1990). *Cooperative learning.* Bloomington, IN: Phi Delta Kappa Educational Foundation.

Hunkins, F. P. (1989). *Teaching thinking through effective questioning.* Boston: Christopher-Gordon.

Kayfetz, J. L., & Stice, R. L. (1987). *Academically speaking.* Belmont, CA: Wadsworth.

Rottier, J., & Ogan, B. J. (1991). *Cooperative learning in middle-level schools.* Washington: National Education Association.

Ruetten, M. K. (1986). *Comprehending academic lectures.* New York: Macmillan.

Slavin, R. E. (1991). Synthesis of research on cooperative learning. *Educational Leadership, 48,* 71–82.

Tobbin, K. (1986). Effects of teacher wait time on discourse in mathematics and language arts classes. *American Educational Research Journal, 23,* 191–200.

Weinstein, C. S. (1987). Seating patterns. In M. J. Dunkin (Ed.). *The international encyclopedia of teaching and teacher education* (pp. 545–548). Oxford: Pergamon Press.

Zumwalt, K. K. (Ed.). (1986). *Improving teaching: 1986 ASCD yearbook.* Alexandria, VA: Association for Supervision and Curriculum Development.

PART III

How Should You Deal with Students' Failure to Cooperate? How Can You Solve Discipline Problems?

Approaching Off-Task Behaviors Systematically

***Purpose of Chapter* 7**

Chapter 7 is designed to help you

1. Deal with student off-task behaviors by applying the Teaching Process Model rather than by reacting without careful consideration of how to teach students to supplant off-task behaviors with on-task behaviors.

2. Develop your own ideas for implementing the following suggestions for responding to student off-task behaviors. (a) Deal with misbehaviors well before they "get to you." (b) Either respond decisively to an off-task behavior or ignore it altogether. (c) Distinguish between teaching students to be on-task and "character building." (d) Distinguish between isolated off-task behaviors and off-task behavior patterns. (e) Control the time and place for dealing with off-task behavior. (f) Provide your students with dignified ways to terminate off-task behaviors. (g) Avoid playing detective. (h) Utilize the help of colleagues. (i) Utilize the help of parents. (j) Utilize alternative lesson plans. (k) Do not use corporal punishment. (l) Know your rights and limitations. (m) Maintain your options. (n) Know your students and know yourself.

DEAL WITH OFF-TASK BEHAVIORS VIA THE TEACHING PROCESS MODEL

A Mechanism for Focusing

Compare Vignette 7.1 to Vignette 7.2.

VIGNETTE 7.1

Ms. Blythe is lecturing to her 26 eighth graders when Jane begins looking around, tapping her pencil on her desk. Ms. Blythe finds Jane's behavior annoying and judges it to be a potential distraction to others in the class. From her position in the front of the room and without much thought, Ms. Blythe interrupts herself to complain to Jane: "Will you stop that infernal tapping, Jane? Can't you ever do what you're supposed to?"

VIGNETTE 7.2

Ms. Guevarra is lecturing to her 26 eighth graders when Jeanne begins looking around, tapping her pencil on her desk. Ms. Guevarra finds Jeanne's behavior annoying and judges it to be a potential distraction to others in the class. Within the span of three seconds and without interrupting her lecture, Ms. Guevarra's thinks to herself: "Jeanne needs to pay attention and quit making that noise. This isn't a chronic behavior for Jeanne and I've never had to deal with it from her before. I will get her to stop and return her attention to the lecture. How should I accomplish this? I'll continue to lecture, but I'll move near her and make eye contact. If that doesn't get her attention or if she continues to tap, I'll gently touch her tapping hand. If that fails, I'll think of another tactic."

Continuing her lecture, she walks to a point near Jeanne. Jeanne ceases looking around and appears to attend to the lecture, but she keeps tapping her pencil. Ms. Guevarra puts her hand on Jeanne's. Jeanne stops tapping and most other class members don't notice the silent communication between them. Ms. Guevarra continues to monitor how well Jeanne and the other students attend to the lecture.

Unlike Ms. Blythe, Ms. Guevarra systematically dealt with an off-task behavior as she would deal with any other student-learning need. She approached Jeanne's off-task behavior using the same steps of the Teaching Process Model that she would use to teach a learning unit in science, social studies, physical education, or any other content area of the curricula. In only a matter of seconds she

1. Identified a student need when she decided that Jeanne should stop tapping and pay attention.
2. Determined a learning objective by deciding that she would somehow get Jeanne to stop tapping and become engaged in the lecture session.
3. Planned a learning activity when she decided to stand by Jeanne, make eye contact, and touch Jeanne's hand as she continued with her lecture.
4. Prepared for the learning activity by moving into position to carry out her plan. (This whole incident happened so fast that Ms. Guevarra had virtually no need to prepare for the rather simple learning activity in this example. Admittedly, a point is stretched here to remind you of all six

steps of the Teaching Process Model. In more complicated examples of dealing with off-task behaviors, preparation for the learning activity may be quite elaborate.)

5. Conducted the learning activity by standing by Jeanne, trying to make eye contact, and gently touching her hand.
6. Evaluated how well the learning objective was achieved by observing Jeanne to see if she would again begin to tap and look around.

Ms. Blythe's response to Jane's off-task behavior appeared to be an unthinking reaction to being annoyed. Instead of focusing on getting Jane to terminate the disruptive behavior in favor of engaged behavior, Ms. Blythe interrupted her lecture and attacked Jane's personality with an irrelevant, rhetorical question. Such tactics may get Jane to stop tapping and look forward, but she would be a very unusual adolescent if she listened to and thought about the substance of Ms. Blythe's lecture immediately after being asked: "Can't you ever do what you're supposed to?" Jane would probably think about Ms. Blythe's insulting and embarrassing attack on her in front of her peers. Furthermore, the engagement of other students was disrupted.

Of course, Ms. Blythe's approach to Jane's off-task behavior was quite understandable. Teachers are continually faced with the problem of orchestrating a group of young people who can manage to display very annoying behaviors. Students ought to behave cooperatively without teachers having to apply creative tactics to lead them to do what they should do on their own. It's no wonder that Ms. Blythe sometimes reacts thoughtlessly to her students' displays of disruptive behaviors. Although Ms. Blythe's tactics were understandable, they're also ineffectual. To overcome the temptation to respond to students' annoying behaviors with ineffective displays of emotion, you, as a teacher, would do well to train yourself to be constantly mindful of the Teaching Process Model. By having your thoughts organized according to the six steps of the Model, you can systematically respond to students' displays of off-task behaviors, even the annoying ones, as did Ms. Guevarra.

More Elaborate Applications

In Vignettes 7.3 and 7.4, teachers deal with off-task behaviors systematically by applying the Teacher Process Model. Unlike Vignettes 7.1 and 7.2, the students' off-task behaviors are behavior patterns rather than simply isolated occurrences. Consequently, the tactics used must be more elaborate than those used by Ms. Guevarra.

VIGNETTE 7.3

Al, one of Ms. Reid's fourth graders, is playing "geography bingo," a small group learning activity with four other students. The game leader calls out: "The largest continent." Paul exclaims: "Bingo! It's Asia and I've got it right here for bingo!"

VIGNETTE 7.3 (continued)

Al stands up and yells at Paul: "You stupid ass-hole! I had that one too! I could've got bingo!" With those words, Al shoves Paul down and upsets the other students' game cards.

Ms. Reid arrives on the scene, firmly grabs Al by the arm, and briskly walks him to a point just outside the classroom door. Looking directly into Al's face, she calmly says: "Wait here while I check to see if Paul is hurt."

Without giving Al a chance to speak, she unhesitatingly turns and walks back to where the incident occurred as other students gather around Paul who, though still lying on the floor, is beginning to communicate his plans for retaliation. Ms. Reid interrupts Paul, saying: "I'm sorry that Al pushed you down, but I'm happy that you are not hurt." Helping Paul to his feet, Ms. Reid continues speaking without giving anyone else a chance to complain about Al or giving Paul a chance to make further threats. Ms. Reid: "Blaine and Carol, I would appreciate you helping each other pick up this mess and getting the bingo game started again. Let's go with just four players this time. Everyone else, please return to your work. Thank you for cooperating."

Ms. Reid quickly returns to Al and says: "Right now, I don't have time to work with you on your misbehavior. Now, I have a class to teach and it's time for you to work on geography. We'll just have to wait until tomorrow morning to discuss this matter. When your bus arrives tomorrow morning, you come immediately to the classroom and meet me at my desk. Will you remember, or should I phone your house tonight to remind you?" Al: "I'll remember." Ms. Reid: "Fine! Now, you still have 13 minutes to work on geography. Get your geography book and bring it to me at my desk." At her desk, Ms. Reid directs Al to complete a geography exercise at a work table located away from the rest of the class. The exercise is a drill on the same geography skills that the bingo game was designed to develop.

At the end of the school day, when Ms. Reid experiences her first solitary moments after the students have been dismissed, she thinks to herself: "I bought myself some time to figure out what to do about Al's outbursts in class. That was a real chance I took grabbing him. With his temper, he might've turned on me. This is the third or fourth time something like this has happened while Al was involved in a small group activity. What makes him so aggressive? Well, that's not what I have to worry about right now. My job is to prevent this from happening again. I'll exclude him from any small group activity for the time being. Today, I hope he didn't think the geography book exercise was a punishment. I don't want to teach him to hate geography. Somehow he's got to understand that antisocial behavior isn't tolerated in my classroom! Look at me, I'm getting myself all worked up just sitting here by myself. What do I do? I could explain my dilemma to him and involve him in the design of a solution. That tactic worked really well with Grayson. But Grayson is different from Al. Al's not ready for that yet. He's too defensive; he'd be telling me how it wasn't his fault at all. I'd love to know more about his home situation and find out why he's so defensive. But I don't have time to worry with that; I've got a more immediate problem to solve. Okay, here's what I'll do.

1. I don't want to give him a chance to argue and be defensive when we meet tomorrow, so I will not even try to explain the reasons for the way I'm dealing with the problem. I'll simply tell him what we're going to do and not defend the plan.

Ms. Reid Has Her Class Back On-Task before Dealing with Al's Misbehavior

---

VIGNETTE 7.3 (continued)

2. I will assign him to work by himself, away from others, whenever he would normally be involved in some small group activity. His independent assignment will deal with content similar to the small group activity in which the others will be engaged.
3. I'll watch for indicators that he is modifying his antisocial behavior pattern and is becoming more willing to cooperate in group activities.
4. Gradually, I'll work him back into group activities as I see encouraging indications that there will be no more trouble. I'll avoid involving him in any sort of competitive activities for a long time.

Okay, how shall I present this plan to him tomorrow? What will I do if he doesn't show up tomorrow? I'd better prepare for that possibility. . . . ''

VIGNETTE 7.4

Mr. Mitchelson routinely assigns his eleventh grade literature class homework that takes students about 45 minutes to satisfactorily complete. Assignments might involve reading a short story, writing an essay, or preparing a reference report. For the first several months of the school session, Mr. Mitchelson finds that only a few students take the time and effort to complete the assignments to his satisfaction. His discussions with students indicate that they view the assignments as busy work that holds little value for them. Most of them fake their way through the assignments, barely doing enough to keep them "out of trouble" with Mr. Mitchelson.

In response to this concern, Mr. Mitchelson begins to incorporate some of the principles of problem-solving learning activities, and he makes certain that students recognize the relation between these homework assignments and problems which they feel a need to solve. Gradually, nearly every student is consistently completing the homework in a satisfactory manner.

However, Wilma is one of the exceptions. Even though Mr. Mitchelson's assignments are now meaningful to the students, Wilma rarely completes homework. The fact that Mr. Mitchelson is now using in-class learning activities that depend on completion of homework assignments compounds Wilma's difficulties because her failure to complete homework makes it nearly impossible for her to participate in class. When queried about homework, Wilma consistently indicates that she tries, but just can't get the assignments finished. Mr. Mitchelson is convinced that Wilma has the ability to satisfactorily complete the work. He decides to do something to help her to consistently choose to do homework.

As he plans the learning activities for teaching her this on-task behavior pattern, he thinks: "I could subtract points from her grade for not getting assignments in on time, but her literature grade should reflect how well she achieves course goals, not how faithfully she finishes work. I want to base grades on test scores. But if she continues not finishing homework; there's no way she'll achieve the goals and consequently she'll get poor grades anyway. Maybe I should just leave her alone and she'll learn a lesson when she receives a failing grade. That would work nicely as naturally occurring punishment. But what is my purpose here, to teach her some life-long lesson about being responsible or to help her achieve course goals? I'm not going to take on the problem of trying to change her life, just teach her literature by trying to get her engaged in my learning activities. No, I won't just let it go.

The next time she doesn't complete an assignment, I could refer her to Mr. Taylor. But even though he's the counselor, I don't think he'd be much help. Scratch that one.

What if I set up a contingency contract with her, working out a system in which privileges depend on completion of homework? I'll save that one for later if something less drastic doesn't work out.

What about requiring her to remain after school to complete unfinished work? Then she'd miss her bus which is fine with me. That would be a nice naturally occurring punishment. But then I'd have to stay with her and I don't want to do that. Although I'm always here until five o'clock, I need that time for other things, not standing over her, pushing her to finish. Scratch another good idea.

What I really need to do is find out why she doesn't finish these assignments and then plan something from there. She doesn't have a job or anything; she must have the time. Grace says she normally turns in her math homework. Let's see, tomorrow's schedule calls for her to turn in an essay on why she thinks the people Charly works with in *Flowers of Algernon* are not his friends. And then most of the class has free reading time scheduled at the library. If she doesn't have the essay completed, I'll have her finish it in class. There'll only be about five others in the room at that time, and I can observe her working on the assignment.''

The next day, Wilma only has the introductory paragraph to her essay. In that one paragraph, the purpose of the essay is accurately stated. As planned, Mr. Mitchelson directs her to complete the essay by the end of the 55-minute class period. Wilma sits and stares at her paper for 10 minutes without writing. Mr. Mitchelson goes to her and looks over her shoulder. She asks: ''Mr. Mitchelson, is my introduction okay?'' ''You've stated the purpose with clarity,'' he replies and moves away. Several minutes later, she come to Mr. Mitchelson and says: ''Were the factory workers Charly's friends or not?'' Mr. Mitchelson: ''That's a matter of opinion. What do you think?'' Wilma: ''I don't know.'' Mr. Mitchelson: ''You don't know what you think?'' Wilma: ''Well, I don't think the workers were very nice to Charly. Am I wrong?'' Mr. Mitchelson: ''You can't be wrong. It's a matter of opinion. There is no way to be right or wrong in this case. As you said in your introduction, the purpose of this essay is to express your opinion on whether or not the workers were Charly's friends. If you say what you believe, then you are correct whether or not anyone else agrees with you.'' Wilma: ''Oh!''

Wilma returns to her seat and writes for five minutes before returning to Mr. Mitchelson with one more line written. ''Is this right, Mr. Mitchelson?'' she asks. . . .

After the school day, Mr. Mitchelson continues thinking about ways to help Wilma choose to complete assignments: ''Wilma really seems reluctant to express her opinions. She finally completed her report in class, but she drove me nuts seeking my approval on each line before she'd write the next. She appears afraid to complete one step in an assignment before having the previous step okayed. Either that, or she doesn't trust people to accept her opinions. Now that I think about it, just about all of the assignments she doesn't do require her to express her opinion. I think Wilma needs to learn that I'm receptive to and value her opinions. It will take some time for her to become convinced of that. In the meantime, as an intermediate step I should help her get in the habit of completing homework. For now, I'll implement the following plan.

VIGNETTE 7.4 (continued)

1. I'll privately tell her just what I've decided and that I expect her to complete every assignment.
2. For at least a week, I won't give her assignments requiring her to express her own opinions. For example, with *Flowers for Algernon,* I'll ask her to write about somebody else's opinion on whether or not Charly's co-workers are his friends. Maybe she could interview a classmate and write about that person's opinion on the question.
3. If Wilma completes these modified assignments every day for a week, I'll gradually begin giving her assignments where she's to express her own opinions. I'll be careful to never judge her opinions; I'll only judge the processes by which she arrives at those opinions. If she doesn't complete all of the first week's assignments, then I'll reevaluate the situation, consider other causes, and maybe move to a contingency contract plan to positively reinforce doing homework.

I need to carefully evaluate how well this works before deciding whether or not to change my strategy.''

Staying Calm and Organizing Thoughts

In Vignettes 7.2, 7.3, and 7.4, Ms. Guevarra, Ms. Reid, and Mr. Mitchelson viewed the problem of eliminating off-task behavior as they would view the problem of helping a student achieve any other learning objective. By applying teaching techniques to help students choose on-task behaviors instead of off-task behaviors, they were able to focus their time, energy, and thoughts on the important issues confronting them. Ms. Reid, for example, did not try to moralize about the evils of fighting with Al. She realized that telling Al about the evils of fighting, something he's likely to have already heard, would serve nothing. Teachers, such as Ms. Blythe, who do not systematically focus on the behavior to be altered, tend to compound difficulties by dwelling on irrelevant issues (e.g., whether or not Jane can ever do what she's supposed to do). Teachers who fail to focus on the goal of getting and keeping students on-task and engaged in learning activities sometimes feel offended when students are disruptive or do not pay attention. These teachers sometimes deal with their own hurt feelings by retaliating against students rather than focusing on getting the students to behave as they should.

The Teaching Process Model provides you with a way of organizing your thoughts about teaching students to behave as they should. As you apply this model, you will need to design strategies for dealing with off-task behaviors. The remainder of this chapter provides you with 14 suggestions. Chapter 8 focuses on strategies that help students supplant off-task behavior patterns with on-task behavior patterns. Chapter 9 is concerned with ideas for dealing with nondisruptive off-task behaviors; Chapter 10's concern is disruptive behaviors.

VIGNETTE 7.5

As part of a process writing lesson, Mr. Edwards' students are paired off, two to a computer, editing one another's essays. Mr. Edwards notices that Clarence and Paige's discussion centers more on gossiping about Florence, one of their classmates, than on writing. Hoping their ratio of on-task talk to gossip will soon increase, Mr. Edwards does not intervene. Three minutes later, he notices their gossiping has spread to a neighboring pair, and now four students are spending less time editing and more time whispering about Florence, who is situated on the other side of the room. In addition to his concern for maintaining student engagement in the activity, he now worries that Florence will overhear the unkind things being said. His anger rises as more and more off-task conversations erupt around the room. No longer containing himself, Mr. Edwards yells: "Since so many of you don't seem to be worried about getting your papers edited, we'll just have you all print out right now and turn in the essays the way they are!" Most students have no idea what Mr. Edwards is talking about as he quips: "Some people in here have to put other people down to make themselves feel better about themselves!"

DEAL WITH MISBEHAVIORS WELL BEFORE THEY "GET TO YOU"

Too often, teachers allow off-task behaviors to continue until the teachers become so irritated that they are too stressed to handle the situation constructively. Consider Vignette 7.5.

By the time Mr. Edwards judged he should no longer tolerate the disruptive talking, he was too agitated to think through an effective intervention plan. His agitation clouded his thoughts; consequently, he badly mishandled the episode. As indicated in Figure 7.1, it is best to decisively deal with off-task behaviors well before they escalate to a point approaching levels you consider intolerable.

RESPOND DECISIVELY TO AN OFF-TASK BEHAVIOR OR IGNORE IT ALTOGETHER

Consider Vignette 7.6.

Although it would have been inadvisable for Ms. Hillyard to ignore her students' inappropriate talking, it would not have been as destructive as her weak, half-hearted response. Not only were her efforts ineffectual, they displayed to the students that they need not seriously consider her directions. In general, an indecisive, perfunctory attempt at dealing with one incident of off-task behavior compounds a teacher's difficulties for effectively dealing with subsequent occurrences. Here is why.

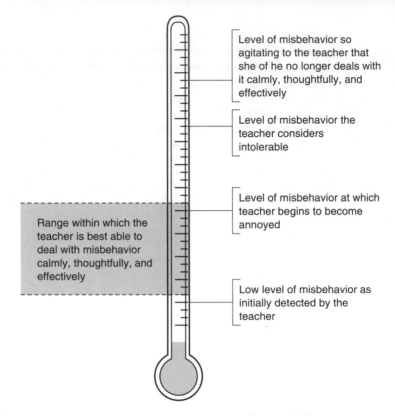

Level of misbehavior so agitating to the teacher that she of he no longer deals with it calmly, thoughtfully, and effectively

Level of misbehavior the teacher considers intolerable

Level of misbehavior at which teacher begins to become annoyed

Range within which the teacher is best able to deal with misbehavior calmly, thoughtfully, and effectively

Low level of misbehavior as initially detected by the teacher

FIGURE 7.1   Deal with Misbehaviors before They "Get to You"

VIGNETTE 7.6

Ms. Hillyard is busy explaining some rules for capitalizing words to her class of 31 fifth graders. "Now, who can tell me which words in this sentence should begin with a capital letter?" she asks as she begins to write on the whiteboard: "my friend eddie said 'looking for ghosts' was a—" Just then, she hears some students talking among themselves. Looking over her shoulder, she sees Don, Abby, and Lyle involved in a conversation. "Hey you chatterboxes, stop talking and pay attention," she says as she finishes writing the sentence: "—funny movie." The three students continue talking. They hardly heard Ms. Hillyard's message as she failed to get their attention before speaking. Ms. Hillyard continues her explanation for several more minutes before once again trying to quiet Don, Abby, and Lyle by saying: "Okay, I told you to knock it off already. This time I mean no more talking!" She continues her lesson as they continue talking.

VIGNETTE 7.7

Mr. Clark, is busy explaining some rules for capitalizing words to his class of 31 fifth graders. "Now, who can tell me which words in this sentence should begin with a capital letter?" he asks as he begins to write on the whiteboard: "my friend eddie said 'looking for ghosts' was a—" Just then, he hears some students talking among themselves. He stops writing, pivots, and faces the class to see Jim, Oral, and Mavis carrying on a conversation. Walking directly over to the three, he picks up the book, paper and pencil off of Jim's desk and says: "Jim, please take these over to that empty seat over there. Mavis, you take your stuff and work from that desk in front of Mike." Confident that his directions will be followed, he quickly returns to the front of the room and continues his explanation.

---

1. When a teacher demonstrates that he or she is aware of off-task behaviors, but does not make the effort to effectively lead the students to supplant the off-task with on-task behaviors, students tend to generalize that the teacher is not serious about expecting them to be on-task. Such an attitude tends to detract from the businesslike climate that should prevail in a classroom.
2. A teacher (e.g., Ms. Hillyard) who only tells students how to behave without taking action to lead students to follow what is said, conditions students to not bother to listen. Some teachers will repeat demands for students to be on-task (e.g., "Pay attention.") over and over without students complying until the teacher finally gets angry and upset. Such a practice conditions students to not listen until the teacher becomes angry and upset.
3. Halfhearted efforts that are nonproductive or counterproductive waste a teacher's valuable energy and time.

If you are confronted with an off-task student behavior, but are not at the time in a position to apply a strategy that has a reasonable chance of working, then you should at least delay your response until help can be obtained or until you can design and apply a suitable strategy.

In Vignette 7.7, Mr. Clark's response to students' off-task behavior is more decisive than was Ms. Hillyard's.

DISTINGUISH BETWEEN TEACHING STUDENTS TO BE ON-TASK AND "CHARACTER BUILDING"

A Teacher's Responsibilities and Capabilities

In Vignette 7.3, Ms. Reid utilized the Teaching Process Model to deal with Al's disruptive behavior; she focused on helping Al to terminate an in-class, antisocial behavior pattern. Ms. Reid recognized that she is responsible for keeping her

---

VIGNETTE 7.8

While her first graders are working in intraclass reading groups, Ms. Blanchard sees Todd yank Celia's hair so hard that she falls over backwards and begins crying. Ms. Blanchard yells to Todd: "Come here, boy!" Todd comes over as all the other students stop their work to watch. "How would you like me to pull your hair? You think you're tough! I can be a lot tougher than you! I'll make you sorry for ever being a bully! Suppose I let Celia pull your hair! Would you like that? Well, would you?" Todd: "I didn't pull that . . ." Ms. Blanchard: "You didn't what? Wait until one of the big second or third graders picks on you! You'll learn not to be so mean!"

VIGNETTE 7.9

Libba, an eleventh grader, stops at a convenience store on her way to school. She buys and consumes three cans of beer before her 8:45 A.M. homeroom period. Neither her homeroom teacher nor her first period history teacher notice anything strange in her behavior. However, as second period begins, she appears tipsy to Mr. Wagoner, her science teacher. Mr. Wagoner directs two students to being setting up an experiment that he plans to demonstrate to the class. While they are doing this, he subtly beckons Libba to the doorway and then out into the hall. Detecting the odor of alcohol on her breath, he says: "It's your business if you want to mess up your own life. But it's my business to teach you science, and I can't teach it to you when you're in this condition. When we've completed this conversation, you go back to your desk. Just keep quiet and concentrate on facing straight ahead. Did you hear me?" Libba: "Yes, sir." Mr. Wagoner: "Fine. Tomorrow morning come to this room at 8:15. We'll discuss the matter then. Can you remember to be here or should I remind you with a call tonight? Libba: "I'll remember; I'll be here."

At 8:15 the next morning, Libba makes her appointment and Mr. Wagoner tells her: "If you ever come into my class again while under the influence of alcohol or any other drug, I will immediately send you to Ms. Swindle's office. I will inform Mr. Giradeau that I refuse to teach you in that condition. And I will inform your parents of the situation. Do you understand?" Libba: "Yes, but I'm not the only . . ." Mr. Wagoner (interrupting): "I am not talking with you about others, only you. I don't discuss your problems with other students, and I won't discuss theirs with you. Do you understand?" Libba: "Yes!" Mr. Wagoner: "Yesterday while you were 'out of it,' we were analyzing this experiment that is described here in my teacher's manual. I want you to take my manual home tonight and analyze the experiment as it is described on pages 79 through 84. Bring in your results, and I'll be happy to give you feedback on them as soon as I find the time. That should catch you up with the rest of the class. You won't be behind anymore. Okay?" Libba: "Okay." Mr. Wagoner: "See you in class. Keep smiling."

SOURCE: Adapted from *Cooperation in the Classroom: Students and Teachers Together*, Second Edition (pp. 63–64) by J. S. Cangelosi, 1990, Washington, DC: National Education Association.

students engaged in learning activities designed to help them achieve worthwhile learning goals. She believes that developing Al's character and teaching him to be an understanding moral human being are outside of the realm of both her responsibilities and capabilities. Her method for stopping the clash between Al and Paul and quickly getting everyone reengaged in the learning activity was effective, because she focused on her responsibilities as a teacher.

Sometimes when teachers understandably react in anger to annoying off-task student behaviors, they lose sight of where their responsibilities begin and end. Vignette 7.8 is an example.

Focusing on the Task

Ms. Blanchard's anger clouded her focus and, instead of taking effective action to prevent a recurrence of such intolerable misbehavior, she got off-track trying to get Todd to be sorry for being "mean." Rather than deal with the incident, she focused on Todd's "meanness."

In Vignette 7.9, Mr. Wagoner helps a student substitute engaged behavior for off-task behavior without allowing himself to be side-tracked into thinking he's building character.

DISTINGUISH BETWEEN ISOLATED OFF-TASK BEHAVIORS AND OFF-TASK BEHAVIOR PATTERNS

Different strategies are used to terminate isolated off-task behaviors than off-task behavior patterns, which are usually more difficult to terminate. However, teachers usually have the luxury of taking time to plan strategies for dealing with patterns; whereas, isolated off-task behaviors should typically be dealt with as they occur. You can effectively utilize the behavior modification principles (e.g., extinction and shaping) explained in Chapter 8 to teach students to eliminate off-task behavior patterns. You need to be mindful of behavior modification principles when dealing with isolated off-task behaviors in order to guard against off-task behavior patterns developing out of the isolated incidents. If an isolated off-task behavior is positively reinforced, then an off-task behavior pattern may emerge.

CONTROL THE TIME AND PLACE FOR DEALING WITH OFF-TASK BEHAVIOR

Once Ms. Reid stopped Al and Paul from fighting in Vignette 7.3, she reengaged the class in learning activities and arranged for a more convenient time to deal with Al's disruptive behaviors. She waited to speak with Al (1) after she had time to collect her thoughts and develop a plan of action, (2) at a time and place in which she wouldn't be burdened with having to supervise other students, (3) when and where no other students would be around so Al would feel free to communicate with her without concern for what his peers were thinking, (4) after they both had time to cool off.

Like Ms. Reid, and Mr. Wagoner in Vignette 7.9, you will be more effective in dealing with off-task behaviors if you manage to control the time and places for interacting with students over their misbehaviors. Typically, students are more concerned with the images they portray for their peers than they are with what you or any other teacher are trying to do for them. Consequently, you are more likely to achieve a productive interchange about preventing recurrences of off-task behaviors in a private conference with a student than you will when both of you are worried about others in the vicinity. Do not make the mistake of making a major issue out of one student's off-task behavior in front of other students in order to exhibit the undesirability of the off-task behavior. Such strategies usually lead to feelings of embarrassment and resentment that detract from the cooperative, businesslike climate you want for your classroom.

PROVIDE STUDENTS WITH DIGNIFIED WAYS TO TERMINATE OFF-TASK BEHAVIORS

Consider Vignette 7.10.

VIGNETTE 7.10

Ms. Fabian is conducting a writing lesson in which her third graders are taking turns writing three-word sentences on the chalkboard. "Okay, Valerie, it's your turn. Please put your sentence on the board," she says. Valerie just looks away and doesn't get out of her seat. Ms. Fabian: "Valerie honey, please write your sentence on the board." Valerie: "I don't have one." Ms. Fabian: "Here, we'll help you. I'll give you two of the three words and you use them in a three-word sentence. How about, 'John loves'? You find a third word and make a sentence that starts John loves'." Valerie: "No!" Ms. Fabian feels threatened by Valerie's refusal. She fears that if she allows Valerie to win the struggle of wills in front of the class, others will also refuse to follow her directions. Ms. Fabian: "Valerie, you had better be up and writing on the board before I count to five!" Valerie: "I won't." Ms. Fabian: "I'm counting! One, two, three, four. Valerie, you'll be sorry . . . five! Okay, young lady, you had your chance, now we'll see that you learn to do what you're told!" Valerie: "Okay, okay! I'll write your sentence." Valerie gets up and walks to the front of the room. Ms. Fabian: "It's too late now. I already counted to five. You had your chance!" Valerie: "I said, I'll write the sentence." Ms. Fabian: "Not until I receive an apology. You tell me you're sorry for your rudeness and you apologize to the class for wasting their time." Valerie faces the class and says, with her head down and a sheepish grin across her face: "Sorry!" Ms. Fabian: "And what do you say to me?" "I'm sorry, Ms. Fabian," she mutters with glaring eyes. Ms. Fabian: "That's more like it!"

Ms. Fabian's mishandling of Valerie's off-task behavior left Valerie feeling stripped of her dignity in front of her peers. What could Ms. Fabian ever expect to gain by insisting that Valerie apologize? Did the apology reestablish Ms. Fabian's authority after her counting-to-five strategy failed? The apology might have temporarily helped Ms. Fabian to feel better about herself, but unfortunately, such power games only create an atmosphere of unhealthy competitiveness between teacher and students. Such competitiveness precludes the development of dignified, businesslike attitudes that are so vital for a classroom to be characterized by cooperative student engagement.

If you expect dignified behaviors from your students, you need to avoid doing anything that leads them to fear that their dignities are in jeopardy. Thus, your strategies for dealing with their off-task behaviors, even rude and annoying ones, should provide them with face-saving ways to supplant off-task behaviors with on-task behaviors. This is not always easily done. When students behave rudely, it is tempting for teachers to respond with clever comebacks or put-downs. Not only does this practice destroy a healthy classroom climate; it can easily backfire on a teacher as it did in Vignette 7.11.

By trying to outwit Ronald instead of providing him with a face-saving way of getting back on-task, Mr. Sceroler turned a self-terminating incident into a most unfortunate confrontation with unhappy consequences for all concerned. Since Mr. Sceroler initially heard Ronald's rude remark, why would he ask him: "What was that you said?" Ronald tried to end the episode by not replying, but Mr. Sceroler persisted and left Ronald with the choice of either lying about what he said or repeating what would surely be interpreted as an obscenity. Had Mr. Sceroler not been such an insecure adult, intent on proving his superiority over an adolescent, he might have left Ronald a dignified way to return to on-task

---

VIGNETTE 7.11

Mr. Sceroler is urging his eighth grade class to get their homework in on time as he says: "There's nothing I can do if you don't have the work in my hands." Ronald from the back of the room, in a barely audible tone, quips to the student next to him: "He could always go jack off!" Having overhead the comment, Mr. Sceroler yells at Ronald: "What was that you said?" Ronald begins to grin and look around at his classmates. Mr. Sceroler: "You were trying to show off for us and now you can't say anything! What did you say?" Ronald whispers with his head down: "Nothing." Mr. Sceroler, seeing Ronald back down, begins to feel confident as he continues: "What was that? Speak up. What did you say?" Now facing Mr. Sceroler, Ronald says in a loud voice: "I said I didn't say nothin'!" Mr. Sceroler retorts: "You can't even use decent English. Of course you didn't say anything. You aren't capable of saying anything, are you?" Some class members laugh. Enjoying the audience, Mr. Sceroler smiles. Ronald, very concerned with what his classmates are thinking, suddenly stands up and shouts at Mr. Sceroler: "I said you could always go jack off, but then I forgot, you don't have a dick!"

behavior by either ignoring the original remark or by politely directing Ronald to visit with him at a more convenient time.

AVOID PLAYING DETECTIVE

You also encourage competitiveness between you and your students by playing the game of "detective," as Mr. Brubacher does in Vignette 7.12.

In Vignette 7.13, Ms. Fisher deals with an on-going disruptive behavior from an unidentified source as did Mr. Brubacher. However, she refuses to play the "detective" game with her students.

VIGNETTE 7.12

Some students in Mr. Brubacher's biology class begin amusing themselves by covertly screeching "Whoop-whoop!" while he speaks to the class. At first, he tries laughing the disruptions off with comments like: "There's a bird in here, and I've got a hunting license!" But after a couple of days, Mr. Brubacher no longer finds any humor whatsoever with the rudeness. To the delight of his students, he vows to catch the pranksters and put an end to the whoop-whooping. Unsuccessfully, he tries to identify the source of the annoying sounds. More and more students get into the act and are becoming bolder and more creative in devising ways to emit the sound without getting caught.

VIGNETTE 7.13

After a day in which Ms. Fisher's students amused themselves by covertly screeching "Whoop-whoop!" when she spoke to the class, she thinks to herself: "I wish I knew who's responsible for that horrible whoop-whooping. But, I'm not going to play their little game with them, so I'm not going to even try to find out. I just won't tolerate it any more. They know that noise annoys me, so I shouldn't try and act as though it doesn't. Tomorrow, I'll be ready with an alternative lesson plan if they try the whoop-whooping while I'm explaining things to them."

The next day, Ms. Fisher is lecturing on the digestive system when "Whoop-whoop" is heard and some of the students begin to laugh. Abruptly, Ms. Fisher stops the lecture and silently and calmly displays a transparency on the overhead with the following message: "I cannot explain the digestive system to you while that noise is going on. I simply won't try to do what you won't allow me to do. But I am responsible for seeing that you learn this material. So please open your book to page 179. Study pages 179 through 191. Most of what I planned to talk about today is covered on those pages. Do not forget that we have a test on the unit objectives scheduled for Monday. Good luck!" Several students glare at two others, who appear rather sheepish.

Ms. Fisher believes that most of her students would prefer listening to her explanations than only reading the text. Thus, she believes that if she continues to abruptly move to her alternative lesson plan each time her lectures and explanations are disrupted, enough peer pressure will be exerted to stop the unidentified sources of the dreaded noise.

UTILIZE ALTERNATIVE LESSON PLANS

When implementing a planned learning activity, you should, of course, expect students to cooperate with you and become engaged. By being confident that they will be on-task, you communicate your expectations and, thus increase the chances that they will be on-task and engaged. However, you also need to be prepared for the possibility that all students' cooperation is not as forthcoming as you expected. In Vignette 7.3, Ms. Reid gets Al engaged in an alternate geography learning activity after his behavior excluded him from the geography bingo plan. Ms. Fisher, in Vignette 7.13 dealt with a recurrence of her students' "whoop-whooping" with an alternative learning activity that communicated she considers learning serious business and demands courteous cooperation in her classroom.

A well-designed, appropriate learning activity should not be aborted simply because things don't go quite as smoothly as planned. Do not give up on your well-thought-out ideas. However, being prepared with alternative plans can sometimes save the day when students' off-task behaviors render your original plan unworkable.

UTILIZE THE HELP OF COLLEAGUES

Refer to Mr. Martin's checklist in Vignette 3.5 for preparing for the opening of a new school year. Item 11 under "Classroom Organization and On-Going Routines" is "Whom, among building personnel, can I depend on to help handle short-ranged discipline problems and whom for long-ranged problems?" In Vignette 5.5, Ms. Williams has an arrangement with her colleague, Mr. Demery, that allows the two of them to more effectively deal with off-task behaviors than they could working alone. You would do well to seek out a few teachers in your school on whom you can depend to (1) work out cooperative arrangements for handling discipline problems, as did Ms. Williams and Mr. Demery; (2) share ideas and provide counsel on how to teach students who get off-task to be on-task.

Dealing with off-task behaviors is one of teachers' more difficult jobs. Do not play "macho teacher" and be too embarrassed to seek help. Routinely share ideas with trusted colleagues and seek help when confronted with particularly difficult situations. Ms. Reid, in Vignette 7.3, arranged some think-time for herself before confronting Al's antisocial behavior. She may have used some of that time to confer with another teacher or an instructional supervisor who has experience dealing with similar problems. Of course, it is assumed that you will seek the help of other professionals like yourself without violating the professional trust that exists between you and your students.

UTILIZE THE HELP OF PARENTS AND INSTRUCTIONAL SUPERVISORS

The Myth of the "Good" Teacher

In *Assertive Discipline: A Take-Charge Approach for Today's Educator,* Canter and Canter (1976) assert:

> Today's teachers must contend with . . . the "Myth of the Good Teacher." This myth basically goes as follows: "A 'good' teacher should be able to handle all behavior problems on her own, and within the confines of the classroom." This means if you are competent, you should never need to go to your principal or the child's parents for assistance. . . . No one teacher, no matter how good she is, or how much experience or training she has, is capable of working successfully with each and every child without support. There are many students today whose behavior is so disruptive that a teacher must have assistance from both the principal and the parent(s) in order to deal effectively with the child and his behavior.
>
> This "myth" places a burden of guilt upon teachers who encounter problems with their students. According to the myth, if they were "really good" they wouldn't have these problems. These guilt-ridden, inadequate feelings tend to keep teachers from asking for the help they need with certain students. (pp. 6–7)*

Canter and Canter (1976) advise you to "ask for assistance from the student's parents," insisting that "you have the right to ask the parents or principal for whatever assistance you deem necessary, in order to maximize your potential influences with a child!" The potential for success of a number of the strategies for dealing with off-task behaviors related in examples throughout this book depends on teachers eliciting the cooperation of students' parents (e.g., Vignette 2.21 and Vignette 7.3 in which Ms. Reid communicated her willingness to involve parents by asking: "Will you remember, or should I phone your house tonight to remind you?").

Undeniably, parents have a responsibility for helping teachers teach their children to cooperate in school. Often, however, obstacles to utilizing the help of parents are difficult to overcome. Some parents, for one reason or another,

---

*From *Assertion Discipline: A Take-Charge Approach for Today's Educator* (pp. 6–7), by L. Canter and M. Canter, 1976, Seal Beach, CA: Canter and Associates. Reprinted by permission.

are simply not available to help. The reasons may or may not be understandable, but an unavailable or unapproachable parent can hardly be utilized, leaving you to seek other alternatives for help in working with the child. The Canters' "Myth of the 'Good' Teacher" leads some misdirected teachers to contact parents only as a last resort, when it is too late to efficiently deal with a discipline problem.

Assertiveness

Some teachers, burdened by the myth, approach parents so apologetically that their lack of assertiveness precludes the effective communications necessary for the teachers to acquire constructive parental help. Canter and Canter (1976) state

> Many teachers feel threatened and overwhelmed by parents, especially if the parents are pushy or manipulative. Thus, many teachers have difficulty in being assertive with parents; they do not clearly and firmly let the parents know what they want or need from them, nor do they stand up for their rights. As a result, all too often we hear teachers being woefully nonassertive. For example, when calling parents:

> - *They apologize for bothering parents:* "I'm really sorry to bother you at home with this . . ."
> - *They downgraded the problem:* "We had a 'small' problem with your son today." (In reality he had a violent tantrum which disrupted the entire class for 20 minutes.)
> - *They belittle themselves:* "I just don't know what to do with your son." (Yes, you do! You need the cooperation of the parents to discipline him at home for his tantrums.)
> - *They do not clearly state their needs:* "I know you are busy, working and all, but if you could find the time I'd appreciate it if you talked to your son about his tantrums." (You want her to discipline her son at home—period!)
> - *They downgrade the consequences of the child's behavior:* "I don't know what will happen if he doesn't change his behavior in class." (Yes, you do! He will need to be suspended.)

> Often teachers confuse being assertive with being hostile. They are afraid that if they are assertive, the parent will be offended and go to the principal. However, hostility means that you express wants and needs in a manner which offends others or violates their self-dignity. The difference between nonassertive, hostile, and assertive communications with parents can best be illustrated by a direct comparison of the different responses.
> *Situation:* You call the parents to discuss the behavior problems of their child. During the conference, the parents become angry and unfairly blame you for their child's problems at school.

> - *Non-Assertive Response:* You sit there and passively take the criticism without expressing your concerns and feelings.
> - *Hostile Response:* You get defensive and tell the parent off, blaming them for their child's problems.

- *Assertive Response:* You listen to the criticism. You express your recognition of their feelings. *Again,* you express that you called them to arrange some constructive cooperation between you, which will help their child's behavior.

Situation: A child comes to school dirty and unkempt. You call the parents to express your concern about the child's cleanliness, and request that he come to school better kempt. The parents balk at your request, as they have in the past.

- *Non-Assertive Response:* You listen to the parents and don't press your demands.
- *Hostile Response:* You tell the parents that it is a disgrace the way they send their child to school, and they should be ashamed of themselves.
- *Assertive Response:* You firmly repeat your demand, and let the parents know that in the best interest of their child you will contact the appropriate agency, if the situation does not improve.

Situation: You call the parents to ask their cooperation in following through at home on the contract you have with their child, as a result of the behavior problems he has in your class. The parents are very reluctant to do so.

- *Non-Assertive Response:* You give up and don't press your wants.
- *Hostile Response:* You tell the parents how inadequate they are, and that they had better learn to discipline their child.
- *Assertive Response:* You firmly repeat your demands, and let the parents know the consequences if their child continues to do poorly in school.

As you have seen, in the assertive responses of each situation, the teacher stated her position and stuck to it. It was firm, not passive, not hostile. You, as a teacher, need to let the parents know where you stand and then allow them to *choose* whether to cooperate with your wishes. When you are non-assertive (passive), you allow the parents to "control you." You feel "lousy" and don't receive the support or action you need to help the child. When you are hostile, you "put down" the parents. They will become threatened and, again, you will not get what you want and need from them.

We have found that teachers can learn to be more assertive and, thus, more effective in their relations with parents. The model we utilize is simple, easily learned and implemented.

1. Assert yourself and contact parents as soon as you see that there is, or possibly will be, a situation with the child where you will need the parents' cooperation.
2. Know what you want from your meeting or conversation with the parents. (Goal)
3. Plan how you will achieve the goal. (Objectives)
4. Know why you want parents' cooperation and assistance. (Rationale)
5. Be prepared to explain what you feel will occur if the parents are not cooperative. (Consequences)
6. Have documentation to support your comments. (pp. 156–160)

Of course, eliciting the help of parents to address students' off-task behavior problems is much easier when you have already established an efficient line of communication with them prior to being confronted by the problems. Mr. Perkins in Vignette 4.35 and Mr. Bertolli with his newsletter (displayed in Figure 4.1) make it easier for themselves to utilize parental help by keeping parents apprised of their goals and expectations. Knowing parents before a discipline problem arises also gives you an advantage in deciding how to handle the problem. Ms. Jackson, in Vignette 9.16, deals with the problem of three students who are high on marijuana. Because prior to the incident she had communicated with the students' parents, she is able to develop her strategy for preventing a recurrence of the misbehaviors in light of what she knows about the kind of help or hindrance she can expect from each individual set of parents. As you will see when you read Vignette 9.16, she decides to involve two of the students' parents, but not those of the third.

DO NOT USE CORPORAL PUNISHMENT

Corporal Punishment

In Chapter 2, a distinction is made between naturally occurring punishment and contrived punishment. A punishment for a person's behavior is naturally occurring if an aversive stimulus is experienced by that person as a direct consequence of that behavior. Punishment that is intentionally and artificially imposed following a behavior is contrived punishment. Vignettes 2.22 and 2.23 illustrate the difference between the two types of punishment.

Corporal punishment is a form of contrived punishment in which physical pain or discomfort is intentionally inflicted upon an individual for the purpose of trying to get that individual to be sorry he or she displayed a particular behavior. Naturally occurring punishment, even if it is physically painful or uncomfortable, is not considered corporal punishment. The pain Henry experiences in Vignette 7.14 is not corporal punishment for his behavior because the pain is a direct consequence of that behavior itself.

Vignettes 7.15–7.19 are examples of corporal punishment.

VIGNETTE 7.14

Ignoring Lakeland Elementary School's "no running in the halls" rule, Henry sprints toward the cafeteria trying to be first in line. He trips and falls suffering a painful bruise on his elbow.

VIGNETTE 7.15

For repeated violations of the school "dress code," Bonnie is sent to Mr. Bailey, the assistant principle, who administers three swats to Bonnie's buttocks with his infamous "board of education." In accordance with local school district policy, Mr. Bailey's secretary witnesses the punishment as a "protection against accusations of abuse."

VIGNETTE 7.16

John is busily carving a picture with the point of a compass in his school desk top when Ms. Salsberry, his fifth grade teacher, surprises him from behind by twisting his ear and asking: "Do you think this will help you remember not to abuse your desk?" John shrieks in pain.

VIGNETTE 7.17

While supervising her prekindergarten class on the playground, Ms. Barfuss notices Raymond running toward a street full of traffic. Ms. Barfuss chases him down and slaps his thigh twice with her hand and says: "No, Raymond! Don't go in that street. You could be killed!" Raymond's leg stings for about 50 seconds after the incident.

VIGNETTE 7.18

Ms. Loycano's third graders are supposed to be quietly working problems in workbooks when she notices Theresa and Eva involved in a conversation. "Would you two please come up here?" Ms. Loycano asks. Theresa: "What in the shit for?" Ms. Loycano responds: "I don't appreciate hearing that kind of language in the classroom, Theresa. You stay in here when the rest go to lunch and we'll help you remember how to speak in here." When the other students leave, Ms. Loycano is ready for Theresa with a bar of soap and wet towel which she uses to literally wash out the inside of Theresa's mouth.

VIGNETTE 7.19

As she is conducting a group discussion on citizenship for her fourth graders, Ms. Xavier notices Lyman starting to pass a note to Becky. Ms. Xavier: "Let's see the note, Lyman." "I don't got no note!" Lyman says as he quickly sits on the note.

Ms. Xavier walks over to Lyman and says: "Stand up." Rather than stand, Lyman squirms in his desk and the note falls to the floor. Ms. Xavier grabs it with a smile says: "I think I'll read it to the class!" Lyman stands up and screams, "No!" as he kicks Ms. Xavier on her shin. "Ouch!" she screams as she kicks him back. "Boy, that'll teach you to never think of touching me again!" she yells.

Do not confuse corporal punishment with other uses of physical force. Vignettes 7.20 and 7.21 are not examples of corporal punishment.

VIGNETTE 7.20

Mr. Triche is conducting his eighth grade mathematics class when a student, not in his class, enters his room and exclaims: "Please Mr. Triche, hurry! Andy and Todd are beating up Bennie!" Mr. Triche dashes out of his room and follows the alarmed student to the site of the assault. Andy and Todd are kicking Bennie as he lies on the floor. Mr. Triche puts a headlock on both offenders and pulls them off Bennie. Andy and Todd struggle in an attempt to free themselves, but Mr. Triche's grip holds firm. Mr. Triche directs the students who had alarmed him to seek first aid for Bennie from a nearby teacher. Maintaining his headlocks, he forcibly escorts Andy and Todd to the school office where he turns the matter over to the principal.

VIGNETTE 7.21

Ms. Marlin is delivering a history lecture to her history school class when she notices John listening to music through the earphones he's wearing. Ms. Marlin: "Would you please put your Walkman away until class is over?" John: "What for?" Ms. Marlin: "Because I don't want you in here unless you are going to pay attention to the lesson." John: "You can't make me leave!" Ms. Marlin walks over to John and says: "John, let's have this discussion out in the hall. We can settle it without the others having to listen to us." John: "I ain't going out there with you." Ms. Marlin puts her hand on John's arm and says: "There's no reason to turn this into a major incident; just come with me and everything will be all right." John stands up and yells: "Don't touch me, you old bitch!" and shoves Ms. Marlin, toppling her over backwards. Standing over her, he starts to throw a punch at her, but before he can, she kicks him viciously in his groin. As John drops to the floor in pain, Ms. Marlin scrambles to her feet, quickly moves away from John, stands in the doorway, and gives the following orders to the class: "Everyone but John, get out in the hall immediately! Cynthia, you run to the Office, tell them what happened and get us some help." Before John can rise from the floor, enough students are already moving out of the room and into the hall so that the path between him and Ms. Marlin is blocked.

Mr. Triche used physical force for the sole purpose of terminating the assault on Bennie. Although Andy and Todd probably experienced pain as a consequence of his force, the purpose of the force was not to inflict that pain. The purpose was to get them under control in order to end the assault and get them to the principal. Similarly, Ms. Marlin's rather violent response to John's attack should not be considered corporal punishment because the purpose of the response was to protect herself and restore order. Had she continued to strike out at John after she had successfully immobilized him, then she would have been administering corporal punishment. On the other hand, Mr. Bailey, Ms. Salsberry, Ms. Barfuss, Ms. Loycano, and Ms. Xavier administered corporal punishment because their physical force was applied with the intent of providing students with physically painful or uncomfortable experiences that would cause them to regret their misbehaviors.

Arguments For and Against Corporal Punishment

Should corporal punishment ever be used in schools? If so, under what circumstances should it be used and how should it be applied? These two questions continue to be debated as they have been for at least the past 200 years. In some school districts corporal punishment, as it is defined herein, is absolutely prohibited; in others it is encouraged (Van Dyke, 1984). Everyone seems to, at least publicly, agree that students need to be protected from abusive corporal punishment in which either serious physical trauma results or in which it is applied thoughtlessly. However, many researchers suggest that all corporal punishment is abusive because of its deleterious effects on both the long-term welfare of students and on the educational environment of the school (Rose, 1984; Welsh, 1985). The National Education Association, the American Federation of Teachers, the Council for Exceptional Children, and the American Psychological Association are only four of the many prominent professional organizations that have issued statements adamantly opposing the use of corporal punishment in schools (National Education Association, 1972; Reardon & Reynolds, 1979; Wood, 1982).

There is a ban on the practice in the public schools of some countries and states (e.g., New South Wales in Australia and New Jersey in the U.S.). Yet, the widespread, but inconsistent, practice of corporal punishment continues to prevail in both public and private schools in the United States and elsewhere. Van Dyke (1984) estimates that nearly 1.5 million times per year corporal punishment is inflicted in over 77,500 U.S. schools.

Supporters of corporal punishment as a response to off-task school behavior in at least some circumstances provide the following arguments.

1. There is the saying: "Spare the rod and spoil the child."
2. The Bible (e.g., Prov. 13:24, 12:15, 23:13) supports corporal punishment as a means of moral development.
3. What else works?
4. Some students do not understand anything else.
5. Teachers need to be able to protect themselves.
6. Corporal punishment builds character and, for boys, masculinity.

7. There are harsher, more dangerous forms of punishment, such as sustained psychological embarrassment.
8. Students want corporal punishment. It provides the firm guidance that students need to feel secure.
9. It leads students to respect teachers and to have respect for authority.
10. Parents want their children disciplined at school.
11. Unlike many other ways of handling off-task behaviors, corporal punishment can be swiftly administered so that the student can quickly return to the business of being engaged in learning activities.
12. Using corporal punishment for one student's off-task behavior may deter others from modeling that off-task behavior.
13. Judicial courts in the United States have consistently upheld the right of school officials to utilize corporal punishment (Kerr & Nelson, 1983, pp. 316–318).
14. The abuses of corporal punishment can be prevented by allowing its application only under clearly specified, strictly controlled circumstances. Different school districts have developed their own guidelines. The following is a sample of rules from the guidelines of a variety of districts.
    a. Corporal punishment shall only be used as a last resort, after other more desirable means have failed.
    b. Corporal punishment may be administered only to students whose parents have provided the school with written permission.
    c. Corporal punishment may only be administered by the school principal or designee.
    d. Corporal punishment shall be prescribed only for those who will profit from it.
    e. Students are not required to submit to corporal punishment providing that they are willing to accept the alternative noncorporal punishment that is prescribed by the school discipline official.
    f. To give those involved a cooling off period, no corporal punishment may be administered within one hour from when the violation that is to be punished occurred.
    g. Whenever corporal punishment is administered, at least two professional adults must be present.
    h. Corporal punishment may be administered only for certain student offenses as specified in the "Disciplinary Code Handbook."
    i. Corporal punishment may be administered to boys only.
    j. The severity of corporal punishment is strictly limited.

The arguments provided to those opposed to any form of corporal punishment in schools seem more compelling.

1. Opposition to corporal punishment is not opposition to firm, strict discipline. "Sparing the rod" does not mean "spoiling the child" if other, more effective means for handling misbehaviors are employed.
2. Research does not support the notion that corporal punishment is an effective tool in teaching students to supplant off-task behaviors with on-task behaviors (Bongiovanni, 1979).

3. Corporal punishment is an extremely destructive form of contrived punishment. Even when it serves to discourage one misbehavior, the long-range side effects can be far less desirable than the original misbehavior (Hyman & Wise, 1979). Welsh (1985) reports that no one has ever demonstrated the utility of spanking a child: "When spanking does work, it is not unlike whacking your watch with your hand to make it tick. This crude procedure may work for a while, but the long-term consequences of hitting one's watch is likely to be detrimental to the delicate mechanism. Our research suggests that the watch analogy also holds for whacking children." The association between children experiencing corporal punishment and their development of aggressive or violent behavior patterns is both well-documented and well-publicized (Azrin, Hake, & Hutchinson, 1965; Azrin, Hutchinson, & Sallery, 1964; Bandura, 1965; Delgado, 1963; Ulrich & Azrin, 1962; Welsh, 1985).

4. Corporal punishment shatters any semblance of a businesslike classroom climate in which mutual respect, cooperation, and seriousness of purpose prevail (Cangelosi, 1990a, pp. 60–64; Kohut & Range, 1979; Strike & Soltis, 1986; Sulzer-Azaroff & Mayer, 1977). The sanctity of the learning environment is violated whenever any sort of violent behavior is tolerated. Corporal punishment is not only tolerated violence; it is condoned violence that is modeled by school personnel.

5. Research findings indicate that school personnel who rely on corporal punishment tend to be less experienced, more close-minded, more neurotic, less thoughtful, and more impulsive than their counterparts who do not use corporal punishment (Rust & Kinnard, 1983).

Corporal Punishment: A Poor Choice

Assuming that it is legal to use corporal punishment in your school, under what circumstances should you either administer it yourself or refer students to another who is authorized to administer it? Although it is still commonly used and may sometimes seem to be a swift, decisive way of dealing with certain off-task behaviors, there are no circumstances when you should depend on corporal punishment. How can one possibly resolve the inconsistency between using corporal punishment and being a professional educator once the following have been considered: (1) the availability of more effective alternatives to dealing with off-task behaviors (e.g., see subsequent chapters of this text), (2) the long-range side effects of corporal punishment, (3) its corrupting influence on the businesslike air of respect and cooperation that contribute so much to maintaining students on-task and engaged in learning activities.

KNOW YOUR RIGHTS AND LIMITATIONS

In many school districts you would surely find yourself with legal problems for ever doing anything that even resembled the use of corporal punishment. In other districts, you may be required to explain why you failed to use corporal punishment in certain circumstances. When addressing off-task behavior problems, you need to be mindful of the limitations of your rights and responsibilities as a professional teacher. Those rights and responsibilities vary considerably from school district to school district. Unfortunately, there is probably no way for you to fully protect yourself from legal suits stemming from circumstances that arise in your school. Mr. Triche was commended by his principal, fellow teachers, and by Andy's parents for the way he handled the delicate situation in Vignette 7.20. Neither Todd nor Andy were injured in the incident and, according to virtually everyone involved, he prevented Bennie from sustaining serious injuries. Yet, several months later, Andy's and Todd's parents sued Mr. Triche for brutality in the incident. The suit failed, but only after two years of expensive litigation. How do you protect yourself from this kind of action? There is no foolproof method, but being aware of school district policies and principles of accepted professional practice can help, as can a habit of being reflective before taking a course of action. Mr. Triche did not, in fact, violate any law or school policy by his actions and he did think about what to do before acting. Repeatedly, he indicated that he did not regret handling the situation as he did. However, he did resent being suspended from his teaching position while having to fight a legal battle as a consequence of "doing the right thing."

Fortunately, legal actions against teachers who fulfill their responsibilities and who do not exceed the limits of their authority when dealing with discipline problems are unlikely occurrences. Before having to wrestle with a sticky situation, find out just what kind of backing you can expect from your school administrators, supervisors, and professional association. Know, for example, if you have the right to bar a student from your classroom until some contingency you've specified has been met. Come to an agreement on these matters with your principal before the start of a school year.

MAINTAIN YOUR OPTIONS

Three clichés, the second one particularly disgusting, may help make the point of this section. "Don't back yourself into a corner." "Don't draw your gun unless you're prepared to use it." "Hold on to your last card." Once you're aware of the extent of your authority, do not exhaust it. If for example, you tell a student: "Either sit down immediately or you're out of this classroom for good," you have committed yourself to what, in most situations, is the extent of any teacher's authority. If the student doesn't sit down immediately, you have left yourself little recourse. Did you really want things to go that far? Before ever exhausting your options regarding a situation, seek the help of supervisors.

KNOW YOURSELF AND KNOW YOUR STUDENTS

Routinely take time to examine your own motives for the methods you use with students. Why do you handle things the way you do? How far are you willing to go with a plan? How much time and energy are you willing and able to invest to solve a particular problem? What are you willing to risk? To effectively handle off-task behaviors, you must provide honest answers to these questions. For some off-task behavior problems under certain circumstances, you should tell yourself that your priorities lead you to be unwilling to spend the time and energy necessary to effect solutions. In each of these instances, implement only the first step of the Teaching Process Model by recognizing that there is a student need with which you are not prepared to deal.

Be receptive to individual differences among your students. Measures that effectively deal with an off-task behavior of one student may be disastrous with another. Be conservative in attempting new ideas with students you don't know well until you have found the ideas to be workable with familiar students. On the other hand, don't give up on an idea because it doesn't work for all students all of the time.

The better you understand yourself and your students, the more effectively you will be able to respond to displays of off-task behavior with decisiveness, sensitivity and flexibility.

TRANSITIONAL ACTIVITIES
FROM CHAPTER 7 TO CHAPTER 8

   I. Ms. Odle follows the Teaching Process Model to plan and conduct a two-week learning unit on drug, alcohol, and tobacco abuse for her fifth grade class. She completed step one by determining that her students need to be aware of the physiological and psychological effects of using such substances. In light of that need, she determines the objectives for the unit and, thus, completes step two. For steps three, four, and five she plans, prepares, and conducts learning activities that include, among other things, small group discussions, guest lecture presentations, poster projects, and formative tests. Near the end of the two-week period, she administers a comprehensive test, the results of which help her complete step six in which she makes a summative evaluation about what students gained from the unit.

   Ms. Odle also utilizes the Teaching Process Model to deal with students' off-task behaviors as they occur during time allocated for the unit's learning activities. Vignettes 7.22 and 7.23 are two such episodes. For each, please specify in writing just what she did for each of the six steps in the Teaching Process in handling the off-task behavior.

VIGNETTE 7.22

Ms. Odle is sitting in the back of her classroom as Mr. Boisvert speaks to the 27 fifth graders about his experiences as a counselor at a drug rehabilitation center. She is disturbed by the general lack of attentiveness to Mr. Boisvert's lecture. Some students are huddled, whispering to one another and giggling; very few appear to be engaged in the learning activity. As she sits in the rear of the room deciding whether she should act and if so how, Mr. Boisvert tends to direct his remarks more to her than to the students. Ms. Odle thinks to herself: "They should be listening to him. He's taking time from his busy schedule to share some very important ideas; the least we can do is to listen courteously. I'm going to do something to get them reengaged in Mr. Boisvert's lecture. But what? I'd live to avoid dramatizing the fact that the students aren't listening. He might find that embarrassing and there's no need to let him know that I know that they don't find his talk engaging. I know!—But, I've got to wait for the opportune moment in his talk. . . ."

". . . and it seems that most of the kids I see just don't think that much of themselves," Mr. Boisvert is saying as Ms. Odle stands up from her place in the back of the room and interrupts: "Excuse me, Mr. Boisvert. You've just made such an important point; I want to make sure everyone understands it." She walks to the front of the room, thinking to herself: "Maybe if I stand up front, just a little behind him, he'll quit directing his remarks to me and I'll be in a position to maintain eye contact with the class. They're more likely to at least pretend to be attending, if they see me watching them. They know me well enough!" Standing near Mr. Boisvert, but looking directly at the class, she asks him: "Would you please explain a little more about what it means for a people not to think much of themselves?" As Mr. Boisvert continues, Ms. Odle positions herself slightly behind him and to one side where she can monitor the class with her best "be quiet, eyes ahead, sit up straight and listen, or else life in here as you now know it will cease to exist" look on her face. For the remainder of the talk, Ms. Odle observes for indications of how well her tactics are working.

VIGNETTE 7.23

For some time, Ms. Odle has believed that Treva should break her habit of making a joke out of what other students say during learning activities. Ms. Odle hadn't decided to do anything about this off-task behavior pattern until a couple of days into the learning unit on substance abuse when Treva went into a "drunken stupor" act in response to another students' very serious comments about the effects of alcohol. After school that day, Ms. Odle thinks to herself: "It wouldn't be so bad if Treva didn't wait for some of the more serious, thought-provoking moments in our discussions to start the class laughing. Then it's hard to get them back into a serious, thoughtful vein. Besides, she's conditioning some students to keep their mouths shut out of fear that their words will be twisted into a joke. I'm going to help Treva reduce the frequency of her clowning. But how should I approach it?"

Ms. Odle designs and implements a plan for, (1) identifying the positive reinforcers (e.g., the attention she receives from others laughing at her) for her clowning; (2) taking steps to prevent her clowning in class to be positively reinforced (e.g., just prior to a discussion session one day, Ms. Odle shows the class a video she thinks will bring home the point that "taking drugs is never funny"); (3) providing positive reinforcers for an appropriate alternative behavior (e.g., drawing attention to Treva when she makes serious, on-task comments in class); (4) gathering data for deciding how well the plan is working.

Check your response to see if it contains the same ideas as this sample response.

Ms. Odle followed the Teaching Process Model in responding to her students' inattentiveness during Mr. Boisvert's guest lecture presentation. (1) She identified student needs by deciding that the students ought to be politely paying attention to the talk. (2) She determined a learning goal by deciding that she would do something to get them to silently attend to the lecture. (3) She determined a learning activity by deciding to discreetly interrupt Mr. Boisvert at an opportune moment and applying her "I mean business" body language technique. (4) She prepared for the learning activity by moving into position. (5) She conducted a learning activity by saying what she did and standing as she did in front of the class. (6) She evaluated how well the goal was achieved by deciding how well her tactics worked.

In Vignette 7.23, she utilized the six steps in dealing with Treva's disruptive behavior pattern. (1) She determined a student need when she decided that Treva should break her habit of inappropriate joking. (2) She determined a learning goal by deciding to do something to help Treva reduce the frequency of clowning in class. (3) She designed a learning activity by developing a plan for getting Treva to extinguish her behavior pattern of clowning in class. (4) She prepared for at least one component of the learning activity by arranging to have the video shown. (5) She conducted a learning activity by showing the film. (6) She evaluated how well Treva is progressing by utilizing the data she gathered.

II. For each of the following, write a half-page essay that either argues for or against the statement.
   A. Although it is not generally advisable to ignore the off-task behaviors of students, ignoring an incident of off-task behavior is preferable to dealing with it half-heartedly.
   B. Teaching students to be on-task differs from molding students' characters.
   C. If a teacher simply terminates a student's disruptive behavior in class and doesn't take measures to prevent recurrences until after class, other students in the class will think that they can get away with disruptive behaviors.
   D. Students are very concerned with what their peers think of them. Thus, humbling a student in front of the class for disruptive behavior is an effective means of preventing such disruptions in the future.
   E. Sometimes it is better for a teacher to fail to identify the perpetrators of a classroom disruption than to play the "detective" game with students.
   F. Experienced teachers who apply sound classroom management principles do not need the help of colleagues, supervisors, or parents in dealing with off-task behaviors.
      Exchange your responses with those of colleagues. Discuss differences and similarities.

III. Design a learning activity for helping students within your teaching specialty achieve a particular learning objective. Now, develop an alternative learning activity that you might use in case students do not cooperate with your first plan.
   Have your plans critiqued by a colleague; return the favor.

IV. The following seven selections from the supplemental readings section at the end of this chapter deal with corporal punishment: Hyman (1978), Hyman & Wise (1979), Rust & Kinnard (1983), Van Dyke (1984), Welsh (1985), and Zirkel (1991). Read as many as you reasonably can. Discuss with colleagues your beliefs about corporal punishment.

V. In preparation for your work with Chapter 8, discuss the following questions with two or more of your colleagues.
   A. What strategies do teachers employ to lead students to supplant off-task behavior patterns with on-task behavior patterns?
   B. How can teachers avoid accidentally encouraging students to develop off-task behavior patterns?
   C. How can teachers avoid accidentally discouraging students to develop on-task behavior patterns?

SUPPLEMENTAL READINGS

Bell, L. C., & Stefanich, G. P. (1984). Building effective discipline using the cascade model. *The Clearing House, 58,* 134–137.

Cangelosi, J. S. (1992). *Teaching mathematics in secondary and middle school: Research-based approaches* (pp. 252–260). New York: Macmillan.

Canter, L., & Canter, M. (1976). *Assertive discipline: A take-charge approach for today's educator* (pp. 155–178). Seal Beach, CA: Canter & Associates.

Cunningham, A. R. (1983). The deportment chart: A student management tool that could help a classroom teacher. *The Clearing House, 56,* 421–422.

Hyman, I. A. (1978). A social science review of evidence cited in litigation on corporal punishment in the schools. *Journal of Child Psychology, 30,* 195–199.

Hyman, I. A., & Wise, J. H. (Eds.). (1979). *Corporal punishment in American education.* Philadelphia: Temple University Press.

Rich, J. M. (1991). Should students be punished? *Contemporary Education, 62,* 180–184.

Rust, J. O., & Kinnard, K. Q. (1983). Personality characteristics of the users of corporal punishment in the schools. *Journal of School Psychology, 21,* 91–105.

Strike, K., & Soltis, J. (1986). Who broke the fish tank? And other ethical dilemmas. *Instructor, 95,* 36–39.

Van Dyke, H. T. (1984). Corporal punishment in our schools. *The Clearing House, 57,* 296–300.

Welsh, R. S. (1985). Spanking: A grand old American tradition? *Children Today, 14,* 25–29.

Wilcox, R. T. (1983). Discipline made gentle. *The Clearing House, 57,* 30–35.

Woolridge, P., & Richman, C. L. (1985). Teachers' choice of punishment as a function of a student's gender, age, race, and IQ level. *Journal of School Psychology, 23,* 19–29.

Zirkel, P. A. (1991). Corporal punishment as a crime. *Principal, 71,* 62–63.

CHAPTER 8

Modifying Off-Task Behavior Patterns

Purpose of Chapter 8

Chapter 8 is designed to help you

1. Design learning activities to teach students to supplant off-task behavior patterns with on-task behavior patterns.
2. Understand how the following principles of behavior modification influence the development of behavior patterns, (a) extinction, (b) alternative behavior patterns, (c) reinforcement schedules, (d) shaping, (e) cuing, (f) generalization and discrimination, (g) modeling, (h) satiation.

SYSTEMATIC TECHNIQUES FOR CHANGING HABITS

The Formation and Elimination of Behavior Patterns

Theories associated with behavioristic psychology provide explanations for how behavior patterns are formed; they also provide a basis for strategies used to teach students to terminate off-task behavior patterns in favor of on-task behavior patterns. Positive reinforcement, punishment, and negative reinforcement in conjunction with behavior modification principles are particularly powerful techniques for you to utilize in dealing with your students' off-task behavior patterns.

Behavior modification principles are continually influencing both the formation and elimination of your students' behavior patterns. Taking advantage of these principles to help students break off-task habits and acquire on-task habits

VIGNETTE 8.1

Jana, one of Mr. Washington's first graders, habitually yells out to him while he is busy working with other students. Mr. Washington decides to apply both the principles of extinction and alternative behavior patterns in devising a scheme to deal with Jana's disruptive behavior pattern. After some thoughtful consideration, he decides that Jana's yelling is positively reinforced by the attention it gains her. Thus, he plans to ignore her whenever she yells for him, and to provide her with special attention when she acts in a more appropriate fashion. He tries his plan, but he doesn't systematically gather data on how the plan is working. Instead, he only depends on his informal perceptions which leave him with the impression that the frequency of Jana's yelling is increasing not decreasing. Figure 8.1 depicts what appears to be happening according to Mr. Washington's unsystematically formed impression. Consequently, Mr. Washington aborts his plan after only three days.

FIGURE 8.1 Mr. Washington's Perception of the Frequency of Jana's Yelling

3 days prior to program	2 days prior to program	1 day prior to program	1st day of program	2nd day of program	3rd day of program
ЖГ ЖГ ЖГ	ЖГ ЖГ ЖГ	ЖГ ЖГ ЖГ	ЖГ ЖГ ЖГ ЖГ ЖГ	ЖГ ЖГ ЖГ ЖГ ЖГ ЖГ ЖГ ЖГ	ЖГ ЖГ ЖГ ЖГ ЖГ ЖГ ЖГ ЖГ ЖГ

is, of course, preferable to having them operate out of your control. You get the behavior modification principles that are explained in this chapter to work for you by (1) consciously considering their influence when planning learning activities and when interacting with students, (2) being very systematic when applying them to off-task behavior problems.

The Need for Systematic Observation

As demonstrated in Vignette 8.1, being systematic is particularly useful in evaluating how well a behavior modification plan is working.

Had Mr. Washington been more systematic and maintained records, he might not have given up so quickly. If, for example, he had kept a tally sheet to mark down every time Jana yelled, a somewhat different picture may have emerged. Figure 8.2 depicts what his results may actually have been.

Is such a discrepancy between perceived frequency of yelling and actual frequency likely? Research results suggest that such differences are quite likely (Cangelosi, 1982, pp. 116–118). Compare the tallies perceived by Mr. Washington in Figure 8.1 to the actual tallies in Figure 8.2 and speculate as to what may have caused the discrepancies.

3 days prior to program	2 days prior to program	1 day prior to program	1st day of program	2nd day of program	3rd day of program
JHT JHT JHT I	JHT JHT IIII	JHT JHT JHT III	JHT JHT JHT JHT JHT I	JHT JHT JHT JHT I	JHT I

4th day of program	5th day of program
IIII	III

FIGURE 8.2   Jana's Actual Frequency of Yelling

The actual baseline data, data collected before any sort of intervention, differ very little from what Mr. Washington thought. According to both Mr. Washington's perception and to the systematically collected tallies, Jana's screams increase in frequency right after the plan is implemented. Does this surprise you? Jana's screaming had gained her attention in the past. When Mr. Washington began ignoring her, she could be expected to initially attempt with greater vigor and frequency what had previously worked.

It is after the plan had been in operation for a couple of days that Mr. Washington's perceptions appear distorted. How might that phenomenon be explained? It may be that Mr. Washington's expectations changed when he began implementing his plan. Jana's yelling is an annoying habit that he wants her to terminate. He's developed a plan that ought to work; he expects it to work. Expecting the plan to work, Jana's every yell appears to echo louder and is more annoying than her yells before he was working to stop the yelling.

APPLYING THE PRINCIPLE OF EXTINCTION

The Principle

Whenever the positive reinforcers for a person's voluntary behavior pattern are removed or cease to exist, the person will begin to discontinue that behavior pattern. This phenomenon is known as the principle of extinction. Students begin to break habits when they discover those habits are no longer rewarding. One voluntarily establishes a particular behavior pattern only in the presence of positive reinforcers. The removal of those reinforcers will, in time, extinguish that behavior pattern. Both desirable (e.g., on-task) and undesirable (e.g., off-task) behavior patterns are extinguished either by conscious design or by unplanned changes in situations.

Unintentional Extinction

Vignette 8.2 is an example of an unplanned extinction of a behavior pattern.

Initially, Ruth's help in the library was positively reinforced by Ms. Tolbert's expressions of appreciation and their companionship. Ruth was motivated to continue to help in the library after school as long as that behavior pattern was positively reinforced. The principle of extinction was unwittingly applied by Ms. Tolbert when she ceased providing the positive reinforcement for Ruth's habit.

Intentional Extinction

You can sometimes take conscious advantage of the principle of extinction to teach students to eliminate certain off-task behavior patterns. (1) Specify the exact behavior pattern to be extinguished. (2) Identify the positive reinforcers for the behavior. (3) Develop a plan for eliminating the positive reinforcement. (4) In light of baseline data, establish a realistic time schedule for reducing the frequency of the behavior. (5) Implement the plan. (6) Evaluate how well the pattern is being broken. In Vignette 8.3, a teacher plans to use the principle of extinction to help students break an off-task behavior habit.

VIGNETTE 8.2

Ruth, a sixth grader, begins stopping by her school's library to browse and pick up books. During some of her initial visits, Ruth helps Ms. Tolbert, the librarian, shelve books and do other chores. Ms. Tolbert enthusiastically expresses her appreciation and carries on lively conversations with Ruth as they work together. Ruth enjoys Ms. Tolbert's companionship and feels that her efforts are appreciated. Ruth begins coming every day after school to help. After about a month, Ms. Tolbert becomes accustomed to Ruth's presence and help and is less attentive to her. She is not as inclined to carry on lively conversations with Ruth and expresses her appreciation for Ruth's help less often than she did before. Soon Ruth's after-school library visits become less frequent until she no longer shows up at all.

VIGNETTE 8.3

Ms. Goldberg, a mathematics teacher, has been using a procedure in which each student's grade is determined by the number of points accumulated during a semester. A student has two means for gaining points. (1) Half of the total possible points are based on test scores. (2) The rest of the points are awarded for homework that, when turned in on time, is scored according to the number of correct responses.

Ms. Goldberg begins to notice that increasingly more students receive high marks on homework, but low marks on test papers. Under her system, these students are still able to pass the course. She analyzes the situation, collects some baseline information, and realizes that these students are simply copying their homework from

---

VIGNETTE 8.3 (continued)

others. Understanding that her grading system positively reinforces this habit of copying instead of actually doing homework, she decided to alter her grading procedure so that those positive reinforcers are eliminated. Under the new system, homework will still be assigned, but no longer factored into the semester grade. Instead, she will use the homework strictly as a learning activity that provides students with practice and feedback relative to the skills that they will be asked to display on the tests. The tests will be the sole source of data for determining semester grades.

After explaining her new grading procedure to the class, she implements it, and assesses whether or not copying homework diminishes and test scores improve.

Extinction is not the only method for helping students eliminate off-task behaviors. Other methods (e.g., punishment, cuing, or satiation) are surely more appropriate whenever the positive reinforcers for an off-task behavior pattern either cannot be identified or cannot be efficiently controlled.

ALTERNATIVE BEHAVIOR PATTERNS

Students, like all living persons, are always behaving in some manner. Sleeping, running, remembering, watching television, doing homework, waiting in line, thinking about schoolwork, thinking about an embarrassing moment, worrying about appearance, listening, talking, being angry, and daydreaming are only a minute portion of the cognitive, affective, and psychomotor behaviors that contribute to a person's behavior complex at any given moment. Because students are always displaying some type of behavior, whenever one behavior pattern is extinguished, an alternate or replacement behavior pattern emerges. Consequently, when you are trying to help a student terminate one undesirable behavior pattern, you should guard against that student replacing the current pattern with another, possibly worse, undesirable pattern. Ms. Goldberg, in Vignette 8.3, needs to guard against students replacing "copying homework" behavior with "cheating on tests" behavior.

When you apply the principle of extinction, you should specify a suitable alternative behavior pattern that you plan to have positively reinforced. Ideally, the alternative on-task behavior pattern is incompatible with the off-task one that is to be extinguished. Ms. Goldberg, for example, would be wise to provide feedback to her students' on their homework that clearly enhances their chances of improving test scores. In this way, students who don't make the effort to do their homework will find that they have placed themselves at a grave disadvantage on tests. Thus, she would be positively reinforcing the alternative on-task behavior pattern of doing one's own homework.

In Vignette 8.4, a teacher deals with an off-task behavior pattern by positively reinforcing an alternative on-task behavior pattern that is incompatible with the off-task pattern.

VIGNETTE 8.4

Jerry habitually litters the area where his teacher, Mr. Archer, conducts shop class. Mr. Archer places Jerry in charge of the daily clean-up crew. The work crew is directed to begin their duties five minutes before the scheduled end of a period. As soon as the area is clean, the class is free to leave. The promise of leaving early and the responsibility of being in charge of the crew are positively reinforcing to Jerry's alternative pattern of cleaning up. Cleaning up is incompatible with the original off-task pattern of littering.

APPLYING THE PRINCIPLE OF SHAPING

Consider Vignette 8.5. Mr. Arata attempted to apply the principle of shaping to help Abby develop an engaged behavior pattern of contributing to discussion sessions. The emergence of a student's behavior pattern is due to shaping when (1) some seemingly random action by the student (e.g., Abby stroking her hair) that has some characteristic similarity to the behavior to be learned (e.g., Abby raising her hand to speak up in class) is positively reinforced; (2) subsequent actions by the student that are more like the behavior to be learned than previous actions are positively reinforced; (3) subsequent actions by the student that are less like the behavior to be learned than previous actions are not positively reinforced.

   In Vignette 8.6, a kindergarten teacher applies the principle of shaping to help students develop a habit of using courteous, thoughtful language.

VIGNETTE 8.5

Abby hardly ever speaks up in Mr. Arata's class. Mr. Arata sets a goal for Abby to voluntarily answer questions, make comments, and raise questions during group learning activity sessions. During a lecture-discussion session on protecting endangered wild animals, Mr. Arata notices Abby bringing her hand up to stroke her hair. Mr. Arata quickly says to her: "Yes, Abby what did you want to say?" Abby: "Nothing." Mr. Arata: "I thought I saw you raise your hand. You looked like you disagreed with the way the location of the dam was decided." Abby: "No, I agree with the process." Realizing that most of the others also agree, Mr. Arata tells the class: "Those of you who agree with Abby raise your hands." Most of the students lift their hands. Mr. Arata: "Danny, why do you agree with Abby?" Danny: "Well, I think she's right because . . ." A faint grin drifts across Abby's face.

   During the ensuing weeks, Mr. Arata controls class discussions so that any move Abby makes that indicates that she is beginning to open up in class is followed by positive reinforcers. Mr. Arata has discovered that while Abby does not enjoy being the center of attention, she does enjoy having what she believes believed by others. He uses this knowledge to design the positive reinforcers for any contribution she makes to class discussions.

VIGNETTE 8.6

When Ms. Harris' students speak to her, she makes a concerted effort to provide them with intense eye contact and displays of interest as long as they are speaking positively about others and using expressions such as "thank you," "please," "excuse me," and "if you don't mind." When they speak unkindly of others, use demanding tones, or fail to use the aforementioned type of expressions, she uses fewer active listening techniques and appears less interested in what they are telling her. At the beginning of any conversation, she searches for any, even accidental, display of thoughtfulness in the student's conversation. She makes sure that the student recognizes her appreciation of that display.

VIGNETTE 8.7

Students in a college class decided to use shaping to play a practical joke on their professor. They appear very attentive to the professor's lecture whenever he makes any movement toward the doorway of the lecture hall. Any movement away from the door or any failure to move at all is met with inattentiveness. After a week, the professor is lecturing from the doorway.

The classic example of shaping is reported in Vignette 8.7.

MAINTAINING DESIRABLE BEHAVIOR CHANGES

Reinforcement Schedules

How long a behavior pattern (either on-task or off-task) persists is largely dependent on the scheduling of positive reinforcers. Two types of reinforcement schedules are of particular concern in dealing with off-task behaviors in the classroom, fixed and intermittent.

Fixed Schedules

Fixed schedules of positive reinforcement can be either fixed intervals or fixed ratios. Fixed interval schedules provide for a positive reinforcer to routinely occur after a set amount of time elapses in which a prescribed behavior has been displayed. Fixed ratio schedules provide for a positive reinforcer to routinely occur after a prescribed behavior has been displayed to a specified degree or with a specified frequency. Students on fixed positive reinforcement schedules should always be able to predict how and when they will be rewarded for displaying the prescribed behavior. In Vignette 8.8, a teacher uses a fixed interval schedule of positive reinforcement; in Vignette 8.9 the schedule is fixed ratio.

VIGNETTE 8.8

Ms. Mecke makes arrangements with a local theater chain to provide enough movie passes for her to carry out a strategy she has devised to help her manage her class. Each day, she checks to see whether or not students have completed all required work and cleaned up their work areas. Those students who have maintained a perfect record for a school week are given a movie pass. Each student begins on Monday morning with a fresh record and the opportunity to receive a pass on Friday.

VIGNETTE 8.9

Nearly every time Mr. Schwartz asks a question in class, David blurts out an answer. Mr. Schwartz speaks to David about the problem, but David has difficulty controlling his tendency to share his thoughts on whatever topic is raised. Finally, Mr. Schwartz and David work out the following agreement: Mr. Schwartz will call on David to answer every fifth question he asks, providing that David has sat quietly through the previous four questions and listened to other give their responses.

Ms. Mecke's students knew exactly what they would have to do for five consecutive days to earn a movie pass on Friday. David understood that he had to display quiet listening behavior through four straight questions and answers before he could be rewarded with a chance to speak out in class. The agreement that Mr. Schwartz and David worked out is a rather simple form of a contingency contract. Contingency contracts are commonly associated with fixed schedules of positive reinforcers. You enter into a contingency contract with a student by agreeing to provide rewards or privileges in return for the student displaying a prescribed behavior. Contingency proclamations are similar, except that the prescription is imposed upon the student by the teacher rather than the two having cooperatively worked out the arrangement. An example of a formalized contingency contract appears in Figure 9.2 in the next chapter.

Intermittent Schedules

Fixed schedules of positive reinforcers are particularly powerful in motivating students to initiate a behavior pattern. However, intermittent schedules are far more powerful in getting students to retain behavior patterns once the pattern has been started (Lewis & Doorlag, 1991, pp. 124–127; Martin & Pear, 1983). With an intermittent schedule, the student whose behavior pattern is being positively reinforced cannot accurately predict when rewards will occur. An intermittent schedule of reinforcement is irregular; the reinforcers do not occur with fixed regularity. Most unplanned reinforcement schedules are intermittent; this is the case in Vignette 8.10 in which an undesirable behavior pattern emerges.

VIGNETTE 8.10

Fourteen-year-old Michelle consumes a significant quantity of wine for the first time. Although the taste does not appeal to her, she begins to feel light-headed and, temporarily, feels relieved of the pressures and anxieties of being an adolescent. Her drinking is positively reinforced by this feeling of relief. A week later, she is feeling down and drinks again. However, this time, she feels no high, so she drinks more until she feels better. On other occasions, she feels no relief, only terribly sick, after drinking. She continues to drink in the hope that it will make her feel better; sometimes it does and sometimes it doesn't. She can't predict how much she must drink to feel better or even if any one drinking bout will provide her with any relief at all.

The intermittent positive reinforcement schedule for Michelle's drinking will likely lead to a permanent habit unless some incompatible, alternative behavior pattern is positively reinforced. The classical example of an intermittent schedule is that of the unpredictable rewards associated with gambling behavior. Gambling, of course, can become quite compulsive.

Planned Schedules of Reinforcement

A planned schedule of positive reinforcers that is commonly used in conjunction with shaping provides (1) a generous fixed schedule during the stage in which the behavior pattern is to be initiated, (2) a meager fixed schedule after the pattern has been exhibited for a time, (3) an intermittent schedule to maintain the pattern until the student becomes intrinsically motivated to continue the pattern without outside intervention. Vignette 8.11 is an example.

VIGNETTE 8.11

Mr. Devlin experiences difficulty in getting Milan to complete reading assignments. After giving the matter considerable thought, Mr. Devlin decides to use shaping to teach Milan to choose to read books. One day, Mr. Devlin sees Milan pick up a magazine, thumb through it, and put it down. Mr. Devlin: "If you read any one article in that magazine, you can tell me about it during the Braves game tomorrow night. I have an extra ticket." Milan: "You mean you'd take me to see the Braves!" Mr. Devlin: "If you read the article." Milan: "It's a deal!" After the game, Mr. Devlin hands Milan a short story on baseball and says: "When you get through reading this, maybe we can talk about it at another game."

In time, Milan reads more, but Mr. Devlin schedules payoffs farther apart and makes them contingent on more ambitious readings by Milan. Eventually, Milan learns to enjoy reading without the anticipation of an extrinsic reward. The extrinsic motivation that stemmed from a desire to attend baseball games is eventually replaced by the intrinsic motivation derived from Milan's enjoyment of reading.

CUING

A cue is a signal that stimulates a person to exhibit a previously learned voluntary behavior pattern. Consider Vignettes 8.12, 8.13, and 8.14.

It appears that Ms. Setzer had conditioned her students to lower their voices in response to the blinking-light cue. Similarly, students responded to Mr. Weaver's lowering his voice as a cue to quiet down. Ms. Petterson's proximity to Tyrone cued him back on-task.

Teaching students to respond to cues, especially non-verbal ones, is invaluable to an efficient, smoothly operating classroom. Recall how Ms. Morrison used posters in her classroom as cues to facilitate smooth transitions between learning activities in Vignette 3.15. As suggested by a number of the examples in Chapters 9 and 10 (see, e.g., Mr. Legget's method of dealing with Rosalie's habitual mind wandering in Vignette 9.5), efficient cues can sometimes be worked out with students to signal that they are exhibiting off-task behaviors and should immediately replace those behaviors with previously agreed to alternative behaviors. Krumboltz and Krumboltz (1972, p. 67) state: "Cuing seems to work better under some circumstances than under others. When cues are verbal, they are sometimes

---

VIGNETTE 8.12

Ms. Setzer's second graders are working in pairs as the noise level in the classroom begins to rise to an unacceptable level. Saying nothing, Ms. Setzer calmly walks over to the light switch and blinks the lights once. The noise level drops to an acceptable level.

VIGNETTE 8.13

Mr. Weaver is vocally giving directions to his chemistry students who are working at laboratory tables. As they follow his directions, they become somewhat noisy in their efforts to help one another. As Mr. Weaver continues to speak, he gradually lowers his voice so that it is no longer audible to those in the noisy room. The students begin signaling one another to quiet down until noise level drops below Mr. Weaver's volume.

VIGNETTE 8.14

Five minutes ago, Ms. Petterson assigned Tyrone and his sixth grade classmates some exercise problems to complete in class. After doing one, Tyrone starts doodling and gazing around the room. Ms. Petterson walks over to Tyrone and silently looks at his paper. Tyrone's attention returns to the exercise problems.

confused with nagging but there is an important distinction. Nagging is persistent unpleasant urging or scolding by finding fault. Cuing is a simple nonhostile direction when the child needs a reminder or when he needs help in learning.''

GENERALIZATION AND DISCRIMINATION

The Idea

The communication style that Ms. Sowel uses with her seventh graders in Vignettes 8.15 and 8.16 should not be emulated in any respect. However, her conversations with two students are related to introduce the ideas of generalization and discrimination.

The Principle of Generalization

In her crude manner, Ms. Sowel attempted, in Vignette 8.15, to help Betty exhibit a behavior pattern in the classroom that Betty practices at home (i.e., disposing of trash in a proper container). Ms. Sowel wanted Betty to generalize a behavior pattern from one situation to another. Students generalize by responding to a new set of stimuli in a manner similar to the way in which they have been conditioned to respond to a different, but similar, set of stimuli. Students tend to generalize between two situations and, thus respond similarly in both situations

---

VIGNETTE 8.15

Betty is busily trying to write an essay in Ms. Sowel's class. She frowns, crumples her paper, and tosses it on the floor. Ms. Sowel turns to Betty and says: "Young lady, pick up that paper right now! Do you throw trash on your living room floor at home?" Betty: "No ma'am. I'm sorry." Ms. Sowel: "Well, if you don't throw trash on the floor of your living room, then you shouldn't throw it on the floor of your classroom either!"

VIGNETTE 8.16

As Ms. Sowel's seventh grade English students file into her room, Roy shoves Hildreth from behind. Hildreth spins around to face Roy and says: "Look mother-fucker, don't start any of your shit with me!" Ms. Sowel dashes to Hildreth, turns him to her by his shoulders and loudly exclaims: "Maybe that filthy language is tolerated around your home, but it will not be tolerated in my classroom!"

because they focus on commonalities instead of differences. You teach students to generalize between two situations by providing them with cues that remind them of what is common to both situations.

The Principle of Discrimination

By throwing paper on her classroom floor when she wouldn't have done so at home, Betty displayed that she was discriminating, rather than generalizing, between the stimuli presented by the classroom and that presented by her home. Ms. Sowel attempted to get her to generalize her disposal-of-trash behavior at home to the classroom. In Vignette 8.16, Ms. Sowel made a poorly conceived attempt to get Hildreth to discriminate between his home—where, according to Ms. Sowel's rude remark, a type of language is acceptable—and her classroom, where that type of language is unacceptable. Students discriminate by responding to a new set of stimuli in a manner dissimilar to the way in which they have been conditioned to respond to a different, but similar, set of stimuli. Students tend to discriminate between two situations and, thus respond differently in one situation than they do in the other because they focus on differences rather than commonalities. You teach students to discriminate between two situations by providing them with cues that remind them of what is different about the two situations.

Discriminating between the Principles of Generalization and Discrimination

In Vignettes 8.17–8.20, Vern, Stephen, Amanda, and Alyson appear to be generalizing.

VIGNETTE 8.17

Whenever Vern watches television at his house, he relaxes, never following what is being said very closely. Vern's teacher shows his class a videotaped lecture on the Declaration of Independence. Although Vern's teacher indicates that they will be tested on the content of the video, Vern is very relaxed as he watches the video monitor, not following what is said very closely.

VIGNETTE 8.18

Eight-year-old Stephen tells his mother: "Sidney took my ball away from me at school today!" "What did you do about it?" his mother asks. "I slugged him and took it back," he replies. "Good!" his mother says, "You have to take care of yourself." A few days later, Stephen's four-year-old brother grabs a book that Stephen is reading. Stephen hits his brother and grabs back the book.

VIGNETTE 8.19

Besides diligently completing history assignments, Amanda reads some unassigned history books. Afterwards, she obtains a grade of "A" in history. Amanda begins diligently working on her science course and seeks additional work in science.

VIGNETTE 8.20

Alyson notes that her mother is more responsive to her requests when she says "please." She asks her teacher: "May I please play with a puzzle?"

In Vignettes 8.21–8.24, Shauna, Mickey, Nancy, and Chris appear to be discriminating.

VIGNETTE 8.21

Whenever Shauna watches television at her house, she relaxes, never following what is being said very closely. Shauna's teacher shows her class a videotaped lecture on the Declaration of Independence. Although the medium is similar to the television in her home, Shauna realizes that she will be tested over the content of the video. Shauna takes notes and listens closely as she watches the video monitor.

VIGNETTE 8.22

Mickey speaks openly about his sexual fantasies to his buddies, but he never mentions them to his father.

VIGNETTE 8.23

Nancy always does homework for Mr. Clancy's class, but she rarely does it for Ms. Taylor's class.

VIGNETTE 8.24

Twelve-year-old Chris tries to win and uses his hardest "slam" when playing table tennis against Amy, his older sister. However, when he plays table tennis against his five-year-old brother, he just pats the ball back to him and never "slams."

APPLYING THE PRINCIPLE OF MODELING

Individuals are modeling behavior when they initiate behavior patterns because they observed others displaying similar behaviors. Marilyn, Sandy, Scott, Phil, Ms. Shelly's students, and Ms. Loyacono's students are learning behavior patterns through modeling in Vignettes 8.25–8.30.

VIGNETTE 8.25

Mr. Bomgars asks his class: "If y equals 6 divided by the quantity $x - 3$ where x is a real number between 0 and 3, what happens to y as x approaches its minimum, George?" George: "Well, I think . . ." Interrupting George, Mr. Bomgars says: "You 'think'! That must be a new experience for you! I've never known you to think before!" A few class members roar with laughter.

The next day, a friend tells Marilyn: "I'm late for a meeting; I'd better hurry." Marilyn in a loud voice says: "You hurry! How can you hurry while carrying around that stomach?"

VIGNETTE 8.26

As part of a problem-solving learning activity for her ninth grade class, Ms. Rogers assigns Sandy to a cooperative group with Ed and Diane. Initially, Sandy has little motivation for working on the task and solving the problem. However, as she associates with Ed and Diane who enthusiastically and diligently work on the project, Sandy gains an interest in working on the task herself.

VIGNETTE 8.27

Several days after Scott's mother spanks him, he hits his younger sister.

VIGNETTE 8.28

Phil and Dudley are confronted by a pusher on their school's grounds with an offer to buy some dope. Phil declines the offer with: "No, I don't use the stuff." Dudley pulls out some money and says: "Okay, I'll try it." As soon as Dudley completes the transaction, Phil pulls out his own money and tells the pusher: "Yea, I'll have some too."

VIGNETTE 8.29

Three times a week, Ms. Shelly makes an hour available to her fifth graders to silently read any selection they choose from a large collection of books available in her classroom. During these periods Ms. Shelly catches up on paperwork. Only about half the students enthusiastically read during these periods.

VIGNETTE 8.30

Three times a week, Ms. Loyacono makes an hour available to her fifth graders to silently read any selection they choose from a large collection of books available in her classroom. During these periods, Ms. Loyacono reads, too. Virtually all of Ms. Loyacono's students enthusiastically read during these periods.

Modeling is a form of generalizing that "if the behavior is okay for them, then it's okay for me." Because children and adolescents tend to follow the examples set by others, modeling is a particularly powerful means for teaching behavior patterns to students. However, you should guard against using the destructive and ineffective tactic of comparing one student's behavior to that of another. If, for example, Tom is told: "Why don't you behave more like Bill? Bill never gives me trouble!" Tom is likely to resent Bill and begin protecting his own ego by acting as un-Bill-like as he can. You effectively use modeling either by quietly serving as an example of the behavior pattern you want students to follow or by grouping students who need to learn to follow the behavior pattern with those who already display it. In Vignette 8.30, Ms. Loyacono applied the former method, while in Vignette 8.26, Ms. Rogers applied the latter.

APPLYING THE PRINCIPLE OF SATIATION

In Vignette 8.31, Ms. Elkins attempts to apply the principle of satiation.

VIGNETTE 8.31

Andy is distributing magazines to his eleventh grade classmates in Ms. Elkins' literature class. Andy places a magazine in front of James who hands it back to Andy and says: "Hey, I don't take anything from you!" "You gotta take it now 'cause you already put your nigger hands on it!" replies Andy. James leaps to his feet and the two square off at each other. Two other students and Ms. Elkins step in and, without further incident, Ms. Elkins sends them both to the dean's office.

Andy and James have been antagonizing one another since school began two months ago. Ms. Elkins does not want to have them suspended, as they are both conscientious students who are progressing nicely toward learning goals. Except for behaviors related to their volatile relationship, neither tends to be disruptive. However, this latest incident is just one more in a continuing series of confrontations between the two. Ms. Elkins refuses to conduct her class under the fear that Andy and James will break out in a fight. She decides to try one more tactic before recommending suspensions.

Her plan calls for Andy and James to work closely on assigned tasks in which the success of one depends on the success of the other. Initially, she assigns them to work on a joint project for which they will receive the same grade. Ms. Elkins believes that while working together, they will become so saturated with antagonizing each other, they might eventually choose to cooperate instead. She knows she is gambling, but she considers the current situation to be intolerable and suspension undesirable.

Ms. Elkins attempted to apply the principle of satiation, which states that if an established learned behavior is allowed to continue unchecked, the person exhibiting that behavior may soon become tired of the pattern and elect to terminate it. If, as in the case of Andy and James, immediate naturally occurring punishment is a consequence of the behavior pattern, the satiation principle may be applicable. Of course, if the naturally occurring punishment is very severe, one may not be able to afford to apply the satiation principle. You wouldn't, for example, apply the satiation principle in dealing with a child who habitually ran out into a busy street. You might consider satiation as a method for terminating off-task behavior patterns only if (1) naturally occurring punishment is a consequence of the behavior pattern, (2) the naturally occurring punishment is not too severe, and (3) you are willing to tolerate the off-task behavior pattern long enough for the satiation principle to take effect.

TRANSITIONAL ACTIVITIES
FROM CHAPTER 8 TO CHAPTER 9

I. Below is a list of 11 concepts or principles from behavioristic psychology that can be used in the design of learning activities to help students supplant off-task behavior patterns with on-task behavior patterns. Write a *T* if the principle focuses on terminating an existing behavior pattern, a *D* if the focus is on developing a new behavior pattern, and an *E* if the focus can be on either terminating an existing pattern or developing a new one.
   A. Positive reinforcement.
   B. Punishment.
   C. Negative reinforcement.
   D. Extinction.
   E. Alternative behavior.
   F. Shaping.
   G. Cuing.

H. Generalization.
I. Discrimination.
J. Modeling.
K. Satiation.

Check your responses against these. B, D, and K focus on terminating existing behaviors; A, C, E, F, and J focus on developing new behaviors; G, H, and I can be either. Cuing can be either because cues can be used to remind students to initiate a behavior or to remind them to stop behavior they are exhibiting. Generalization can be either because students can either generalize that what is appropriate under one circumstance is also appropriate under another, or they could generalize that what is inappropriate in one situation is also inappropriate in another. Discrimination can be either because students can recognize that because a behavior is appropriate in one situation does not mean it's appropriate in another, or they can recognize that inappropriate behavior for one set of circumstances may be appropriate for another set.

II. Give an example for each of the following.
  A. A student generalizes between two situations and is on-task.
  B. A student generalizes between two situations and is off-task.
  C. A student discriminates between two situations and is on-task.
  D. A student discriminates between two situations and is off-task.
  E. A teacher (1) identifies an off-task behavior pattern exhibited by a student, (2) identifies an alternative on-task behavior pattern for that student to develop, and (3) devises a plan for applying the principle of extinction to help the student eliminate the off-task pattern and for positively reinforcing the alternative pattern.
  F. A teacher unknowingly uses a destructive positive reinforcer to encourage an alternative behavior pattern.
  G. A teacher uses the principle of shaping to help a student develop an on-task behavior pattern.
  H. A teacher unwittingly uses the principle of shaping to lead a student to develop an off-task behavior pattern.
  Compare and discuss your examples with those of colleagues.

III. Milton is a seventh grader who habitually fails to bring the required uniform to physical education class.
  A. Describe a scenario in which his teacher uses contrived punishment to deal with this off-task behavior pattern.
  B. Describe a scenario in which the teacher uses naturally occurring punishment.
  C. Describe a scenario in which the teacher uses negative reinforcement.
  Compare and discuss your scenarios with those of colleagues.

IV. In preparation for your work with Chapter 9, discuss the following questions with two or more of your colleagues.
  A. Why is it critical for teachers to discourage students from being off-task even when the off-task behaviors are nondisruptive?
  B. What strategies do teachers employ to deal with the following types of off-task behaviors?
    1. Mind-wandering and daydreaming.
    2. Refusing to participate in class activities.
    3. Failing to complete homework assignments.
    4. Being under the influence of debilitating drugs.
    5. Being absent or tardy.
    6. Cheating on tests.

SUPPLEMENTAL READINGS

Brown, D. (1971). *Changing student behavior: A new approach to discipline.* Dubuque, IA: W. C. Brown.

Curwin, R. L., & Mendler, A. N. (1988). *Discipline with dignity.* Alexandria, VA: Association for Supervision and Curriculum Development.

Homme, L. (1973). *How to use contingency contracting in the classroom.* Champaign, IL: Research Press.

Kerr, M. M., & Nelson, C. M. (1983). *Strategies for managing behavior problems in the classroom* (pp. 3–79). Columbus, OH: Merrill.

Krumboltz, J. D., & Krumboltz, H. B. (1972). *Changing children's behavior.* Englewood Cliffs, NJ: Prentice-Hall.

Presbie, R. J., & Brown, P. L. (1985). *Behavior modification* (2nd ed.). Washington: National Education Association.

Walker, J. E., & Shea, T. M. (1984). *Behavior management: A practical approach for educators* (3rd ed.), (pp. 24–121). St. Louis: Times Mirror/Mosby College Publishing.

Wolf, M. M., Hanley, E. L., King, L. A., Lachowicz, J., & Giles, D. K. (1970). The timer game: A variable interval contingency for the management of out-of-seat behavior. *Exceptional Children, 37,* 113–117.

Dealing with Nondisruptive Off-Task Behaviors

Purpose of Chapter 9

Chapter 9 is designed to help you develop strategies for effectively handling both isolated incidents and patterns of nondisruptive off-task student behaviors. In particular the following types of nondisruptive off-task behaviors are addressed. (1) mind-wandering and daydreaming, (2) refusing to participate in class activities, (3) failing to complete homework assignments, (4) failing to brings materials, (5) being under the influence of debilitating drugs during class, and (6) being absent or tardy, and (7) cheating on tests.

NONDISRUPTIVE OFF-TASK BEHAVIORS

Nondisruptive off-task behaviors can easily be disregarded by teachers. Such behaviors do not interfere with the learning activities of a class as a whole; students only interfere with their own learning by exhibiting nondisruptive off-task behaviors. A student usually suffers only minor consequences from one isolated incident of nondisruptive off-task behavior. However, there are three reasons why you should not generally disregard nondisruptive off-task behaviors, even isolated ones.

1. Whenever students are off-task, they are failing to benefit from your planned learning activities and consequently are diminishing their chances of achieving learning goals. Since, as a teacher, you are responsible for helping students achieve learning goals, it follows that you are responsible for helping students be on-task.
2. Off-task behavior patterns begin with isolated off-task behaviors that are positively reinforced.

3. Students exhibiting nondisruptive off-task behaviors tend to fall behind in a lesson. Once students miss one part of a learning activity, they are unlikely to understand subsequent parts (even if they become reengaged). Students who are unable to follow a learning activity may well become bored, frustrated, and disruptive.

The efficacy of the solutions you prescribe for any off-task behavior problem is dependent on your understanding of the students, the peculiarities of the situation, and yourself. Please keep in mind that the examples of teachers dealing with off-task behaviors that are given in this chapter and the next, are only examples. The teachers' methods in these examples worked or didn't work (examples of teachers' mishandling situations are also included) because of individual characteristics of the involved persons and circumstances. You and other teachers can learn from them, but you must develop your own unique style for handling the unique cases you confront.

MIND-WANDERING AND DAYDREAMING

Detection and Response

Mind-wandering and daydreaming may be the most common forms of student off-task behaviors. Mind-wandering is an uncontrolled coursing of ideas and mental images (Dewey, 1933, pp. 3–12). Daydreaming is similar to mind-wandering except that the daydreamer cognitively controls the thoughts and images (Klinger, 1978). Although children have been traditionally reprimanded, embarrassed, and punished for allowing their thoughts to deviate from school tasks, daydreaming seems to serve a critical purpose in cognitive development (Gold & Cundiff, 1980). There appears to be a direct relation between the frequency at which individuals daydream and their level of creative achievement (Lyerly, 1982). Mind-wandering and especially daydreaming per se shouldn't be discouraged by teachers, but students need to learn to control mind-wandering and time their daydreams so that engagement in learning activities isn't disrupted.

Because teachers cannot directly observe mind-wandering and daydreaming as they can other off-task behaviors (e.g., inappropriate talking), it is difficult to detect this form of student disengagement from learning activities. Shrewd and concerned teachers learn to read body language, recognize vacant stares in students' eyes, and use questioning techniques to detect incidences of students' quietly drifting out of touch with learning activities. Consider three contrasting vignettes (Vignettes 9.1, 9.2, and 9.3).

If Amelia continues to enjoy her daydreaming during Mr. Minchot's lecture, she may soon develop a pattern of daydreaming in his classes. The beginning of a lecture may serve as a cue for Amelia to daydream. Ms. Searcy dealt with Amy's daydreaming, but she disrupted her own learning activity to belabor Amy's behavior and destructively characterize Amy as a daydreamer. Ms. Smith's one question for Anita, hopefully, cued her back on-task without disrupting the rest of the class and without positively reinforcing the daydreaming.

VIGNETTE 9.1

Mr. Minchot is explaining to his ninth grade science class how Darwin and Wallace each arrived at his theory of natural selection. Most of the class listens intently. Amelia sits erectly, staring directly at Mr. Minchot as she imagines herself galloping on a horse along a river bank. Mr. Minchot, pleased with his class silence, continues unaware of Amelia's disengagement.

VIGNETTE 9.2

Ms. Searcy is explaining to her ninth grade science class how Darwin and Wallace each arrived at his theory of natural selection. Most of the class listens intently. Amy sits erectly, staring directly at Ms. Searcy as she imagines herself galloping on a horse along a river bank. Ms. Searcy, who watches her students' faces as she lectures, notices the blank look in Amy's eyes. Suspicious that Amy is not engaged in the lesson, she pauses and asks: "What do you think about that, Amy?" Amy: "About what?" Ms. Searcy: "About what I said." Amy: "I don't know what you said." Ms. Searcy: "You don't know what I said because you were daydreaming. Amy, the daydreamer, off in a world of her own! Okay daydreamer, let's listen from now on." Amy: "Yes, ma'am. I will."

   "Off in a world of her own—Amy, the daydreamer!" Amy thinks to herself as she stares directly at Ms. Searcy and nods her head as if agreeing with what Ms. Searcy is saying. Amy keeps pondering those words; she likes the sound of "a daydreamer, off in her own world."

VIGNETTE 9.3

Ms. Smith is explaining to her ninth grade science class how Darwin and Wallace each arrived at his theory of natural selection. Most of the class listens intently. Anita sits erectly, staring directly at Ms. Smith as she imagines herself galloping on a horse along a river bank. Ms. Smith, who watches her students' faces as she lectures, notices the blank look in Anita's eyes. Suspicious that Anita is not engaged in the lesson, she pauses and asks the class: "Why do you suppose Darwin waited so long before publishing his theory? Anita?" Anita: "What's the question?" Ms. Smith: "Please repeat the question for those of us who missed it, Michael." Michael: "You asked why Darwin took so long before publishing his stuff." Ms. Smith: "Thanks, Mike. What's your opinion, Debbie?" Debbie expresses her opinion and the lecture/discussion continues. Ms. Smith subtly observes Anita to see if her strategy worked.

Strategies

Teachers employ strategies to check mind-wandering in Vignettes 9.4 and 9.5.

VIGNETTE 9.4

Mr. Cavallaro's second graders are working on independent computational exercises. He circulates among them, checking on their engagement. He notices Richard staring off into space. Mr. Cavallaro moves into Richard's line of vision and makes eye contact. Richard seems to return to work. However, Mr. Cavallaro begins noticing that more and more students appear to have wandering minds. Convinced their attention spans are inadequate for the exercise to efficiently continue uninterrupted, he calls for their attention, directs them to stop their computing, and takes them outside where he conducts a five-minute session of calisthenics. After the exercises, they return to the classroom and complete the computations.

VIGNETTE 9.5

Mr. Legget detects that a number of his seventh grade English students frequently allow their minds to wander off the planned topic during learning activities. By watching students' faces and raising questions, he determines that this form of disengagement is particularly prevalent during large group sessions in which he lectures and conducts discussions. He decides to attempt a strategy with Rosalie, who appears to habitually daydream, and to evaluate how well it works with her. If successful, he will try the strategy with others and eventually develop a plan for the entire class. In a one-to-one conference with Rosalie, they define the problem and agree to the following plan.

Mr. Legget is to provide Rosalie with a tiny, flat rubber image of a frog that can easily be attached to and removed from her desk top. Mr. Legget will keep a statue of a frog facing the class on his desk. During large group learning activities, Rosalie is to attach the rubber frog to her desk top. Every time she sees the frog on her desk "looking" at her, she is to glance at the frog on Mr. Legget's desk and be reminded that it is not the time to daydream.

The success of the plan depends on the frog cuing Rosalie to discriminate between when daydreaming is appropriate and when it is not. She does not attach the frog to her desk at times when daydreaming is appropriate. After a two-week trial, Rosalie and Mr. Legget both agree that the frequency at which she daydreams during large group learning activities is significantly lower than it was before they started the program. The time frame for the plan is extended.

Pleased with Rosalie's success, Mr. Legget initiates a similar strategy with Mike. However, it seems that Mike tends to stare upward and not see anything when he daydreams; the plan fails. Mr. Legget decides to use a sound cue approach with Mike and they agree that Mr. Legget will watch for signs that Mike's attention is drifting. When he believes Mike's thoughts have wandered, he will wait for an appropriate point in the lecture or discussion and rap a pencil, which he always carries, against the backside of the ring he wears. Upon hearing the unique sound, Mike is to remind himself to focus his thoughts on the lesson.

The plan works fairly well with Mike, and Mr. Legget experiments with other cues for other students. Some work well, others do not. After a month, Mr. Legget is having trouble keeping up with what cues whom. Finally, he calls a class meeting

VIGNETTE 9.5 (continued)

to explain that he will trigger the beeper on the chronograph he wears on his wrist anytime he detects at least three students drifting off. (He chose this signal because of the mobility it afforded him.) After implementing his plan for two weeks, he evaluates its success, and decides that, although it doesn't seem to help some students, it is worthwhile continuing because it is working for others.

REFUSING TO PARTICIPATE IN CLASS ACTIVITIES

In Vignettes 9.6–9.9, teachers effectively deal with students' disengagement during in-class learning activities. In these examples, reasons other than mind-wandering or daydreaming interfere with the students' in-class participation.

VIGNETTE 9.6

Ms. Webb has just directed her first grade students to carry out assignments in five-member cooperative groups. Sophonia, Scott, April, Heather, and Louis are assigned to work together and plan a mural for the classroom. Scott, April, Heather, and Louis move to their work areas and begin discussing the project. Sophonia remains at her desk on the other side of the room. Ms. Webb observes the situation for a minute, collects her thoughts, and discreetly goes to Sophonia and says to her in a soft voice: "You are not working with your group. May I help you?" Sophonia; "No, I'm okay." Ms. Webb: "Why did you decide to stay here instead of working with your group?" Sophonia: "Because of Scott; he makes me mad." Ms. Webb: "Why do you get mad?" Sophonia: "He calls me 'dummy'!" Ms. Webb: "I understand why you would get mad. I don't like it when someone calls me 'dummy'." Ms. Webb reads Sophonia's expression and believes she has received the supportive communication. Hoping that Sophonia has dealt with her feelings, Ms. Web confidently says: "Now, hurry and get with your group. They need your ideas so that they'll have the best mural possible!" As Sophonia moves toward her task group, Ms. Webb decides to be especially attentive to Sophonia and Scott's group, thinking that her presence will reduce the chances that Scott will call Sophonia "dummy." As Ms. Webb continues to supervise the activities in the room, she thinks to herself: "What, if anything, should I do if I hear Scott call Sophonia 'dummy?'"

VIGNETTE 9.7

Mr. Sabid directs his French class to translate 12 sentences before the end of the class period. He plans to collect their work and provide then with feedback the next day. As other students begin the work, Derald puts his head down on his desk and falls asleep. Mr. Sabid thinks: "I could just let him sleep and require him to complete those translations before he leaves school today. But I'd rather stop his sleeping in class before it becomes a distraction to others. I wonder what's going on with him today. It's not like him to do this. Well, for whatever reason, I'm not going to allow him to develop a habit of sleeping in my class. I know! I'll write a note to him. A note won't be disturbing to the others, nor will it call attention to him." Mr. Sabid writes

Derald,
  If I do not receive you translations before I leave today at 4:30, I will not be able to provide you with feedback in tomorrow's class. If you don't finish them by the end of the period, turn them in to me at 4:20 P.M. today in Room 143.
  Mr. Sabid

  Quietly, Mr. Sabid walks over to Derald, inconspicuously shakes him until he opens his eyes, and hands him the note. Mr. Sabid immediately walks away, not giving Derald an opportunity to comment. If Derald does not comply with Mr. Sabid's request, Mr. Sabid plans to contact Derald's parents.

Mr. Sabid Discreetly Wakes Derald and Hands Him a Note

VIGNETTE 9.8

Mr. Burns-Whittle notices that one of his fifth graders, Jamie, is just sitting at his desk instead of working on the assigned in-class word recognition exercise. Mr. Burns-Whittle discreetly goes over to Jamie, makes eye contact, and signals him to begin working. Jamie just looks away without taking the cue. Mr. Burns-Whittle then whispers directly to Jamie: "I would like you to begin the exercise now." Assuming Jamie will begin, Mr. Burns-Whittle confidently walks away. Twenty seconds later, he sees that Jamie has still not begun. He beckons Jamie to meet him in the hall just outside the room. There, he softly asks: "Why have you not begun your work?" Jamie: "Because I don't want to." Mr. Burns-Whittle: "I understand that you don't want to do this exercise, but I suggest that you get it over with now so you won't need to worry about it later today." Jamie: "I'm not going to do it." Mr. Burns-Whittle: "Jamie, do you know what the word 'option' means?" Jamie: "No." Mr. Burns-Whittle: "An option is a choice. It's an opportunity to choose. Right now, you have an option. You have a choice to make. What did I just say?" Jamie: "I have a choice." Mr. Burns-Whittle: "You have the option of going to Ms. Cook's office and waiting there for me until two o'clock when I have the time to work with you. Or, you have the option of quietly returning to your desk and completing the assignment. Which option do you choose?" Jamie: "I don't want to go to Misses Cook's office." Mr. Burns-Whittle: "So, tell me your choice. I have to get back to our class." Jamie: "Okay, I won't go to Misses Cook." Mr. Burns-Whittle: "Whatever you say, Jamie. You've made your choice."

Jamie returns to his place and reluctantly begins working. Mr. Burns-Whittle thinks: "If he doesn't continue working, I'll send him to the office and instruct them to have him wait for me until I get there at two. That'll give me time to think through what to do."

VIGNETTE 9.9

Mr. Cobb is a junior high school social studies teacher who does not design problem-solving learning activities. Throughout his years as a teacher, Mr. Cobb has had difficulty with students habitually failing to participate in class activities, failing to complete homework assignments, failing to bring materials to class, and skipping his classes. Consequently, he now finds it necessary to initiate the following plan for each of his classes that meet five days a week for 55 minutes per session.

The last 30 minutes of each Wednesday's class and the entire 55 minutes of each Friday's class, are designated as "option times" in which students may spend their time in one of the following ways

Option 1: In a supervised study hall in which students are required to individually and silently work on school-related tasks of their choice.

Option 2: In a free activity in which students do as they please (e.g., watch a videotape, listen to CDs, socialize, play games, go to the library, or attend supervised study hall) within a predetermined set of specific guidelines.

CONTINGENCY CONTRACT

Contract Period:

    Beginning   Ending

    We the undersigned,   (here referred to as "Teacher") and   (hereafter referred to as "Student") do hereby enter into a contract with the following provisions:

    The teacher will maintain a record of option credits* for the student in a ledger book (hereafter referred to as "the ledger") during the contract period according to the following schedule:

ATTENDANCE (10 credits per day maximum):
10 credits for each regularly scheduled social studies class at which the student attends for a complete 55 minutes. 5 credits for each such class that the student attends for less than the 55 minutes.

HOMEWORK (10 credits per day maximum):
Homework assignments completed and returned by the deadline established by the teacher will be rated for completeness and effort on a scale of 1 to 10 by the teacher. Homework received after the deadline will be rated for completeness and effort on a scale of 1 to 5.

IN-CLASS ASSIGNMENTS (10 credits per day maximum):
In-class assignments completed and returned by the deadline established by the teacher will be rated for completeness and effort on a scale of 1 to 10 by the teacher. In-class assignments received after the deadline will be rated for completeness and effort on a scale of 1 to 5.

HAVING MATERIALS IN CLASS (5 credits per day maximum):
5 credits are earned each day that the student has all of his/her materials (e.g., books, pens, and paper) for full class participation.

    The student may choose to exercise option 2** during option times on a Wednesday by forfeiting 50 of his/her option credits. Otherwise the student is required to exercise option 3** on the Wednesday. The student may exercise option 2 during option time on a Friday by forfeiting 100 of his/her option credits. Otherwise

FIGURE 9.1 Mr. Cobb's Contingency Contract

VIGNETTE 9.9 (continued)

the student is required to exercise option 3 on Friday. The student must have a ledger balance of at least 50 option credits before a Wednesday class period begins and 100 option credits before a Friday class begins to be in a position to choose option 2 on that day.

The student's option credit balance shall not in any way influence decisions which the teacher makes (e.g., course grades) other than whether or not the student may choose option 2 on Wednesdays and Fridays.

Nothing in this contract shall supersede classroom, school, or school system policies and regulations.

This contract may be voided before its ending date by mutual agreement of both the student and the teacher.

---

*Option Credits are defined on page 6 of "Classroom Regulations."
**Options 2 and 3 are defined on page 8 of "Classroom Regulations."

Teacher   /   date

Student   /   date

Witness   /

Witness   /

FIGURE 9.1 (continued)

Option 3: Working under Mr. Cobb's direction, students complete certain tasks (e.g., filing, collating papers, cleaning the classroom, duplicating materials, or performing classroom maintenance) within a predetermined set of specific guidelines.

The specific guidelines are printed in a book of classroom regulations given to every student. Mr. Cobb provides each student with the opportunity to sign a contingency contract similar to one that appears in Figure 9.1. Students who do not sign such a contract automatically exercise Option 1 during each option time. Those who do sign will exercise either Options 2 or 3 depending on how well they have fulfilled the contingencies of their contract during any given week.

Although some of Mr. Cobb's colleagues criticize his plan because it cuts into regularly scheduled class time, Mr. Cobb continues to use it. He believes that the plan's overall impact leads to a richer participation in learning activities because students are more diligent with in-class activities, homework, and attendance. His data indicate that each student lost far more than 85 minutes of class time per week prior to implementation of the plan simply because of time Mr. Cobb spent dealing with student disengagement.

FAILING TO COMPLETE HOMEWORK ASSIGNMENTS

Meaningful Homework

Consider Vignette 9.10. For many learning objectives, in-class learning activities only provide direction, stimulate thinking, and explain assignments, while actual student objective achievement occurs after class when students individually think, practice, and work out problems on their own. In many circumstances, the most efficient time for students to conceptualize, memorize, or polish skills is when they are working on out-of-class assignments. Unfortunately, some teachers don't keep the eight ideas listed on pages 179–180 in mind when designing homework assignments, they tend to mindlessly assign homework. Mr. Davis' students, in Vignette 9.11, are given busy work that is hardly relevant to student attainment of any goal that address any of their needs.

VIGNETTE 9.10

While conducting a learning activity within a unit on modern poetry for one of her high school English classes, Ms. Ramsen provides definitions and explanations of the following concepts: rhythm, meter, iamb foot, trochee foot, anapest foot, and dactyl foot. Ronny, Stacy, and most of the other students listen to Ms. Ramsen and record the definitions in their notes. Ms. Ramsen then assigns homework in which they are to read and analyze several poems, classifying them according to rhythm and meter. The assignment specifies exactly what is expected. At the end of the period, Ronny complains to Stacy: "How can Ramsen expect me to do this when I don't even know what she's talking about? Iambs! Trochees! She must be crazy! Those definitions don't make any sense to me. She didn't teach them to us!" Stacy: "No one understood her today; I don't know how to do the homework either." That night as Ronny struggles through Ms. Ramsen's assignment, the concepts introduced in class that day begin to come clear to him. After analyzing several poems, the differences between an iamb foot and a trochee foot are apparent.

VIGNETTE 9.11

Mr. Davis to his history class: "For tonight's homework, complete Exercise 5–3 beginning on page 83 of your workbook. I will check it first thing tomorrow. Anyone who doesn't have every blank filled with get 10 points deducted from his grade total. Is that clear?"

VIGNETTE 9.11 (continued)

Exercise 5–3 consists of 27 fill-in-the-blank statements, such as: "The first state to enter the union after the original _____ colonies was _____ in _____." The workbook was published as a supplement to a history text used in Mr. Davis' class. To complete the assignment, a student spends about an hour finding information from the textbook to fill in the blanks. Chapter 5 of the text contains each of the 27 completed statements nearly verbatim. Few students recognize value in doing this assignment, other than to keep them in Mr. Davis' good graces and prevent them from losing points from their grades.

The concern of this section is how teachers, such as Ms. Ramsen, can deal with situations in which students choose not to attempt meaningful homework assignments. It is debatable as to whether or not it is even desirable for students to complete assignments, such as the one Mr. Davis gave, for which there is no worthwhile rationale. There are no naturally occurring consequences for failing to complete meaningless assignments. With his point deduction scheme, Mr. Davis imposed a contrived punishment for students' failure to fill in all the blanks.

Strategies

Recall how Ms. Hanzlik dealt with students' failure to complete homework in Vignette 6.26; In Vignette 9.12, Mr. Benge uses another strategy.

VIGNETTE 9.12

The goal of Mr. Benge's first unit in the eighth grade English course he is just starting involves improving students' essay-writing abilities. His first homework assignment requires students to choose a topic for a two-page essay dealing with something from their neighborhood and then construct an outline listing the subtopics for the intro- duction, the main body, and the ending. A number of students ask Mr. Benge ques- tions regarding how to do the assignment "right." He brushes off their questions and tries to assure them that if they will only do it the best way they know how, it will help him help them learn how to do it "right." He tells them that he will collect the work the next day and make suggestions on it that will help them fix it up so that eventually they will be ready to start writing the complete two-page essay. He tries to assure them that, although he will collect and comment on the work, it will not be graded. "How many points is this worth?" asks one student. "Zero," replies Mr. Benge.

Christine, who like most members of the class does not yet know Mr. Benge well enough to trust what he says, thinks to herself: "I've never made an outline before. I don't know how to do this and since he's not grading on it, I won't do it." The next day, Christine and several others do not have topics and outlines ready. Others present their attempts to Mr. Benge, but, as he expected, few are anything near a finished product. Mr. Benge analyzes each outline he receives and returns it to its owner with helpful suggestions and encouraging comments. Students refine their outlines in class by taking Mr. Benge's suggestions and individually showing them to him. He either makes further suggestions for refinement or okays the work and directs them to begin writing the essay.

Christine feels left out of the activities as she did not give Mr. Benge the opportunity to help her. She asks Mr. Benge if she can turn in the work the next day. He replies: "If you bring a draft of your outline tomorrow, I'll do my best to get to it and make suggestions. But, I may not have time. Do not write your essay until after I've approved your outline." At no time does Mr. Benge either ask Christine or others why they did not do the initial assignment, nor is he receptive to hearing their excuses. He only concerns himself with the business of getting the work done, not with why it was not done in the past.

The following day, Mr. Benge busies himself helping those who are on schedule with their assignments and does not find time to annotate the "late" ones in class. He takes those home and returns with them the next day. Until all those students who have kept up with the work have satisfactory essays in hand, the procedures continue with students presenting homework to Mr. Benge who then makes suggestions and the next assignment. Mr. Benge administers a unit test that includes an item requiring an essay to be written. Christine feels her chances of doing well on the test are diminished because she was one day behind schedule throughout the unit and never had the opportunity to have her final homework checked by Mr. Benge before taking the test. She vows to more diligently keep up with Mr. Benge's assignments in the future.

FAILING TO BRING MATERIALS

Teachers deal with students' failure to bring materials in Vignettes 9.13–9.15.

VIGNETTE 9.13

Ms. Watham directs her class to begin an in-class written assignment. Instead of beginning, Andrea tells her: "I don't have anything to write with. I forgot my pencil." Ms. Watham: "Here, you may borrow one of mine this time. Please don't make a habit of this." Andrea: "I won't. Thank you." Ms. Watham thinks to herself, "I'd better develop some strategies if this forgetting' becomes habitual."

VIGNETTE 9.14

Because failing to bring supplies and borrowing among students became a problem for Ms. Murphy's fourth grade class, the class established the following rules.

Borrowing supplies among students is not allowed during class. A student who does not have needed school supplies may choose to either (1) purchase the needed items from the class storeroom, paying the marked price immediately, (2) take the

---

VIGNETTE 9.14 (continued)

needed items from the storeroom and provide twice as many items to the storeroom supply the morning of the very next school day (e.g., if three sheets of paper are taken, six are provided the next day). Students failing to replace twice what they take will be required to work off the price of the items during the free period the day after the items are taken. The work tasks will be determined by Ms. Murphy and will involve such jobs as cleaning out the classroom or straightening up the storeroom.

VIGNETTE 9.15

Mr. Emery requires his junior high male physical education classes to wear clean uniform shorts, t-shirts, socks, sneakers, and athletic supporters. Mark, one of his students, tells Mr. Emery before class while others are changing into their uniforms: "Coach, I brought my P.E. clothes home to wash and I forgot to bring them back today." Mr. Emery: "Well, you need to workout today, but not in those street clothes. What are you missing?" Mark: "My shirt, shorts, socks, and jock." Mr. Emery: "You've got your sneakers?" Mark: "Yes." Mr. Emery: "Wait here, I can lend you some extra stuff, but you'll have to bring them back tomorrow cleaned." Mark: "Okay, Coach." Mr. Emery goes to his supply of P.E. clothes and purposely selects shorts that are baggy and an oversized shirt. Returning, he gives them to Mark. As he dresses, Mark looks at the ill-fitting outfit and thinks: "I hope I never forget my uniform again!"

BEING UNDER THE INFLUENCE OF DEBILITATING DRUGS

Teachers' Attitudes

Every school day in numerous urban, suburban, and rural school districts, tens of thousands of elementary, middle, junior high, and high school students attend classes under the debilitating influences of drugs (e.g., alcohol, marijuana, cocaine, crank, legal prescription drugs, barbiturates, amphetamines, and heroin) (Elam, Rose & Gallup, 1991; McLaren, 1989, p. 7; Shannon, 1986; Towers, 1987). Strangers to a community who are seeking a source for an easy buy of illegal drugs typically try areas near high schools and junior high schools first. Teachers respond to drug use by their students in a variety of ways.

1. Many teachers never become aware of their students' drug use although it is occurring at their schools and affecting the success of their learning activities. Such teachers remain naive because they do not "see" individual personalities in their classes. They visualize their classes as a mass of faceless students and think, for example, of their "third period European

literature class'' rather than ''Clarence, Jean, Barbara, Mono, Sam, Oramya, . . .'' Typically, such teachers spend much of their time talking to their groups while staring at the back walls of their classroom. They do not look into any one student's eyes and do not distinguish between glassy-eyed stupors and bright-eyed alertness. Subtle and even dramatic personality changes go undetected. Students who are depressive in the morning and manic in the afternoon appear the same all day to these teachers.

2. Some teachers, who believe they have never before been around drug users, are so frightened by the prospect of drugs in their classrooms that they do not allow themselves to accept the possibility. ''Deny what you don't like and you won't have to deal with it,'' is the deceptive message in which they find comfort. These teachers avoid drug awareness seminars and depend on their experiences sitting in motion picture theaters watching dramatizations of heroin addicts in the acute stages of withdrawal as indicative of how drug users act. They are not familiar with the wealth of resources on dealing with drugs in schools (e.g., Ray & Ksir, 1990; Rogers & McMillin, 1989; Towers, 1987, 1989).

3. Some teachers welcome the mellow, nondisruptive behaviors displayed by many students when under the influence of some drugs (e.g., marijuana and barbiturates). ''I wish he didn't use drugs at all, but I'd rather have him doped up than misbehaving,'' one teacher admitted. She continues: ''He can sleep it off in my class. That way, he's not disturbing those who want to learn. I can't control their habits, so why try?'' Similarly, there are teachers who encourage parents to obtain medication for their ''hyperactive'' children.

4. There are teachers who react to student drug use by initiating a personal crusade against this ''evil.'' Moralizing on the reasons why drugs should be avoided is usually ineffectual. Teachers who preach to students about the evils of drug use are often dealing with their own feelings of inadequacy. They may not be doing anything to effectively stem drug usage, but they can tell themselves: ''I'm trying to do something about the problem.''

5. Some teachers do not moralize about drug usage, but they do attempt to help students become more knowledgeable regarding the effects of drugs. These teachers alter curricula so that specific units about drugs are taught and so that problems involving drugs are used to intrinsically motivate students to engage in learning activities in science, mathematics, social studies, physical education, language arts, music, and other academic areas. The section ''Problem-Solving Learning Activities'' from Chapter 6 treats this type of learning activity. These teachers believe that it is better for students to choose whether or not to use drugs from an enlightened posture than to have to make that choice from a position of ignorance.

6. There are teachers who realize that they cannot be ''all things'' to their students and concentrate on helping students attain only those goals for which they are responsible. But, they also realize that students cannot be completely engaged in learning activities and, thus efficiently achieve

those goals while under the influence of crack, crank, marijuana, uppers, downers, acid, cocaine, and other commonly used mind-altering substances (Santrock, 1984, pp. 606–635). Such teachers believe that while they may not be able to control drug use outside their own classrooms, they are responsible for and can teach students to choose not to be under the influence of such substances when under their supervision.

Strategies

The teachers in Vignettes 9.16–9.19 use the last of the aforementioned six approaches to student drug use.

VIGNETTE 9.16

Royal, Paul, and Jake return from lunch to their sixth grade classroom grinning and glancing at one another. Ms. Jackson, their teacher, observes them carefully and finds their behavior, while not disruptive, strange for them. Ms. Jackson ignores the three boys for the first 10 minutes while she conducts a large group activity. As the class divides into smaller work groups and begins a second learning activity, Ms. Jackson individually engages each of the three in a conversation. She notices that Paul and Jake are less coherent than usual and that all three respond slower to questions than they normally do. Their eyes seem dilated more than one would expect in the daytime and she detects a sweet, musky odor when near Royal. She believes the three smoked marijuana during the lunch break. She thinks to herself: "I'm pretty sure this is the first time they've shown up in class stoned. I need to make sure it's the last. I have to prevent others from modeling what they've done. They first need to understand that this won't be tolerated in our classroom. I should get them out of here while I think of what to do, but they should also be kept apart. I don't want them enjoying each other's company right now. . . ."

Ms. Jackson goes over to Royal, takes him by the hand, walks him out of the room, and without anger says: "You're in no condition right now to learn. There is no sense in you remaining here for this lesson." Royal: "But I didn't do anything!" Ms. Jackson: "You're just not thinking as well as you usually do, and I think it's because you've been smoking marijuana or something else that messes up your mind. You wait for me in the time-out room until I have time to come and get you." Royal enters the time-out room adjoining the classroom. Ms. Jackson thinks: "Now, for the other two. I don't want them together. They should be alone to think. Where can I put Paul? Let's see. . . . The library! No, Ms. Green wouldn't understand. She'd likely do something stupid. . . . I know, I'll send a note to Mrs. Lobianco in the office and ask if she can find a couple of inconspicuous places for both Paul and Jake to wait separately. She'll understand." Ms. Jackson writes the following note and seals it in an envelope addressed to Ms. Lobianco, the principal's receptionist secretary.

Mrs. Lobianco:

I need to send Jake Abramson and Paul Guidry out of my room until 2:20 when I can retrieve them. Can you immediately locate two inconspicuous, quiet places (one for each as I don't want them together or anyone talking to them now)? My time-out room is occupied and I don't want either in the library.

Please return this note by way of Tyrone indicating whether or not you can work this out. If you can, I'll send Paul first and then Jake five minutes later. If either doesn't make it, send an aide to my room to let me know.

Thanks for your help.

Wilma Jackson

Ms. Jackson directs Tyrone to take the note. In two minutes, he returns with a reply from Ms. Lobianco: "It's all worked out. Glad to help." Ms. Jackson directs Paul and then Jake to the office in a manner similar to the way she handled Royal. She thinks: "Now, what do I do? I'd like to turn the whole matter over to their parents. Jake's parents would handle it effectively. But Royal's parents would just beat him. I don't want that. I don't really know Paul's parents. Actually, I wouldn't be surprised if Paul's mother and father share their dope with him. They seem so emotionally immature. . . . I'll call Jake's and Paul's houses tonight. But the Van Harpers will just mishandle it and not help Royal at all. I'm going to refer him to the guidance office; Hodge will handle it right. . . ."

After school, Ms. Jackson enters the time-out room and tells Royal, "I never want you to come into our class after smoking marijuana."

ROYAL: I didn't smoke anything.
MS. JACKSON: I'm surprised, because you show the signs of having smoked something.
ROYAL: Well, I didn't!
MS. JACKSON: I really don't care what you've already done or not done. I just want to make sure that you won't ever take anything like marijuana before coming to class in the future. Do you understand?
ROYAL: Yes, but I didn't!
MS. JACKSON: What is it that I'm trying to tell you?
ROYAL: Not ever to show up in our class stoned.
MS. JACKSON: Very well, you understand. Now to help you, I am going to ask Mr. Hodge to assist you. If he agrees, he'll be calling you into his office to speak with you either tomorrow or the next day. Do you have anything you'd like to say?
ROYAL: What about Paul and Jake? Don't they have to do nothin'?
MS. JACKSON: We're not concerned with Paul and Jake right now, only with you. Do you have anything else to say?
ROYAL: No, nothing.
MS. JACKSON: Now hurry along so you won't miss your bus. Have a pleasant night; I'll see you tomorrow.

Ms. Jackson brings Paul to the time-out room and engages him in a conversation.

MS. JACKSON: Paul, I never want you to come to class after smoking marijuana.
PAUL: Who said I smoked it? Was it Royal? He smoked a lot more than me? Why are you puttin' it on me?
MS. JACKSON: Be cool, Paul. I don't want to talk about Royal. I'm asking you to never use any kind of dope before or during school. I can't teach you when your mind's messed up. Tonight, I'm going to call your parents to

---

VIGNETTE 9.16 (continued)

get their help in preventing this from happening again. I don't expect it to happen again, but if it does, I'm not going to call your parents again, I'm going to send you to Principal Bannon. Do you know what that means?

Paul shrugs his shoulders.

MS. JACKSON: What do you suppose Ms. Bannon will do if I send you to her office?

Paul shrugs again.

MS. JACKSON: I don't know what that means.
PAUL: I don't know what she'll do.
MS. JACKSON: Let's brainstorm the possibilities. You go first.
PAUL, grinning shyly: She could just let it go.
MS. JACKSON, not grinning at all: That's one possibility. Here's another. She could expel you. Now it's your turn.
PAUL: She could call the police.
MS. JACKSON: That's a very real possibility. Or she could call the juvenile authorities. I think we understand one another. That's good. Now, I know you've got somewhere to go, so be on your way. But first, how about a nice firm handshake? Take care; I'll see you tomorrow.

Jake takes his turn speaking to Ms. Jackson in the time-out room.

MS. JACKSON: Jake, I think you smoked marijuana or something that messes up your mind at lunch break today.
JAKE: Yes.
MS. JACKSON: Thank you for being up front with me. I never expect you to come into our class in that condition again.
JAKE: Okay.
MS. JACKSON: Now, I have a favor to ask you.
MS. JACKSON, watching to see if he appears to understand: I want you to relate the whole incident to either your mother or your father after you get home. Have one of them call me to discuss it at this number and time.

She writes down her phone number and a time interval and hands it to Jake.

MS. JACKSON: That's between seven and 10 o'clock tonight. If I haven't heard from one of them by 10, I'll call your house. Okay?
JAKE: All right.
MS. JACKSON: You take care; I'll see you tomorrow.

VIGNETTE 9.17

For the first two months that Joel is in Ms. Bazinski's second grade class, he always appears alert and active. At times, Ms. Bazinski finds Joel's behavior to be exhausting as he displays a high-energy level. But she always manages to help him direct that energy into constructive activities. Ms. Bazinski makes lesson plans so that when she wants Joel in a quiet, sedentary learning activity, she precedes it with a vigorous psychomotor activity.

One morning, Joel is uncharacteristically listless. He seems to want to just sit and stare. His eyes do not seem bright and mischievous as they normally do. She asks him: "Are you feeling poorly?" Joel: "No." To Ms. Bazinski's amazement, Joel's listlessness continues through the next school day and she decides to contact his mother.

Over the phone, Ms. Bazinski speaks to Ms. Logan, Joel's mother.

MS. LOGAN: Hello.

MS. BAZINSKI: Hi, Ms. Logan. This is Susan Bazinski, Joel's teacher at school. How are you tonight?

MS. LOGAN: Just fine. Is anything the matter?

MS. BAZINSKI: I'm not sure; that's what I've called to find out. Did I catch you at an inconvenient time? We can arrange for another time to talk.

MS. LOGAN: Oh, no. Things are quiet around here for a change. Is Joel giving you some kind of trouble? Is he failing?

MS. BAZINSKI: No, Joel is not giving me trouble and he's not failing.

MS. LOGAN: Then what's the matter?

MS. BAZINSKI: Joel is always so energetic in class, always eager to participate. But yesterday and today, he acted tired and out of it.

MS. LOGAN: Really!

MS. BAZINSKI: Yes, it is worrying me and I wonder if you have any explanations?

MS. LOGAN: He shouldn't be tired. He used to hardly ever sleep through the night, but since he started his medication, he's gotten 10 good hours a night. Plus, he naps in the afternoon. So he shouldn't be tired.

MS. BAZINSKI: What medication, Ms. Logan?

MS. LOGAN: Oh, the doctor prescribed something to settle him down.

MS. BAZINSKI: Why? Is he sick?

MS. LOGAN: No, he's just hard to handle—always wiggling, won't sit still. He drives me up a wall and when the school bus driver complained about him, I checked with the doctor.

MS. BAZINSKI: Who is the doctor?

MS. LOGAN: Dr. Herrold. He said Joel is hyperactive.

MS. BAZINSKI: What is the medication.

MS. LOGAN: Dr. Herrold says it's a tranquilizer. Joel takes it twice a day. Life sure is easier around here since he's been on it. It really works.

MS. BAZINSKI: I guess that explains Joel's peculiar behavior at school.

MS. LOGAN: What do you mean "peculiar"?

MS. BAZINSKI: I mean it's just not like him to sit and stare and not participate the way he needs to participate.

MS. LOGAN: But how can he learn if he won't sit down and be quiet?

MS. BAZINSKI: Ms. Logan, Joel can learn much better when he's active and alert than he can in a stupor. I would like you to call Dr. Herrold tomorrow, and discuss this with him. I'd like to speak with him myself, after you've had a chance to explain the problem to him.

MS. LOGAN: Maybe he can change his prescription.

MS. BAZINSKI: Maybe so. I know I'd like to have the real Joel back in my classroom.

MS. LOGAN: Okay, I'll call the doctor tomorrow.

VIGNETTE 9.17 (continued)

MS. BAZINSKI: Thank you very much. I'll call you at this time tomorrow night and you can let me know about your discussion with Dr. Herrold and what you decided.

MS. LOGAN: All right.

MS. BAZINSKI: You have been so helpful. I look forward to speaking with you tomorrow. Have a pleasant night and tell Joel "good night" for me.

MS. LOGAN: Oh, he's already asleep. Good-bye.

VIGNETTE 9.18

Jim comes into Mr. Terrell's fourth-period business law class glassy-eyed and moving in a peculiar, mechanical fashion. Mr. Terrell watches him sit at his desk with his head seeming to bob around his shoulders like a doll with a spring neck. Jim seems to be making an effort to appear "straight," but Mr. Terrell is not deceived. Mr. Terrell decides not to deal with the situation at present. After class, he writes out an anecdotal account describing Jim's behavior in class that day. He sends copies to the principal and a trusted school counselor with notes requesting advice as to how he should handle the matter.

VIGNETTE 9.19

Through 10 years of schooling, Ray was never instructed by a teacher who utilized problem-solving learning activities. Not being intrinsically motivated to participate, Ray learned in ninth grade that by coming to class high on drugs, time seemed to pass more quickly and the boredom was not as insufferable. The drugs also seemed to relieve the anxiety he felt over his concern for peer approval.

Early in Ray's eleventh school year, Ms. Koo-Kim, Ray's literature teacher, becomes aware that he is habitually stoned in her class. She thinks to herself: "I will not tolerate Ray or any other student wasting time in my class by being strung out. I'll definitely do something to either teach him to show up straight or not at all. But how? What strategy should I try? Maybe I should give him one warning and then let the office handle him if he shows up out of it again. But unless they catch him with the stuff on him, what can they do? There's no school rule against being high, just for possession and trafficking. I'll first see if I can entice him into wanting to participate in class. Maybe intrinsic motivation isn't just a textbook dream. First of all, I need to find out more about Ray."

After some observations, Ms. Koo-Kim thinks that Ray might have some interest in being an entertainer. She decides to assign him the role of Macbeth in an upcoming class play during a unit on Shakespeare. She hopes he will discover that he cannot learn to perform to the satisfaction of his classmates when he is high. She figures that the responsibility of having them depend on him will either make or break him in the literature class.

Ms. Koo-Kim implements her plan and Ray begins to realize that he is unable to remember the lines he studies the night before when he is under the influence of drugs in class. Classmates' performances are affected by how well Ray does. Several times, Ray and other students suggest that he be replaced for the production. Ms. Koo-Kim persists in her expressions of confidence in Ray's will to succeed. Ray resolves to control his drug usage at least so that it does not interfere with his ability to be engaged during the unit on Shakespeare. Ms. Koo-Kim hopes that this is the beginning of the end of Ray's attending her class while under the influence of drugs.

BEING ABSENT OR TARDY

School-wide Policies for Extrinsically Motivating Student Attendance

The policy related in Vignette 9.20 typifies those of many secondary and middle schools.

VIGNETTE 9.20

Gloster High's handbook includes the following attendance policy:

A student who is absent for an entire school day or from an entire class during a school day may not be admitted back into any of the missed classes before bringing a note, signed by a parent, explaining the reason for the absence. The note will be evaluated by the school attendance official to classify the absence as either "excused" or "unexcused." The official will provide the student with an "admit slip," which teachers are required to initial prior to allowing the student to return to individual classes.

A student who either arrives at school after the beginning of homeroom period or is late for any class must explain the reason for the tardiness to the attendance officer who will provide the student with an admit slip and categorize the tardiness either as "excused" or "unexcused." Teachers shall not admit tardy students into their classes without admit slips.

A student who accumulates three unexcused absences for a class during one grade-reporting period or a student who accumulates a combined total of five unexcused absences and incidences of tardiness for a class period during one grade-reporting period shall receive a failing grade for that class for that period.

A student will be allowed by make up work missed during an excused absence and excused tardiness. Students may not be allowed to make up work missed during any unexcused absence or unexcused tardiness.

A student will be suspended from attending school for a week each time a total of five unexcused absences for entire school days are accumulated.

Teachers' Policies for Extrinsically Motivating Student Attendance

Sometimes individual teachers, especially secondary school teachers, have rules for their classes similar to the one in Vignette 9.21.

Irrationality of Some Popular Attendance Policies

Schools and teachers with policies similar to those in Vignettes 9.20 and 9.21 attempt to extrinsically motivate students to attend classes with a system of rewards and punishments that largely depend on students' desires to obtain high grades. Such systems are inherently irrational for at least four reasons.

1. The purpose of grades is to communicate teachers' summative evaluations of students' achievement of learning goals. If in-class learning activities are relevant to student attainment of goals and grades are assigned based

---

VIGNETTE 9.21

Ms. Keane includes the following in her course syllabus:

Each student's course grade will be based on attendance, completion of assignments, scores on weekly tests, score on the final examination, and conduct in class. During the 45-day grading period, students have the opportunity to earn up to 500 points distributed as follows:

1. *Attendance (90 points):* For each complete class attended, the student will receive 2 points. A student who is tardy receives 1 point for that day. No points are received on days a student is absent.
2. *Completion of Assignments (90 points):* For each day a student satisfactorily turns in assigned homework on time and completes all in-class work, that student is credited with 2 points. Only 1 point is given on days in which assignments are either turned in late or unsatisfactory done. No points are given on days assignments are not turned in at all.
3. *Scores on Weekly Tests (160 points):* Eight 20-point weekly tests will be given.
4. *Final Exam Score (100 points):* The final exam will be an opportunity for each student to earn up to 100 points.
5. *In-Class Conduct (60 points):* Each student will begin the grade reporting period with 60 points. A student who is disruptive or violates a classroom regulation will have points subtracted from that total in proportion to the seriousness of each offense.

A student's report card grade will be determined by the number of points obtained during the grading period, ''A'' for 468 to 500 points, ''B'' for 428 to 467 points, ''C'' for 388 to 427 points, ''D'' for 348 to 387 points, and ''F'' for 0 to 347 points.

on students' achievement of those goals, then there is no need to artificially tie grades to class attendance. Students who are absent from classes in which worthwhile learning activities take place are far less likely to receive high grades than students who engage in those worthwhile learning activities. It is only when what goes on in class does not help students achieve goals that making grades directly contingent on attendance even remotely makes sense. In such unfortunate cases, the rationale is: "We want students to attend classes. Since what goes on in classes doesn't really help them achieve and, thus does not naturally help their grades, we'll fabricate a relation between attendance and grades."

2. Many students, especially those with a history of obtaining low grades, are simply not motivated by the desire for high grades or the fear of low grades.

3. Not allowing a student to make up work missed for unexcused absences or tardiness is an admission that school work is unimportant. If work missed by an absent student is critical to that student's goal attainment, then not allowing the student to do that work is leaving that student with a learning gap. How is a teacher supposed to deal with that student for the remainder of the school year when the student lacks some knowledge, skill, ability, or attitude that is a prerequisite for subsequent learning?

4. Responding to habitual absenteeism with suspension seems counterproductive. Is the principle of satiation being applied?

Strategies

Rather than depend on schemes for artificially tying grades to attendance, you, as a teacher, can make sure that students discover the natural connection among attendance, achievement, and grades. Teachers deal with students' absenteeism in Vignettes 9.22–9.24.

VIGNETTE 9.22

As part of a language arts exercise, Mr. Kacala's third grade students compose letters to the mayor of their city suggesting ideas for reducing crime. The letters are written in class on a day when April is not in attendance. The next day when April returns, Mr. Kacala has the letters displayed on the classroom walls. He tells the students: "I want you to select a letter to talk about. In your talk, explain what you agree with and disagree with. You may talk about a letter only if its author agrees to talk about your letter, too."

As the students make their selections, April tells Steve: "I want to talk about your letter!" Steve: "Okay, then I get to do yours." April: "I don't have one because I wasn't here yesterday." Steve: "Let's ask Mr. Kacala what to do."

Hearing about their problem, Mr. Kacala replies: "I'm sorry, but if April does not have a letter, then she won't be able to talk about one today." April: "But it wasn't my fault; I was sick yesterday!" Mr. Kacala: "I'm really sorry that you were

---

VIGNETTE 9.22 (continued)

sick yesterday. It's terrible that you didn't get to write a letter.'' April: ''But I wanna . . .'' Mr. Kacala: ''I know you do. I'll tell you what. Just listen to the others talk about the letters today and after you get home, you write your letter. Bring it tomorrow. Gretchen isn't here today. If she agrees, you can talk about each other's letters tomorrow or on whatever day she's back in school.'' April: ''But I want to do Steve's today!'' Mr. Kacala has already moved toward another group of students and is conversing with them.

VIGNETTE 9.23

Due to a dental appointment, Singh misses Mr. Shapiro's health science class one Tuesday. The next day, Singh listens to Mr. Shapiro's lecture befuddled and unable to follow the trend of thought. Several times within his lecture, Mr. Shapiro prefaces statements with: ''As we discussed yesterday, . . .'' Not having ''discussed'' anything with the class yesterday, Singh feels frustrated.

Afterwards, Singh approaches Mr. Shapiro with: Man! I'm absent one day and now I'm two days behind! I couldn't follow a thing you said today just because I had to go to the dentist yesterday.'' Mr. Shapiro: ''Yes, I was just thinking it was unfortunate that you couldn't schedule that appointment at another time. Anyway, after class, find someone who is willing to let you copy yesterday's notes. After you've gone over the notes, check with me in here at 7:45 tomorrow morning. I'll answer any questions I can before homeroom period begins. I'll also lend you some reading matter that'll help you catch up.'' Singh: ''Thank you.''

VIGNETTE 9.24

Willie approaches Ms. Grimes, his college botany teacher, and says: ''Ms. Grimes, are we having a test next Tuesday?'' Ms. Grimes: ''I'm not sure yet. It depends on how much progress we make before then. If the test isn't on Tuesday, it'll be on Thursday.'' Willie: ''I have to be out of town on Tuesday and I don't want to miss a test. If we have one, will I be allowed to make it up? I really hate to miss, but I can't help it because . . .'' Ms. Grimes (interrupting): ''Why you'll be absent is irrelevant. Let's concern ourselves with what we should do about it.'' Willie: ''Okay.'' Ms. Grimes: ''Actually, I'd much rather you miss a test than a regular class meeting. I can easily administer an equivalent form of the test to you at another time.'' Willie: ''And you won't take off because it's a make-up?'' Ms. Grimes: ''Why would I do that?'' Willie: ''That's what other teach—Hey, that's great!'' Ms. Grimes: ''But, if we have a regular class on Tuesday, that does present us with a problem. Whom do you know in class that you can easily get in touch with?'' Willie: ''Lamona or Edgar.'' Ms. Grimes: ''Ask one of them to bring some cassettes and a recorder to class that Tuesday. I'll record the session for you. As soon as you return to town, listen to the tapes, get their notes, find out the assignment, and discuss the session with Lamona or Edgar. After you've done that, you can give me a call and we'll either talk about it on the phone or make an appointment to clear up any further questions you might have." Willie: "Thank you. I'll do it. Really, I wouldn't miss your class if it wasn't for . . ." Ms. Grimes (interrupting): "Good-bye, Willie."

CHEATING ON TESTS

Nine Incidents

Some students are quite resourceful in devising ways to cheat. Consider Vignettes 9.25–9.33.

VIGNETTE 9.25

Angee gets out of her seat, walks over to the classroom pencil sharpener, and returns to her desk to complete the multiple-choice science test she and the rest of her sixty grade classmates are taking. During her walk, Angee looked on several other students' papers to find out how they responded to certain items that she couldn't answer.

VIGNETTE 9.26

A calculus teacher, Mr. Kruhl, scores test papers by writing down the number of "points off" by each item a student doesn't correctly answer. Mr. Kruhl does not mark anything by correctly answered items; he simply subtracts the total number of points off from the maximum possible score of 100. Jack, one of Mr. Kruhl's students, realizes this after his first calculus test is returned. When Jack is about to begin taking the second test, he thinks: "I'll never have time to complete this 12 page monster in the 90 minutes Kruhl's allowing us. I'll just rip out pages 6 and 9 and discard them. He'll probably just pass over them and not realize they're missing. If he does catch it, I'll just say they were never there." Several days later, Mr. Kruhl returns Jack's paper. Jack's score is the same as it would have been if Jack had correctly responded to all of the items on pages 6 and 9.

VIGNETTE 9.27

June did not study for the history exam that Ms. Tolbert is giving today. Instead, June memorized the answers to an old unit test that Ms. Tolbert had administered to one of June's friends in a previously held class. June is overjoyed when Ms. Tolbert hands her a test identical to the one her friend shared.

VIGNETTE 9.28

Twelfth graders Kraemer, Tom, and Arthur engage Ms. Hubert in a lively conversation before school as their coconspirator, Mary Ellen, steals four copies of the final physics exam schedules for that afternoon off of Ms. Hubert's desk. During the morning study hall, the four students jointly figure out the answers and each fills out a copy of the test. To avoid suspicion, they make sure that there are some discrepancies among their papers. When Ms. Hubert administers the test, the four carefully substitute their completed copies for the ones distributed by Ms. Hubert.

VIGNETTE 9.29

Sonia, an eighth grade student, runs a popular service for her schoolmates at Abraham Lincoln Middle School. Sonia searches trash containers for used duplicating carbons and masters that have been discarded in the faculty lounge or school office. From her growing "test file," she provides test information to her many "friends." Sonia feels very popular with her peers.

VIGNETTE 9.30

"May I please be excused to the restroom?" Mickey asks Mr. Green during a fourth grade spelling test. Mr. Green: "Yes, but hurry so you will have plenty of time to finish your test." Mickey: "I will. Thank you very much." In the restroom, Mickey extracts his spelling list that earlier in the day he had hidden under a toilet. He quickly checks the spelling of the four words from the test that he does not know.

VIGNETTE 9.31

Freda takes a lengthy psychology test and leaves several short-answer, written-response items blank. Her teacher, Mr. Zabriski, scores the test and returns them to the class the following day. The items Freda left blank are marked with zeroes, but she quickly fills in the answers and approaches Mr. Zabriski: "Mr. Zabriski, don't I get any credit for these? I thought they were at least partially correct!"

VIGNETTE 9.32

As Mr. Duetchman supervises a large group of high school students taking a two-day achievement test battery, he finds it curious that Donna frequently brings her elbow together and stares down the neckline of her dress. Not knowing what to do, he dismisses her behavior as a reflection of adolescent self-consciousness. Actually, Donna has crib notes or a "cheat sheet" attached to the inside of her bra.

VIGNETTE 9.33

Ms. Bolden instructs her first graders to keep their test papers covered and not to let classmates see their answers while taking a mathematics tests. Ashley and Monica are sitting at the same table taking the test when Monica turns to Ashley and, pointing to one of her test items, says: "I forgot what this one is." Ashley: "Ms. Bolden said you weren't supposed to show me your paper! Cover it up." Monica: "Sorry! But I need some help on this one." Ashley: "Okay, don't show me your paper. Just read it to me." Monica: "What's this called?" Monica draws a rectangle in the air with her finger. Ashley: "Let me see what I just put for that. But don't look on my paper while I look. It's not allowed." Ashley turns back to Monica, still carefully covering her paper, and says, "It's a rectangle."

Primary Grade Children, like Ashley and Monica, Do Not Have an Adult's Concept of Cheating

Strategies

By violating rules under which a test is administered so they can correctly answer items which they otherwise could not answer, students contaminate the validity of the test. In other words, besides being an unethical, distasteful practice, cheating leads to inaccurate and misleading test results. Students would have no inclination to cheat on a test if they believed that accurate information about their achievement in the hands of their teachers is more beneficial to them than is misinformation that deceives their teachers. Once again, three vital principles become apparent.

1. The self-worth students perceive and the respect, love, and esteem others (including teachers) feel for them should never be dependent upon their achievements.
2. Formative evaluations of students' achievements should be emphasized to a far greater degree than should summative evaluations.
3. Grades should only be used to communicate summative evaluations; they should not be used as a reward for achievements.

Given the unfortunate fact that there is almost universal violations of these principles, you are virtually assured of encountering students with inclinations for cheating on tests. But even with these students, cheating is unlikely in the following situations.

1. You set a businesslike tone and display an attitude that communicates that students are not expected to cheat.
2. Test administrations are closely supervised. (Please note, however, that, as indicated by Vignette 9.33, the concept of cheating is not well-developed in young children (e.g., under the age of nine). Primary school children do not differentiate between obtaining a correct response with unauthorized aid and obtaining it without unauthorized aid (Pulaski, 1980; Rogoff, 1990, pp. 42–61). Teachers should observe whether or not young children respond on their own or with unauthorized aid. Steps should be taken so that such aid is not attainable. However, warning young students not to cheat or to punish them for behaviors that adults consider to be cheating is, for them, a frustrating experience that only teaches them they are not trusted. Even with older students, warnings are futile and should be avoided. However, students should not be given reasonable opportunities to cheat.)
3. The same form of a test is not used repeatedly.
4. You account for each copy of a test that is duplicated (copies can be numbered) and materials, such as duplicating masters, are secured.
5. You mark test papers so that points are added for correct responses rather than subtracting points for incorrect ones.
6. You annotate, as well as score, test papers. (Not only does this practice provide helpful feedback to students, but it also helps you remember why you scored items as you did. Students are less likely to manipulate answers after the tests are returned if you have already commented on their answers.

7. Students are directed to check on whether or not their test copies contain all pages and are properly collated prior to beginning.
8. Students are not tested on their recall of material that seems unnecessary to memorize. (When obtaining a grade on a test is the sole perceived purpose students have for memorizing, what they know will be forgotten after the test, using crib notes seems like a sensible thing to do.)

Because a student cheats on a test is not a reason for recording a low score. Cheating does not reflect learning goal attainment (expect in the rare case in which the learning goal is for the student to be honest). Thus, if a teacher knows that a student has cheated on a test, then the test results are not valid and no score should be recorded. A student's understanding of biology, for example, should not be judged by whether or not that student cooperated with the test-taking procedures. Judgments of how well learning goals are achieved should be withheld until after the student no longer displays the dishonest behavior and a valid measurement of achievement can be obtained (Cangelosi, 1982, pp. 237–238). Teachers in Vignettes 9.34–9.36 deal with some sticky situations.

VIGNETTE 9.34

While scoring a unit test he had administered to his tenth grade first-aid class, Mr. Broussard notices some inconsistencies in Joe's test responses. Joe's answers to a couple of the more difficult items on the test are correct, while he missed a number of items that measured simple rudimentary knowledge. Mr. Broussard asks himself: "How could he get these correct without knowing these?" Later, while scoring Remy's paper, Mr. Broussard notices that Remy answers the same difficult items using words very similar to those in Joe's responses. Mr. Broussard compares their two sets of responses and notices some peculiar similarities. On the multiple-choice portions of the test, Joe's choices nearly always agree with Remy's. He finds it curious that the two would consistently choose the same distractors or foils for multiple-choice items that they both missed.

Highly suspicious that Joe copied from Remy's paper, Mr. Broussard begins planning how to deal with the situation. He thinks: "I should confront them both with this. Scare the hell out of them! But if I'm wrong, I'll only teach them they're not trusted. That could be damaging. They just might cheat from now on because they figured there'd be no trust to lose. But I really can't put any stock in Joe's test results and I need to know what he got out of this unit. I need an accurate score on him. Also, I don't want Joe to get away with this. I don't think he's cheated before. I should block any positive reinforcement so this doesn't become a pattern. I'll just disregard his test paper and schedule a retest for him with an equivalent form."

The next day, Mr. Broussard distributes the scored and annotated test papers. Joe, from his desk: "Mr. Broussard, you didn't give my test back." Mr. Broussard: "I didn't? Please come up here." Joe arrives and Mr. Broussard says softly: "You didn't get your paper back. What do you think happened?" Joe: "I don't know. I took the test." Mr. Broussard: "Yes, I know. I remember going over it." Mr. Broussard pulls out his grade book and says: "Here, Joe, let's see if I recorded a score for you.

VIGNETTE 9.34 (continued)

No, there's no score here. Look.'' Joe sees the empty square. Mr. Broussard: ''We'll just schedule a retest. How about tomorrow? I'll give you a retest tomorrow.'' Joe: ''That's not fair for me to have to take another test.'' Mr. Broussard: ''Things don't always seem fair. Now, let's see when we can schedule it . . . .''

VIGNETTE 9.35

Mr. Stoddard validates each sociology test that he administers to his classes before allowing the test results to influence evaluations he makes regarding students' achievement levels. From analysis of one set of test results and from his observations of some curious student behaviors during the administration of that test, Mr. Stoddard suspects that student cheating contaminated the accuracy of the test results. At the next class meeting, Mr. Stoddard announces: ''The results I received from the test are invalid. There are some major discrepancies among the scores. Statistical analyses indicate the test was too unreliable to accurately indicate your levels of achievement. Therefore, I discarded the results and we will take a refined version of the test under more controlled conditions on Wednesday.''

VIGNETTE 9.36

Ms. Maggio administers a problem-solving test to her fourth graders in which they are directed to work out in their heads a sequence of tasks that are presented in pages 39 and 40 in one of their textbooks. She instructs them to look at only those two pages in their books while completing the test. Ms. Maggio notices that Nettie, keeps glancing up at her. Furthermore, Nettie seems to manipulate her book suddenly whenever Ms. Maggio comes near or looks at her. Ms. Maggio suspects that Nettie has surreptitiously turned to the back of the book in which answers to the problems are given.

    After the test, Ms. Maggio examines Nettie's answer sheet. Most of the responses are correct. She then engages Nettie in a private conference and presents one of the test problems to Nettie and asks her to solve it. Nettie is unable to come up with a solution this time. Nettie fails twice more to reproduce answers which she had written on the test earlier in the day. Ms. Maggio: ''Nettie, I do not understand why you cannot figure out these answers now if you solved the problems during the test.'' Nettie: ''I don't know.'' Ms. Maggio: ''I will not check-off that you can do these types of problems until you demonstrate to me that you can.''

TRANSITIONAL ACTIVITIES
FROM CHAPTER 9 TO CHAPTER 10

  I. Which of the six approaches to students' abuse of drugs (pp. 256–258) do you most closely associate with your philosophy? Explain in a paragraph why you prefer this approach. Argue your point of view with a colleague whose opinion differs.

II. Observe the students in a colleague's classroom. Search for indicators of student daydreaming and mind-wandering. Describe what you observed in those students' behaviors that led you to believe that they had quietly become disengaged from the learning activity.

III. Write one or two paragraphs explaining your view of the advantages and disadvantages of the way the teacher handled the off-task behavior in each of the following vignettes; suggest how the approach could have been improved. Vignettes 9.2, 9.4, 9.5, 9.8, 9.12, 9.14, 9.16, 9.34, and 9.36.

Exchange copies of what you wrote with those of colleagues. After reading one another's papers, discuss the differences and similarities among your responses.

IV. In preparation for your work with Chapter 10, discuss the following questions with two or more of your colleagues.

    A. Why is it necessary for teachers to control disruptive student behaviors in order to fulfill their responsibilities to all of their students?

    B. What strategies do teachers employ to deal with these disruptive behaviors.

        1. Talking.

        2. Interrupting a speaker.

        3. Clowning.

        4. Being generally discourteous.

        5. Failing to clean up following a learning activity.

        6. Vandalizing property.

        7. Threatening or assaulting a student or teacher.

SUPPLEMENTAL READINGS

Maifar, L. L. (1986, October). Helping kids resist drugs. *Instructor, XCVI* (3), 72–74.

Ray, O., & Ksir, C. (1990). *Drugs, society, and human behavior* (5th ed.). St. Louis: Time Mirror/Mosby College Publishing.

Rogers, R. L., & McMillin, C. S. (1989). *Freeing someone you love from alcohol and other drugs: A step-by-step plan starting today!* Los Angeles: The Body Press.

Seeman, H. (1984). A major source of discipline problems. *Educational Horizons, 62,* 128–131.

Shannon, J. (1986). In the classroom stoned. *Phi Delta Kappan, 68,* 60–62.

Tillman, M. (1982). *Trouble-shooting classroom problems.* Glenview, IL: Scott, Foresman.

Towers, R. L. (1987). *How schools can help combat student drug and alcohol abuse.* Washington: National Education Association.

Dealing with Disruptive Behaviors

Purpose of Chapter 10

Chapter 10 is designed to help you develop strategies for effectively handling both isolated incidents and patterns of disruptive behaviors. In particular the following types of disruptive behaviors are addressed. (1) talking, (2) interrupting, (3) clowning, (4) being generally discourteous, (5) failing to clean up, (6) vandalizing, (7) perpetrating violence against students, and (8) perpetrating violence against teachers.

DISRUPTIVE BEHAVIORS

When students reject opportunities to learn by displaying nondisruptive off-task behaviors, they suffer the consequences of their own choices. But students who behave disruptively also tread on the rights of other students to learn. You, as their teacher, can hardly ignore disruptive student behaviors. This chapter includes 29 vignettes in which teachers deal one way or another with disruptive student behaviors. From these examples, you are urged to extract ideas and develop strategies that will work for you and your students. Reflect on the pros and cons of how these teachers handled disruptions; please don't simply copy their methods.

DISRUPTIVE TALKING

Consider Vignettes 10.1–10.5.

VIGNETTE 10.1

Ms. Bravo usually plans each school day so that her fourth grade students alternate learning activities in which they need to be rather quiet and learning activities in which talking with one another is not disruptive. Her students typically look forward to the learning activities that have hardly any restrictions on talking. One day during a quiet session in which the class is supposed to be engaged in an independent learning activity, sporadic conversations erupt among the students. Ms. Bravo finds the noise disturbing to those working on the assigned task. Realizing that students are anticipating playing "Who Am I?" in 30 minutes, she blinks the classroom lights to get their attention and announces: "There is much too much talk for us to think on our own. I am starting my stopwatch now." She pushes a button on the chronograph on her wrist and continues: "I will keep my stopwatch running as long as there is noise in here. When the noise stops, my watch will stop. When the noise starts again, my watch will also. We will begin playing 'Who Am I?' only after 30 more minutes of silence for working out these problems." In five minutes, the class is quiet and working, and Ms. Bravo stops her watch. Eight minutes later, talking disrupts the work and Ms. Bravo accumulates another six minutes on the stopwatch waiting for silence. The required total of 30 minutes of silence is finally obtained after one more three minute interruption. She directs the class to begin playing "Who Am I?" 14 minutes after the game was scheduled to start. However, the starting time for the silent learning activity scheduled right after "Who Am I?" is not delayed. A number of students complain that the game was too short and they did not have enough time to finish.

VIGNETTE 10.2

There are 30 minutes remaining in Ms. Allen's fourth period Russian II class when she directs the students to begin work on a translation exercise from their textbooks. A number of students carry on conversations that are disturbing to others. Ms. Allen motions for silence, but talking continues to spring up around the classroom. Ms. Allen calls a halt to the translations saying: "Class, please let me have your attention. . . . I think each of us needs silence to properly translate these sentences. I'm sorry, but I see this isn't working. Let's hold off on these translations until you can get away by yourselves, either at home or during your free period. Just have them ready for class tomorrow. Right now, put your books away and we'll work together on our conversational Russian. Here's what we'll do. . . ."

VIGNETTE 10.3

Mr. Haimowitz is explaining Ohm's Law to his physics class when he becomes annoyed by a conversation between two students, Walt and Henry. Without missing a word in his explanation, he moves between the students and continues speaking

VIGNETTE 10.3 (continued)

to the class. The two boys stop talking and appear to pay attention as long as Mr. Haimowitz is between them. Five minutes later, with Mr. Haimowitz lecturing from another area of the room, Walt and Henry are conversing again. This time, Mr. Haimowitz continuing with his lecture, goes over to them, picks up Henry's papers from the top of his desk, and motions Henry to follow him to another part of the room where there is a vacant desk. Mr. Haimowitz places Henry's papers on the desk top and Henry takes a seat. At no time during the incident did Mr. Haimowitz speak directly to either Henry or Walt, nor did he miss a word in his explanation of Ohm's Law.

VIGNETTE 10.4

Mr. Eglin is lecturing to a political science class when several students' conversations develop in the crowded lecture hall. Mr. Eglin lowers his voice below the level of the combined students' voices. Other students, who are now straining to hear Mr. Eglin's inaudible words, turn to those near them who are talking and tell them to be quiet. As the conversations cease, Mr. Eglin raises his voice so that he can again be heard.

VIGNETTE 10.5

Leora and Nan, two sixth graders, consider themselves best friends. At school they are almost constant companions. Ms. Helmick, their teacher, believes their relationship is healthy and she doesn't want to discourage it. However, they have developed a pattern of talking, note passing, giggling, and looking at one another during quiet learning activities. Ms. Hemlick has dealt with their disruptive talking individually as she would for isolated off-task behaviors. She now decides that their pattern of disruptive talking must somehow be modified. Careful thought leads Ms. Helmick to formulate three alternative plans.

1. Ms. Helmick will confront the two with the problem they have been creating. She will indicate that each time she recognizes that they are talking at an inappropriate time, she will signal them to leave the area where the learning activity is going on and to continue their conversation in the time-out room. They are to remain there until the learning activity that they disturbed is over.

2. Ms. Helmick will frequently schedule "free talk" sessions, in which students can socialize within certain guidelines, after quiet learning activities. Participation in the free talk sessions will be contingent on all students having quietly engaged in the previous quiet learning activity. Time wasted during the quiet activity due to disruptive talking will be made up from time scheduled for the free talk session.

3. Each time Leora and Nan's talking disrupts a learning activity, Ms. Helmick will use the stopwatch she wears on her wrist to keep account of the amount of time wasted. Leora and Nan will then be required to make up the lost time after school that day. Leora's and Nan's parents will be made aware of this plan so they can cooperate in having the two students get home on days they miss their buses.

Ms. Helmick is not yet sure which of the three plans she will try first. She has confidence in the first plan because she doesn't believe that Leora and Nan want to be excluded from class activities. In fact, incidents during class activities often stimulate their in-class talking. Furthermore, the principle of satiation may take effect and the girls could become "talked out." In the time-out room they would be deprived of much of the stimulations (e.g., seeing other students) for their conversations. Ms. Helmick thinks the second plan would bring peer pressure on Leora and Nan to control their disruptive talking. The third plan utilizes the power of negative reinforcement because they would control when Ms. Helmick stops her timer.

INTERRUPTING

What motivates Sandy's behavior in Vignette 10.6? As we see Sandy did not help Lorene at all. Unfortunately, students are often conditioned into believing that all teachers want from them are the right answers. They don't think processes and thinking skills are of concern to teachers. Furthermore, these students have learned to believe that they are constantly being tested. Thus, by popping up with the right answer, Sandy felt she could seize an opportunity to show off her knowledge and she could either gain Lorene's favor for "helping" her or outdo Lorene in a competiton of "who knows the answer." Mr. Caldwell faced a dilemma. On one hand, he did not want to discourage the interrupting student's enthusiasm for the lesson. On the other hand, he needed to discourage such disruptions. Of course, teachers who apply research-based principles for conducting questioning and discussion sessions, such as those elaborated in "Ideas for Questioning Sessions" in Chapter 6, are less likely to be faced with this dilemma.

Teachers effectively deal with students' interruptions in Vignettes 10.7–10.9.

VIGNETTE 10.6

During a questioning session, Mr. Caldwell asks Lorene: "What number multiplied by 7 is 42?" Lorene: "Uhh, let's see. I think . . ." Sandy interrupts: "Six because 42 divided by 7 is 6!" Lorene appears relieved to be "off the hook." Sandy smiles. Mr. Caldwell is frustrated because his planned strategy in which Lorene was to reason deductively has been disrupted. Sandy's interruption deprived Lorene of a learning experience. Mr. Caldwell, appearing quite disgusted, turns to Sandy: "Why did you interrupt?" Sandy: "I was just helping her out."

VIGNETTE 10.7

Ms. Brittain has established the following procedure for her fourth graders to use during large group discussions.

> During a discussion session only the person who has the floor may speak. Students may obtain the floor by raising their hands and being recognized by the student who has the floor. A student who has the floor must relinquish it within one minute after someone raises a hand. Ms. Brittain may intervene at any time in the process to assure each student a fair opportunity to speak and to keep the discussion focused on the agreed upon topic.

> While discussing the differences between living in a large city and in a small town, Crystal is explaining why she thinks it is easier to travel in a small town. Without raising his hand, Oral interrupts with: "Yeah, but in a big city you can take a subway and—" Crystal (interrupting): "I have the floor! I didn't call on you!" Oral: "But,—" Ms. Brittain (interrupting): "Oral, the procedure is to raise your hand and wait to be recognized before speaking. Now, I want to hear what Crystal was saying about traveling in a small town." The discussion continues as Ms. Brittain carefully monitors the session, watching to see if the less bold students are encouraged to speak.

VIGNETTE 10.8

Mr. Rutknecht is explaining how to bisect an angle with a straight-edge and compass when Debbie, one of his 34 students, interrupts with: "What size radius do you need for the first arc?" Mr. Ruthknecht appreciates that Debbie has asked a question that is relevant to the topic. He wants to encourage her interest and that type of question. However, he doesn't want to positively reinforce interruptions. He responds to Debbie's out-of-turn question with only a frown and continues his explanation, watching for Debbie and other students to raise their hands. Momentarily, Lynn raises her hand and Mr. Rutknecht immediately recognizes her. Lynn asks a questions and raises a point on which Mr. Rutknecht elaborates. Five students, including Debbie, raise their hands and two speak out without being recognized. Mr. Rutkneckt cuts off the interrupting students and calls on those with hands raised. At one point, he thanks a student for her patience in waiting to be recognized.

VIGNETTE 10.9

"People moved west because—," Maureen is saying to Mr. Peck's class when another student, Hugh, interrupts with: "They never would have moved if . . ." Mr. Peck has had to deal with Hugh's interruptions in the past; he resolves to do something about the pattern.

That night, Mr. Peck thinks: "I will use the principle of extinction to help Hugh break this habit of interrupting speakers during class. I first need to identify the payoff he realizes from interrupting. What's the positive reinforcement? I think he likes being noticed, wanting the rest of the class and me to know what he knows. He thinks others are upstaging him by talking. It is a competitive thing. If it's attention he wants, I'll make sure he gets it when he's patiently waiting for his turn to talk; I'll keep him from getting attention when he interrupts. Each time he interrupts, I'll cut him off immediately by repeating the last words of whomever he interrupted. I won't even look at him. I'll just jump in and say: 'You were saying' and repeat the words of the other student. If he interrupts Sue, for example, I'll interrupt him and say to Sue something like: 'Excuse me Sue, you were saying you thought that . . .' and I'll let Sue go on. When Hugh remains quiet, I'll ask him for a comment or an opinion. That should positively reinforce a desirable alternative behavior. Now, I'd better work up a tally sheet to help me measure how much progress Hugh makes while he's on this plan."

Clowning

Consider how teachers in Vignettes 10.10–10.12 deal with students clowning.

VIGNETTE 10.10

Mr. Holts' sixth grade class is engaged in a large group learning activity on nutrition when Vickie responds to one of Mr. Holt's questions with: "I'm not just going to eat anything. I'm careful about what I stick in my body." Woodrow stands up and yells out: "Here's something you can stick in your body!" Woodrow momentarily grabs his crotch. Laughter erupts around the room. Because Mr. Holt has thought about how to handle this type of situation and because he follows the Teaching Process Model, he is able to process the following thoughts in his mind without a moment's delay: "Woodrow has never pulled this stunt before. He's only looking for attention. It's too bad they laughed at him. That's positive reinforcement and this could be the beginning of a pattern. I need to prevent this from happening again. But how? I have numerous options. I could just laugh along and not make a big deal of it. But no, I cannot display approval. I might just ignore it and try not to focus any more attention on it. But, damn it, they've already laughed at him! It's too late to ignore it. I could jerk him out of his seat and give him a good tongue lashing, but that would just call more attention to him. That's what he wants. Of course, he's left himself very vulnerable for a comeback. It would be easy for me to turn this around and embarrass him with his own words. Maybe that could serve as a punishment. But that would also be destructive; I'd never do that. It's never helpful to have a child lose face in front of peers. That could easily turn into a competitive thing between us; I can't afford that. I'm only glad no one in the class had a comeback for him. I must make sure I don't label him in any way. If I called him 'dirty' or 'rude,' he might learn to live up that expectation. I could pretend that I did not understand the sexual connotation of his comment and respond as if he were really talking about nutrition. But that would be obvious dishonesty. No, I've got to handle this one head on."

VIGNETTE 10.10 (continued)

Because Mr. Holt's mind is busy thinking in the moments immediately following the outburst of laughter, he is able to maintain a serious expression throughout. The class quickly realizes that Mr. Holt does not find Woodrow's clowning humorous. He turns to Woodrow and says: "I know you are trying to make us laugh. But I do not like to hear that kind of joke. You and I will talk about this right after the class leaves for lunch today." Turning to Vickie, Mr. Holt says: "Excuse the interruption Vickie. You were telling us that you choose your food carefully. Please continue."

VIGNETTE 10.11

It is the first week of the school year in Ms. Giminski's kindergarten class. Students have just begun working individually on a language arts task. Brian jumps up and begins dancing and gyrating in front of the others saying: "Watch me! Watch me!" Two students stop their work and giggle, but most just ignore him. Ms. Giminski

Mr. Holt's Response to Woodrow's Clowning Is Systematic, Thoughtful, and Decisive

thinks: "I hope this isn't a pattern for Brian. I'll bet this is what he does for attention at home." She picks up Brian's paper, takes him by the hand, and walks him over to an area of the room that is out of the view of the other students. She softly tells Brian: "Please sit here and finish your paper. Bring it to me only after all of these spaces are colored in. What are you going to do?" Brian: " Color all this and bring it to you." Ms. Giminski: "That is what you are to do."

Over the next several days, Ms. Giminski watches for signs of Brian wanting to show off. She makes an effort to see that he gets attention at times when he is not trying to show off.

VIGNETTE 10.12

Holly's frequent out-loud quips, gestures, and facial contortions evoke laughter among her peers in Mr. Smith's tenth grade English class. Mr. Smith considers occasional clowning humorous and a healthy diversion from work. However, Holly's clowning has become so frequent that it is impeding class progress. Mr. Smith is beginning to fear what Holly will come up with and, consequently, phrases his words with care to avoid having Holly turn a serious comment into a joke. He decides to help her control her in-class clowning and thinks to himself: "I'm not going to continue to stand for Holly's habitual clowning. She's modifying my behavior so that I'm not as relaxed in class as I used to be. I'm afraid to smile for fear she'll think it's her cue to be on stage. If I asked her why she was clowning or if I turned her jokes back on her, it'd embarrass her and she might quit. Or would she? She'd more likely try to regain face with the class by trying even harder to be funny. No, I don't want to embarrass her. That would make matters worse. She does it to gain favor and to relieve her boredom. I know! I'll call her in for a private conference and be perfectly frank with her. I'll explain how her clowning is making it difficult for me to do my job. I'll request her cooperation. If she agrees to try, I'll agree to help her succeed. We'll set up a secret code between us so that I can signal her when she is being disruptive and should stop whatever she's doing at the moment. The rest of the class doesn't need to know. She can also have a signal worked out for me when she feels the urge to clown; I'll help her pick an appropriate time and set her stage. We'll establish a cooperative relationship. But I'd better come up with some alternative plans in case she doesn't go for this one. I hope she goes for the original idea or else I may have to sacrifice her welfare for the good of the class."

BEING GENERALLY DISCOURTEOUS

Learning activities are generally more effective when they are conducted in a businesslike atmosphere of cooperation and mutual respect among participants. Thus, it is usually disruptive for students to treat others in the classroom in a disrespectful or thoughtless manner. Although conventional customs of decorum and courtesy vary among the subcultures of many school populations, a teacher is responsible to establish an environment where students are unlikely to feel insulted, uncomfortable, or inconvenienced as a consequence of the rudeness of others. In Vignettes 10.13–10.16, teachers deal with discourteous student behavior.

VIGNETTE 10.13

Mr. Lowder assigns Mitch and Ward to be on the same basketball team during one physical education session. Mitch complains aloud in front of the class: "I don't want Ward on my team; he's gay! I'd rather not play." Mr. Lowder immediately thinks: "Mich is so competitive. I should just tell him, Fine! Then you don't play.' He could just sit on the sidelines. Maybe I could play in his place and show Ward that I'd like to be on his team. But I don't want to give the class the impression that their participation isn't critical. I'd like to do something to protect Ward's feelings. I know he's already allowed them to be damaged and I may make things worse by making a big deal out of the incident. I'll let it slide for now; if it recurs, I'll intervene. Maybe I should catch Mitch by himself and let him know that I don't approve of such behavior. I will. In fact, I'll use Glasser's approach in a conference with Mitch."

VIGNETTE 10.14

Several of Ms. Belcher's second graders begin jockeying and shoving to obtain a place near the front of the line that they are forming in preparation for going to the auditorium for a puppet show. "Hey, I'm first; get away!" Jack yells as Ellis pushes his way to the front. Ms. Belcher observes the scene for a minute, noticing that the more aggressive students are near the front of the line, crowding toward the exit. In a very calm voice, Ms. Belcher announces: "Okay, keep your places in line. We're going to stretch our legs a bit and take a walk around the room before leaving." Noticing that Cheri is last in line, Ms. Belcher continues: "Cheri, you lead the line around the back wall, over along the side wall, past the front, and then lead the line out of the door. I'll get in behind Ellis and shut the door as I leave." Surprised by the strange route they take exiting the room, the students silently turn and follow Cheri to the auditorium. Cheri beams as Ellis and Jack roll their eyes in disgust.

VIGNETTE 10.15

Susan, a seventh grader, is working on a problem-solving assignment when she exclaims in a rather curt voice to Ms. Comeaux, her teacher: "I can't do this ass-hole crap! It's so stupid!" Ms. Comeaux: "I can tell you're frustrated. The problems are difficult. When you are ready for me to help you with them, tell me in a courteous way using only words that are acceptable to me."

VIGNETTE 10.16

Mr. Turner's social studies students are engaged in cooperative group discussions when he overhears Kendall tell Russ: "You wouldn't think that if you weren't such an ugly slob!" Mr. Turner: "Kendall, I get so angry when you speak rudely that I cannot understand what you're trying to say." Mr. Turner hopes that he has reminded the group that impolite, thoughtless talk is unacceptable during learning activities. He wants to avoid an inane, nonproductive exchange on why Kendall spoke rudely. He does not think that it would be wise to appear as if he were trying to protect Russ, so he doesn't say anything like: "Russ is not an ugly slob! I like him very much." He believes that would display a lack of confidence in Russ being able to deal with his other feelings. The focus is on terminating the rude behavior and getting on with the business at hand.

FAILING TO CLEAN UP

A classroom in disarray, a littered playing field, inaccessible equipment, unattractive surroundings, damaged supplies, and an unprepared activity area interfere with the effectiveness of learning activities. Thus, by failing to clean-up after themselves, students can be disruptive. Teachers in Vignettes 10.17–10.19 deal with this problem.

VIGNETTE 10.17

Ms. Johnson frequently schedules her third graders' school days so that learning activities that require cleanup time are followed by activities that students genuinely enjoy. Initiation of an anticipated enjoyable activity is always contingent on the orderliness of the classroom as specified by Ms. Johnson.

VIGNETTE 10.18

Ms. Lambert usually gives her tenth grade biology students some time to begin their homework assignment in class. However, she never informs them of the assignment until after the lab area meets her standards for cleanliness and order.

VIGNETTE 10.19

Each student in Mr. Ditty's art class has a container for supplies. Mr. Ditty directs his students to clean their materials and put them away for the next day. Juan and Candy leave out some of their brushes, paints, cloth, and paper. Mr. Ditty notices

---

VIGNETTE 10.19 (continued)

this before they leave, but says nothing. He cleans up after them, placing their equipment in the general art supply closet. The next day, Juan complains: "Where's my thin brush? And I'm out of paper; I had plenty yesterday!" Candy: "I can't find my green paint. Mr. Ditty: "Oh, that must have been your stuff I cleaned up yesterday. I'm sorry, but I mixed them up with the general supplies. You need to purchase more."

VANDALIZING

Vandalism, like general discourtesy and an unkempt classroom, can be extremely disruptive to a learning environment. School-level vandalism (e.g., breaking windows or arson) should be handled by school administrators and law enforcement authorities. It is wise for you, as a teacher, to avoid playing the role of detective with your own students. Antagonism between teacher and students is a likely consequence of the teacher trying to detect the identities of culprits among students. Repeat vandalism may be encouraged by students' desires to continue the "cops and robbers" game that a teacher has been duped into playing. Besides reporting vandalism to authorities and cooperating with their investigations, you may try to prevent acts of vandalism from being positively reinforced. Consider Vignette 10.20.

VIGNETTE 10.20

Ms. Romano enters her equipment room to prepare for the day's physical education classes when she discovers the soccer balls she plans to use are deflated and flattened. The nets of the six portable soccer goals are cut and unusable. In horror she thinks: "Who would have done this? This screws up my whole day! The girls will be on the field in six minutes and we are scheduled to play soccer first period. If I ever catch the little—!" Ms. Romano composes herself and begins thinking: "Barbara, Evelyn, Tamaria, and some of the others have been complaining about having to play soccer during first period. They said it was too hot and their hair was a mess the rest of the day. I wonder if it's one of them. Well, I don't know that. I could hardly find out if I tried. But I do know that a lot of the girls would love to use this as an excuse to avoid going out and working up a sweat."

Ms. Romano walks over to the locker room where her students are changing. She announced: "Let's go ladies! We meet on the soccer field at exactly 9:20." "Do we have to? It'll be too hot today?" complains one student. Ms. Romano makes no response and heads for the field. Outside, she tells the class: "We will not be able to play soccer today because the equipment has been damaged." Barbara: "Then why are we out here?" Ms. Romano: "Because it is critical that we do an aerobic type activity today and the soccer field is as good a place as any to get your hearts and lungs working. Just because we can't play soccer, doesn't mean we can't get the same benefits that a vigorous soccer game affords us." Some students begin to moan and complain to one another. Ms. Romano puts them through an especially fatiguing routine of calisthenics. After the session, the students are dragging and perspiring as they enter the showers. Ms. Romano reports the vandalism to her immediate supervisor who makes arrangements to repair the damages and prepares a report for the principal.

PERPETRATING VIOLENCE AGAINST STUDENTS

Generally speaking, if a students strikes a teacher or other adult school personnel, that student is in serious trouble with school authorities and possibly with law enforcement authorities. Expulsion or suspension from the school is a likely consequence. Although society tends to view an unarmed assault of one student on another as less serious than on an adult, students have as much right as do their teachers to feel safe and secure from violence at school.

In Vignette 10.21, a teacher develops a plan for dealing with student violence.

VIGNETTE 10.21

Ms. Duke found it odd that Frank, Maunsell, Mickey, and a few other of her fifth grade boys chose to spend their time before school and during their recess break in the classroom with her. "Why don't you men go out and get some fresh air while you still have the chance?" she asks. They shrug sheepishly and remain with her. She finds Mickey's absentee pattern curious. He seems perfectly healthy on Monday, Wednesday, and Friday of a week, while being excused for "illness" on Tuesday and Thursday. Other puzzling occurrences involving the boys (e.g., their homework papers wet and crumpled all on the same day with no apparent explanation) cause Ms. Duke to wonder just what is going on. These boys choose to spend virtually all their time at school in her company, yet Ms. Duke has the distinct impression that they are uncomfortable around her and prefer being elsewhere. The students offer no explanation.

Ms. Duke begins making observations. Instead of staying in her room just before school begins in the mornings, she walks the grounds where most of her students are at that time. She notices that Bobby, Ronald, Stan, and Winslow nearly always hang around together and that her "followers," Frank, Maunsell, and Mickey, appear particularly uneasy as Bobby and his companions greet her with: "Good morning, Ms. Duke!" Soon, Ms. Duke surmises that Ronald, Stan, and Winslow are terrorizing fellow students to the point that Frank's, Mickey's, and Maunsell's opportunities to learn are being hindered.

She thinks to herself: "I can't stand bullying! What do those creeps think they get out of terrorizing others? They must really be miserable with themselves to act so miserably toward their classmates! I can't conduct effective learning activities in an environment filled with fear. What should I do? If I confront that gang with what I suspect, they'll think Maunsell and the rest of the victims tattled on them and they'll just make life more miserable for them. We need intense adult supervision

---

VIGNETTE 10.21 (continued)

on the school grounds, the bus stop, the buses, the halls! Good grief! Do we need a police state? I'll try one tactic and if it doesn't work, I'll find a way to sit on those bullies so they become the ones having to hang around me all day. But first I'll try this. I'll pair Maunsell and Bobby in a project where they have to meet me before school. That'll begin breaking up the gang before school, and maybe the two of them will start cooperating. If I notice any progress, I'll work some of the other bullies into cooperating roles with the victims. Oh! Listen to me! I'm labeling them. I'd better watch my language and not even think such characterizations as 'bullies' and 'victims . . . .' I don't know if this plan will work at all. Why should I force them together? Maybe I should call a class meeting instead, we can discuss the problem openly and have the group initiate a proposal. . . . They'd probably come up with a vigilante plan with Bobby and his gang as the main 'hit squad.' That's an idea! Put them in charge of keeping the school grounds peaceful. Forget it. I'll stick with the plan of splitting the gang and motivating some cooperation between the antagonists. I need to work out the details . . . .''

Ms. Duke's plan has a chance of working because she focused on her task of making the learning environment conducive to on-task behavior. She was not overly concerned with punishing those that perpetrated the terror or teaching them some lifelong moral lesson. She concentrated on stopping the disruptive behaviors and preventing recurrences. She controlled her anger. She abhorred Bobby's, Ronald's, Stan's, and Winslow's antisocial behaviors and determined not to tolerate such activities. But she also recognized that they need a more constructive way of dealing with their own insecurities, a way that doesn't step on the rights of others. This realization made it possible for her to calmly think through a plan for dealing with the situation.

Vignettes 10.22 and 10.23 are two more examples of teachers dealing with student violence.

VIGNETTE 10.22

Ms. Saunders, a librarian at Bishop Vincent High School, is supervising activities in the library when Stanley, an eleventh grade student, bursts into the room and confronts Ronny, another student who is seated at a table. Stanley: "You little piece of shit! You owe me!" Ronny pulls a small knife from his pocket, gets up, and faces Stanley. Displaying the knife, he says: "Get away from me, or I'll cut your goddamn throat out!" Stanley: "You wouldn't—"

Ms. Saunders has made her way to the two and yells: "Enough!" Convinced the two see her, she steps between them with her back to Stanley, facing Ronny. She attempts to present a stern, but nonthreatening posture to Ronny. She does not want to raise either student's level of anxiety. "Stanley," she firmly says, "I want you to turn around and walk out of the door right now. You can wait for us in the hall." Some of the other students in the library are gathering around as others back away from the scene. Stanley: "I don't have to—" Ms. Saunders (still with her back to Stanley): "Be cool, Stanley. You're right. You don't have to, but be cool and do it anyway." Ronny: "Yeah, why don't—" Ms. Saunders (interrupting): "Ronny, shut up! And the rest of you in here get back to what you were doing. This whole incident is over. Hurry up! You've got work to do."

Surprised, Stanley leaves and the other students hesitatingly move back to their places. Ronny and Ms. Saunders are left alone, standing face-to-face with the knife between them. Calmly and softly, Ms. Saunders tells Ronny: "It's okay now. There's no longer a need for that knife to be out, so put it back in your pocket. After I report this incident to Mr. Civello, he'll be calling you to his office. If I were you, I'd get rid of that knife before he calls you. You can dispose of it yourself after you're through working here or, if you like, I'll get rid of it for you now. If you give it to me, no one will ever see it again."

Ronny lowers the knife and puts it back in his pocket. Ms. Saunders walks back to her desk where she calls Mr. Civello's office to report the situation. Ronny returns to where he was seated before, but then immediately gets up, goes over to Ms. Saunders, and asks: "If you get rid of this for me, will it go easier on me?" Ms. Saunders: "It might." Ronny: "Here." He hands her the knife. With Ronny still standing there, Ms. Saunders completes her report over the phone. The dean of students, Mr. Civello, handles the matter, taking disciplinary action against both students.

VIGNETTE 10.23

Ms. Silverstein's fourth graders are working individually at their places on an assignment as she helps Zachary at his desk. Suddenly from behind her, she hears Beth scream: "Stop it!" She turns to see Roxanna on the floor crying: "Ow! Oh, ow!" Roxanna has fresh scratch marks extending from one cheek down to the side of her neck. Beth is standing over her. "She clawed me!" screams Roxanna as she continues to cry. Ms. Silverstein is uncertain as to what happened, but rather than investigate the cause, she decides to deal with Roxanna's immediate need. She bends over Roxanna, cradles her head with an arm, and says: "You are hurt. I'm sorry." Ms. Silverstein softly strokes Roxanna's hair and says: "I can see why you're crying." Roxanna: "She clawed me! I hate—" Ms. Silverstein (interrupting): "Don't talk now, we have to clean those scratches." Beth: "Well, she poked me firs—" Ms. Silverstein (interrupting and not even looking at Beth): "Enough talk. I don't want to hear anything until we've taken care of Roxanna's scratches. Zachary, please get two tissues from my desk. Wet one at the sink and leave one dry and bring them both to me. Nadine, bring me the first aid kit, please. The rest of you get back to work."

As Ms. Silverstein helps Roxanna to her feet and walks her to the back of the room, she thinks to herself: "I've bought some time to figure out how to handle this and prevent recurrences. This'll also give those two time to cool off. I can deal with them more effectively when they've over their anger." She thanks Nadine and Zachary for their help and administers to Roxanna's scratches. Ms. Silverstein thinks: "I'll talk to both of them together and get them to examine their own actions. But when? This has to be handled before they leave school today. It's going to be inconvenient, but I must meet them after school; it'll be a lot easier in the long

VIGNETTE 10.23 (continued)

run if I deal with this today. If this becomes a pattern with Beth, I'll have hell to pay for the rest of the year. The inconvenience today will be a good investment for the future."

Nine minutes after everyone is back on-task, Ms. Silverstein beckons Beth and Roxanna to her desk. Ms. Silverstein: "Roxanna, what are you planning to do after the final bell today?" Roxanna: "I have a Girl Scout meeting. Mrs. Sheirer is picking us up." Ms. Silverstein: "Where is the meeting and how long will it last?" Roxanna: "At Ellie's house." Ms. Silverstein: "When will it be over?" Roxanna: "I don't know." Ms. Silverstein: "Is Ellie's house far from here?" Roxanna: "It's just over the other side of the hill." Ms. Silverstein: "Could you show me how to get there?" Roxanna: "Yes." Ms. Silverstein: "Thank you. Beth, what do you have to do after school today?" Beth: "I catch bus 57." Ms. Silverstein: "Do you go straight home from the bus?" Beth: "Yes." Ms. Silverstein: "Who will be there when you arrive?" Beth: "My dad." Ms. Silverstein: "Is your dad there now?" Beth: "Probably, he works the night shift. He's probably sleeping." Ms. Silverstein: "Thank you." Beth: "Ms. Silverstein, Roxanna poked—" Ms. Silverstein (interrupting): "Not now, Beth. We'll talk about it after school." Roxanna: "But I've got a Girl Sc—" Ms. Silverstein (interrupting): "You will miss your bus today, Beth. So I will call your dad and make arrangements for you to get home. Roxanna, I'll meet Ms. Sheirer and explain to her that you'll be late for Girl Scouts. Both of you are to stay right here after the last bell so we can talk about how to prevent today's incident from ever happening again. I'll make arrangements for you to get to where you need to be after our talk. Now, go back to your places and get on with your work."

After the last bell, Roxanna and Beth wait in the classroom as Ms. Silverstein informs Ms. Sheirer that Roxanna will be late for the meeting and that she'll drive her to Ellie's house herself. Ms. Silverstein then phones Beth's father and arranges for him to pick up Beth in 30 minutes. Arriving back in the classroom, she sits with Beth and Roxanna. Ms. Silverstein: "Beth, your father will pick you up in front of school in 30 minutes. We have until then to talk about what happened today." Roxanna: "I didn't do nothin' to her!" Beth (interrupting): "I guess jabbin' me through my ribs is nothing!" Roxanna: "I was just playing. You didn't have to try and kill me with your claws!" Beth (holding up her hands in a claw-like manner): "You ain't seen nothin' yet!" Roxanna (flinching): "Look Ms. Silverstein, she's gonna do it again!" Ms. Silverstein: "No she isn't. Would you like to know what I think, Beth?" Beth (returning to a normal, nonthreatening posture): "What?" Ms. Silverstein: "Please answer me with a more pleasant tone." Beth: "Yes, ma'am." Ms. Silverstein: "Roxanna, are you ready to hear what I think?" Roxanna: "Yes, ma'am." Ms. Silverstein: "I think Roxanna poked Beth as she passed her desk. And Roxanna did it to be friendly, sort of like saying, 'Hello, Beth. Look at me. I'm here.' Is that right, Roxanna?" Roxanna: "Yes." Beth: "But—" Ms. Silverstein (interrupting): "Shh! But Roxanna poked Beth too hard and it disturbed her while she was working. Is that right, Beth?" Beth: "Yes, ma'am." Ms. Silverstein: "And Beth got so annoyed that without thinking, she struck out at Roxanna and hurt her. If Beth had thought first, she never would have scratched Roxanna. Now, I don't care who was right and who was wrong. I only care that none of my students hurts one another again. If Beth hadn't lost control of her temper, and just ignored Roxanna's poke, everything would be okay now. And if Roxanna hadn't bothered Beth while she was working, this wouldn't have happened. Am I correct?'' Beth and Roxanna both nod in agreement. Ms. Silverstein: ''Beth, will this ever happen again?'' Beth: ''Not if she doesn't—'' Ms. Silverstein (interrupting): ''Beth, either one of you is capable of keeping this from happening again. No matter what anyone else does, are you going to let this happen again?'' Beth: ''No, I won't.'' Roxanna: ''Me neither.'' Ms. Silverstein: ''Wonderful! We'll wait here until it's time for Beth's dad to be out front. Then I'll take Roxanna to her Girl Scout meeting.

PERPETRATING VIOLENCE AGAINST TEACHERS

Causes

There are many reasons students make the mistake of physically abusing teachers. Here are four of them.

1. The student feels backed into a corner and striking out at the teacher is the only way to maintain ''face'' with peers. Vignette 10.24 is an example.
2. The teacher is an accessible target for the student at a moment when the student is reacting angrily. Vignettes 10.25–10.27 are examples.
3. The student attempts to either experience control over authorities, win favor with peers, seek revenge on an authority, or relieve boredom by carrying out a prank that endangers the well-being of a teacher. Vignette 10.28 is an example.
4. The student defends against a perceived danger posed by the teacher. Vignette 10.29 is an example.

VIGNETTE 10.24

Ms. Mildred is lecturing to one of her eighth grade classes when she become annoyed by Jim and Jan's off-task conversation. Ms. Mildred stops her lecture and scolds: ''Can't you two be quiet? You're forever chattering. Jim, if you'd listen in class instead of mooning over Jan all the time, you wouldn't be flunking!'' Jim is overwhelmed with embarrassment. He, in fact, is very fond of Jan and feels that Ms. Mildred has challenged his status with Jan and his other peers. He tries to save face by verbally striking out. ''I never mooned anybody!'' Jim curtly barks. Ms. Mildred gets embarrassed herself and yells: ''What? That's not what I meant! You come right here, young man, and apologize to me!'' Jim slowly shuffles up to Ms. Mildred with a grin on his face, shifting his eyes to see who is watching him. Ms. Mildred: ''Wipe that stupid grin off your face! There's nothing funny about your impudence!'' Jim looks down, trying not to laugh, but he is overcome by his concern for what his classmates are thinking and covers his fear and anger with laughter. ''You wipe off that smile and apologize,'' says Ms. Mildred standing face-to-face with Jim. Jim wipes his mouth with his hand and says: ''There, I wiped it off.'' But he bursts out laughing as he

VIGNETTE 10.24 (continued)

hears others in the room giggling. Furiously thinking Jim is making her look bad in front of the class, Ms. Mildred tries to gain the upper hand with a show of authority. Ms. Mildred: "You know I can make you sorry you ever set foot in this school! You either say 'I'm sorry' to me right now or you'll find out just how tough I can be!" Jim believes that this confrontation has gone too far for him to back down without losing the respect of his classmates. Panicked and knowing no desirable way out of the situation, he suddenly appears very serious. Gritting his teeth, he says in a low voice: "Go play with yourself, you old bitch!" Jim shoves Ms. Mildred, using both hands on her shoulders. She tumbles over backwards as he runs out of the room.

Within a week, Jim is expelled from the school and enrolled in an alternative school for students who have committed "first class" offenses according to school based policy.

VIGNETTE 10.25

Mr. Diel is returning to his classroom where a class of tenth graders are waiting for the beginning of the next period. Suddenly, he observes Kraemer leap at Danny and yell: "What did you call me? Don't ever say that to me again! Understand?" Danny is about to respond when Mr. Diel arrives and from behind touches Kraemer on the right shoulder and says: "Easy, Kraemer." Kraemer wheels around, swinging his right arm so that his elbow catches Mr. Diel in the mouth. A tooth is broken and blood spurts from Mr. Diel's lip.

VIGNETTE 10.26

Finis is a 15-year-old student participating in an intramural basketball game refereed by Mr. Leblanc, a physical education teacher. The game is closely contested when Mr. Leblanc calls a personal foul on Finis. "You, number three-two," Mr. Leblanc yells coming face-to-face with Finis in the tradition of basketball officials. Finis believes that he is not guilty of the foul; he thinks he was fouled instead. "Get your hand up, 32!" Mr. Leblanc yells in Finis' face. Finis: "I didn't do—" Mr. Leblanc (interrupting): "Technical foul!" Finis, feeling frustrated and helpless, lashes out at the nearest accessible target by striking Mr. Leblanc on the nose with his fist.

VIGNETTE 10.27

Ms. Blouin teaches a class of 11 students who are classified as emotionally handicapped. Two of her students, Suzanne and Paul, habitually express their feelings by physically striking out at Ms. Blouin. Ms. Blouin has been kicked, bitten, pushed, scratched, and slapped by these two students. To help her deal with the situation, avoid being victimized by them, and prepare for similar situations in the future, Ms. Blouin completes a course in self-defense techniques especially designed for teachers. Ms. Blouin is now able to protect herself from such abuse without a high risk of injury to Suzanne, Paul, or any other student who might attack her or attack another student. The self-defense techniques she uses are designed to immobilize students without harming them.

VIGNETTE 10.28

Ms. Heidingsfelder, a teacher at Blackhawk High School, is driving home after work when she is startled by the sound of an explosion from under her car. A tire blows out, she loses control of the vehicle, crosses a lane with on-coming traffic, and comes to a stop in a ditch on the side of the road. Fortunately, she is uninjured and the car suffers only a damaged tire.

Ms. Heidingsfelder does not suspect that the accident is anything more than that until the following school day. Several students in her third period class question her. "Ms. H, are you okay?" "Did you drive your bug to school today?" "Did anything happen to you after school yesterday?" Thinking quickly, she concludes that she had been a victim of a booby trap. Believing she can hardly find the responsible criminals among the students, she decides not to give them the satisfaction of knowing that the prank worked. She replies: "I'm fine; it's awfully nice of you to ask. Why do you ask if anything out of the ordinary happened after school yesterday?"

VIGNETTE 10.29

Mr. Moe, an assistant principal at Greenfield Creek Junior High, is six-feet-five and weighs nearly 300 pounds. He believes his reputation as a strict disciplinarian who'll "knock off your head rather than look at you" helps him with his primary responsibility of maintaining order in the school. One day, Mr. Moe surprises Rudolph, an eighth grader who is smoking crack in a restroom. Panicked at the sight of the towering figure of the man with the infamous reputation, Rudolph spots a large wrench, inadvertently left on the floor by a custodian. He grabs it and throws it at Mr. Moe's head.

Strategies

You can reduce your chances of being a victim of student violence by adhering to these six principles.

1. You are not intimidated by the threat of violence.
2. You do not pose a threat to students. This includes not perpetrating violence on them (e.g., by using corporal punishment, by roughly touching them, or violating their space) nor competing with them for esteem from others (especially their peers). You never try to show up a student.

3. You use physical force with students only in drastic situations in which it is the only reasonable means for restraining them from harming themselves or others. Physical force is never used to punish or hurt, only to restrain in certain unusual situations.
4. You are sensitive to potentially volatile situations and do not make yourself available as a target when students might unthinkingly react aggressively.
5. You avoid making ultimatums in which the consequence of a student's noncompliance is the most severe sanction you can levy. (If you commit yourself to administering the severest penalty available to you, then students have nothing left to lose by displaying even less desirable behaviors than those that initially led to the unpleasant situation.)
6. You never tolerate violent behavior in your presence. You have every right to use the full power of the legal system to prevent violence or the threat of violence from preventing you from effectively meeting your professional responsibilities.

TRANSITIONAL ACTIVITIES
FROM CHAPTER 10 TO CHAPTER 11

  I. Observe the students in a colleague's classroom. Identify three incidents of disruptive student behavior. For each, write two paragraphs describing the disruptive behavior and what the teacher did to deal with it. Limit your report to descriptions of what happened; do not include your value judgments regarding the teacher's method of handling the disruption. Discuss the episode with the teacher, eliciting the teacher's rationale for the methods of responding to the disruptions.
 II. For each of the vignettes cited below, write one or two paragraphs giving your view of the advantages and disadvantages of the way the teacher handled the disruptive behavior. Suggest how the approach could have been improved. Vignettes 10.1, 10.2, 10.3, 10.5, 10.7, 10.9, 10.10, 10.12, 10.13, 10.14, 10.19, 10.21, 10.22, 10.23, 10.24, and 10.28.

   Discuss your views with those of colleagues. Debate the pros and cons of the different strategies.
III. In preparation for your work with Chapter 11, discuss the following questions with two or more of your colleagues.
   A. Why do proven methods for managing student behavior sometimes fail?
   B. What advantages do experienced teachers have over beginning teachers in gaining and maintaining students' cooperation?
   C. How can instructional supervision, self-assessments, and action research be used to refine a teacher's classroom management strategies?

SUPPLEMENTAL READINGS

Burke, J. (1991). Teenagers, clothes, and gang violence. *Educational Leadership, 49,* 11–13.
Curwin, R. L., & Mendler, A. N. (1988). *Discipline with dignity* (pp. 94–158). Alexandria, VA: Association for Supervision and Curriculum Development.

Karlin, M. S., & Berger, R. (1972). *Discipline and the disruptive child: A practical guide for elementary teachers* (pp. 102–130). West Nyack, NY: Parker.

Petty, R. (1989). Managing disruptive students. *Educational Leadership, 46,* 26–28.

Swick, K. J. (1985). *Disruptive student behavior in the classroom* (2nd ed.). Washington: National Education Association.

Walker, H., & Sylwater, R. (1991). Where is school along the path to prison? *Educational Leadership, 49,* 14–16.

Wilde, J., & Sommers, P. (1978). Teaching disruptive adolescents: A game worth winning. *Phi Delta Kappan, 59,* 342–343.

PART IV

Why Do Proven Methods Sometimes Fail? How Do You Make Proven Methods Work For You?

CHAPTER **11**

Incorporating New Ideas into Your Teaching Style

Purpose of Chapter 11

Chapter 11 serves as a reminder for you to continually cultivate your teaching style so that your ability to apply classroom management strategies for gaining and maintaining students' cooperation improves as your experiences grow. The art of teaching is far too complex for even proven strategies to fully succeed in the hands of novices who have yet to accumulate adequate experiences for refining their teaching talents.

BUILDING ON EXPERIENCES

Some methods for gaining students' cooperation may not work as effectively as you'd like until you've had some experiences trying them out and tailoring them to your own situations. Consider these examples.

- In Chapter 4 it was suggested that you establish more productive communication patterns with your students by using descriptive instead of judgmental language. However, most people are not in the habit of considering their words carefully enough to consistently express themselves descriptively. Consequently, you may find that it takes consistent effort in practicing descriptive language with your students before descriptive phrases flow from your tongue and you begin to reap the benefits of this technique.

- In Chapter 6 you were urged to use problem-solving learning activities (e.g., Vignettes 6.5 and 6.6) to intrinsically motivate student engagement. However, teachers need to have observed students a while and be thoroughly familiar with the subject matter before being readily able to identify interesting problems on which to focus. Familiarity with both students and subject matter increases with teaching experience. If you are not used to conducting problem-solving learning activities, but are convinced of the advantages of doing so, begin on a small scale, only with teaching units that readily lend themselves to that approach. In time, you will build both your repertoire of teaching units that utilize the problem-solving approach and your abilities to design such units.

- Throughout this text, especially in Chapter 7, you have been encouraged to respond to your students' off-task behaviors via the Teaching Process Model, just as you do for academic teaching units. In Vignette 7.3, Ms. Reid effectively handled a rather nasty situation because she organized her thoughts around the Teaching Process Model. You may have to face a number of discipline problems before you have utilized the Teaching Process Model enough times to make it consistently and efficiently work to your advantage.

- As indicated in Chapter 8, the principle of extinction can be a powerful weapon in your arsenal against off-task behavior patterns. However, unless you can identify positive reinforcers that lead students habitually off-task, you can hardly take advantage of extinction. As an observant, thinking teacher you will, with experience, develop your abilities to identify what positively reinforces your students' habits.

INSTRUCTIONAL SUPERVISION

Pre-service teacher preparation programs provide beginning teachers with necessary, but insufficient, competencies to be successful in-service teachers. The success of instructional practice depends on teachers further developing these competencies from inservice experiences (Duke, Cangelosi, & Knight, 1988). To be consistently effective, especially in the first few years of their careers, in-service teachers gravely need support, guidance, and feedback as they practice their complex art (Evans, 1989).

Instructional supervision is collaborating with teachers to help them enhance their effectiveness with students (Cangelosi, 1991b, pp. 6, 122–158). Two promising and flourishing instructional supervisory models are *peer coaching* (Bang-Jensen, 1986; Brandt, 1989; Chrisco, 1989; Raney & Robbins, 1989) and *mentoring* (Duke, Cangelosi, & Knight, 1988; Stallion, 1988). Peer coaching involves two or more teachers sharing ideas and providing formative feedback on one another's teaching (Swartz & Perkins, 1990, pp. 198–203). Mentor teachers work with beginning teachers to help them through their first few years.

Vignette 11.1 illustrates the type of collegial communications that grows out of peer coaching and mentoring relationships.

VIGNETTE 11.1

Two primary grade teachers, Kristine Scott and Ebony Del Rio, engage in the following conversation.

KRISTINE: Do you have any ideas on dealing with a student who habitually interrupts classmates when they have the floor?

EBONY: The prescription has to fit the student and the situation. Why do you ask? Does one of your students have that problem?

KRISTINE: I don't really know. Tim Ziegler seems to be developing a pattern of interrupting classmates. I'm not sure if he needs me to teach him to break the habit, or if I should treat it as an isolated disruption, instance by instance.

EBONY: Apparently it's bothering you enough that the problem merits some attention.

KRISTINE: In the last three days, I'd bet he's interrupted someone at least four times.

EBONY: What were the circumstances, group discussions, recitations, what?

KRISTINE: At least twice that I can remember, it was during a class meeting when we have very strict rules governing who may speak. That's when I first began thinking he might be developing a habit. In the past, I hadn't really paid attention to it.

EBONY: Sounds like you need to collect some baseline data. That'll give us a better idea if it's habitual or not. Why don't you keep a chart indicating . . .

The conversation continues with the two deciding to meet to analyze the baseline data Kristine collects. If they decide that Kristine should treat Tim's interruptions as a habit, Kristine will propose an intervention plan that Ebony will critique.

After three days of collecting baseline data, Kristine is convinced that Tim has a persistent pattern that she needs to teach him to modify. Thus, she already has an objective formulated, which she hands to Ebony the next time she meets with her.

KRISTINE: Tim's definitely developed a habit. What do you think of this objective?

EBONY [reading]: "Tim will reduce the frequency of interrupting classmates who are speaking from his baseline ratio of 35% of the time to a ratio of less than 10% of the time within two weeks." Wow! Pretty ambitious.

KRISTINE: It's either that or I have to keep reacting to each incident one at a time, and he's just going to get deeper and deeper in trouble.

EBONY: We don't want that. But I have one question. This objective suggests you're going to focus on him breaking the habit. What have you got in mind for intervention?

KRISTINE: I haven't worked it out yet, but I guess I should apply the principle of extinction.

EBONY: But then you'd have to identify the positive reinforcers. For this type of behavior, that's going to be difficult to do and then to control.

KRISTINE: I agree. Do you have a suggestion?

VIGNETTE 11.1 (continued)

EBONY: If you change your objective so that it focuses on teaching him an on-task behavior pattern that's incompatible with his pattern of interruptions—

KRISTINE: Oh! Like quietly listening when others are speaking and raising his hand to speak.

EBONY: Exactly. Then a principle like shaping would apply and that would be more efficient for this situation.

KRISTINE: So, I'll restate the objective. Give me a minute. . . . How does this sound? "Tim will exhibit a pattern of quiet listening behaviors by waiting his turn to speak and raising his hand to be recognized at least 90% of the time that classmates are speaking. Two weeks after intervention begins, this pattern will have emerged." What do you think?

EBONY: I think your chances of succeeding with that objective are favorable.

KRISTINE: Now, I've got to design the intervention. I'll work on it tonight. May I pass it by you tomorrow?

EBONY: You bet; I'm anxious to see what you come up with.

The following day, their conversation focuses on the next stage of the Teaching Process Model.

EBONY: So what have you planned for your intervention?

KRISTINE: My plans aren't finalized, but I'll continue to maintain a record of his behavior during relevant situations, just like for baseline. I'll try to anticipate the times when other students have the floor and be near Tim so I can use non-attention-getting body language to quickly intercept his interruptions. Now if that'll control his interruptions, then there's a chance shaping can work.

EBONY: How do you propose to use shaping?

KRISTINE: I'll really have to monitor him closely and then when he's displaying some patience and makes any kind of movement that even vaguely resembles raising his hand, I'll call on him to make a comment. Then I'll have to get on a gradually decreasing schedule of reinforcement for waiting to speak in turn.

EBONY: Do you think he finds attention rewarding?

KRISTINE: Not in general; I think he's just got a lot to say.

EBONY: Okay, so you'll give him opportunities to talk as rewards for waiting.

KRISTINE: Right, but first I've got to get him to begin raising his hand. That's a real key.

EBONY: I think it'll work if you consistently stick to your reinforcement schedule.

KRISTINE: But I really have to know when to jump in and when to back off. It's not going to be easy. Will you spot check me occasionally with a few observations?

EBONY: Yes, and you can also share what happens each day with me—we can discuss how closely you're sticking to the plan.

Three times during the first week of Kristine's attempt to teach Tim to habitually raise his hand and patiently wait his turn to speak, she and Ebony discuss how the plan is progressing. Here is a portion of the next conference.

VIGNETTE 11.1 (continued)

KRISTINE: This morning, just before I pulled the four reading groups together to share stories with one another, I moved right by Tim, and then stayed with him for the whole discussion. Anytime he even looked like he was going to interrupt, I'd be right between him and the rest of the class.

EBONY: Did he ever interrupt?

KRISTINE: Not once this morning. But here's the best part! Because I was blocking his view, he began to wiggle in his chair to look around me. That's when I pretended to think he was raising his hand and I called on him, thanking him for raising his hand.

EBONY: What did he say?

KRISTINE: What didn't he say? He talked on and on about the story his group read! I let him talk longer than I usually do to reinforce his waiting to be called on.

EBONY: But did others get bored?

KRISTINE: Some got real restless.

EBONY: So that's going to be a complicating factor.

KRISTINE: That's not the only . . .

Ebony observes Kristine's class twice the following week. As they continue to discuss strategies for Tim and assess his progress, they learn from one another, stimulating each other's abilities to formulate strategies for a wide variety of complex situations.

SOURCE: Adapted from *Evaluating Classroom Instruction* (pp. 148–157) by J. S. Cangelosi, 1991, White Plains, NY: Longman, Copyright 1991 by Longman Publishing Group.

SELF-ASSESSING YOUR OWN TEACHING

Some teachers expertly and systematically evaluate their own instruction; others use more haphazard approaches. But none can avoid making judgements about their own performances. Teachers' self-assessments, accurate or not, influence their strategies, preparation, and activities. Now that videotape camcorders are generally available for classroom and household use, you can easily view your own instructional performances in the privacy of your own home. However to realize the potential of this resource, you should acquaint yourself with some of the recently developed systematic self-assessment tools (Cangelosi, 1991b, pp. 127–130). Struyk (1990), for example, developed and validated a video-based instrument and procedure by which teachers evaluate the efficiency of their own transition-time classroom management strategies.

ACTION RESEARCH

In their quest to improve their own performances and to be better prepared to exchange ideas with colleagues, many teachers experiment with contrasting strategies and techniques and compare outcomes. Vignette 11.2 is an example.

VIGNETTE 11.2

Although convinced of the values of cooperative learning activities and knowledge-able on how to use them, Ms. Olson worries that her students will display far more disruptive off-task behaviors during such activities than they normally do during the large group and independent work sessions she's used to conducting. She's simply not ready to commit a major share of her instructional time to cooperative learning activities if the consequences are an increase in off-task behaviors—no matter what the academic benefits might be.

To help her resolve the question, she experiments with the lessons in a writing unit by conducting six comparable learning activities over a two-week period so that two of the activities are large group, two are independent work sessions, and two involve cooperative small groups. To compare the three types of activities relative to levels of student cooperation and on-task behaviors, she videotapes the sessions with a camcorder stationed on a tripod in the rear of the room. To reduce the effects of being videotaped on the students' behaviors during the experimental sessions, she videotaped class sessions during the previous week so the students would be used to having the camcorder in the classroom.

After the six experimental sessions are complete, she views the videotapes, carefully counting incidences of student off-task behaviors and noting evidence of student cooperation. Her comparisons reveal no major differences in students' cooperation and on-task behaviors according to the type of activity. She also gains insights as to what she might do to improve her classroom management techniques. She concludes that as long as cooperative learning activities are carefully planned and orchestrated, students are just as likely to be on-task as they are during other types of learning activities. Thus, she plans to include more cooperative group activities in subsequent units.

SOURCE: Adapted from *Systematic Teaching Strategies* (pp. 30–31) by J. S. Cangelosi, 1992, White Plains, NY: Longman. Copyright 1992 by Longman Publishing Group.

YOUR UNIQUENESS

Because of differences among teachers and their circumstances, what is advisable for one teacher may be inadvisable for you. However, your knowledge of what other teachers do to teach their students to be on-task is a major source of ideas for originating your own systematic approaches. Consider these examples.

- Ms. Phegley's activities in Vignette 3.7 exemplify the use of research-based strategies for the first week of a school term to establish a learning environment that encourages students to cooperate. There are probably legitimate reasons why you should not try to copy exactly what Ms. Phegley did when you begin your next new term as a teacher. Unlike Ms. Phegley, you may not feel comfortable putting your hands on your head as a cue for your students to listen to your directions. Maybe your students are too old for that sort of thing. But surely, you can learn from Ms. Phegley's methods by thinking of ways that you can, nonverbally, but comfortably, establish cues for your students to follow your directions during the first week of a school term.

- Mr. Cooper used a democratic process to determine a classroom procedure in Vignette 5.7. Perhaps a democratic process is too inefficient for you to use in establishing your own classroom procedures or rules of conduct. Even if you choose not to follow Mr. Cooper's example, your knowledge of what he did can serve you with ideas on how to clearly distinguish for your students those times when the class is to focus on management matters and those times when the concern is on achieving some academic learning objective.

- In Vignette 9.5, Mr. Legget took some rather extraordinary steps to deal with the problem of students' mind-wandering and daydreaming. Most teachers would not choose to try Mr. Legget's elaborate scheme. However, his method illustrates some important strategies that can be incorporated into more conventional approaches.

It is inadvisable for you to try to revolutionize your teaching style all at once; ideas and new methods should be tried cautiously and conservatively. But they should be tried if they have a documented record of success. Those suggested by this book do have such success records for gaining students' cooperation. For some that you try, you can expect immediate success; others must be practiced for a while before the benefits are enjoyed. Please reread the first section of Chapter 1, "The Difference between Satisfying and Frustrating Teaching Experiences."

May your teaching career be dominated by satisfying teaching experiences.

Glossary

Action Research. Experiments teachers perform in their own classrooms to help them make decisions about the efficacy of different instructional strategies.

Allocated Time. Periods of a day when a teacher intends for students to be participating in planned learning activities.

Alternative Behavior Pattern, Principle of. Whenever one behavior pattern is extinguished, an alternate or replacement behavior pattern emerges.

Antisocial Behavior. Hostile and sometimes violent conduct that threatens the rights of others.

Assertive Communication. An expression in which a person openly and directly sends a message without being either intimidated or intimidating.

Assertive Discipline. A model, based on principles forwarded by Canter and Canter (1976), for school-wide programs designed to encourage students to be on-task.

Baseline Data. Information or data collected prior to an intervention and used as a point of comparison to data collected during and after the intervention is completed.

Behavioristic Psychology. The study of learned behaviors emphasizing responses to stimuli and the effects of stimuli presented after responses.

Behavior Modification. Application of principles of behavioristic psychology by which environments are manipulated to increase the chances that desirable behaviors are rewarded while undesirable behaviors are unrewarded or punished.

Behavior Pattern. A habit displayed by an individual.

Body Language. Messages expressed by individuals as a function of their physical posture, location, movements, and countenance.

Businesslike Classroom. A learning environment in which the students and teacher conduct themselves as if achieving specified learning goals takes priority over other concerns.

Contingency Contract. Agreement between a student and teacher specifying rewards or privileges the student will receive in return for displaying a prescribed behavior.

Contingency Proclamation. Prescription imposed by a teacher specifying rewards or privileges a students will receive in return for displaying particular behaviors.

Contrived Punishment. Punishment controlled and administered to one individual by another.

Cooperative Learning Activities. Experiences from which students learn from one another. Typically, students are organized into intraclass task groups; task-group patterns include (1) *peer instruction groups* in which one student teaches others, either presenting a brief lesson, tutoring, or providing help with a particular exercise, (2) *practice groups* in which students review, drill, and provide one another with feedback as part of a knowledge-level or skill-level lesson; (3) *interest or achievement-level groups* which are organized around interests, achievement levels, or combinations of interest and achievement; (4) *problem-solving groups* in which students use a team approach to undertake projects or formulate solutions.

Corporal Punishment. Contrived punishment in which physical pain or discomfort is intentionally inflicted upon an individual for the purpose of trying to get that individual to be sorry for having displayed a particular behavior.

Cue. A signal that prompts a learned behavior.

Daydreaming. Fantasizing experiences, imaginative episodes, or mental images.

Descriptive Language. Nonjudgmental expression verbally portraying a situation, behavior, achievement, or feeling.

Destructive Positive Reinforcer. A positive reinforcer for one behavior that has undesirable side effects on another behavior.

Destructive Punishment. Punishment that produces undesirable side effects in addition to discouraging some targeted behavior.

Discrimination, The Principle of. A new behavior pattern can emerge as a consequence of responding to a new set of stimuli in a manner dissimilar to the way in which an individual is conditioned to respond to a different, but similar, set of stimuli.

Disruptive Student Behavior. Student conduct that is not only off-task, but also interferes with other students being on-task.

Engaged Student Behavior. A student's attempts to participate in a learning activity as planned by the teacher (i.e., on-task behavior during allocated time).

Extinction, Principle of. Whenever the positive reinforcers for a person's voluntary behavior pattern are removed or cease to exist, the person will begin to discontinue that behavior pattern.

Extrinsic Motivation. Motivation to engage in an activity stimulated by the desire to receive rewards that have been artificially associated with engagement or by the desire to avoid consequences artificially imposed on failing to engage in the activity.

Fixed Interval Schedule of Positive Reinforcement. Schedule providing for a positive reinforcer to routinely occur after a set amount of time elapses in which a prescribed behavior has been displayed.

Fixed Ratio Schedule of Positive Reinforcement. Schedule providing for a positive reinforcer to routinely occur after a prescribed behavior has been displayed to a specified degree or with a specified frequency.

Formative Evaluation of Student Achievement. Judgment of student progress used solely to regulate instruction and the design of learning activities.

Functional Rule for Classroom Conduct. Rule for classroom conduct stated in terms that focus on the purpose or function for having the rule in the first place.

Generalization, The Principle of. A new behavior pattern can emerge as a consequence of responding to a new set of stimuli in a manner similar to the way in which an individual is conditioned to respond to a different, but similar, set of stimuli.

Group Dynamics. The psychological forces and processes operating within a relatively small human group (e.g., classroom size group) that determine sociological characteristics of the group as a whole and influence the individual behaviors of the group's members. As a singular term, group dynamics refers to the scientific study of group influences on individuals as well as group characteristics (e.g., organization, composition, aims, and stability.)

Higher-Level Questioning Session. Learning activity in which a teacher raises questions to stimulate students to think, discover, and reason.

Hostile Communication. A nonassertive expression intended to be intimidating, typically including insults and personal innuendoes.

Individualized Education Program (IEP). As mandated by P.L. 94-142 for each mainstreamed student, a description of the student's individualized curriculum including statements of learning goals, prescriptions for educational services, and a delineation of the assessment procedures to be used for placement decisions and evaluation of the program's success.

Interclass Grouping. Assigning students to a classroom or section of a course on the basis of some specified criteria (e.g., achievement test scores).

Intermittent Schedule of Positive Reinforcement. A schedule of positive reinforcement for a behavior pattern that is so irregular that the individual exhibiting the behavior cannot predict which episodes of the behavior will be followed by a positive reinforcer and which ones will not.

Intraclass Grouping. Subdividing of the students within a class into individual task groups for a learning activity.

Intrinsic Motivation. Motivation to engage in an activity stimulated by the belief that engagement in the activity directly satisfies a need.

Instructional Supervision. Collaborating with teachers to help them enhance their effectiveness with students.

Isolated Behavior. An event in which a person displays conduct that is not habitual.

Judgmental Language. Expression verbally summarizing an evaluation of a behavior, achievement, or person with a characterization or label.

Mainstreaming. The social and instructional integration of handicapped students in regular education classes for at least a portion of the school day (Schulz & Turnbull, p. 49).

Mentor Teacher. Classroom teacher who provides one-to-one instructional supervisory services to another, usually a beginning, teacher.

Mind-Wandering. Uncontrolled coursing of ideas and mental images.

Modeling, The Principle of. A behavior pattern can emerge because an individual observes others displaying similar behaviors.

Motivation. What prompts an individual to voluntarily engage in specific activity.

Naturally Occurring Punishment. Punishment that is a direct consequence of a person's behavior (i.e., the punishment is not artificially imposed by another as in the case of contrived punishment).

Necessary Rule for Classroom Conduct. Rule for classroom conduct designed to serve at least one of the following four purposes: (1) to maximize on-task behaviors and minimize off-task, especially disruptive, behaviors; (2) to secure the safety and comfort of the learning environment; (3) to prevent the activities of the class from disturbing other classes and persons outside of the class; (4) to maintain acceptable standards of decorum among students, school personnel, and visitors to the school campus (Cangelosi, 1990a, pp. 28–29).

Negative Reinforcement. Stimuli in which the removal of an existing punishment is contingent upon a specified change in the behavior of the individual experiencing the punishment.

Nonsupportive Response. Reply to an expression of feelings indicating that the expression of feelings has not been understood or the feelings are not acceptable.

Off-Task Student Behavior. Student conduct during either allocated or transition time that is inconsistent with attempts to cooperative and follow a teacher's directions.

On-Task Student Behavior. A student's attempts to cooperate and follow a teacher's directions either during allocated or transition time.

Passive Communication. A nonassertive expression that fails to send the message to be conveyed because the sender is intimidated or fearful of the recipient's reaction.

Peer Coaching. Instructional supervisory activity in which two or more teachers share ideas and provide formative feedback to one another's teaching.

Positive Reinforcer. A stimulus presented after a response that increases the probability of that response being repeated in the future.

Problem-solving Learning Activities. Lesson in which students are confronted with problems they have a perceived need to solve, and pursue solutions to those problems as they progress toward achievement of learning objectives.

Procedures for Classroom Routines. Mechanisms by which students move through transition periods and learning activities.

Public Law 94-142. Education for All Handicapped Children Act of 1975 which mandates that free, appropriate public education be available to all handicapped students between the ages of three and 18, that they be educated to the maximum extent possible, and that their education take place in the "least restrictive" learning environment.

Punishment. A stimulus presented after a response that decreases the probability of that response being repeated in the future.

Recitation Session. Learning activities in which students respond to questions raised by the teacher for the purpose of helping students remember content.

Rules for Classroom Conduct. Formalized statements providing students with general guidelines for the types of behaviors that are required and the types of behaviors that are prohibited.

Satiation, The Principle of. If an established learned behavior is allowed to continue unchecked, the person exhibiting that behavior may soon become tired of the pattern and elect to terminate it.

Shaping, The Principle of. A new behavior pattern will emerge if isolated behaviors with some semblance of the new behavior are positively reinforced and then subsequent positive reinforcers are applied only as the individual exhibits closer and closer approximations of the new behavior.

Smoothness of a Transition. The degree to which a transition time between two planned learning activities is efficient, with students simultaneously terminating the first learning activity and simultaneously beginning the second.

Special Students. Students with special learning needs who require instructional adaptations to learn successfully; handicapped students, gifted and talented students, culturally diverse students, and students at risk for school failure are included (Lewis & Doorlag, 1991, p. 480).

Summative Evaluation of Student Achievement. Judgment of student success relative to the goal of completed lessons.

Supportive Response. Nonjudgmental reply to an expression of feelings indicating the expression of feelings has been understood and accepted.

Teaching Process Model. The following sequence of activities engaged in by teachers whenever completing a cycle of instruction. (1) determine needs of students; (2) determine learning goal; (3) design learning activities; (4) prepare for the learning activities; (5) conduct the learning activities; (6) determine how well students have achieved the learning goal.

Transition Time. Periods of a school day when a teacher intends for students to be between learning activities (i.e., school time that is not allocated time).

Wait Time. Variable interval of time between when a teacher finishes asking a question and when a student verbalizes a response to the question; in a questioning session, how long the teacher allows students to formulate an answer to a question.

Withitness. A teacher's level of awareness of what is going on in the classroom.

References

Abernathy, S., Manera, E., & Wright, R. (1985). What stresses student teachers most? *The Clearing House, 58,* 361–362.

Adkins, G. (1990). Educating the handicapped in the regular classroom. *The Educational Digest, 56,* 24–27.

Alderman, M. K. (1990). Motivation for at-risk students. *Educational Leadership, 48,* 27–30.

Allen, L. A., & Patton, D. M. (1990, November). *Effects of sound field amplification on students' on-task behavior.* Paper presented at the Listening in the Classroom Teleconference, Logan, UT.

Allen, R. R. (1988, April). *Mathematics, reform, and excellence—Japan and the U.S.* A presentation at the annual meeting of the National Council of Teachers of Mathematics, Chicago.

Ames, C., & Ames, R. (Eds.). (1985). *Research on motivation in education: Vol. 1. Student motivation.* Orlando: Academic Press.

Anderson, L. W. (1976). An empirical investigation of individual differences in time to learn. *Journal of Educational Psychology, 68,* 226–233.

Arnold, D., Atwood, R., & Rogers, V. (1974). Question and response levels and lapse time intervals. *Journal of Experimental Education, 43,* 11–15.

Ashlock, R. B. (1990). *Error patterns in computation: A semiprogrammed approach* (5th ed.). Columbus, OH: Merrill.

Augustine, D. K., Gruber, K. D., & Hanson, L. R. (1990). Cooperation works! *Educational Leadership, 47,* 4–7.

Axelrod, S., & Bailey, S. A. (1979). Drug treatment for hyperactivity: Controversies, alternatives, and guidelines. *Exceptional Children, 45,* 544–550.

Azrin, N. H., Hake, D. G., Holz, W. C., & Hutchinson, R. R. (1965). Motivational aspects of escape from punishment. *Journal of Experimental Analysis of Behavior, 8,* 31–44.

Azrin, N. H., Hake, D. G., & Hutchinson, R. R. (1965). Elicitation of aggression by a physical blow. *Journal of Experimental Analysis of Behavior, 8,* 55–57.

Azrin, N. H., Hutchinson, R. R., & Sallery, R. D. (1964). Pain-aggression toward inanimate objects. *Journal of Experimental Analysis of Behavior, 7,* 223–228.

Bandura, A. (1965). Behavior modification through modeling procedures. In L. Krasner & L. P. Ullman (Eds.), *Research in behavior modification* (pp. 310–340). New York: Holt, Rinehart, & Winston.

Bang-Jensen, V. (1986). The view from next door: A look at peer "supervision." In K. K. Zumwalt (Ed.), *Improving teaching* (pp. 51–62). Alexandria, VA: Association for Supervision and Curriculum Development.

Bell, L. C., & Stefanich, G. P. (1984). Building effective discipline using the cascade model. *The Clearing House, 58,* 134–137.

Berg, F. S. (1987). *Facilitating classroom listening.* Boston: College-Hill Press.

Berg, F. S. (1990). Sound field FM: A new technology for the classroom. *The Clinical Connection, 4,* 14–17.

Biehler, R. F., & Snowman, J. (1990). *Psychology applied to teaching* (6th ed.). Boston: Houghton Mifflin.

Bongiovanni, A. F. (1979). An analysis of research on punishment and its relation to the use of corporal punishment in the schools. In I. A. Hyman & J. Wise (Eds.), *Corporal punishment in American education* (pp. 351–372). Philadelphia: Temple University Press.

Boostrom, R. (1991). The nature and function of classroom rules. *Curriculum Inquiry, 21,* 193–216.

Borg, W. R. (1980). Time and school learning. In C. Denham & A. Lieberman (Eds.), *Time to Learn.* Washington: National Institute of Education.

Boynton, P., Di Geronimo, J., & Gustafson, G. (1985). A basic survival guide for new teachers. *The Clearing House, 59,* 101–103.

Brandt, R. (1989). A changed professional culture. *Educational Leadership, 46,* 2.

Bridges, E. M. (1986). *The incompetent teacher.* Philadelphia: Falmer Press.

Brody, N. (1983). *Human motivation: Commentary on goal-directed action.* New York: Academic Press.

Brophy, J. E. (1987). Synthesis on strategies for motivating students to learn. *Educational Leadership, 45,* 40–48.

Brophy, J. E., & Putnam, J. G. (1979). Classroom management in the elementary school. In D. L. Duke (Ed.). *Classroom management: The seventy-eighth yearbook of the National Society for the study of education* (pp. 182–216). Chicago: University of Chicago Press.

Brough, J. A. (1990). Changing conditions for young adolescents: Reminiscences and realities. *Educational Horizons, 68,* 78–81.

Brown, D. (1971). *Changing student behavior: A new approach to discipline.* Dubuque, IA: W. C. Brown.

Burke, J. (1991). Teenagers, clothes, and gang violence. *Educational Leadership, 49,* 11–13.

Cangelosi, J. S. (1980). *Project G.R.E.A.T. needs assessment report.* Tallahassee: Florida Department of Education.

Cangelosi, J. S. (1982). *Measurement and evaluation: An inductive approach for teachers.* Dubuque, IA: W. C. Brown.

Cangelosi, J. S. (1990a). *Cooperation in the classroom: Students and teachers together* (2nd ed.). Washington: National Education Association.

Cangelosi, J. S. (1990b). *Designing tests for evaluating student achievement.* New York: Longman.

Cangelosi, J. S. (1991a, April). *Assessing on-task student behavior.* Paper presented at the Listening in the Classroom Teleconference, Logan, UT.

Cangelosi, J. S. (1991b). *Evaluating classroom instruction.* New York: Longman.

Cangelosi, J. S. (1992a). *Systematic teaching strategies.* New York: Longman.

Cangelosi, J. S. (1992b). *Teaching mathematics in secondary and middle school: Research-based approaches.* New York: Macmillan.

Cangelosi, J. S., Struyk, L. R., Grimes, M. L., & Duke, C. (1988, April). *Classroom management needs of beginning teachers.* Paper presented at the annual meeting of the American Educational Research Association, New Orleans.

Canter, L. (1978). Be an assertive teacher. *Instructor, 88,* 60.

Canter, L., & Canter, M. (1976). *Assertive discipline: A take-charge approach for today's educator.* Seal Beach, CA: Canter & Associates.

Chandler, T. A., & Kindsvatter, R. (1991). Complementary approaches for effective discipline. *Middle School Journal, 22,* 34–37.

Charles, C. M. (1989). *Building classroom discipline: From models to practice* (3rd ed.). New York: Longman.

Chrisco, I. M. (1989). Peer assistance works. *Educational Leadership, 46,* 31–32.

Coolican, J. (1988). Individual differences. In R. McNergney (Ed.), *Guide to classroom teaching.* Boston: Allyn and Bacon.

Cooper, H. (1989a). *Homework.* New York: Longman.

Cooper, H. (1989b). Synthesis of reserach on homework. *Educational Leadership, 47,* 85–91.

Corno, L., & Snow, R. E. (1986). Adapting teaching to individual differences among learners. In M. C. Wittrock (Ed.), *Handbook of research on teaching* (3rd ed., pp. 605–629). New York: Macmillan.

Cunningham, A. R. (1983). The deportment chart: A student management tool that could help a classroom teacher. *The Clearing House, 56,* 421–422.

Curwin, R. L., & Mendler, A. N. (1988). *Discipline with dignity.* Alexandria, VA: Association for Supervision and Curriculum Development.

Delgado, J. M. R. (1963). Cerebral heterostimulation in a monkey colony. *Science, 141,* 161–163.

Dewey, J. (1933). *How we think* (rev. ed.). Boston: D. C. Heath.

Doenau, S. J. (1987). Soliciting. In M. J. Dunkin (Ed.). *The international encyclopedia of teaching and teacher education* (pp. 407–413). Oxford: Pergamon Press.

Doyle, W. (1986). Classroom organization and management. In M. C. Wittrock (Ed.). *Handbook of research on teaching* (3rd ed., pp. 392–431). New York: Macmillan.

Dreikurs, R. (1968). *Psychology in the classroom* (2nd ed.). New York: Harper & Row.

Dreikurs, R., Grunwald, B., & Pepper, F. (1982). *Maintaining sanity in the classroom* (2nd ed.). New York: Harper & Row.

Duke, C. R., Cangelosi, J. S., & Knight, R. S. (1988, February). *The Mellon Project: A collaborative effort.* Colloquium presentation at the annual meeting of the American Association of Colleges for Teacher Education, New Orleans.

Dunlap, K. (1919). Are there instincts? *Journal of Abnormal Psychology, 14,* 307–311.

Elam, S. M. (1989). The second Gallup Phi Delta Kappa Poll of teachers' attitudes toward the public school. *Phi Delta Kappan, 70,* 785–798.

Elam, S. M., Rose, L. C., & Gallup, A. M. (1991). The 23rd Annual Gallup Poll of the public's attitudes toward the public schools. *Phi Delta Kappan, 73,* 41–56.

Emmer, E. T., Evertson, C. M., & Anderson, L. M. (1980). Effective classroom management at the beginning of the school year. *Elementary School Journal, 80,* 219–231.

Evans, R. (1989). The faculty in midcareer: Implications for school improvement. *Educational Leadership, 46,* 10–15.

Evertson, C. M. (1989). Classroom organization and management. In M. C. Reynolds (Ed.), *Knowledge base for the beginning teacher* (pp. 49–70). Oxford: Pergamon Press.

Evertson, C. M., & Emmer, E. T. (1982). Effective management at the beginning of the school year in junior high classes. *Journal of Educational Psychology, 82,* 329–350.

Fisher, C. W., Berliner, D. C., Filby, N. N., Marliave, R., Cahen, L. S., & Dishaw, M. M. (1980). Teaching behaviors, academic learning time, and student achievement: An overview. In C. Denham & A. Lieberman (Eds.), *Time to learn* (pp. 7–32). Washington: National Institute of Education.

Foyle, H. C., Lyman, L., & Thies, S. A. (1991). *Cooperative learning in the early childhood classroom.* Washington: National Education Association.

Ginott, H. G. (1965). *Parent and child.* New York: Avon.

Ginott, H. G. (1972). *Teacher and child.* New York: Avon.

Glasser, W. (1965). *Reality therapy: A new approach to psychiatry.* New York: Harper & Row.

Glasser, W. (1969). *Schools without failure.* New York: Harper & Row.

Glasser, W. (1977). Ten steps to good discipline. *Today's Education, 66,* 60–63.

Glasser, W. (1978). Disorders in our schools: Causes and remedies. *Phi Delta Kappan, 59,* 331–333.

Glasser, W. (1985). *Control theory in the classroom.* New York: Perennial Press.

Glasser, W. (1988). On students' needs and team learning: A conversation with William Glasser. *Educational Leadership, 45,* 38–41.

Glickman, C., & Wolfgang, C. (1979). Dealing with student misbehavior: An eclectic review. *Journal of Teacher Education, 30,* 7–13.

Gold, S. R., & Cundiff, G. (1980). Increasing the frequency of daydreaming. *Journal of Clinical Psychology, 36,* 116–121.

Goodlad, J. I. (1984). *A place called school: Prospects for the future.* New York: McGraw-Hill.

Gordon, T. (1974). *T.E.T.: Teacher effectiveness training.* New York: Peter H. Wyden.

Harris, T. A. (1969). *I'm OK—You're OK: A practical guide to transactional analysis.* New York: Harper & Row.

Hilke, E. V. (1990). *Cooperative learning.* Bloomington, IN: Phi Delta Kappa Educational Foundation.

Homme, L. (1973). *How to use contingency contracting in the classroom.* Champaign, IL: Research Press.

Hunkins, F. P. (1989). *Teaching thinking through effective questioning.* Boston: Christopher-Gordon.

Hyman, I. A. (1978). A social science review of evidence cited in litigation on corporal punishment in the schools. *Journal of Child Psychology, 30,* 195–199.

Hyman, I. A., & Wise, J. H. (Eds.). (1979). *Corporal punishment in American education.* Philadelphia: Temple University Press.

Jesunathadas, J. (1990). *Mathematics teachers' instructional activities as a function of academic preparation.* Unpublished doctoral dissertation, Utah State University, Logan.

Jones, F. (1979). The gentle art of classroom discipline. *National Elementary Principal, 58,* 26–32.

Jones, V. F., & Jones, L. S. (1990). *Comprehensive classroom management: Motivating and managing students* (3rd ed.). Boston: Allyn & Bacon.

Karlin, M. S., & Berger, R. (1972). *Discipline and the disruptive child: A practical guide for elementary teachers.* West Nyack, NY: Parker.

Kauffman, J. M. (1989). *Characteristics of children's behavior disorders* (4th ed.). Columbus, OH: Merrill.

Kayfetz, J. L., & Stice, R. L. (1987). *Academically speaking.* Belmont, CA: Wadsworth.

Kerr, M. M., & Nelson, C. M. (1983). *Strategies for managing behavior problems in the classroom.* Columbus: Merrill.

Klinger, E. (1978). Modes of normal conscious flow. In K. S. Pope & J. L. Singer (Eds.), *The stream of consciousness*. New York: Plenum Press.

Kobrin, D. (1992). *In there with kids: Teaching in today's classrooms*. Boston: Houghton Mifflin.

Kohut, S., & Range, D. G. (1979). *Classroom discipline: Case studies and viewpoints*. Washington: National Education Association.

Kounin, J. (1970). *Discipline and group management in classrooms*. New York: Holt, Rinehart, & Winston.

Kounin, J. S., & Doyle, P. H. (1975). Degree of continuity of a lesson's signal system and the task involvement of children. *Journal of Educational Psychology, 67*, 159–164.

Kounin, J. S., & Gump, P. V. (1974). Signal systems of lesson settings and the task related behavior of preschool children. *Journal of Educational Psychology, 66*, 554–562.

Kounin, J., & Sherman, L. (1979). School environments as behavior settings. *Theory into Practice, 18*, 145–151.

Krumboltz, J. D., & Krumboltz, H. B. (1972). *Changing children's behavior*. Englewood Cliffs, NJ: Prentice-Hall.

Lasley, T. J. (1985). Fostering nonaggression in the classroom: An anthropological perspective. *Theory into Practice, 24*, 247–255.

Latham, G. I. (1984). *Time-on-task and other variables affecting the quality of education of handicapped students*. Logan, UT: Utah State University.

Lessinger, L. (1970). *Every kid a winner: Accountability in education*. New York: Simon & Schuster.

Lewis, R. B., & Doorlag, D. H. (1991). *Teaching special students in the mainstream* (3rd ed.). New York: Macmillan.

Loo, C. M. (1977). *The differential effects of spatial density on low and high scorers on behavior problem indices*. Paper presented at the annual meeting of the Western Psychological Association, Seattle.

Lyerly, K. Z. (1982). *Daydreaming and its implications to reading instruction among gifted children*. Master's Thesis, University of North Florida, Jacksonville.

Lyman, L., & Foyle, H. C. (1990). *Cooperative grouping for interactive learning: Students, teachers, and administrators*. Washington: National Education Association.

MacNaughton, R. H., & Jones, F. A. (1991). Developing a successful schoolwide discipline program. *NASSP Bulletin, 75*, 47–57.

Maifair, L. L. (1986, October). Helping kids resist drugs. *Instructor, 96*(3), 72–74.

Margolis, H., & Schwartz, E. (1989). Facilitating mainstreaming through cooperative learning. *The High School Journal, 72*, 83–88.

Martin, G., & Pear, J. (1983). *Behavior modification: What it is and how to do it* (2nd ed.). Englewood Cliffs, NJ: Prentice-Hall.

Maslow, A. (1962). *Toward a psychology of being*. New York: Van Nostrand.

McGarity, J. R., & Butts, D. P. (1984). The relationship among teacher classroom management behavior, student engagement, and student achievement of middle and high school science students of varying aptitude. *Journal of Research in Science Teaching, 21*, 55–61.

McLaren, P. (1989). *Life in schools: An introduction to critical pedagogy in the foundations of education*. New York: Longman.

Merriam-Webster, Inc. (1986). *Webster's third new international dictionary*. Chicago: Author.

Morganett, L. (1991). Good teacher-student relationship: A key element in classroom motivation and management. *Education, 112*, 260–264.

Mudd, R. (1990). Editorial comment on video program *Learning in America: Schools that work*. Alexandria, VA: PBS Videos.

National Commission on excellence in Education. (1983). *A nation at risk: The imperative of educational reform.* Washington: U.S. Government Printing Office.

National Education Association. (1972). *Report of the task force on corporal punishment.* Washington: Author.

Ornstein, A. C. (1990). *Strategies for effective teaching.* New York: Harper & Row.

Paley, V. G. (1986). On listening to what children say. *Harvard Educational Review, 56,* 122–131.

Parker, W. C., & Gehrke, N. J. (1986). Learning activities and teacher decisionmaking: Some grounded hypotheses. *American Educational Research Journal, 23,* 227–242.

Petreshene, S. (1986, October). What can you do in 10 minutes? Transition activities that make kids think! *Instructor, XCVI*(3), 68–70.

Petty, R. (1989). Managing disruptive students. *Educational Leadership, 46,* 26–28.

Presbie, R. J., & Brown, P. L. (1985). *Behavior modification* (2nd ed.). Washington: National Education Association.

Pulaski, M. A. S. (1980). *Understanding Piaget: An introduction to children's cognitive development* (2nd ed.). New York: Harper & Row.

Pysch, R. (1991). Discipline improves as students take responsibility. *NASSP Bulletin, 75,* 117–118.

Quina, J. (1989). *Effective secondary teaching: Going beyond the bell curve.* New York: Harper & Row.

Raney, P., & Robbins, P. (1989). Professional growth and support through peer coaching. *Educational Leadership, 46,* 35–38.

Ray, O., & Ksir, C. (1990). *Drugs, society, and human behavior* (5th ed.). St. Louis: Time Mirror/Mosby College Publishing.

Reardon, F. J., & Reynolds, R. N. (1979). A survey of attitudes toward corporal punishment in Pennsylvania schools. In I. A. Hyman & J. H. Wise (Eds.), *Corporal punishment in American education.* Philadelphia: Temple University Press.

Rich, J. M. (1991). Should students be punished? *Contemporary Education, 62,* 180–184.

Robert, S. C. (Ed.). (1970). *Robert's rules of order* (rev. ed.). Glenview, IL: Scott Foresman.

Rogers, R. L., & McMillin, C. S. (1989). *Freeing someone you love from alcohol and other drugs: A step-by-step plan starting today!* Los Angeles: The Body Press.

Rogoff, B. (1990). *Apprenticeship in thinking.* New York: Oxford University Press.

Rose, T. L. (1984). Current uses of corporal punishment in American public schools. *Journal of Educational Psychology, 76,* 427–441.

Rosenshine, B., & Stevens, R. (1986). Teaching functions. In M. C. Wittrock (Ed.) *Handbook of research on teaching* (3rd ed., pp. 376–391). New York: Macmillan.

Rosenthal, R., & Jacobson, L. (1968). *Pygmalion in the classroom: Teacher expectations and pupils' intellectual development.* New York: Holt, Rinehart & Winston.

Rottier, J., & Ogan, B. J. (1991). *Cooperative learning in middle-level schools.* Washington: National Education Association.

Ruetten, M. K. (1986). *Comprehending academic lectures.* New York: Macmillan.

Rust, J. O., & Kinnard, K. Q. (1983). Personality characteristics of the users of corporal punishment in the schools. *Journal of School Psychology, 21,* 91–105.

Sabornie, E. J. (1985). Social mainstreaming of handicapped students: Facing an unpleasant reality. *Remedial and Special Education, 6,* 12–16.

Salter, A. (1949). *Conditioned reflex therapy.* New York: Farrar, Straus & Giroux.

Santa, C. M., & Havens, L. T. (1991). Learning through writing. In C. M. Santa & D. E. Alverman (Eds.). *Science learning: Process and applications* (pp. 122–133). Newark, DE: International Reading Association.

Santrock, J. W. (1984). *Adolescence: An introduction* (2nd ed.). Dubuque, IA: W. C. Brown.

Schultz, J. B., & Turnbull, A. P. (1983). *Mainstreaming handicapped students* (2nd ed.). Boston: Allyn and Bacon.

Seeman, H. (1984). A major source of discipline problems. *Educational Horizons, 62,* 128–131.

Shannon, J. (1986). In the classroom stoned. *Phi Delta Kappan, 68,* 60–62.

Skinner, B. F. (1953). *Science and human behavior.* New York: Macmillan.

Skinner, B. F. (1954). The science of learning and the art of teaching. *Harvard Educational Review, 24,* 86–97.

Slavin, R. E. (1991a). *Student team learning: A practical guide to cooperative learning* (3rd ed.). Washington: National Education Association.

Slavin, R. E. (1991b). Synthesis of research on cooperative learning. *Educational Leadership, 48,* 71–82.

Smith, D. D. (1981). *Teaching the learning disabled.* Englewood Cliffs, NJ: Prentice-Hall.

Smith, H. A. (1985). The marking of transitions by more or less effective teachers. *Theory into Practice, 24,* 57–62.

Stallion, B. K. (1988, April). *Classroom management intervention: The effects of mentoring relationships on the inductee teacher's behavior.* Paper presented at the annual meeting of the American Educational Research Association, New Orleans.

Strike, K., & Soltis, J. (1986). Who broke the fish tank? And other ethical dilemmas. *Instructor, 95,* 36–39.

Struyk, L. R. (1990). *A self-evaluation model for examining transition time in the classroom.* Unpublished doctoral dissertation, Utah State University, Logan.

Sulzer-Azaroff, B., & Mayer, G. R. (1977). *Applying behavior analysis procedures with children and youth.* New York: Holt, Rinehart, & Winston.

Swartz, R. J., & Perkins, D. N. (1990). *Teaching thinking: Issues and approaches* (rev. ed.). Pacific Grove, CA: Midwest Publications.

Swick, K. J. (1985). *Disruptive student behavior in the classroom* (2nd ed.). Washington: National Education Association.

Tillman, M. (1982). *Trouble-shooting classroom problems.* Glenview, IL: Scott, Foresman.

Tobbin, K. (1986). Effects of teacher wait time on discourse in mathematics and language arts classes. *American Educational Research Journal, 23,* 191–200.

Towers, R. L. (1987). *How schools can help combat student drug and alcohol abuse.* Washington, DC: National Education Association.

Towers, R. L. (1989). *Children of alcoholics/addicts.* Washington, DC: National Education Association.

Ulrich, R. E., & Azrin, N. H. (1962). Reflexive fighting in response to aversive stimulation. *Journal of Experimental Analysis of Behavior, 5,* 511–520.

Van Dyke, H. T. (1984). Corporal punishment in our schools. *The Clearing House, 57,* 296–300.

Van Horn, K. L. (1982, April). *The Utah pupil/teacher self-concept program: Teacher strategies that invite improvement of pupil and teacher self-concept.* Paper presented at the annual meeting of the American Educational Research Association, New York.

Voorhies, R. (1989). Cooperative learning: What is it? *Social Studies Review, 28,* 7–10.

Walker, H., & Sylwater, R. (1991). Where is school along the path to prison? *Educational Leadership, 49,* 14–16.

Walker, H. M. (1979). *The acting-out child: Coping with classroom disruptions.* Boston: Allyn and Bacon.

Walker, J. E., & Shea, T. M. (1984). *Behavior management: A practical approach for educators* (3rd ed.). St. Louis: Times Mirror/Mosby College Publishing.

Watson, J. B. (1914). *Behavior: An introduction to comparative psychology.* New York: Holt, Rinehart & Winston.

Weber, W. A. (1990). Classroom management. In J. M. Cooper (Ed.), *Classroom teaching skills* (4th ed., pp. 229–306). Lexington, MA: D. C. Heath.

Weinstein, C. S. (1987). Seating patterns. In M. J. Dunkin (Ed.). *The International encyclopedia of teaching and teacher education* (pp. 545–548). Oxford: Pergamon Press.

Welsh, R. S. (1985). Spanking: A grand old American tradition? *Children Today, 14,* 25–29.

Wilcox, R. T. (1983). Discipline made gentle. *The Clearing House, 57,* 30–35.

Wilde, J., & Sommers, P. (1978). Teaching disruptive adolescents: A game worth winning. *Phi Delta Kappan, 59,* 342–343.

Wittrock, M. C. (1986). Students' thought processes. In M. C. Wittrock (Ed.) *Handbook of Research on Teaching* (3rd ed., pp. 297–314). New York: Macmillan.

Wolf, M. M., Hanley, E. L., King, L. A., Lachowicz, J., & Giles, D. K. (1970). The timer game: A variable interval contingency for the management of out-of-seat behavior. *Exceptional Children, 37,* 113–117.

Wolpe, J., & Lazarus, A. A. (1966). *Behavior therapy techniques: A guide to the treatment of neuroses.* Oxford: Pergamon Press.

Wood, F. H. (1982). The influence of public opinion and social custom on the use of corporal punishment in the schools. In F. H. Wood & K. C. Lakin (Eds.), *Punishment and aversive stimulation in special education: Legal, theoretical and practical issues in their use with emotionally disturbed children and youth* (pp. 29–39). Reston, VA: Council for Exceptional Children.

Woolridge, P., & Richman, C. L. (1985). Teachers' choice of punishment as a function of a student's gender, age, race, and IQ level. *Journal of School Psychology, 23,* 19–29.

Worner, W. (1988). An inexpensive group FM amplification system for the classroom. *The Volta Review, 90,* 29–39.

Zirkel, P. A. (1991). Corporal punishment as a crime. *Principal, 71,* 62–63.

Zumwalt, K. K. (Ed.). (1986). *Improving teaching; 1986 ASCD yearbook.* Alexandria, VA: Association for Supervision and Curriculum Development.

Index